Marmottan!

W9-CSM-798

Rick Steves'
PARIS
2003

by Rick Steves, Steve Smith & Gene Openshaw

AVALON
TRAVEL

Other ATP travel guidebooks by Rick Steves

Rick Steves' Best of Europe
Rick Steves' Europe 101: History and Art for the Traveler (with Gene Openshaw)
Rick Steves' Europe Through the Back Door
Rick Steves' Mona Winks: Self-Guided Tours of Europe's Top Museums
   (with Gene Openshaw)
Rick Steves' Postcards from Europe
Rick Steves' France (with Steve Smith)
Rick Steves' Germany, Austria & Switzerland
Rick Steves' Great Britain
Rick Steves' Ireland (with Pat O'Connor)
Rick Steves' Italy
Rick Steves' Scandinavia
Rick Steves' Spain & Portugal
Rick Steves' Amsterdam, Bruges & Brussels (with Gene Openshaw)
Rick Steves' Florence (with Gene Openshaw)
Rick Steves' London (with Gene Openshaw)
Rick Steves' Rome (with Gene Openshaw)
Rick Steves' Venice (with Gene Openshaw)
Rick Steves' Phrase Books: German, Italian, French, Portuguese, Spanish, and
   French/Italian/German

Avalon Travel Publishing, 1400 65th Street, Suite 250, Emeryville, CA 94608

Printed in the USA by R.R. Donnelley Norwest, Inc. Second printing March 2003.
Distributed by Publishers Group West.

Portions of this book were originally published in *Rick Steves' Mona Winks*, © 2001,
1998, 1996, 1993, 1988 by Rick Steves and Gene Openshaw; *Rick Steves' France,
Belgium & the Netherlands* © 2002, 2001, 2000, 1999, 1998 by Rick Steves and Steve
Smith; and in *Rick Steves' France* © 2003 by Rick Steves and Steve Smith.

ISBN 1-56691-456-6 • ISSN 1522-3299

For the latest on Rick's lectures, guidebooks, tours, and public television series, contact
Europe Through the Back Door, Box 2009, Edmonds, WA 98020, tel. 425/771-8303,
fax 425/771-0833, www.ricksteves.com, or e-mail: rick@ricksteves.com.

Europe Through the Back Door Managing Editor: Risa Laib
Europe Through the Back Door Editors: Cameron Hewitt, Jill Hodges
Avalon Travel Publishing Editor: Mia Lipman
Avalon Travel Publishing Series Manager: Laura Mazer
Copy Editor: Kate McKinley
Research Assistance: Karen Lewis Smith
Indexer: Stephen Callahan
Production & Typesetting: Kathleen Sparkes, White Hart Design
Cover & Interior Design: Janine Lehmann
Maps & Graphics: David C. Hoerlein, Rhonda Pelikan, Zoey Platt
Photography: pp. 78, 85, 178: David C. Hoerlein; p. 319: Dominic Bonucelli;
   all others by Rick Steves
Front cover photo: Tour Eiffel, Paris, France © Blaine Harrington III
Front matter color photos: p. i, Paris, France © Alex Bartel/PHOTOPHILE;
   p. viii, Place du Tertre, Paris, France © FOLIO, Inc.

*Although the author and publisher have made every effort to provide accurate, up-to-date
information, they accept no responsibility for loss, injury, bad crêpes, or inconvenience
sustained by any person using this book.*

CONTENTS

NUMBERS INDICATE ARRONDISSEMENTS (DISTRICTS)

1/2 MILE

INTRODUCTION

Paris—the City of Lights—has been a beacon of culture for centuries. As a world capital of art, fashion, food, literature, and ideas, it stands as a symbol of all the fine things that human civilization can offer. Come prepared to celebrate, rather than judge, the cultural differences, and you'll capture the romance and joie de vivre that Paris exudes.

Paris offers sweeping boulevards, chatty crêpe stands, chic boutiques, and world-class art galleries. Sip decaf with deconstructionists in a sidewalk café, then step into an Impressionist painting in a tree-lined park. Climb Notre-Dame and rub shoulders with the gargoyles. Cruise the Seine, zip up the Eiffel Tower, and saunter down the Champs-Elysées. Master the Louvre and Orsay museums. Save some after-dark energy for one of the world's most romantic cities.

This Information Is Accurate and Up-to-Date

This book is updated every year. Most publishers of guidebooks that cover a city from top to bottom can afford an update only every two or three years. Since this book is selective, covering only the places we think make the top week or two in and around Paris, we can update it each summer (we even do a winter checkup). Even with an annual update, however, things change. But if you're traveling with the current edition of this book, we guarantee you're using the most up-to-date information available in print (for the latest, check www.ricksteves.com/update). This book will help you have an inexpensive, hassle-free trip. Use this year's edition. Saving a few bucks by traveling on old information is not smart. If you're packing an old book, you'll learn the seriousness of your mistake . . . in Paris. Your trip costs at least $10 per waking hour. Your time is valuable. This guidebook saves lots of time.

Welcome to Our Paris City Guide

This book is organized in the following way:

Paris Orientation includes tourist information, public-transportation basics, and easy-to-read maps. The "Planning Your Time" section offers a suggested schedule with thoughts on how best to use your limited time.

Sights provides a succinct overview of Paris' most important sights. They're arranged by neighborhood and include ratings: ▲▲▲—Don't miss; ▲▲—Try hard to see; ▲—Worthwhile if you can make it; no rating—Worth knowing about.

The **Walks** cover five of Paris' most enjoyable neighborhoods: Historic Paris (Notre-Dame and Sainte-Chapelle), Champs-Elysées, the Marais, rue Cler (near the Eiffel Tower), and Montmartre.

The **Self-Guided Museum Tours** take you through Paris' most interesting museums: Louvre, Orsay, Rodin, Marmottan, Cluny, Carnavalet, Pompidou Center, and Les Invalides, including Napoleon's Tomb.

Day Trips covers nearby sights, including the great châteaux of Versailles (includes self-guided tour), Vaux-le-Vicomte, Fontainebleau, and Chantilly; Chartres' majestic cathedral (includes self-guided tour); the Impressionist retreats of Monet's Giverny and van Gogh's Auvers-sur-Oise; and, *finalement*, Disneyland Paris. Accommodations are listed for Versailles, Fontainebleau, Chartres, Giverny, and Auvers-sur-Oise.

Sleeping is a guide to our favorite hotels, from budget deals to cushy splurges in three cozy neighborhoods, with orientation tips geared to make you feel at home.

Eating offers good-value restaurants ranging from inexpensive eateries to romantic bistros, arranged by neighborhood, with a special section on "Grand Cafés."

Paris with Children includes our top 10 recommendations to help keep your kids (and you) happy in Paris.

Shopping helps you shop painlessly and enjoyably, without letting it overwhelm your vacation or ruin your budget. Read up on Paris' great department stores, neighborhood boutiques, flea markets, and outdoor food markets.

Nightlife is a guide to entertainment and evening fun, with music, bus tours, and river cruises, plus information on how to easily translate *Pariscope*, the weekly entertainment guide.

Transportation Connections lays the groundwork for your smooth arrival and departure, covering connections by train and plane, with detailed information on Paris' two airports and six train stations.

The **French History** chapter takes you from Celtic times right up to the present.

Tips for Tackling Our Self-Guided Tours

Sightseeing can be hard work. Our self-guided tours are designed to help make your visits to Paris' finest museums meaningful, fun, fast, and painless. To make the most of our tours, read the tour the night before your visit.

When you arrive at the sight, use the overview map to get the lay of the land and the basic tour route. Expect a few changes—paintings can be on tour, on loan, out sick, or shifted at the whim of the curator. Even museum walls are often moved. To adapt, pick up any available free floor plan as you enter. If you can't find a particular painting, just ask any museum worker. Point to the photograph in this book and ask, *"Où est?"* (pron. oo`ay; meaning, "Where is?").

We cover the highlights at sights. You might want to supplement with an audioguide (dry-but-informative recorded descriptions in English, about €5) or a guided tour (usually €6 or more). If guided tours in English are available, they're most likely to occur during peak season (though key museums offer them year-round). The quality of a tour depends on the guide's knowledge, fluency, and enthusiasm.

Museums have their rules; if you're aware of them in advance, they're no big deal. Keep in mind that many sights have "last entry" times 30 to 60 minutes before closing. Guards usher people out before the official closing time. Cameras are normally allowed in museums, but no flashes or tripods (without special permission). A handheld camera with ASA-400 film and an F-2 aperture will take a fine picture (or buy slides at the museum bookstore). Video cameras are usually allowed. For security reasons, you're often required to check even small bags. Most museums have a free checkroom at the entrance. They're safe. Prepare to stash anything that you can't bear to part with in a purse or pocket.

At the museum bookshop, thumb through the biggest guidebook (or scan its index) to be sure you haven't overlooked something that is of particular interest to you. If there's an on-site cafeteria, it's usually a good place to rest and have a snack or light meal. Museum WCs are free and generally clean.

The **appendix** includes a pronunciation guide, a climate chart, telephone tips, French survival phrases, and a handy almanac of resources.

Throughout the book, when you see a ✪ in a listing, it means that the sight is covered in much more depth in one of our walks or self-guided tours—a page number will tell you just where to look to find more information.

Browse through this book and choose your favorite sights. Then have a *fantastique* trip! You'll become your own guide with our self-guided walks and museum tours. Traveling like a temporary local, you'll get the absolute most out of every mile, minute, and dollar. You won't waste time on mediocre sights because, unlike other guidebooks, this one covers only the best. Since lousy, expensive hotels are a major financial pitfall, we've worked hard to assemble the best accommodations values. And, as you explore the city we know and love, we're happy you'll be meeting some of our favorite Parisians.

Trip Costs

Five components make up your trip costs: airfare, surface transportation, room and board, sightseeing/entertainment, and shopping/miscellany.

Airfare: Don't try to sort through the mess. Find and use a good travel agent. A basic round-trip U.S.–Paris flight costs $700–1,100 (even cheaper in winter), depending on where you fly from and when.

Surface Transportation: For a typical one-week visit, allow about $50 for Métro tickets and a couple of day trips. Add an additional $70 if you opt for taxi rides to and from the airport (or you could save money taking a shuttle, airport bus, or the RER).

Room and Board: You can thrive in Paris on $80 a day per person for room and board. An $80-a-day budget allows $5 for breakfast, $10 for lunch, $20 for dinner, and $45 for lodging (based on 2 people splitting the cost of a $90 double room). That's doable. Students and tightwads do it on $40 ($20 per bed, $15–20 for meals and snacks). But budget sleeping and eating require using the skills and information covered in this book (and in much greater depth in *Rick Steves' Europe Through the Back Door*).

Sightseeing and Entertainment: Get the Paris Museum and Monument Pass, which covers most sights in Paris (for more information, see Sights chapter, page 29). You'll pay about $15 for a one-day pass, $30 for a three-day pass, and $45 for a five-day pass. (While you can buy the pass through some U.S. travel agents, it's easy and cheaper to buy in Paris). Without a museum pass, figure $5–7.50 per major sight (e.g., Rodin Museum-$5, Louvre-$7.50),

$4 for minor ones (climbing church towers), and $25 for bus tours and splurge experiences (concerts in the Sainte-Chapelle). An overall average of $15 a day works for most. Don't skimp here. After all, this category directly powers most of the experiences all the other expenses are designed to make possible.

Shopping and Miscellany: Figure $3 per ice-cream cone, coffee, or soft drink. Shopping can vary in cost from nearly nothing to a small fortune. Good budget travelers find that this category has little to do with assembling a trip full of lifelong and wonderful memories.

Exchange Rate

We've priced things throughout this book in the euro currency.

---

1 euro (€) = about $1.

One euro is broken down into 100 cents. You'll find coins ranging from 1 cent to 2 euros, and bills from 5 euros to 500 euros.

Prices, Times, and Discounts

The prices in this book, as well as the hours and telephone numbers, are accurate as of mid-2002. Europe is always changing, and we know you'll understand that this, like any other guidebook, starts to yellow even before it's printed.

In Europe—and in this book—you'll use the 24-hour clock. After 12 noon, keep going—13:00, 14:00, and so on. For anything over 12, subtract 12 and add p.m. (14:00 is 2:00 p.m.).

While discounts for sights and transportation are listed for only the most important sights in this book, students with International Student Identification Cards, teachers with proper identification, and youths under 18 often get discounts—but only if they ask.

When to Go

Late spring and fall have the best weather and the biggest crowds. Summers are generally hot and dry; if you wilt in the heat, look for a room with air-conditioning. It's fairly easy to find rooms in summer, and though many French businesses close in August, you'll hardly notice. Paris makes a great winter getaway. Airfares are cheap, the cafés are cozy, and the city feels lively but not touristy. The only problem—weather—is fixed by dressing correctly. Expect cold and rain, but no snow.

Red Tape and Business Hours

You need a passport, but no visa or shots, to travel in France.

Most shops are open Monday through Saturday (10:00–19:00)

and closed Sunday, though many small markets, *boulangeries* (bakeries), and street markets are open Sunday mornings until noon. On Mondays, some businesses are closed until 14:00, and possibly all day. Saturdays are like weekdays (but most banks are closed).

Banking
Bring your ATM, credit, or debit card, along with a couple hundred dollars in cash as a backup. Traveler's checks are a waste of your time and money.

The best and easiest way to get cash in euros is to use the omnipresent French bank machines (always open, lower fees, quick processing; you'll need a PIN code—numbers only, no letters—with your Visa or MasterCard). Before you go, verify with your bank that your card will work. Bring two cards in case one gets damaged. "Cash machines" in French are signed *distributeur des billets;* the French just say *"distributeur"* (pron. dee-stree-bew-tur). Also look for signs indicating *point d'argent* (pron. pwan dar-jahn).

Just like at home, credit or debit cards work easily at larger hotels, restaurants, and shops. Smaller businesses prefer payment in local currency. Smart travelers function with hard local cash and a major credit or debit card.

The Language Barrier and that French Attitude
You've no doubt heard that Parisians are "mean and cold and refuse to speak English." This is an out-of-date preconception left over from the de Gaulle days. Parisians are as friendly as any other people and no more disagreeable than New Yorkers. Like many big cities, Paris is a massive melting pot of international cultures (your evening hotel receptionist is just as likely to speak French with an accent as not). And, without any doubt, Parisians speak more English than Americans speak French. Be reasonable in your expectations: Waiters are paid to be efficient, not chatty. And Parisian postal clerks are every bit as speedy, cheery, and multilingual as ours are back home.

The biggest mistake most Americans make when traveling in France is trying to do too much with limited time. Hurried, impatient travelers who miss the subtle pleasures of people-watching from a sun-dappled café often misinterpret French attitudes. By slowing your pace and making an effort to understand French culture, you're much more likely to have a richer experience. Parisians take great pride in their customs, clinging to their belief in cultural superiority despite the fact that they're no longer a world superpower. Let's face it—it's tough to keep on smiling when you've been crushed by a Big Mac, Mickey-Moused by Disney, and drowned in instant coffee. Your hosts

are cold only if you decide to see them that way. Polite and formal, the French respect the fine points of culture and tradition.
In France, strolling down the street wearing a big grin on your
face and saying hello to strangers is a sign of senility, not friendliness (seriously). Parisians think that Americans, while friendly, are
hesitant to pursue more serious friendships. Recognize sincerity
and look for kindness. Give them the benefit of the doubt.

Communication difficulties are exaggerated. To hurdle the
language barrier, bring a small English/French dictionary, a phrase
book (look for ours), a menu reader, and a good supply of patience.
In transactions, a small notepad and pen minimize misunderstand-
ings about prices; have vendors write the price down. If you learn
only five phrases, learn and use these: *bonjour* (good day), *pardon*
(pardon me), *s'il vous plaît* (please), *merci* (thank you), and *au revoir*
(goodbye). The French place great importance on politeness. Begin
every encounter with "*Bonjour, madame/monsieur*" and end every
encounter with "*Au revoir, madame/monsieur.*"

The French are language perfectionists—they take their
language (and other languages) seriously. Often they speak more
English than they let on. This isn't a tourist-baiting tactic, but
timidity on their part to speak another language less than fluently.
Start any conversation with, "*Bonjour, madame/monsieur. Parlez-vous
anglais?*" and hope they speak more English than you speak French.

Travel Smart

Your trip to Paris is like a complex play—easier to follow and
really appreciate on a second viewing. While no one does the same
trip twice to gain that advantage, reading this book in its entirety
before your trip accomplishes much the same thing.

Reread this book as you travel, and visit local tourist information offices (abbreviated as "TI" in this book). Buy a phone card
or cell phone and use it for reservations and confirmations. Be
positive and don't let one rude Parisian ruin your day. Ask questions.
Most locals are eager to point you in their idea of the right direction.
Wear your money belt. Those who expect to travel smart, do.

Plan ahead for banking, laundry, post-office chores, and picnics. Mix intense and relaxed periods. Every trip (and every traveler)
needs at least a few slack days. Pace yourself. Assume you will return.

As you read through this book, plan your itinerary. Note the
days when sights are closed. Sundays have pros and cons, as they
do for traveling in the United States (special events and weekly
markets, limited hours, shops and banks closed, limited public
transportation, no rush hours). Saturdays are virtually weekdays.
Popular places are even more popular on weekends and inundated
on three-day weekends.

In 2003, be ready for unusually big crowds during these holiday periods: Easter week (April 19–26), Labor Day weekend
(May 1–4), VE Day (May 8–10), Ascension weekend (May 29–31),
Pentecost weekend (June 7–9), Bastille Day (July 14), Assump-
tion (Aug 15), All Saints' Day weekend (Oct 30–Nov 1), Armistice
Day (Nov 11), and the winter holidays (late Dec–early Jan). Many
sights close on the actual holiday (check with a local tourist information office).

French Tourist Offices in the United States

France's national tourist offices in the United States are a wealth of
information. Before your trip, request any specific information you
may want (such as city maps and schedules of upcoming festivals).

French Government Tourist Offices: For questions and
brochures (on regions, barging, the wine country, and so on), call
410/286-8310. Ask for the Discovery Guide. Materials delivered
in four to six weeks are free; if you want the information delivered
in three to four days, there's a $4 shipping fee.

Their Web site is www.franceguide.com, and their offices
are in...

New York: 444 Madison Ave., 16th floor, New York, NY
10022, fax 212/838-7855, e-mail: info@francetourism.com.

Illinois: 676 N. Michigan Ave. #3360, Chicago, IL 60611-
2819, fax 312/337-6339, e-mail: fgto@mcs.net.

California: 9454 Wilshire Blvd. #715, Beverly Hills, CA
90212, fax 310/276-2835, e-mail: fgto@gte.net.

Recommended Guidebooks

For most travelers, this book is all you need. But if you'd like more
information, you may want to buy an additional guidebook. The
Michelin Green Guide, which is somewhat scholarly, and the more
readable *Paris Access* guide are both well-researched. Of the multi-
tude of other guidebooks on France and Paris, many are high on
facts and low on opinion, guts, or personality. To better understand
the French, read *French or Foe* (by Polly Platt) and *Fragile Glory* (by
Richard Bernstein). *The Course of French History* (by Pierre Goubert)
provides a good, succinct summary of French history. If you'll be
traveling elsewhere in France, consider *Rick Steves' France 2003*.

Rick Steves' Books and Videos

Rick Steves' Europe Through the Back Door 2003 gives you budget
travel tips on minimizing jet lag, packing light, planning your
itinerary, traveling by car or train, finding budget beds without
reservations, changing money, avoiding rip-offs, outsmarting
thieves, hurdling the language barrier, using cell phones,

staying healthy, taking great photographs, using your bidet, and lots more. The book also includes chapters on 35 of Rick's favorite "Back Doors."

Rick Steves' **Country Guides** are a series of eight guidebooks covering France (co-written with Steve Smith); Great Britain; Ireland (co-written with Pat O'Connor); Italy; Spain and Portugal; Scandinavia; Germany, Austria, and Switzerland; and the Best of Europe. They're updated annually and come out in December and January.

Rick's **City Guides** include this book, Rome, Venice, Florence, London, and—new for 2003—*Rick Steves' Amsterdam, Bruges & Brussels.* By the sleek Eurostar train, London is just three hours from Paris, and by the just-as-sleek Thalys train, Amsterdam is only four hours away. Consider combining two or all three of these cities (and books) for a great visit.

Rick Steves' Europe 101: History and Art for the Traveler (with Gene Openshaw, 2000) gives you the story of Europe's people, history, and art. Written for smart people who were sleeping in their history and art classes before they knew they were going to Europe, *101* really helps Europe's sights come alive.

Rick Steves' Mona Winks (with Gene Openshaw, 2001) gives you fun, easy-to-follow, self-guided tours of Europe's top 25 museums and cultural sites. All of the *Mona Winks* chapters on Paris are included in this Paris guidebook (except the Orangerie Museum, which is closed for renovation in 2003). But if you'd like similar coverage for the great museums in London, Amsterdam, Venice, Florence, Rome, and Madrid, *Mona*'s for you.

Rick Steves' French Phrase Book is a fun, practical tool for independent budget travelers. This handy book has everything you'll need, including a menu decoder, conversation starters for connecting with locals, and an easy-to-follow telephone template for making hotel reservations.

Rick's new PBS TV series, *Rick Steves' Europe*, keeps churning out shows. Of 82 episodes (including the new series and *Travels in Europe with Rick Steves*), two shows cover Paris and seven half-hour shows cover other parts of France. These air nationally on public television stations and the Travel Channel. They are also available in information-packed home videos and DVDs (order online at www.ricksteves.com, or call 425/771-8303 for our free newsletter/catalog).

Rick Steves' Postcards from Europe, Rick's autobiographical book, packs 25 years of travel anecdotes and insights into the ultimate 3,000-mile European adventure. Through his guidebooks, Rick shares his favorite European discoveries with you. *Postcards* introduces you to his favorite European friends.

All of Rick's books are published by Avalon Travel Publishing (www.travelmatters.com).

Maps

The black-and-white maps in this book, drawn by Dave Hoerlein, are concise and simple. Dave, who is well-traveled in Paris, designed these maps to help you quickly orient and painlessly get where you want to go. Once in Paris, simply check the color city map (and handy Métro map) at the front of this book, and you're ready to travel.

For a longer trip, consider the new Rick Steves' France Planning Map, which shows France on one side and Paris on the other. Designed for the traveler, it lists sightseeing destinations prominently (order online at www.ricksteves.com, or call 425/771-8303 for a our free newsletter/catalog).

Tours of Paris and France by Rick Steves and Steve Smith

Travel agents will tell you about all the normal tours of Paris and France, but they won't tell you about ours. At Europe Through the Back Door, we organize and lead one-week tours of Paris and longer tours covering the highlights of France. The Paris tours, limited to 20 people, run March–July and October–December. For a longer tour, choose from "Paris and the Heart of France" (14 days), "Provence and the South of France" (15 days), and "The Best of Village France" (18 days). These depart each year April–October, are limited to 22–26 people per group, and have big, roomy buses and two great guides. For details, call us at 425/771-8303 or check www.ricksteves.com.

Transportation

Transportation concerns within Paris are limited to the subway, buses, and taxis, all covered extensively in the Orientation chapter. If you have a car, stow it (for parking information, see the Transportation Connections chapter on page 324). You don't want to drive in Paris.

For all the specifics on transportation throughout France by train or car, see *Rick Steves' France 2003*.

Telephones, Mail, and E-Mail

You'll want a locally purchased phone card *(une carte téléphonique)* for making hotel/restaurant reservations, verifying hours at sights, and phoning home. There are two basic types: a *télécarte* (pron. tay-lay-kart) that can be used only in a public phone booth, and a *carte téléphonique prépayée* (pron. kart tay-lay-foh-neek pray-pay-yay) with a dial-up code that can be used in any phone. Either card can be purchased at any post office and from most newsstands and tobacco shops *(tabacs)*, which you'll find everywhere in Paris, including at train stations and airports.

The *télécarte* is an efficient card-operated system that has replaced coin-operated public phones throughout Europe. Insert the card in the phone and dial away. There are two denominations: *une petite* costs about €7; *une grande* about €15. When you use the *télécarte* (simply take the phone off the hook, insert the card, and wait for a dial tone), the price of the call (local or international) is automatically deducted.

There are a variety of prepaid cards *(carte téléphonique prépayée)* that work like those sold in the United States, allowing you to dial from the comfort of your hotel (or anywhere) and charge the call to the card at low rates. The *Carte Kertel* (pron. kart kare-tel) and *Carte 365* are the most common (€7 and €15 cards available). There's even an international card *(Le Ticket de Téléphone International)* that offers cheaper rates for international calls. These cards all work the same way and are simple to use, once you learn the rules. Scratch to get your PIN code. After you dial the access code, the message tells you to enter your PIN code followed by #; once the next message arrives, dial your number, again followed by # (you don't have to listen to the sales pitch for more minutes). While per-minute rates are cheaper with a *carte téléphonique prépayée* than with a *télécarte*, it's slower to use (more numbers to dial), so local calls are quicker with a *télécarte* from a phone booth.

U.S. Calling Card Services: Since direct-dialing rates have dropped, calling cards (offered by AT&T, MCI, and Sprint) are no longer the good value they used to be. In fact, they are a rip-off. You'll likely pay $3 for the first minute with a $4 connection fee; if you get an answering machine, it'll cost you $7 to say, "Sorry I missed you." Now it's much cheaper to make your international calls using a phone card purchased in Europe.

Dialing Direct: France has a direct-dial 10-digit telephone system. There are no area codes. To call to or from anywhere in France, including Paris, you dial the 10 numbers directly. All Paris numbers start with 01.

To call France from another country, start with the international access code (00 if you're calling from a European country; 011 from the United States and Canada), dial France's country code (33), and then drop the initial 0 of the 10-digit local number and dial the remaining nine digits. For example, the phone number of a good hotel in Paris is 01 47 05 49 15. To call it from home, dial 011-33-1 47 05 49 15.

To dial out of France, start your call with its international code (00), then dial the country code of the country you're calling, then the number you're calling. For example, to call our office in the United States, dial 00 (France's international access code), 1 (U.S. country code), then 425/771-8303 (our area code plus local number).

For a list of international access codes and country codes, see the appendix. European time is six/nine hours ahead of the East/West Coast of the United States.

Cell Phones: You can buy inexpensive cell phones—about $70 on up—to make local and international calls. The cheapest phones work only in the country where they're sold; the pricier phones work throughout Europe (but it'll cost you about $40 per country to outfit the phone with the necessary chip and prepaid phone time). Because of their expense, cell phones are most economical for travelers staying in one country for two weeks or more. If you're interested, stop by one of the ubiquitous phone shops or at a cell-phone counter in a department store. Find an English-speaking clerk to help you. To understand all the extras, get a brand that has instructions in English. Confirm with the clerk whether the phone works only in France or throughout Europe. Make sure the clerk shows you how to use the phone—practice making a call to the store. You'll need to pick out a policy; different policies offer, say, better rates for making calls at night or for calling cell phones rather than fixed phones. We always get the basic fixed rate: a straight 30 cents per minute to the United States and 15 cents per minute to any fixed or cell phone in the home country at any hour. Receiving calls is generally free. When you run out of calling time, buy more time at a newsstand. Upon arrival in a different country, purchase a new chip (which comes with a new phone number). If you're on a tight budget, skip the cell phone and buy phone cards instead.

Mail: The hours of French post offices (called PTT for "Post, Telegraph, and Telephone") vary, though most are open weekdays 8:00–19:00 and Saturday morning 8:00–12:00. Stamps and phone cards are also sold at *tabac* (tobacco) shops. It costs about €0.70 to mail a postcard to the United States.

To arrange for mail delivery, reserve a few hotels along your route in advance and give their addresses to friends. Or you can use the American Express Company's mail services (free for AmEx cardholders and a minimal fee for anyone else). Allow 10 days for a letter to arrive. Phoning is so easy that we've dispensed with mail stops altogether.

E-mail: E-mail has caught on among hoteliers; very few lack an e-mail address. As for Internet access, ask at your hotel for the nearest Internet (pron. an-ter-net) café; some hoteliers even have Internet terminals in their lobbies. If the extension .com doesn't work, try .fr for France.

If you're planning to go online from your hotel room, you'll need an Internet service provider (ISP) that has local phone numbers for each country you visit. While an American modem cable plugs into a European phone jack, you may have to tweak your settings to make your computer recognize a pulse instead of the U.S. dial tone. Bring a phone jack tester that reverses line polarity as needed.

Tipping

Tipping in France isn't as automatic and generous as it is in the United States, but for special service, tips are appreciated, if not expected. As in the United States, the proper amount depends on your resources, tipping philosophy, and the circumstance, but some general guidelines apply.

Restaurants: At cafés and restaurants, the service charge is included in the bill, though it's customary to tip 5 percent extra for good service (for details, see page 285). If you order a meal at a counter, don't tip.

Taxis: To tip the cabbie, round up. For a typical ride, round up to the next euro on the fare (to pay a €13 fare, give €14); for a long ride, round to the nearest €10 (for a €75 fare, give €80). If the cabbie hauls your bags and zips you to the airport to help you catch your flight, you might want to toss in a little more. But if you feel like you're being driven in circles or otherwise ripped off, skip the tip.

Special services: Tour guides at public sites and tour bus drivers sometimes hold out their hands for tips after the tour; since we've already paid for the tour, we don't tip extra—but some tourists do give a euro or two, particularly for a job well done. We don't tip at hotels, but if you do, give the porter a euro for carrying bags and leave a couple of euros in your room at the end of your stay for the maid if the room was kept clean. In general, if someone in the service industry does a super job for you, a tip of a couple euros is appropriate . . . but not required.

When in doubt, ask. If you're not sure whether (or how much) to tip for a service, ask your hotelier or the tourist information office; they'll fill you in on how it's done on their turf.

Stranger in a Strange Land

We travel all the way to Europe to enjoy differences—to become temporary locals. You'll experience frustrations. Certain truths that we find "God-given" or "self-evident," like friendly waiters, ice in drinks, bottomless cups of coffee, hot showers, body odor smelling bad, and bigger being better, are suddenly not so true. One of the benefits of travel is the eye-opening realization that there are logical, civil, and even better alternatives. Paris is an understand-ably proud city. To enjoy its people, you need to celebrate the differences. A willingness to go local ensures that you'll enjoy a full dose of Parisian hospitality.

Back Door Manners

While updating our guidebooks, we hear over and over again that our readers are considerate and fun to have as guests. Thank you for traveling as temporary locals who are sensitive to the culture. It's fun to follow you in our travels.

Send Us a Postcard, Drop Us a Line

If you enjoy a successful trip with the help of this book and would like to share your discoveries, please fill out the survey at the end of this book and send it to Europe Through the Back Door, Box 2009, Edmonds, WA 98020. We personally read and value all feedback. Thanks in advance—it helps a lot.

For our latest travel information, tap into our Web site: www.ricksteves.com. To check for any updates to this book, visit www.ricksteves.com/update. Rick's e-mail address is rick @ricksteves.com. Anyone is welcome to request a free issue of our Back Door quarterly newsletter (call 425/771-8303 or order it online at www.ricksteves.com).

Judging from all the positive feedback and happy postcards we receive from travelers who have used this book, it's safe to assume you'll enjoy a great, affordable vacation—with the finesse of an independent, experienced traveler.

From this point, "we" (your co-authors) will shed our respective egos and become "I."

Thanks, and *bon voyage*!

BACK DOOR TRAVEL PHILOSOPHY
From *Rick Steves' Europe Through the Back Door*

Travel is intensified living—maximum thrills per minute and one of the last great sources of legal adventure. Travel is freedom. It's recess, and we need it.

Experiencing the real Europe requires catching it by surprise, going casual . . . "Through the Back Door."

Affording travel is a matter of priorities. (Make do with the old car.) You can travel—simply, safely, and comfortably—anywhere in Europe for $80 a day plus transportation costs. In many ways, spending more money only builds a thicker wall between you and what you came to see. Europe is a cultural carnival and, time after time, you'll find that its best acts are free and the best seats are the cheap ones.

A tight budget forces you to travel close to the ground, meeting and communicating with the people, not relying on service with a purchased smile. Never sacrifice sleep, nutrition, safety, or cleanliness in the name of budget. Simply enjoy the local-style alternatives to expensive hotels and restaurants.

Extroverts have more fun. If your trip is low on magic moments, kick yourself and make things happen. If you don't enjoy a place, maybe you don't know enough about it. Seek the truth. Recognize tourist traps. Give a culture the benefit of your open mind. See things as different but not better or worse. Any culture has much to share.

Of course, travel, like the world, is a series of hills and valleys. Be fanatically positive and militantly optimistic. If something's not to your liking, change your liking. Travel is addictive. It can make you a happier American, as well as a citizen of the world. Our Earth is home to six billion equally important people. It's humbling to travel and find that people don't envy Americans. They like us, but, with all due respect, they wouldn't trade passports.

Globetrotting destroys ethnocentricity. It helps you understand and appreciate different cultures. Travel changes people. It broadens perspectives and teaches new ways to measure quality of life. Many travelers toss aside their hometown blinders. Their prized souvenirs are the strands of different cultures they decide to knit into their own character. The world is a cultural yarn shop. And Back Door Travelers are weaving the ultimate tapestry.

Come on, join in!

ORIENTATION

Many people fall in love with Paris. Some see the essentials and flee, overwhelmed by the big city. With the proper approach, you'll fall head over heels for Europe's capital city.

This orientation to the City of Lights will illuminate your trip. The day plans—for visits of one to seven days—will help you prioritize the many sights. You'll tap into Paris' information sources for current events. Most important, you'll learn to navigate Paris by Métro, bus, taxi, or foot. For most travelers, the key to the city is a Métro ticket.

Arrival in Paris

For a comprehensive rundown on Paris' six train stations and two airports, see the Transportation Connections chapter on page 324.

Planning Your Time

Paris in One, Two, or Three Busy Days

Sights are listed in descending order of importance. If you have only one day, just do Day 1 (below); for two days, add Day 2. If you want to fit in Versailles on a three-day visit, try the afternoon of the second day (easier) or third day.

Day 1

Morning: Follow Historic Paris Walk, featuring Ile de la Cité, Notre-Dame, Latin Quarter, and Sainte-Chapelle (consider lunch at nearby Samaritaine view café).
Afternoon: Tour the Louvre.
Evening: Cruise Seine River or take "Paris Illumination" nighttime bus tour.

Day 2
Morning: Follow Champs-Elysées Walk from Arc de Triomphe down the grand Champs-Elysées boulevard to Tuileries Garden (consider lunch at a café in the Tuileries Garden).
Midday: Cross the pedestrian bridge from the Tuileries Garden, then tour the Orsay Museum.
Afternoon: Tour the Rodin Museum or Napoleon's Tomb, or visit Versailles (take RER direct from Orsay).
Evening: Enjoy Trocadéro scene and twilight ride up the Eiffel Tower.

Day 3
Morning: Follow Marais Walk.
Afternoon: Stay in the Marais and tour your choice of the Carnavalet Museum, Pompidou Center, or Jewish Art and History Museum. (Or visit Versailles.)
Evening: Take Montmartre Walk, featuring Sacré-Coeur.

Paris in Five to Seven Days without Going In-Seine
Day 1
Morning: Follow Historic Paris Walk, featuring Ile de la Cité, Notre-Dame, Latin Quarter, Cluny Museum, and Sainte-Chapelle.
Afternoon: Enjoy the Luxembourg Garden and relax in a nearby café (see "Les Grands Cafés de Paris" in the Eating chapter) or tour the nearby Pompidou Center.
Evening: Cruise Seine River or take "Paris Illumination" nighttime bus tour.

Day 2
Morning: Tour the Louvre (arrive 20 min before opening). Lunch at Café le Nemours.
Afternoon: Follow Champs-Elysées Walk from Arc de Triomphe down the grand Champs-Elysées boulevard to Tuileries Garden. (Reversing the morning and afternoon also works well because the Champs-Elysées Walk leaves you near the Louvre, though most have more energy for museums in the morning.)
Evening: Take Montmartre Walk, featuring Sacré-Coeur.

Day 3
Morning: Tour Orsay Museum (arrive 15 min before opening).
Midday: Tour Rodin Museum (picnic or café lunch in gardens).
Afternoon: Visit Napoleon's Tomb, then take the Rue Cler Walk and relax at the Café du Marché.
Evening: Enjoy dinner on the Ile St. Louis.

Daily Reminder

Monday: These sights are closed today—Orsay, Rodin, Marmottan, Montmartre, Carnavalet, Petit Palais, Catacombs, Giverny, and Versailles; the Louvre is more crowded because of this, but the Denon wing (with *Mona Lisa*, Venus de Milo, and more highlights) stays open until 21:45. Napoleon's Tomb is closed the first Monday of the month. Some small stores don't open until 14:00. Street markets such as rue Cler and rue Mouffetard are dead today. Some banks are closed. It's discount night at most cinemas.

Tuesday: Many museums are closed today, including the Louvre, Picasso, Cluny, and Pompidou Center, as well as the châteaux of Chantilly (except July–Aug) and Fontainebleau. The Eiffel Tower, Orsay, and Versailles are particularly busy today.

Wednesday: All sights are open (Louvre until 21:45). The weekly *Pariscope* magazine comes out today. Most schools are closed, so many kids' sights are busy. Some cinemas offer discounts.

Thursday: All sights are open (except the Sewer Tour). The Orsay is open until 21:45. Department stores are open late.

Friday: All sights are open (except the Sewer Tour). Afternoon trains and roads leaving Paris are crowded; TGV reservation fees are higher.

Saturday: All sights are open (except the Jewish Art and History Museum). The fountains run at Versailles (July–Sept) and Vaux-le-Vicomte hosts candlelight visits (May–Oct); otherwise avoid weekend crowds at area châteaux. Department stores are busy. The Jewish Quarter is quiet.

Sunday: Some museums are two-thirds price all day and/or free the first Sunday of the month, thus more crowded (e.g., Louvre, Orsay, Rodin, Cluny, Pompidou, and Picasso). The fountains run at Versailles (early April–early Oct). Most of Paris' stores are closed on Sunday, but shoppers will find relief in the Marais neighborhood's lively Jewish Quarter and in Bercy Village, where many stores are open. Look for organ concerts at St. Sulpice and possibly other churches. The American Church sometimes offers a free evening concert at 18:00 (Sept–May only). Most recommended restaurants in the rue Cler neighborhood are closed for dinner.

Day 4
Morning: Catch the RER and arrive early (9:00) at Versailles. Tour palace interior.
Midday: Have lunch on Versailles' market square.
Afternoon: Take the shortcut from the market square to Versailles' gardens, and visit Le Hameau and Trianon Palaces. Return to Paris with some time for shopping.
Evening: Attend a concert at Sainte-Chapelle.

Day 5
Morning: Follow Marais Walk and tour the Carnavalet Museum. Lunch at Nectarine on place des Vosges or have a falafel on rue des Rosiers.
Afternoon: Tour the Pompidou Center and/or the Jewish Art and History Museum.
Evening: Enjoy Trocadéro scene and twilight ride up the Eiffel Tower.

Days 6 and 7
Choose from:
Shopping and cafés
Montmartre and Sacré-Coeur (by day)
Picasso, Cluny, Marmottan, or Jacquemart-André Museums, or Garnier Opéra
Day trip to Chartres
Day trip to Vaux-le-Vicomte and Fontainebleau
Day trip to Disneyland Paris
Evening: Night bus or boat tour (whichever you have yet to do)

Paris: A Verbal Map
Paris is split in half by the Seine River, divided into 20 *arrondissements* (proud and independent governmental jurisdictions), and circled by a ring-road freeway (the *périphérique*). You'll find Paris easier to navigate if you know which side of the river you're on, which *arrondissement* you're in, and which subway (Métro) stop you're closest to. If you're north of the river (the top half of any city map), you're on the Right

Paris Arrondissements

Bank (*rive droite*). If you're south of it, you're on the Left Bank (*rive gauche*). Most of your sightseeing will take place within five blocks of the river.

Arrondissements are numbered, starting at the Louvre and moving in a clockwise spiral out to the ring road. The last two digits in a Parisian zip code are the *arrondissement* number. The abbreviation for the Métro stop is "Mo." In Parisian jargon, Napoleon's tomb is on *la rive gauche* (the Left Bank) in the *7ème* (7th *arrondissement*), zip code 75007, Mo: Invalides. Paris Métro stops are used as a standard aid in giving directions, even for those not using the Métro. As you're tracking down addresses, these definitions will help: *place* (square), *rue* (road), and *pont* (bridge).

Tourist Information

Avoid the Paris tourist offices (abbreviated as "TI" in this book) because of their long lines, short information, and charge for maps. This book, the *Pariscope* magazine (described below), and one of the freebie maps available at any hotel (or in the front of this book) are all you need. The main TI is at 127 avenue des **Champs-Elysées** (daily 9:00–20:00, tel. 08 36 92 31 12—phone tree), but the other TIs are less crowded: at **Gare de Lyon** (daily 8:00–20:00), at the **Eiffel Tower** (May–Sept daily 11:00–18:42, yes, 18:42, closed off-season, tel. 01 45 51 22 15), and at the **Louvre** (Wed–Mon 10:00–19:00, closed Tue). Both **airports** have handy TIs (called ADP) with long hours and short lines (see the Transportation Connections chapter). If you want to call a Paris TI from the States, dial 011 33 8 92 68 31 12 (wait for message in English).

Paris' TIs have an official Web site (www.paris-touristoffice .com) offering practical information on hotels, special events, museums, children's activities, fashion, nightlife, and more. Two other Web sites that are entertaining and at times useful are www.bonjourparis.com (which claims to offer a virtual trip to Paris with interactive French lessons, tips on wine and food, and news on the latest Parisian trends) and the similar www .paris-anglo.com (with informative stories on visiting Paris, plus a directory of over 2,500 English-speaking businesses).

For a complete schedule of museum hours and English-language museum tours, pick up the free *Musées, Monuments Historiques, et Expositions* booklet from any museum.

Pariscope: The *Pariscope* weekly magazine (or one of its clones, €0.50 at any newsstand) lists museum hours, art exhibits, concerts, music festivals, plays, movies, and nightclubs. Smart tour guides and sightseers rely on this for all the latest (www.pariscope.fr, in French). See "Tour of *Pariscope*" on page 319.

Maps: While Paris is littered with free maps, they don't show all the streets. You may want the huge Michelin #10 map of Paris. For an extended stay, I prefer the pocket-size, street-indexed *Paris Pratique* (about €6) with an easy-to-use Métro map.

Bookstores: There are many English-language bookstores in Paris where you can pick up guidebooks (for nearly double their American prices). A few of the best: Shakespeare & Company (daily 12:00–24:00, some used travel books, 37 rue de la Boucherie, across the river from Notre-Dame, tel. 01 43 26 96 50), W. H. Smith (248 rue de Rivoli, Mo: Concorde, tel. 01 44 77 88 99), and Brentanos (37 avenue de L'Opéra, Mo: Opéra, tel. 01 42 61 52 50). The friendly Red Wheelbarrow Bookstore in the Marais neighborhood sells our books (13 rue Charles V, Mo: St Paul, tel. 01 42 77 42 17).

American Church: The American Church is a nerve center for the American émigré community. It distributes a free, handy, and insightful monthly English-language newspaper called the *Paris Voice* (with useful reviews of concerts, plays, and current events; available at about 200 locations in Paris, http://parisvoice.com) and an advertisement paper called *France—U.S.A. Contacts* (full of useful information for those seeking work or long-term housing). The church faces the river between the Eiffel Tower and Orsay Museum (reception open Mon–Sat 9:30–22:30, Sun 9:00–19:30, 65 quai d'Orsay, Mo: Invalides, tel. 01 40 62 05 00).

Helpful Hints

Theft Alert: Pickpockets seem more numerous and determined than ever. Métro and RER lines that serve popular sights are infested with thieves. Wear a money belt, put your wallet in your front pocket, loop your day bag over your shoulders (consider wearing it in front), and keep a tight grip on a purse or shopping bag. If you're out late, avoid the riverfront quays if the lighting is dim and pedestrian activity minimal.

Paris Museum Pass: This worthwhile pass, covering most sights in Paris, is available at major Métro stations, TIs, and museums. For detailed information, see page 29.

Museum Strategy: Arriving 20 minutes before major museums open is line-time well spent. Remember, most museums require you to check daypacks and coats, and important museums have metal detectors that will slow your entry. If you're still ahead of the pack when you enter, consider hustling to the most popular works first.

Street Safety: Be careful on foot! Parisian drivers are notorious for ignoring pedestrians. Look both ways (many streets are one-way) and be careful of seemingly quiet bus/taxi lanes. Don't assume you have the right of way, even in a crosswalk. When crossing a street, keep your pace constant and don't stop suddenly. By law, drivers must miss pedestrians by one meter/three feet

(1.5 meters/5 feet in the countryside). Drivers carefully calculate your speed and won't hit you, provided you don't alter your route or pace. Watch out for a lesser hazard: *merde.* Parisian dogs decorate the city's sidewalks with 16 tons of droppings a day. People get injured by slipping in it.

Toilets: Carry small change for pay toilets, or walk into any sidewalk café like you own the place and find the toilet in the back. The toilets in museums are free and generally the best you'll find, and if you have a museum pass, you can drop into almost any museum for the clean toilets. Modern, super-sanitary, street-booth toilets provide both relief and a memory (coins required, don't leave small children inside unattended). Keep some toilet paper or tissues with you, as some toilets are poorly supplied.

Getting around Paris

By Métro: Europe's best subway is divided into two systems—the Métro (for puddle-jumping everywhere in Paris; see map in this book) and the RER (connects suburban destinations with a few stops in central Paris). You'll use the Métro for almost all your trips (daily from 5:30 until 00:30). Occasionally, you'll find the RER more convenient, as it makes fewer stops (like an express bus).

Tickets and Passes: In Paris, you're never more than a 10-minute walk from a Métro station. One ticket takes you anywhere in the system with unlimited transfers. Save 40 percent by buying a *carnet* (pron. car-nay) of 10 tickets for €10 at any Métro station (a single ticket is €1.40, kids 4–10 pay €5 for a *carnet*). Métro tickets work on city buses, though one ticket cannot be used as a transfer between subway and bus. If you're staying in Paris for a week or more, consider the **Carte Orange** (pron. kart oh-rahnzh), which gives you free run of the bus and Métro system for one week (about €15, ask for Carte Orange *coupon vert* and supply a passport-size photo) or a month (about €50, ask for Carte Orange *coupon orange*). These passes cover only central Paris; you can pay more for passes covering regional destinations (like Versailles). The weekly pass begins Monday and ends Sunday, and the monthly pass is valid from the first to last day of the month, so mid-week or mid-month pass purchases aren't worthwhile. All passes can be purchased at any Métro station, most of which have photo booths where you can get the photo required for the pass. While some Métro agents may hesitate to sell you Carte Orange passes because you're not a resident (and encourage you to buy the bad-value Paris Visite pass instead), Carte Orange passes are definitely not limited to residents; if you're refused, simply go to another station to buy your pass. The overpriced **Paris Visite** passes were designed for tourists, offering minor reductions at minor sights but costing

Key Words for the Métro and RER

- *direction* (pron. dee-rek-see-ohn): direction
- *ligne* (pron. leen-yuh): line
- *correspondance* (pron. kor-res-pohn-dahns): transfer
- *sortie* (pron. sor-tee): exit
- *carnet* (pron. kar-nay): cheap set of 10 tickets
- *Pardon, madame/monsieur* (pron. par-dohn, mah-dahm/ mes-yur): Excuse me, lady/sir.
- *Je descend* (pron. juh day-sahn): I'm getting off.
- *Donnez-moi mon porte-feuille!* (pron. doh-nay mwah mohn port-foo-ay): Give me my wallet!

Etiquette

- When waiting at the platform, get out of the way of those exiting the train. Board only once everyone is off.
- Avoid using the hinged seats near the doors when the car is jammed; they take up valuable standing space.
- In a crowded train, try not to block the exit. If you're blocking the door when the train stops, step out of the car and to the side, let others off, then get back on.
- Talk softly in the cars. Listen to how quietly Parisians can communicate and follow their lead.
- On escalators, stand on the right, pass on the left.

more than a *carnet* of 10 tickets or a Carte Orange (1 day-€9, 2 days-€14, 3 days-€19, 5 days-€28).

How the Métro works: To get to your destination, determine the closest "Mo" stop and which line or lines will get you there. The lines have numbers, but they're best known by their direction or end-of-the-line stop. (For example, the La Défense/ Château de Vincennes line runs between La Défense in the west and Vincennes in the east.) Once in the Métro station, you'll see blue-and-white signs directing you to the train going in your direction (e.g., "*direction:* La Défense"). Insert your ticket in the automatic turnstile, pass through, and reclaim and keep your ticket until you exit the system. Fare inspectors regularly check for cheaters and accept absolutely no excuses from anyone. I repeat, keep that ticket until you leave the Métro system. Also keep in mind that if you travel beyond the center city, you'll need to buy an RER ticket for your destination before getting on the RER (see below for details).

Transfers are free and can be made wherever lines cross.

When you transfer, look for the orange *correspondance* (con-nections) signs when you exit your first train, then follow the proper direction sign.

While the Métro whisks you quickly from one point to another, be prepared to walk significant distances within stations to reach your platform (most noticeable when you transfer). Escalators are usually available for vertical movement, but they're not always in working order. To avoid excessive walking, avoid transfering at these stations: Montparnasse, Chatelet/Les Halles, Etoile, Gare du Nord, and Bastille.

Before taking the *sortie* (exit), check the helpful *plan du quartier* (map of the neighborhood) to get your bearings, locate your destination, and decide which *sortie* you want. At stops with several *sorties*, you can save lots of walking by choosing the best exit.

After you exit the system, toss or tear your used ticket so you don't confuse it with your unused ticket—they look virtu-ally identical.

Thieves spend their days in the Métro. Be on guard. For example, if your pocket is picked as you pass through a turnstile, you end up stuck on the wrong side while the thief strolls away. Any jostle or commotion (especially when boarding or leaving trains) is likely the sign of a thief or team of thieves in action.

Paris has a huge homeless population and higher than 11 percent unemployment; expect a warm Métro welcome by pan-handlers, musicians, and those selling magazines produced by the homeless community.

By RER: The RER (Réseau Express Régionale; pron. air-euh-air) is the suburban train system serving destinations such as Versailles, Disneyland Paris, and the airports. These routes are indicated by thick lines on your subway map and identified by letters A, B, C, and so on. The RER works like the Métro but can be speedier (if it serves your destination directly) because it makes only a few stops within the city. One Métro ticket is all you need for RER rides within central Paris. You can transfer between the Métro and RER systems with the same ticket. Unlike in the Métro, you need to insert your ticket in a turnstile to exit the RER system, and also unlike the Métro, signage can vary between RER stations, meaning you have to pay attention and verify that you're head-ing the right direction (RER lines often split at the end of the line leading to different *destination* signs—study your map or confirm with a local and you'll do fine). To travel outside the city (to Ver-sailles or the airport, for example), you'll need to buy a separate, more expensive ticket at the station window before boarding; make sure your stop is served by checking the signs over the train platform. Not all trains serve all stops. If you see *toutes les gares* on the platform sign, your train will stop at all of the stations.

By City Bus: The trickier bus system is worth figuring out. Métro tickets are good on both bus and Métro, though you can't use the same ticket to transfer between the two systems. One ticket gets you anywhere in central Paris, but if you leave the city center (shown as zone 1 on the diagram on board the bus), you must validate a second ticket. While the Métro shuts down about 00:30, some buses continue much later. Schedules are posted at bus stops. Handy bus-system maps *(plan des autobus)* are available in any Métro station and are provided in your *Paris Pratique* map book if you invest €6.

Big system maps, posted at each bus and Métro stop, display the routes. Individual route diagrams show the exact routes of the lines serving that stop. Major stops are painted on the side of each bus. Enter through the front doors. Punch your Métro ticket in the machine behind the driver, or pay the higher cash fare. Get off the bus using the rear door. Even if you're not certain you've figured it out, do some joyriding (outside of rush hour). Lines #24, #63, and #69 are Paris' most scenic routes and make a great introduction to the city. Bus #69 is particularly handy, running between the Eiffel Tower and the Père Lachaise Cemetery by way of rue Cler (recommended hotels), the quai d'Orsay, the Louvre, and the Marais (recommended hotels). The handiest bus routes are listed for each hotel area recommended (see the Sleeping chapter, page 258).

By Taxi: Parisian taxis are reasonable—especially for couples and families. The meters are tamper-proof. Fares and supplements (described in English on the back windows) are straightforward. There's a €5 minimum. A 10-minute ride costs about €8 (versus €1 to get anywhere in town on the Métro). You can try waving one down, but it's easier to ask for the nearest taxi stand (*Où est une station de taxi?*; pron. oo ay oon stah-see-ohn duh taxi). Taxi stands are indicated by a circled *T* on many city maps, including Michelin's #10 Paris. A typical taxi takes three people (maybe 4 if you're polite and pay €2.50 extra); groups of up to five can use a *grand taxi*, which must be booked in advance (ask your hotel to call). If a taxi is summoned by phone, the meter starts as soon as the call is received—adding €3 or €4 to the bill. Higher rates are charged at night from 19:00 to 7:00, all day Sunday, and to either airport. There's a €1 charge for each piece of baggage and for train station pick-ups. To tip, round up to the next euro (minimum €0.50). Taxis are tough to find on Friday and Saturday nights, especially after the Métro closes (around 00:30). If you need to catch a train or flight early in the morning, consider booking a taxi the night before.

Organized Tours of Paris

Bus Tours—Paris Vision offers handy bus tours of Paris, day and night (advertised in hotel lobbies); their "Paris Illumination" night tour is much more interesting and is explained on page 321.

Far better daytime bus tours are the hop-on, hop-off, double-decker buses that connect Paris' main sights while providing running commentary (ideal in good weather when you can sit on top; see also Bâtobus under "Boat Tours," below). Two companies provide hop-on, hop-off bus service: **L'Open Tours** and **Les Cars Rouges** (pick up their brochures showing routes and stops from any TI or on their buses). L'Open Tours, which uses yellow buses, provides more extensive coverage and offers three different routes rolling by most of the important sights in Paris (the Paris Grand Tour offers the best introduction). Tickets are good for any route. Buy your tickets from the driver (€25/1-day ticket, €27/2-day ticket, kids 4–11 pay €12.50 for 1 or 2 days, 20 percent less if you have a *Carte Orange* Métro pass). Two or three buses depart hourly from about 10:00 to 18:00; expect to wait 10–20 minutes at each stop (stops can be tricky to find). You can hop off at any stop, then catch a later bus following the same circuit. You'll see these bright-yellow topless double-decker buses all over town—pick one up at the first important sight you visit, or start your tour at the Eiffel Tower stop (the first street on other side of the tower from the river, tel. 01 42 66 56 56). **Les Cars Rouges'** bright red buses offer largely the same service with fewer stops on a single Grand Tour Route, for less money (2-day tickets, €22-adult, €11-kids 4–12, tel. 01 53 95 39 53).

Boat Tours—Several companies offer one-hour boat cruises on the Seine (by far best at night). The huge, mass-production **Bâteaux-Mouches** boats depart every 20–30 minutes from the pont de l'Alma's right bank, and right in front of the Eiffel Tower, and are convenient to rue Cler hotels (€7.50, €4.50 for ages 4–12, daily 10:00–22:30, useless taped explanations in 6 languages and tour groups by the dozens, tel. 01 40 76 99 99). The smaller and more intimate **Vedettes de pont Neuf** depart only once an hour from the center of pont Neuf (twice an hour after dark), but they come with a live guide giving explanations in French and English and are convenient to Marais and Contrescarpe hotels (€9.50, €5 for ages 4–12, tel. 01 46 33 98 38).

From April through October, **Bâtobus** operates hop-on, hop-off boats on the Seine, connecting eight popular stops every 15–25 minutes: Eiffel Tower, Champs-Elysées, Orsay/place de la Concorde, Louvre, Notre-Dame, St. Germain-des-Prés, Hôtel de Ville, and Jardin des Plantes. Pick up a schedule at any stop (or TI) and use them as a scenic alternative to the Métro. Tickets are available for one day (€10, €5.50 under 12) and two days (€12.50, €6.50 under 12); boats run from 10:00 to 19:00, or 21:00 June through September.

Paris Canal departs twice daily for three-hour, one-way cruises between the Orsay Museum and Parc de la Vilette. You'll cruise up the Seine then along a quiet canal through non-touristy Paris, accompanied by English explanations (€17, €9.50 for kids 4–11, €12.50 for ages 12–25, tel. 01 42 40 96 97); the one-way trips depart at 9:30 from quai Anatole France (near the Orsay), and from Parc de la Vilette (at Folie des Visites du Parc) at 14:30.

Canauxrama offers a 2.5-hour cruise on a peaceful canal without the Seine in sight, starting from Place de la Bastille and ending at Bassin de la Vilette, near Métro stop Stalingrad (€14, €9 for kids, €11 for seniors and students, departs at 9:45 and 14:30 across from Opéra Bastille, just below boulevard de la Bastille, opposite #50, where the canal meets place de la Bastille, tel. 01 42 39 15 00).

Walking Tours—The company **Paris Walking Tours** offers a variety of excellent two-hour walks, led by British or American guides, nearly daily for €10 (tel. 01 48 09 21 40 for recorded schedule in English, fax 01 42 43 75 51, see www.paris-walks.com for their complete schedule). Tours focus on the Marais, Montmartre, Ile de la Cité and Ile St. Louis, and Hemingway's Paris. Ask about their family-friendly tours. Call ahead a day or two to learn their schedule and starting point. No reservations are required. These are thoughtfully prepared, relaxing, and humorous. Don't hesitate to stand close to the guide to hear.

Private Guide Service—For many, Paris merits hiring a Parisian as your personal guide. Two excellent licensed local guides who freelance for individuals and families are Arnaud Servignat, who runs Accueil-France-Paris-Guide (also does car tours of countryside around Paris, tel. 06 72 77 94 50, fax 01 42 57 00 38, e-mail: arnotour@noos.fr or franceparisguide@noos.fr), and Marianne Siegler (€150/4 hrs, €250/day, reserve in advance if possible, tel. 01 42 52 32 51).

Bike Tours—**Mike's Bullfrog Bike Tours** attract a younger crowd for boisterous three- to four-hour rolls through Paris (€20, May–Nov daily at 11:00, also at 15:30 June–July, no CC, in English, no bikes or reservations needed, meet at south pillar of Eiffel Tower, cellular 06 09 98 08 60, www.mikesbiketours.com).

Excursion Tours—Many companies offer minivan and big bus tours to regional sights, including all of the day trips described in this book. **Paris Walking Tours** are the best, with informative though infrequent tours of the Impressionist artist retreats of Giverny and Auvers-sur-Oise (€47–56, includes admissions, tel. 01 48 09 21 40 for recording in English, fax 01 42 43 75 51, www.paris-walks.com).

Paris Vision offers mass-produced, full-size bus and minivan tours to several popular regional destinations, including the Loire Valley, Champagne region, D-Day beaches, and Mont St. Michel. Their minivan tours are more expensive but more personal, given in English, and offer pick-up at your hotel (€130–200/person). Their full-size bus tours are multilingual and cost about half the price of a minivan tour—worth it for some simply for the ease of transportation to the sights (full-size buses depart from 214 rue de Rivoli, Mo: Tuileries, tel. 01 42 60 30 01, fax 01 42 86 95 36, www.parisvision.com).

SIGHTS

These sights are arranged by neighborhood for handy sightseeing. When you see a ✪ in a listing, it means the sight is covered in much more depth in one of my walks or self-guided tours.

Paris Museum Pass: In Paris, there are two classes of sightseers—those with a Paris museum pass and those who stand in line. Serious sightseers save time and money by getting this pass.

Most of the sights listed in this chapter are covered by the Paris museum pass, except for the Eiffel Tower, Montparnasse Tower, Marmottan Museum, Garnier Opéra, Notre-Dame treasury, Jacquemart-André Museum, Jewish Art and History Museum, Grande Arche de La Défense, Jeu de Paume Exhibition Hall, Catacombs, *Paris Story* film, and the ladies of Pigalle. Outside Paris, the pass covers the châteaux of Versailles, Chantilly, and Fontainebleau.

The pass pays for itself in two admissions and gets you into most sights with no lining up (1 day-€15, 3 consecutive days-€30, 5 consecutive days-€45, no youth or senior discount). It's sold at museums, main Métro stations (including Ecole Militaire and Bastille stations), and TIs (even at the airports). Try to avoid buying the pass at a major museum (such as the Louvre), where supply can be spotty and lines long.

The pass isn't activated until the first time you use it (you enter the date on the pass). Think and read ahead to make the most of your pass, since some museums are free (e.g., Carnavalet, the Petit Palais, and Victor Hugo's house) and many are discounted on Sundays, and your pass must be used on consecutive days.

The pass isn't worth buying for children, as most museums are free for those under 18. Note that kids can skip the lines with their passholder parents.

The free museum and monuments directory that comes with

your pass lists the latest hours, phone numbers, and specifics on what kids pay. The cutoff age for free entry varies from 5 to 18. Most major art museums let young people under 18 in for free, but anyone over age 5 has to pay to tour the sewers—go figure.

Included sights you're likely to visit (and admission prices without the pass): Louvre (€7.50), Orsay Museum (€7), Sainte-Chapelle (€5.50), Arc de Triomphe (€7), Les Invalides Museums/Napoleon's Tomb (€6), Conciergerie (€5.50), Panthéon (€5.50), Sewer Tour (€4), Cluny Museum (€7), Pompidou Center (€5.50), Notre-Dame towers (€5.50) and crypt (€3.50), Picasso Museum (€5.50), Rodin Museum (€5), and the Cité des Sciences et l'Industrie museum (€9). Outside Paris, the pass covers the Palace of Versailles (€7.50) and its Trianon châteaux (€5); Château of Fontainebleau (€5.50); and Château of Chantilly (€6).

Tally up what you want to see—and remember, an advantage of the pass is that you skip to the front of some lines, saving hours of waiting, especially in summer (though everyone must pass through the slow-moving metal-detector lines at some sights, and a few places, such as Notre-Dame's tower, can't accommodate a bypass lane). With the pass, you'll pop freely into sights that you're walking by (even for a few minutes) that otherwise might not be worth the expense (e.g., Notre-Dame crypt, Conciergerie, Picasso Museum, and the Panthéon).

Museum Tips: The Louvre and many other museums are closed on Tuesday. The Orsay, Rodin, Marmottan, and Carnavalet Museums and Versailles are closed Monday. Most museums offer reduced prices on Sunday. Many sights stop admitting people 30–60 minutes before they close, and many begin closing rooms 45 minutes before the actual closing time. For the fewest crowds, visit very early, at lunch, or very late. Most museums have slightly shorter hours October through March. French holidays can really mess up your sightseeing plans (Jan 1, May 1, May 8, July 14, Nov 1, Nov 11, and Dec 25). The best Impressionist art museums are the Orsay and Marmottan (see the self-guided tours of these in this book). Another excellent Impressionist museum, L'Orangerie, is closed until 2004.

Paris Museums near the Tuileries Garden

Paris' grandest park, the Tuileries Garden, was once the private property of kings and queens and now links the museums of the Louvre, L'Orangerie (closed until 2004), Jeu de Paume, and the Orsay.

▲▲▲**Louvre (Musée du Louvre)**—This is Europe's oldest, biggest, greatest, and second-most-crowded museum (after the Vatican). It's packed with Greek and Roman masterpieces, medieval jewels, Michelangelo statues, and paintings by the greatest artists from the Renaissance to the Romantics (mid-1800s).

Museums near Tuileries Garden

Cost: €7.50, €5 after 15:00 and on Sun, free on first Sun of month and for those under 18, covered by museum pass.

Hours: Wed–Mon 9:00–18:00, closed Tue. All wings open Wed until 21:45. On Mon, only the Denon wing is open until 21:45. Galleries start closing 30 minutes early. Closed Jan 1, Easter, May 1, Nov 1, and Dec 25. Tel. 01 40 20 51 51, recorded info tel. 01 40 20 53 17, www.louvre.fr.

Location: At Palais Royal/Musée du Louvre Métro stop. (The old Louvre Métro stop, called Louvre Rivoli, is farther from the entrance.) ✪ See Louvre Tour on page 100.

▲**Orangerie (Musée de l'Orangerie)**—This Impressionist museum, lovely as a water lily, is due to reopen sometime in early 2004 after renovation (for the latest, ask at a Paris TI or any Paris museum). When it opens, you can step out of the tree-lined, sun-dappled Impressionist painting that is the Tuileries Garden, and into L'Orangerie (pron. loh-rahn-zheh-ree), a little *bijou* of select works by Utrillo, Cézanne, Renoir, Matisse, and Picasso. On the ground floor, you'll find a line of eight rooms dedicated to these artists. Downstairs is the finale: Monet's water lilies. The museum's collection is small enough to enjoy in a short visit, but complete enough to see the bridge from Impressionism to the Moderns. And it's all beautiful (located in Tuileries Garden near place de la Concorde, Mo: Concorde). If you need a Monet fix, the Marmottan Museum (described under "Southwest Paris," below) is a good replacement until L'Orangerie reopens.

Jeu de Paume—Once home to the Impressionist art collection now located in the Musée d'Orsay, this museum now hosts rotating exhibits of top contemporary artists (€6, not covered by museum pass, Tue 12:00–21:30, Wed–Fri 12:00–19:00, Sat–Sun 10:00–19:00, closed Mon, on place de la Concorde, just inside Tuileries Garden on rue de Rivoli side, Mo: Concorde).

▲▲▲Orsay Museum (Musée d'Orsay)—Paris' 19th-century art museum (actually, 1848–1914) includes Europe's greatest collection of Impressionist works.

Cost: €7; €5 after 16:15, on Sun, and for ages 18–25; free for youth under 18 and for anyone first Sun of month; covered by museum pass. English-language tours usually run at 11:30 daily except Sun, cost €6, take 90 minutes, and are also available on audioguide (€5). Tel. 01 40 49 48 48.

Hours: June 20–Sept 20 Tue–Sun 9:00–18:00, Sept 21–June 19 Tue–Sat 10:00–18:00, Sun 9:00–18:00, Thu until 21:45 all year, always closed Mon. Last entrance is 45 min before closing.

Location: Above the RER-C stop called Musée d'Orsay; the nearest Métro stop is Solferino, three blocks south of the Orsay. From the Louvre, it's a lovely 15-minute walk through the Tuileries and across the pedestrian bridge to the Orsay. ❂ See Orsay Museum Tour on page 121.

Historic Core of Paris: Notre-Dame, Sainte-Chapelle, and More

❂ All of these sights are covered in detail in the Historic Paris Walk (plus map) on page 47. Only the essentials are listed here.

▲▲Notre-Dame Cathedral—This 700-year-old cathedral is packed with history and tourists (free, daily 8:00–18:45; treasury-€2.50, not covered by museum pass, daily 9:30–17:30; ask about free English tours, normally Wed and Thu at 12:00 and Sat at 14:30; Mo: Cité, Hôtel de Ville, or St. Michel; clean €0.50 toilets in front of church near Charlemagne's statue). ❂ See page 48.

You can climb to the top of the facade between the towers and then to the top of the south **tower** (€5.50, daily April–Sept 9:30–19:30, until 21:00 July–Aug on Sat and Sun, Oct–March 10:00–17:30, last entry 45 min before closing, covered by museum pass, arrive early to avoid long lines), or descend to the **crypt.** The Paris Archaeological Crypt is a worthwhile 15-minute stop with your museum pass (€3.50, Tue–Sun 10:00–17:30, closed Mon, enter 100 meters in front of church). You'll visit Roman ruins, trace the street plan of the medieval village, and see diagrams of how early Paris grew and grew, all thoughtfully explained in English.

▲▲**Deportation Memorial (Mémorial de la Déportation)**— This memorial to the 200,000 French victims of the Nazi concentration camps draws you into their experience (free, April–Sept daily 10:00–12:00 & 14:00–19:00, Oct–March daily 10:00–12:00 & 14:00–17:00, east tip of the island Ile de la Cité, behind Notre-Dame and near Ile St. Louis, Mo: Cité). ✪ See page 54.

Ile St. Louis—This residential island behind Notre-Dame is known for its restaurants (see Eating chapter), great Berthillon ice cream (31 rue St. Louis en l'Ile), and shops (along rue St. Louis en l'Ile). ✪ See page 54.

Cité "Métropolitain" Stop and Flower Market—On place Louis Lepine, between Notre-Dame and Sainte-Chapelle, you'll find an early-19th-century subway entrance and a flower market (that chirps with a bird market on Sun).

▲▲▲**Sainte-Chapelle**—This triumph of Gothic church architecture is a cathedral of glass like no other (€5.50, €8 combo-ticket covers Conciergerie, both covered by museum pass, daily 9:30–18:00, Mo: Cité, tel. 01 44 07 12 38 for concert information). ✪ See page 60.

▲**Conciergerie**—Marie Antoinette was imprisoned here, as were 2,600 others on the way to the guillotine (€5.50, €8 combo-ticket covers Sainte-Chapelle, both covered by museum pass, daily April–Sept 9:30–18:30, Oct–March 10:00–17:00, good English descriptions). ✪ See page 65.

▲**Samaritaine Department Store Viewpoint**—For a great view, take the elevator to the ninth floor and walk to the 11th-floor rooftop panorama (€2, daily 9:30–19:00, reasonably priced café on 10th-floor terrace, supermarket in basement, Mo: Pont Neuf, tel. 01 40 41 20 20). ✪ See page 66.

Southwest Paris: Eiffel Tower Neighborhood

▲▲▲**Eiffel Tower (La Tour Eiffel)**—It's crowded and expensive, but worth the trouble. Go early (by 8:45) or late in the day (after 18:00, after 20:00 in summer, last entry 1 hour before closing) to avoid most crowds; weekends are worst. The Pilier Nord (north pillar) has the biggest elevator and, therefore, the fastest-moving line. A TI/ticket booth is between the Pilier Nord and Pilier Est (east pillar). The stairs (yes, you can walk up partway) are next to the Jules Verne restaurant entrance. A sign in the jam-packed elevator tells you to beware of pickpockets.

The tower is 300 meters/1,000 feet tall; in hot weather, it's

Southwest Paris: Eiffel Tower Neighborhood

15 centimeters/6 inches taller. It covers 2.5 acres and requires 50 tons of paint. Its 7,000 tons of metal are spread out so well at the base that it's no heavier per square inch than a linebacker on tiptoes. Visitors to Paris may find *Mona Lisa* to be less than expected, but the Eiffel Tower rarely disappoints, even in an era of skyscrapers.

Built a hundred years after the French Revolution (and in the midst of an Industrial one), the tower served no function but to impress. Bridge-builder Gustave Eiffel won the contest for the 1889 Centennial World's Fair by beating out such rival proposals as a giant guillotine. To a generation hooked on technology, the tower was the marvel of the age, a symbol of progress and of man's ingenuity. To others it was a cloned-sheep monstrosity. The writer Guy de Maupassant routinely ate lunch in the tower just so he wouldn't have to look at it.

Delicate and graceful when seen from afar, it's massive—even a bit scary—from close up. You don't appreciate the size until you walk toward it; like a mountain, it seems so close but takes forever to reach. There are three observation platforms, at 60, 120, and 270 meters/200, 400, and 900 feet; the higher you go, the more you pay. Each requires a separate elevator (and line), so plan on at least 90 minutes if you want to go to the top and back. For most, the view from the second level is plenty. As you ascend through the metal beams, imagine being a worker, perched high above nothing, riveting this giant erector set together. On top, all of Paris lies before you, with a panorama guide. On a good day, you can see for 65 kilometers/40 miles.

The **first level** has exhibits, a post office (daily 10:00–19:00, cancellation stamp will read Eiffel Tower), a snack bar, WCs, and souvenirs. Read the informative signs (in English) describing the major monuments, see the entertaining free movie on the history of the tower, and don't miss a century of fireworks—including the entire millennium blast—on video. Then consider a drink or a sandwich overlooking all of Paris at the snack café (outdoor tables in summer) or at the city's best view bar/restaurant, **Altitude 95** (€19–28 lunches, €46 dinners, dinner seatings at 19:00 and 21:00, reserve well ahead for a view table; before you ascend to dine, drop by the booth between the north *(nord)* and east *(est)* pillars to buy your Eiffel Tower ticket and pick up a pass that enables you to skip the line; tel. 01 45 55 20 04, fax 01 47 05 94 40).

The **second level** has the best views (walk up the stairway to get above the netting), a small cafeteria, WCs, and an Internet gimmick to have your photo at the Eiffel Tower sent into cyber-space (La Gallerie des Visiteurs).

Cost and Hours: It costs €4 to go to the first level, €7 to the second, and €10 to go all the way for the 270-meter/900-foot view (not covered by museum pass). On a budget? You can climb the stairs to the second level for only €3 (daily March–Sept 9:00–24:00, Oct–Feb 9:30–23:00, last entry 1 hour before closing, shorter lines at night, can catch Bâteaux-Mouches boat for Seine cruise at base of tower, Mo: Trocadéro, RER: Champ de Mars, tel. 01 44 11 23 23).

The best place to view the tower is from **Trocadéro Square** to the north (a 10-min walk across the river, and a happening scene at night); for a kid's angle on the tower and Trocadéro, see the Paris with Children chapter (page 306). Consider arriving at the Trocadéro Métro stop for the view, then walking toward the tower. Another great viewpoint is the long, grassy field, le Champ de Mars, to the south (after about 20:00, the *gendarmes* look the other way as Parisians stretch out or picnic on the grass). However impressive it may be by day, the tower is an awesome thing to see at twilight, when it becomes engorged with light and virile Paris lies back and lets night be on top.

▲**Paris Sewer Tour (Les Egouts de Paris)**—This quick and easy visit takes you along a few hundred meters of underground water tunnel. Its interesting displays and English descriptions explain the evolution of the world's longest sewer system. (If you straight-ened out Paris' sewers, they would reach beyond Istanbul.) Don't miss the slide show, the fine WCs just beyond the gift shop, and the occasional tours in English (€4, covered by museum pass, Sat–Wed 11:00–17:00, closed Thu–Fri, where pont de l'Alma greets the Left Bank, Mo: Alma Marceau, RER Pont de l'Alma, tel. 01 47 05 10 29).

▲▲**Napoleon's Tomb and Les Invalides Army Museum
(Tombeau de Napoléon et le Musée de l'Armée)**—The
emperor lies majestically dead inside several coffins under a grand
dome—a goose-bumping pilgrimage for historians. Napoleon is
surrounded by Europe's greatest military museum in the Hôtel
des Invalides, providing fascinating coverage of Napoleon, World
War I, and World War II. The dome glitters with 26 pounds of
gold (€6, students-€5, under 18 free, covered by museum pass,
daily April–Sept 9:00–17:45, mid-June–mid-Sept until 18:45, Oct–
March 10:00–16:45, closed first Mon of month; Mo: La Tour
Maubourg or Varennes, tel. 01 44 42 37 72, www.invalides.org).
✪ See Napoleon's Tomb & Les Invalides Tour on page 194.

▲▲**Rodin Museum (Musée Rodin)**—This user-friendly
museum is filled with passionate works by the greatest sculptor
since Michelangelo. See *The Kiss, The Thinker, The Gates of
Hell,* and many more (€5, €3 on Sun and for students, free for
youth under 18 and for anyone first Sun of month, covered by
museum pass; €1 for gardens only, which may be Paris' best
deal, as many works are well displayed in the beautiful gardens;
April–Sept Tue–Sun 9:30–17:45, closed Mon, gardens close
18:45, Oct–March Tue–Sun 9:30–17:00, closed Mon, gardens
close 16:45; near Napoleon's Tomb, 77 rue de Varennes, Mo:
Varennes, tel. 01 44 18 61 10, www.musee-rodin.fr). ✪ See
Rodin Museum Tour on page 178.

▲▲**Marmottan Museum (Musée Marmottan)**—In this private,
intimate, less-visited museum, you'll find more than 100 paintings by Claude Monet (€6.50, not covered by museum pass,
Tue–Sun 10:00–18:00, closed Mon, 2 rue Louis Boilly, Mo: La
Muette, follow brown museum signs 6 blocks down chaussée de
la Muette through park to museum, tel. 01 44 96 50 33). Take
a post-museum stroll down one of Paris' most pleasant (and upscale) shopping streets, the rue de Passy (2 blocks up chaussée
de la Muette in opposite direction from La Muette Métro stop).
✪ See Marmottan Museum Tour on page 187.

Southeast Paris: Latin Quarter

✪ The Historic Paris Walk, on page 47, dips into the Latin Quarter.
▲**Latin Quarter (Quartier Latin)**—This Left Bank neighborhood, just opposite Notre-Dame, was the center of Roman Paris.
But the Latin Quarter's touristy fame relates to its intriguing,
artsy, bohemian character. This was perhaps Europe's leading
university district in the Middle Ages, when Latin was the language of higher education. The neighborhood's main boulevards
(St. Michel and St. Germain) are lined with cafés—once the haunts
of great poets and philosophers, now the hangout of tired tourists.

Southeast Paris: Latin Quarter

While still youthful and artsy, the area has become a tourist ghetto filled with cheap North African eateries.

▲▲Cluny Museum (Musée National du Moyen Age)—This treasure trove of medieval art fills the old Roman baths, offering close-up looks at stained glass, Notre-Dame carvings, fine gold-smithing and jewelry, and rooms of tapestries (€7, €5.50 on Sun, free first Sun of month, covered by museum pass, Wed–Mon 9:15–17:45, closed Tue, near corner of boulevards St. Michel and St. Germain, Mo: Cluny, tel. 01 53 73 78 00). ✪ See Cluny Museum Tour on page 209.

St. Germain-des-Prés—A church was first built on this site in A.D. 452. The church you see today was constructed in 1163 and is all that's left of a once sprawling and powerful monastery. The colorful interior reminds us that Gothic churches originally were painted in bright colors. The area around the church hops at night with venerable cafés, fire-eaters, mimes, and scads of artists (Mo: St. Germain-des-Prés).

▲St. Sulpice Organ Concert—For pipe-organ enthusiasts, this is a delight. The Grand-Orgue at St. Sulpice has a rich history, with a succession of 12 world-class organists (including Widor and Dupré) going back 300 years. Widor started the tradition of opening the loft to visitors after the 10:30 service on Sundays. Daniel Roth continues to welcome guests in three languages while playing five keyboards at once. The 10:30 Sunday Mass is followed by a high-powered 25-minute recital at 11:40. Then, just after noon, the small, unmarked door is opened (left of entry as you face the rear). Visitors scamper like 16th notes up spiral stairs, past the 18th-century Stairmasters that were used to fill the billows, into a world of 7,000 pipes, where they can watch the master play during the next Mass. You'll generally have 30 minutes to kill (there's a plush lounge) before the organ plays; visitors can leave at any time. If late or rushed, show up around 12:30 and wait at the little door. As someone leaves, you can slip in (Mo: St. Sulpice or Mabillon). The Luxembourg Garden and St. Germain market are both nearby and open seven days a week (the St. Germain market is between St. Sulpice and Métro stop Mabillon on rue Clément).

▲▲**Luxembourg Garden (Jardin du Luxembourg)**—Paris' most beautiful, interesting, and enjoyable garden/park/recreational area is a great place to watch Parisians at rest and play. (See Paris with Children, page 306.) These private gardens are property of the French Senate (housed in the château) and have special rules governing their use (e.g., where cards can be played, where dogs can be walked, where joggers can run, when and where music can be played). The brilliant flowerbeds are completely changed three times a year, and the boxed trees are brought out of the *orangerie* in May. Challenge the card and chess players to a game (near the tennis courts), or find a free chair near the main pond and take a breather. Notice any pigeons? The story goes that a poor Ernest Hemingway used to hand-hunt (read: strangle) them here. Paris Walking Tours offers a good tour of the park (see "Organized Tours of Paris," page 26). The grand neoclassical-domed Panthéon, now a mausoleum housing the tombs of several great Frenchmen, is a block away and only worth entering if you have a museum pass. The historic cafés of Montparnasse are a few blocks from the southwest-corner exit of the park (on rue Vavin, see "Les Grands Cafés de Paris," page 302). The park is open until dusk (Mo: Odéon, RER: Luxembourg). If you enjoy the Luxembourg Garden and want to see more, visit the more elegant Parc Monceau (Mo: Monceau) and the colorful Jardin des Plantes (Mo: Jussieu or Gare d'Austerlitz, RER: Luxembourg).

Montparnasse Tower (La Tour Montparnasse)—This 59-floor superscraper is cheaper and easier to get to the top of than the Eiffel Tower, and has the added bonus of offering one of Paris' best views—since the Eiffel Tower is in it and the Montparnasse Tower isn't. Buy the photo guide to the city, then go to the roof-top and orient yourself (€8, not covered by museum pass, daily in summer 9:30–23:30, off-season 10:00–22:00, disappointing after dark, entrance on rue l'Arrivé, Mo: Montparnasse). The tower is an efficient stop when combined with a day trip to Chartres, which begins at the Montparnasse train station.

▲Catacombs—These underground tunnels contain the anony-mous bones of six million permanent Parisians. In 1785, the Rev-olutionary Government of Paris decided to make its congested city more spacious and sanitary by emptying the city cemeteries (which traditionally surrounded churches) into an official ossuary. The perfect locale was the many kilometers of underground tunnels from limestone quarries, which were, at that time, just outside the city. For decades, priests led ceremonial processions of black-veiled, bone-laden carts into the quarries, where the bones were stacked into piles 1.5 meters/5 feet high and as much as 24 meters/ 80 feet deep behind neat walls of skull-studded tibiae. Each trans-fer was completed with the placement of a plaque indicating the church and district from which that stack of bones came and the date they arrived.

From the entry of the catacombs, a spiral staircase leads 18 meters/60 feet down. Then you begin a 1.5-kilometer-long (1 mile) subterranean walk. After several blocks of empty passageways, you ignore a sign announcing: "Halt, this is the empire of the dead." Along the way, plaques encourage visitors to reflect upon their destiny: "Happy is he who is forever faced with the hour of his death and prepares himself for the end every day." You emerge far from where you entered, with white limestone-covered toes, telling anyone in the know you've been underground gawking at bones. Note to wannabe Hamlets: An attendant checks your bag at the exit for stolen souvenirs. A flashlight is handy (€5, not cov-ered by museum pass, 1 place Denfert-Rochereau, Mo: Denfert-Rochereau, Wed–Sun 9:00–16:00, Tue 11:00–16:00, closed Mon, tel. 01 43 22 47 63).

Northwest Paris: Champs-Elysées, Arc de Triomphe, and Beyond

✪ Take the Champs-Elysées Walk (page 69) for a pleasant downhill stroll connecting the sights from the enduring Arc de Triomphe to the historic place de la Concorde.

▲▲Champs-Elysées—This famous boulevard is Paris' back-bone, and has the greatest concentration of traffic. From the Arc de Triomphe down the Champs-Elysées, all of France seems to converge on place de la Concorde, the city's largest square.

Northwest Paris: Champs-Elysées, Arc de Triomphe, and Beyond

While the boulevard has become a bit Americanized, a walk here is a must. Take the Métro to the Arc de Triomphe (Mo: Etoile) and saunter down the Champs-Elysées (Métro stops every few blocks: Etoile, George V, FDR).

▲▲▲**Arc de Triomphe**—Napoleon had the magnificent Arc de Triomphe commissioned to commemorate his victory at the battle of Austerlitz. Climb to the top for a mesmerizing view of the traffic that swirls around the arch (€7, covered by museum pass, April–Sept daily 10:00–23:00, Oct–March daily 10:00–22:30, Mo: Etoile, use underpass to reach arch, tel. 01 55 37 73 77). ✪ See page 69.

▲**Old Opera (Le Palais Garnier)**—This grand palace of the belle époque was built for Napoleon III and finished in 1875. (After completing this project, the architect—Garnier—went south to do the casino in Monte Carlo.) From the grand avenue de l'Opéra, once lined with Paris' most fashionable haunts, the newly restored facade seems to say "all power to the wealthy." While huge, the actual theater seats only 2,000. The real show was before and after, when the elite of Paris—out to see and be seen—strutted their elegant stuff in the extravagant lobbies. Think of the grand marble stairway as a theater itself. As you wander the halls and gawk at the decor, imagine the place filled with the beautiful people of the day. The massive foundations straddle an underground lake (creating the mysterious world of the *Phantom of the Opera*). Tourists can peek from two boxes into the actual red-velvet theater to see Marc Chagall's colorful ceiling (1964) playfully dancing around the eight-ton chandelier.

Note the box seats next to the stage—the most expensive in the house, with an obstructed view of the stage but just right if you're there only to be seen. The elitism of this place prompted Mitterand to have a people's opera house built in the 1980s (symbolically on place de la Bastille, where the French Revolution started in 1789). This left the Garnier Opéra home only to a ballet and occasional concerts (usually no performances mid-July–mid-Sept). While the library/museum is of interest to opera buffs, anyone will enjoy the second-floor grand foyer and Salon du Glacier, iced with decor typical of 1900 (€6, not covered by museum pass, daily 10:00–17:00 except when in use for performance, €10 English tours summers only, normally at 12:00 and 14:00, 90 min, includes entry, call to confirm; enter through the front off place de l'Opéra, Mo: Opéra, tel. 01 40 01 22 53). American Express and the *Paris Story* film are on the left side of the Opéra, and the venerable Galeries Lafayette department store is just behind.

Paris Story **Film**—This entertaining film gives a good and pain-less overview of Paris's turbulent and brilliant past, covering 2,000 years in 45 fast-moving minutes. The theater's wide-screen projection and cushy chairs provide an ideal break from bad weather and sore feet and make it fun with kids (€8, kids 6–18-€5, families with 2 kids and 2 parents-€21, not covered by museum pass, claim a 20 percent discount with this book, shows are on the hour daily 9:00–19:00, next to Opéra at 11 rue Scribe, Mo: Opéra, tel. 01 42 66 62 06).

▲▲**Jacquemart-André Museum (Musée Jacquemart-André)**—This thoroughly enjoyable museum showcases the lavish home of a wealthy, art-loving, 19th-century Parisian couple. After wander-ing the grand boulevards, you now get inside for an intimate look at the lifestyles of the Parisian rich and fabulous. Edouard André and his wife Nélie Jacquemart—who had no children—spent their lives and fortunes designing, building, and then decorating a sumptuous mansion. What makes this visit so rewarding is the fine audioguide tour (in English, free with admission). The place is strewn with paintings by Rembrandt, Botticelli, Uccello, Man-tegna, Bellini, Boucher, and Fragonard—enough to make a paint-ing gallery famous. Plan on spending an hour with the audioguide (€8, not covered by museum pass, daily 10:00–18:00, elegant café, 158 boulevard Haussmann, Mo: Miromesnil, tel. 01 42 89 04 91).

Petit Palais (and its Musée des Beaux-Arts)—This free muse-um, built for the Universal Exposition of 1900, houses a broad collection of painting and sculpture from the 1600s to the 1900s. It feels like a museum of second-choice art, as the more famous museums in Paris have better collections from the same periods. Still, you'll find a few diamonds in the rough from Monet, Renoir,

Boudin, and others; some interesting Art Nouveau pieces; and a smattering of works from Dutch, Italian, and Flemish Renaissance artists (free, Tue–Sun 10:00–17:40, last entry at 17:00, closed Mon, across from Grand Palais, avenue Winston-Churchill, just west of place de la Concorde, tel. 01 40 05 56 78).

▲**Grande Arche de La Défense**—On the outskirts of Paris, the centerpiece of Paris' ambitious skyscraper complex (La Défense) is the Grande Arche. Inaugurated in 1989 on the 200th anniversary of the French Revolution, it was dedicated to human rights and brotherhood. The place is big—38 floors holding offices for 30,000 people on more than 200 acres. Notre-Dame Cathedral could fit under its arch. The complex at La Défense is an interesting study in 1960s land-use planning. More than 100,000 workers commute here daily, directing lots of business and development away from downtown and allowing central Paris to retain its more elegant feel. This makes sense to most Parisians, regardless of whatever else they feel about this controversial complex. You'll enjoy city views from the Arche elevator (€7, under 18–€5.50, not covered by museum pass, daily 10:00–19:00, includes a film on its construction and art exhibits, RER or Mo: La Défense, follow signs to Grande Arche or get off 1 stop earlier at Esplanade de la Défense and walk through the interesting business complex, tel. 01 49 07 27 57).

Northeast Paris: Marais Neighborhood and More

✪ To connect the sights with a fun, fact-filled stroll leading from place de la Bastille to the Pompidou Center, take the Marais Walk on page 78. To locate these sights, see the Marais map on page 79.

▲▲**Pompidou Center (Centre Pompidou)**—Europe's greatest collection of far-out modern art is housed in the Musée National d'Art Moderne, on the top floor of this colorful, exoskeletal building. Once ahead of its time, this 20th-century (remember that century?) art has been waiting for the world to catch up with it. After so many Madonnas-and-Children, a piano smashed to bits and glued to the wall is refreshing. Ride the escalator for a great city view from the top, and don't miss the free exhibits on the ground floor (€5.50, covered by museum pass, audioguide-€4, Wed–Mon 11:00–21:00, closed Tue and May 1; to use escalator you need museum ticket or museum pass, good mezzanine-level café is cheaper than cafés out-side, Mo: Rambuteau, tel. 01 44 78 12 33).

The Pompidou Center and its square are lively, with lots of people, street theater, and activity inside and out—a perpetual street fair. Kids of any age enjoy the fun, colorful fountain (called *Homage to Stravinsky*) next to the Pompidou Center.

✪ See Pompidou Center Tour on page 148.

Northeast Paris: Marais Neighborhood and More

▲▲**Jewish Art and History Museum (Musée d'Art et Histoire du Judaïsme)**—This fascinating museum is located in a beautifully restored Marais mansion and tells the story of Judaism throughout Europe, from the Roman destruction of Jerusalem to the theft of famous artworks during World War II. Helpful, free audioguides and many English explanations make this an enjoyable history lesson (red numbers on small signs indicate the number you should press on your audioguide). Move along at your own speed. The museum illustrates the cultural unity maintained by this continually dispersed population. You'll learn about the history of Jewish traditions from bar mitzvahs to menorahs, and see the exquisite traditional costumes and objects around which daily life revolved. Don't miss the explanation of "the Dreyfus affair," a major event in early 1900 French politics. You'll also see photographs of and paintings by famous Jewish artists, including Chagall, Modigliani, and Soutine. A small but moving section is devoted to the deportation of Jews from Paris (€6.50, ages 18–26-€4, under 18 free, not covered by museum pass, Mon–Fri 11:00–18:00, Sun 10:00–18:00,

closed Sat, 71 rue du Temple, Mo: Rambuteau or Hôtel de Ville a
few blocks farther away, tel. 01 53 01 86 60).

▲**Picasso Museum (Musée Picasso)**—Hidden in a far corner of
the Marais and worth ▲▲▲ if you're a Picasso fan, this museum
contains the world's largest collection of Picasso's paintings, sculptures, sketches, and ceramics, and includes his small collection of
Impressionist art. The art is well-displayed in a fine old mansion
with a peaceful garden café. The room-by-room English introduc-
tions help make sense of Picasso's work—from the Lautrec-like
portraits at the beginning of his career, to his gray-brown Cubist
period, to his Salvador Dalí–like finish. The well-done €3 English
guidebook helps Picassophiles appreciate the context of his art and
learn more about his interesting life. Most will be happy reading
the posted English explanations while moving at a steady pace
through the museum—the ground and first floors satisfied my
curiosity (€5.50, free first Sun of month, covered by museum pass,
Wed–Mon 9:30–18:00, closes at 17:30 Oct–March, closed Tue,
5 rue Thorigny, Mo: St. Paul or Chemin Vert, tel. 01 42 71 25 21).

▲▲**Carnavalet Museum (Musée Carnavalet)**—The tumultuous
history of Paris is portrayed well in this converted Marais mansion.
Explanations are in French only, but many displays are fairly self-
explanatory. You'll see paintings of Parisian scenes, French Revolution paraphernalia, old Parisian store signs, a small guillotine, a
model of 16th-century Ile de la Cité (notice the bridge houses),
and rooms full of 15th-century Parisian furniture (free, Tue–Sun
10:00–18:00, closed Mon, 23 rue de Sévigné, Mo: St. Paul, tel. 01
44 59 58 58). ○ See Carnavalet Museum Tour on page 162.

Victor Hugo's House—France's literary giant lived in this
house on place des Vosges from 1832 to 1848. Inside are posters
advertising theater productions of his works, paintings of some of
his most famous character creations, and a few furnished rooms
(free, Tue–Sun 10:00–17:40, closed Mon, 6 place des Vosges,
tel. 01 42 72 10 16).

▲**Promenade Plantée Park**—This three-kilometer-long (2 miles),
narrow garden walk on a viaduct was once used for train tracks and
is now a joy. It runs from place de la Bastille (Mo: Bastille) along
avenue Daumesnil to Saint-Mandé (Mo: Michel Bizot). Part of the
park is elevated. At times, you'll walk along the street until you pick
up the next segment. To reach the park from place de la Bastille,
take avenue Daumesnil (past Opéra building) to the intersection with
avenue Ledru Rollin; walk up the stairs and through the gate (free,
opens Mon–Fri at 8:00, Sat–Sun at 9:00, closes at sunset). The shops
below the viaduct's arches make for entertaining window-shopping.

▲**Père Lachaise Cemetery (Cimetière Père Lachaise)**—
Littered with the tombstones of many of the city's most illustrious

dead, this is your best one-stop look at the fascinating, romantic world of "permanent Parisians." More like a small city, the place is confusing, but maps will direct you to the graves of Chopin, Molière, Edith Piaf, Oscar Wilde, Gertrude Stein, Jim Morrison, and Héloïse and Abélard. In section 92, a series of statues memorializing World War II makes the French war experience a bit more real (helpful €1.50 maps at flower store near entry, closes at dusk, across street from Métro stop, Mo: Père Lachaise or bus #69).

North Paris: Montmartre

◯ Connect the sights with the Montmartre Walk on page 92.

▲▲Sacré-Coeur and Montmartre—This Byzantine-looking church, while only 130 years old, is impressive (daily until 23:00). One block from the church, the place du Tertre was the haunt of Toulouse-Lautrec and the original bohemians. Today, it's mobbed with tourists and unoriginal bohemians, but it's still fun (go early in the morning to beat the crowds). Take the Métro to the Anvers stop (1 Métro ticket buys your way up the funicular and avoids the stairs) or the closer but less scenic Abbesses stop. A taxi to the top of the hill saves time and avoids sweat.

Pigalle—Paris' red-light district, the infamous "Pig Alley," is at the foot of butte Montmartre. *Oo la la.* It's more shocking than dangerous. Walk from place Pigalle to place Blanche, teasing desperate barkers and fast-talking temptresses. In bars, a €150 bottle of cheap champagne comes with a friend. Stick to the bigger streets, hang on to your wallet, and exercise good judgment. Cancan can cost a fortune, as can con artists in topless bars. After dark, countless tour buses line the streets, reminding us that tour guides make big bucks by bringing their groups to touristy nightclubs like the famous Moulin Rouge (Mo: Pigalle or Abbesses).

Near Paris: Versailles

▲▲▲Versailles—Every king's dream, Versailles was the residence of the French king and the cultural heartbeat of Europe for about 100 years—until the Revolution of 1789 ended the notion that God deputized some people to rule for Him on earth. Louis XIV spent half a year's income of Europe's richest country turning his dad's hunting lodge into a palace fit for a divine monarch. Louis XV and Louis XVI spent much of the 18th century gilding Louis XIV's lily. In 1837, about 50 years after the royal family was evicted, King Louis-Philippe opened the palace as a museum. Europe's next-best palaces are Versailles wannabes.

Cost and Hours: €7.50 (main palace and both Trianons covered by museum pass); €5.50 after 15:30, under 18 free. There are extra charges for tours, the gardens, and the Grand and Petit Trianon châteaux. On summer weekends, the fountains perform in the garden. The palace is open April–Oct Tue–Sun 9:00–18:30, Nov–March Tue–Sun 9:00–17:30, closed Mon (last entry 30 min before closing). ✪ See Versailles Tour on page 215.

Disappointments de Paris

Here are a few negatives to help you manage your limited time:

La Madeleine is a big, stark, neoclassical church with a postcard facade and a postbox interior.

Paris' **Panthéon** (nothing like Rome's) is another stark neoclassical edifice, filled with the mortal remains of great Frenchmen who mean little to the average American tourist.

The **Bastille** is Paris' most famous non-sight. The square is there, but confused tourists look everywhere and can't find the famous prison of Revolution fame. The building's gone, and the square is good only as a jumping-off point for the Marais Walk (see page 78) or Promenade Plantée Park (see page 44).

Finally, the **Latin Quarter** is a frail shadow of its characteristic self. It's more Tunisian, Greek, and Woolworth's than old-time Paris. The café life that turned on Hemingway and endeared "boul' Miche" and boulevard St. Germain to so many poets is also trampled by modern commercialism.

HISTORIC PARIS
WALK

From Notre-Dame to Sainte-Chapelle

Paris has been the capital of Europe for centuries. We'll start where it did, on the Ile de la Cité, with forays into both the Left and Right Banks, on a walk that laces together the story of Paris: Roman, medieval, the Revolution, café society, the literary scene of the 1920s, and the modern world. Allow four hours to do this five-kilometer/three-mile walk justice.

Orientation

Many sights that charge admission are covered by the Paris museum pass, which for many is a great time and money saver (see page 29).

Notre-Dame: Free, church open daily 8:00–18:45; treasury-€2.50 (not covered by museum pass), daily 9:30–17:30; Sunday Mass at 8:00, 8:45, 10:00 (Gregorian), 11:30 (international), 12:30, and 18:30. Organ performances daily at 16:30. Leaflet with church schedule at booth inside entrance. Free English tours, normally Wed and Thu at 12:00 and Sat at 14:30. The tower climb takes 400 steps and €5.50—worth it for the gargoyle's-eye view of the cathedral, Seine, and city (daily April–Sept 9:30–19:30, Oct–March 10:00–18:00, last entry 45 min before closing, covered by museum pass, no bypass line for passholders, long lines at peak times—thanks to that Disney movie).

Paris Archaeological Crypt: €3.50, covered by museum pass, Tue–Sun 10:00–18:00, closed Mon, entry 100 meters/330 feet in front of the cathedral.

Deportation Memorial: Free, April–Sept daily 10:00–12:00 & 14:00–19:00, Oct–March daily 10:00–12:00 & 14:00–17:00.

Sainte-Chapelle and Conciergerie: €5.50 each, €8 together, both covered by museum pass, daily 9:30–18:00, tel. 01 44 07 12 38, Mo: Cité.

Historic Paris Walk

NOTRE-DAME

• *Start at the Notre-Dame Cathedral on the island in the River Seine, the physical and historic bull's-eye of your Paris map (closest Métro stops are Cité, Hôtel de Ville, and St. Michel, each requiring a short walk). On the square in front of the cathedral, stand far enough back to take in the whole facade. Look at the circular window in the center.*

For centuries, the main figure in the Christian "pantheon" has been Mary, the mother of Jesus. Catholics petition her in times of trouble to gain comfort and to ask her to convince God to be compassionate with them. The church is dedicated to "Our Lady" (Notre-Dame), and there she is, cradling God, right in the heart of the facade, surrounded by the halo of the rose window. Though the church is massive and imposing, it has always stood for the grace and compassion of Mary, the "mother of God."

Imagine the faith of the people who built this. They broke ground in 1163 with the hope that someday their great-great-great-great-great-great grandchildren might attend the dedication Mass two centuries later. Look up the 60-meter/200-foot bell towers and imagine a tiny medieval community muster-ing the money and energy to

build this. Master masons supervised, but the people did much of the grunt work themselves for free—hauling the huge stones from distant quarries, digging a 9-meter-deep (30 feet) trench to lay the foundations, and treading like rats on a wheel designed to lift the stones up, one by one. This kind of backbreaking, arduous manual labor created the real hunchbacks of Notre-Dame.

• *"Walk this way" toward the cathedral, and view it from the bronze plaque on the ground marked . . .*

Point Zero

You're standing at the very center of France, the point from which all distances are measured. The Cité started here in the third cen-tury B.C. In 52 B.C., the Romans conquered the Parisii tribe and built their government palace at the end of the square behind you, and the Temple of Jupiter where the cathedral sits. Two thousand years of dirt and debris have raised the city's altitude. The archaeo-logical crypt nearby offers a fascinating look at the remains of the earlier city and church below today's street level.

Still facing the church, you see on your right a grand eques-trian statue of Charlemagne ("Charles the Great"), whose reign marked the birth of modern Europe. Crowned in A.D. 771, he briefly united much of Europe during the Dark Ages, becoming the First Holy Roman Emperor in 800. (Maybe even greater than Charles are the nearby pay toilets—the cleanest you'll find in downtown Paris.)

Before renovation 150 years ago, this square was much smaller, a characteristic medieval shambles facing a run-down church, surrounded by winding streets and higgledy-piggledy buildings. (Yellow bricks in the pavement show the medieval street plan and even identify some of the buildings.) The church's huge bell towers rose above this tangle of smaller buildings, inspiring Victor Hugo's story of a deformed bell-ringer who could look down on all of Paris.

Notre-Dame Facade

GREAT VIEW!

← GARGOYLES

MARY IN ROSE WINDOW

28 KINGS OF JUDAH →

ST. DENIS (HOLDING HEAD) →

PORTAL OF MARY

LAST JUDGMENT

PORTAL OF ST. ANNE

SEINE RIVER

TOWER ENTRANCE

EXIT

ENTER

TO VIEW OF FLYING BUTTRESSES

← TO RIGHT BANK

POINT ZERO

WC →

CHARLEMAGNE STATUE →

PLACE DU PARVIS

↓ TO STE CHAPELLE

TO PLACE ST. MICHEL ↘

DCH

• *Now turn your attention to the church facade. Look at the left doorway and, to the left of the door, find the statue with his head in his hands.*

Notre-Dame Facade

When Christianity began making converts in Roman Paris,

the bishop of Paris (St. Denis) was beheaded. But those early Christians were hard to keep down. St. Denis got up, tucked his head under his arm, headed north, paused at a fountain to wash it off, and continued until he found just the right place to meet his maker. The Parisians were convinced by this miracle, Christianity gained ground, and a church soon replaced the pagan temple.

By the way, Christians think Montmartre (the one hill overlooking Paris) is named for this martyr, but pagans think it was named after a Roman temple of Mars (Mount of Mars) that once stood there. Bishop Denis eventually died on the edge of town where the church of St. Denis was built (famous in history books as the first Gothic church).

• *Now look above the central doorway, where you'll find scenes from the Last Judgment.*

Central Portal

It's the end of the world, and Christ sits on the throne of judgment (just under the arches, holding his hands up). Below him, an angel and a demon weigh souls in the balance. The good people stand to the left, looking up to heaven. The naughty ones to the right are chained up and led off to a six-hour tour of the Louvre on a hot day. Notice the crazy sculpted demons to the right, at the base of the arch. Find the

cauldron with the sinner diving into it headfirst. The lower panel shows Judgment Day, as angels with trumpets remind worshipers that all social classes will be judged—clergy, nobility, army, and peasants. Below that, Jesus stands between the 12 apostles—each barefoot and with their ID symbol.

• *Above the arches is a row of 28 statues, known as . . .*

The Kings of Judah

In the days of the French Revolution (1789–1793), these Biblical kings were mistaken for the hated French kings, and Notre-Dame represented the oppressive Catholic hierarchy. The citizens stormed the church, crying, "Off with their heads!" Plop, they lopped off the crowned heads of these kings with glee, creating a row of St. Denises that wasn't repaired for decades.

But the story doesn't end there. A schoolteacher who lived nearby collected the heads and buried them in his backyard for

safekeeping. There they slept until 1977, when they were accidentally unearthed. Today, you can stare into the eyes of the original
kings in the Cluny Museum, a few blocks away (see page 209).
• *Enter the church and find a spot where you can view the long, high
central aisle. (Be careful: Pickpockets attend church here regularly.)*

Notre-Dame Interior

Remove your metaphorical hat and become a simple bareheaded
peasant, entering the dim medieval light of the church. Take a
minute to let your pupils dilate, to take in the subtle, mysterious
light show God beams through the stained-glass windows. Follow
the slender columns up to the praying-hands arches of the ceiling
and contemplate the heavens. Let's say it's dedication day for this
great stone wonder. The priest intones the words of the Mass
that echo through the hall: *"Terribilis est locus iste"*—"This place
is *terribilis*," meaning awe-inspiring or even terrifying. It's a huge,
dark, earthly cavern lit with an unearthly light.

This is Gothic. Taller and filled with light, this was a major
improvement over the earlier Romanesque style. Gothic architects needed only a few structural columns, topped by pointed
arches that crisscross the columns to support the weight of the
roof. This let them build higher than ever, freeing up the walls
for windows.

Notre-Dame is designed in the shape of a cross, with the
altar where the cross beams intersect. The church can hold up
to 10,000 faithful.
• *Walk up to the main altar.*

The Altar

This marks the spot where Mass is said and the bread and wine
of Communion are blessed and distributed. In olden days, there
were no chairs. Join the statue of Joan of Arc (Jeanne d'Arc, in
the right transept) in gazing up to the blue and purple rose-
shaped window, the only one of the three still with its original
medieval glass.

This was the holy spot for Romans, Christians … and even
atheists. When the Revolutionaries stormed the church, they
gutted it and turned it into a "Temple for the Cult of Reason."
A woman dressed up like the Statue of Liberty held court at the
altar as a symbol of the divinity of Man. France today, while
nominally Catholic, remains aloof from Vatican dogmatism.
Instead of traditional wooden confessional booths, notice the
open, glass-walled room where modern sinners seek counseling
as much as forgiveness.

Just past the altar are the walls of the choir, where more

intimate services can be held in this spacious building. The aisles are lined with chapels, each dedicated to a particular saint. The faithful can pause at their favorite, light a candle as an offering, and meditate in the cool light of the stained glass. (The nearby treasury, containing lavish robes and golden reliquaries, lacks English explanations and probably isn't worth the €2.50 entry fee.)

Behind the altar, you'll see a fine 17th-century *pietà* flanked by two kneeling kings: Louis XIII and Louis XIV.

• *Amble around the ambulatory, spill back outside, and make a U-turn left. Walk to the back end of the church along the side that faces the river.*

Notre-Dame Side View

Along the side of the church, you'll notice the flying buttresses. These 15-meter/ 50-foot stone "beams" that stick out of the church were the key to the complex architecture of Gothic. The pointed arches we saw inside caused the weight of the roof to push outward rather than downward. The "flying" buttresses support the roof by pushing back inward. Gothic architects were masters at playing architectural forces against each other to build loftier and loftier churches.

Picture Quasimodo limping around along the railed balcony at the base of the roof among the gargoyles. These grotesque beasts sticking out from pillars and buttresses represent souls

caught between heaven and earth. They also function as rain spouts when there are no evil spirits to battle.

The neo-Gothic 90-meter/300-foot spire is a product of the 1860 reconstruction of the dilapidated old church. Around its base are apostles and evangelists (the green men) as well as Viollet-le-Duc, the architect in charge of the work. Notice how the apostles look outward, blessing the city, while the architect (at top) looks up the spire, marveling at his fine work.

• *Behind Notre-Dame, squeeze through the tourist buses, cross the street, and enter the iron gate into the park at the tip of the island.*

Deportation Memorial
(Mémorial de la Déportation)

This memorial to the 200,000 French victims of the Nazi concentration camps draws you into their experience. As you descend the steps, the city around you disappears. Surrounded by walls, you have become a prisoner. Your only freedom is your view of the sky and the tiny glimpse of the river below.

Enter the dark, single-file chamber up ahead. Inside, the circular plaque in the floor reads, "They went into the earth and they did not return."

The hallway stretching in front of you is lined with 200,000 lighted crystals, one for each French citizen who died. Flickering at the far end is the eternal flame of hope. The tomb of the unknown deportee lies at your feet. Above, the inscription reads, "Dedicated to the living memory of the 200,000 French deportees sleeping in the night and the fog, exterminated in the Nazi concentration camps." The side rooms are filled with triangles—reminiscent of the identification patches inmates were forced to wear—each bearing the name of a concentration camp. Above the exit as you leave is the message you'll find at all Nazi sights: "Forgive, but never forget."

Ile St. Louis

Back on street level, look across the river to the Ile St. Louis. If the Ile de la Cité is a tug laden with the history of Paris, it's towing this classy little residential dinghy laden only with boutiques, characteristic restaurants, and famous sorbet shops.

This island wasn't developed until much later (17th century) than the Ile de la Cité. What was a swampy mess is now harmonious Parisian architecture and one of Paris' most exclusive neighborhoods. Its uppity residents complain that the local ice cream shop—Berthillon—draws crowds until late into the night. (See Eating chapter for plenty of Ile St. Louis restaurant ideas.)

• *From the tip of Ile de la Cité, cross the bridge to the Left Bank and turn right. Walk along the river, toward the front end of Notre-Dame. Stairs detour down to the riverbank if you need a place to picnic. This side view of the church from across the river is one of Europe's great sights.*

Ile St. Louis

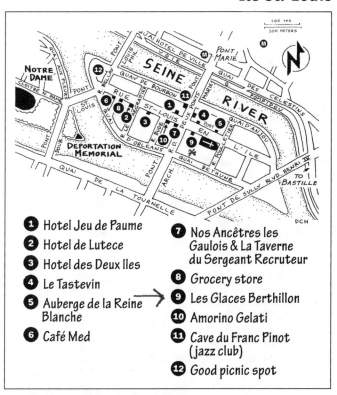

- ❶ Hotel Jeu de Paume
- ❷ Hotel de Lutece
- ❸ Hotel des Deux Iles
- ❹ Le Tastevin
- ❺ Auberge de la Reine Blanche
- ❻ Café Med
- ❼ Nos Ancêtres les Gaulois & La Taverne du Sergeant Recruteur
- ❽ Grocery store
- ❾ Les Glaces Berthillon
- ❿ Amorino Gelati
- ⓫ Cave du Franc Pinot (jazz club)
- ⓬ Good picnic spot

LEFT BANK (RIVE GAUCHE)

The Left Bank of the Seine—"left" if you were floating downstream—still has many of the twisting lanes and narrow buildings of medieval times. The Right Bank is more modern and business-oriented, with wide boulevards and stressed Parisians in suits. Here

along the riverbank, the "big business" is secondhand books, displayed in the green metal stalls on the parapet. These literary entrepreneurs pride themselves on their easygoing business style. With flexible hours and virtually no overhead, they run their businesses as they have since medieval times.

• *When you reach the bridge (pont au Double) that crosses over in front of Notre-Dame, veer to the left across the street to a small park (square Viviani). Go through the park to the small rough-stone church of St. Julien-le-Pauvre. You'll pass Paris' oldest inhabitant, a kind of acacia tree—nicknamed Robinier for the name of the guy who planted it in 1602—that may once have shaded the Sun King.*

Medieval Paris (1000–1400)

The church of St. Julien-le-Pauvre dates from the 12th century, and the area around it keeps the same feel. A half-timbered house stands to the right of the entrance. Many buildings in medieval times were built like this, with a wooden frame filled in with a plaster of mud, straw, and dung. Back then, the humble "half-timbered" structure would have been hidden by a veneer of upscale stucco.

Looking along nearby rue Galande, you'll see a few old houses built every which way. In medieval days, people were piled on top of each other, building at all angles, as they scrambled for this prime real estate near the main commercial artery of the day—the Seine. The smell of fish competed with the smell of neighbors in this knot of humanity.

These narrow dirt (or mud) streets sloped from here down into the mucky Seine, until modern quays and embankments cleaned that up.

• *Return to the river and turn left on rue de la Bûcherie. At #37, drop into the . . .*

Shakespeare & Company Bookstore

In addition to hosting butchers and fishmongers, the Left Bank has been home to scholars, philosophers, and poets since medieval times. This funky bookstore—a reincarnation of the original shop

from the 1920s—has picked up the literary torch. Sylvia Beach, an American with a passion for free thinking, opened this bookstore for Americans fleeing the uptight, Prohibition-era United States. In the '20s, her bookstore was famous as a meeting place of Paris' literary expatriate elite. Ernest Hemingway, who is said to have strangled and cooked pigeons in the park to keep fed, borrowed books from here regularly. James Joyce struggled to find a publisher for his now-classic novel *Ulysses*—until the progressive Sylvia Beach published it. F. Scott Fitzgerald and Ezra Pound also got their English fix here.

Today, the bookstore does its best to carry on that literary tradition. Struggling writers are given free accommodations upstairs in tiny, book-lined rooms with views of Notre-Dame. Downstairs, travelers enjoy the best selection of used English books in Paris. Pick up *Paris Voice*, a newspaper published for today's American expatriates, and say hi to George and his daughter Sylvia.

Notice the fine green water fountain (c. 1900) in front of the bookstore. Paris is dotted with these "Wallace Fountains," a gift to the city from the English philanthropist Sir Richard Wallace. He wanted the regular Parisians to have a handy source of clean drinking water. The little hooks below each of the caryatids once tethered metal mugs. The water is still cool and drinkable—but you need to B.Y.O.B.

• *Continue to the busy rue du Petit Pont (which becomes rue St. Jacques). Way back in Roman times, this was the main north-south access road for Paris—a straight, wide, paved road that brought chariots racing in and out of the city. (Roman-iacs can see remains from the 3rd-century baths, along with a fine medieval collection, at the nearby Cluny Museum, 4 blocks away; see tour on page 209.) Walking away from the river for one block, turn right at the Gothic church of St. Séverin and walk into the Latin Quarter.*

St. Séverin

Don't ask me why, but it took a century longer to build this church than Notre-Dame. This is flamboyant, or "flame-like," Gothic, and you can see the short, prickly spires meant to make this build-

ing flicker in the eyes of the faithful. The church gives us a close-up look at gargoyles. This weird, winged species of flying mammal, now extinct, used to swoop down on unwary peasants, occasionally carrying off small children in their beaks. Today, they're most impressive in thunderstorms, when they vomit rain.

• *Continue down rue St. Séverin deeper into . . .*

The Latin Quarter

While it may look more like the Tunisian Quarter today, this area is the Latin Quarter, named for the language you'd have heard on these streets if you walked them in the Middle Ages. The university, one of the leading educational institutions of medieval Europe, was (and still is) nearby.

A thousand years ago, the "crude" or vernacular local languages were sophisticated enough to communicate basic human needs, but if you wanted to get philosophical, the language of choice was Latin. The educated elite of Dark Ages Europe was a class that transcended nations and borders. From Sicily to Sweden, they spoke and corresponded in Latin. Now the most Latin thing about this area is the beat you may hear coming from some of the subterranean jazz clubs.

Along rue St. Séverin, you can still see the shadow of the medieval sewer system. (The street slopes into a central channel of bricks.) In the days before plumbing and toilets, when people still went to the river or neighborhood wells for their water, flushing meant throwing it out the window. Certain times of day were flushing times. Maids on the fourth floor would holler, "*Garde de l'eau!*" ("Look out for the water!") and heave it into the streets, where it would eventually wash down into the Seine.

As you wander, remember that before Baron Haussmann modernized the city with grand boulevards, Paris was just like this—a medieval tangle. The ethnic feel of this area is nothing new—it's been a melting pot and university district for 800 years.
• *At #22 rue St. Séverin, you'll find the skinniest house in Paris, two windows wide. Continue along rue St. Séverin to . . .*

Boulevard St. Michel

Busy boulevard St. Michel (or "boul' Miche") is famous as the main artery for Paris' café and artsy scene, culminating a block away (to the left), where it intersects boulevard St. Germain. Although nowadays you're more likely to find pantyhose at 30 percent off, there are still many cafés, boutiques, and bohemian haunts nearby.

The Sorbonne—the University of Paris' humanities department—is also close, if you want to make a detour. (Turn left on boulevard St. Michel and walk two blocks. Gaze at the dome from the place de la Sorbonne courtyard or, when school is in session, poke your head into some of the buildings. The entrance at 17 rue de la Sorbonne can sell you an overpriced guidebook.) Originally founded as a theological school, the Sorbonne began attracting more famous professors (such as St. Thomas Aquinas) and students as its prestige grew. By the time the school expanded to include other subjects, it had a reputation for bold, new ideas. Nonconformity is a tradition here, and Paris remains a world center for new intellectual trends.
• *Cross boulevard St. Michel. Just ahead is . . .*

Place Saint André des Arts

This tree-filled square is lined with cafés. In Paris, most serious thinking goes on in cafés. (For more information, see "Les Grands Cafés de Paris," page 302.) For centuries, these have been social watering holes, where you can buy a warm place to sit and stimulating conversation for the price of a cup of coffee. Every great French writer—from Voltaire and Rousseau to Sartre—had a favorite haunt.

Paris honors its writers. If you visit the Panthéon (a few blocks up boulevard St. Michel and to the left), you will find French writers and scientists buried in a setting usually reserved for warriors and politicians.

• *Adjoining this square on the river side is the triangular place St. Michel, with a Métro stop and a statue of St. Michael killing a devil.*

Place St. Michel

You're standing at the traditional core of the Left Bank's artsy, liberal, hippie, bohemian district of poets, philosophers, and winos. You'll find international eateries, far-out bookshops, street singers, pale girls in black berets, jazz clubs, and—these days— tourists. Small cinemas show avant-garde films, almost always in the *version originale* (v.o.). For colorful wandering and café-sitting, afternoons and evenings are best. In the morning, it feels sleepy. The Latin Quarter stays up late and sleeps in.

In less commercial times, place St. Michel was a gathering point for the city's malcontents and misfits. Here, in 1871, the citizens took the streets from the government troops, set up barricades *Les Miz*–style, and established the Paris Commune. In World War II, the locals rose up against their Nazi oppressors (read the plaques under the dragons at the foot of the St. Michel fountain).

And in the spring of 1968, a time of social upheaval all over the world, young students battled riot batons and tear gas, took over the square, and declared it an independent state. Factory workers followed their call to arms and went on strike, toppling the de Gaulle government and forcing change. Eventually, the students were pacified, the university was reformed, and the Latin Quarter's original cobblestones were replaced with pavement, so future scholars could never again use the streets as weapons.

• *From place St. Michel, look across the river and find the spire of the*

Sainte-Chapelle church, with its weathervane angel below. Cross the river on pont St. Michel and continue along the boulevard du Palais. On your left, you'll see the doorway to the Sainte-Chapelle. But first, carry on another 30 meters/100 feet and turn right at a wide pedestrian street, the rue de Lutèce.

Cité "Metropolitain" Stop

Of the 141 original early-20th-century subway entrances, this is one of only a few survivors—now preserved as a national art treasure. (New York's Museum of Modern Art even exhibits one.) The curvy, plantlike ironwork is a textbook example of Art Nouveau, the style that rebelled against the erector-set squareness of the Industrial Age. In Paris, only the stations at Abbesses and Porte Dauphine survive with their canopies.

The flower and plant market on place Louis Lépine is a pleasant detour. On Sundays, this square is all aflutter with a busy bird market. And across the way is the Prefecture de Police, where Inspector Clouseau of *Pink Panther* fame used to work, and where the local resistance fighters took the first building from the Nazis in August of 1944, leading to the allied liberation of Paris a week later.

• *Pause here to admire the view. The Sainte-Chapelle is a pearl in an ugly architectural oyster, part of a complex of buildings that includes the Palace of Justice (to the right of the Sainte-Chapelle, behind the iron and bronze gates).*

Return to the entrance of the Sainte-Chapelle. You'll need to pass through a metal detector to get into the Sainte-Chapelle. Walk through the security scanner. Toilets are ahead on the left. The line into the church may be long. (Museum passholders can go directly in.) Enter the humble ground floor (pick up an English info flier and check the concert schedule if you're interested).

SAINTE-CHAPELLE

The Sainte-Chapelle, the triumph of Gothic church architecture, is a cathedral of glass like no other. It was built in 1248 for King Louis IX (the only French king who is now a saint) to house the supposed Crown of Thorns. Its architectural harmony is due to the fact that it was completed under the direction of one architect and in only five years—unheard of in Gothic times. Recall that Notre-Dame took over 200 years.

The exterior is ugly. But those fat buttresses are all the support needed to hold up the roof, opening up the walls for stained glass. The design clearly shows an Old Regime approach to worship. The basement was for staff and more common folks—worshiping under a sky filled with painted fleurs-de-lis, a symbol of the king. Royal Christians worshiped upstairs. The paint job, a 19th-century restoration, helps you imagine how grand this small, painted, jeweled chapel was. (Imagine Notre-Dame painted like this....)

• *Climb the spiral staircase to the Haute Chapelle. Leave the rough stone of the earth and step into the light.*

The Stained Glass

Fiat lux. "Let there be light." From the first page of the Bible, it's clear—light is important. Light shining through stained glass was a symbol of God's grace shining down to earth, and Gothic architects used their new technology to turn dark stone buildings into lanterns of light. For me, the glory of Gothic shines brighter here than in any other church.

There are 15 separate panels of stained glass, with more than 1,100 different scenes, mostly from the Bible. These cover the entire Christian history of the world, from the Creation in Genesis (first window on the left), to the coming of Christ (over the altar), to the end of the world (the round "rose-shaped" window at the rear of the church). Each individual scene is interesting, and the whole effect is overwhelming.

Let's look at a single scene. Head toward the altar to the fourth big window on the right. Look at the bottom circle, second from the left. It's a battle scene (the campaign of Holophernes), showing three soldiers with swords slaughtering three men. The background is blue. The men have different-colored clothes—red, blue, green, mauve, and white. Notice

Sainte-Chapelle

some of the details. You can see
the folds in the robes, the hair,
and facial features. Look at the
victim in the center—his head
splotched with blood.

It takes 13 tourists to build a Gothic church: six columns, six buttresses, and one steeple.

Craftsmen made glass
(which is, essentially, melted
sand), coloring it by mixing
in metals like cobalt (blue) or
copper (green). Then they'd
assemble pieces of different-
colored glass to make, say, the
soldier in blue with a green
shield (upper right). The pieces
were held together by lead. Details like the folds in the robes (see
the victim in white, lower left) came either by scratching on the
glass or by baking on paint. It was a painstaking process of finding
just the right colors, fitting them together to make a scene . . . and
then multiplying by 1,100. (Note: The sun lights up different
windows at different times of day. Overcast days give the most
even light. On bright, sunny days, some sections are glorious
while others look like a sheet of lead.)

Other scenes worth a look:

1) Cain clubbing Abel (first window on the left, second row
of circles, far right—Cain wears red; this window is always dark
because of a building butted up against the other side).

2) The life of Moses (second window, the bottom row of
diamond panels). The first panel shows baby Moses in a basket,
placed by his sister in the squiggly brown river. Next, he's found
by the pharaoh's daughter. Then, he grows up. And finally, he's
a man, a prince of Egypt on his royal throne.

3) In the next window (third on left, in middle and upper
sections), you'll see various scenes of Moses. He's the guy with
the bright yellow horns. He's often shown horned because in
medieval times, the Hebrew word for "rays of light" (halo) was
mistranslated as "horns."

4) Over the altar are scenes from Jesus' arrest and crucifixion.
Stand 9 meters/30 feet in front and look over the altar and through
the canopy to find Jesus being whipped (left) and Jesus in purple
being crowned with thorns (right). Walk closer to the altar to
see Jesus in yellow carrying his cross (a little above), and, finally,
Jesus on the cross being speared by a soldier (high as you can see).

5) Helena, the mother of Constantine—the first Christian
Roman emperor—travels to Jerusalem to find and collect relics
of Jesus' Crucifixion (window nearest the entry, lowest level).

6) The glorious rose window showing Judgment Day is 200 years newer then the rest, from the flamboyant period. Facing west and the sunset, it's best late in the day.

If you can't read much into the individual windows, you're not alone. For some tutoring, a little book with color photos is on sale downstairs with the postcards.

The altar was raised up high (notice the staircase for the priest) to better display the relic around which this chapel was built—the Crown of Thorns. This was the crown put on Jesus when the Romans were torturing and humiliating him before his execution. King Louis, convinced he'd found the real McCoy, paid three times as much money for the thorns as was spent on this entire chapel. Today, the supposed Crown of Thorns is kept in the Notre-Dame Treasury (and shown only every first Friday).

Notice the little private viewing window in the wall to the right of the altar. Louis was both saintly and shy. He liked to be able to go to church without dealing with the rigors of public royal life. Here

he could worship still dressed in his jammies.

Lay your camera on the ground and shoot the ceiling. Those pure and simple ribs growing out of the slender columns are the essence of Gothic structure.

Palais de Justice

As you walk around the church exterior, look down and notice how much Paris has risen in the 800 years since the Sainte-Chapelle was built. You're in a huge complex of buildings that has housed the local government since ancient Roman times. It was the site of the original Gothic palace of the early kings of France. The only surviving medieval parts are the Sainte-Chapelle and the Conciergerie prison.

Paris' Palais de Justice in 1650, with Sainte-Chapelle, the Conciergerie, and Pont Neuf (then 30 years old) in the background.

Most of the site is now covered by the giant Palais de Justice, built in 1776, home of France's supreme court. The motto *Liberté, Egalité, Fraternité* over the doors is a reminder that this was also the headquarters of the Revolutionary Government. Here, they doled out justice, condemning many to imprisonment in the Conciergerie downstairs or to the guillotine.

• *Now pass through the big iron gate to the noisy boulevard du Palais and turn left (toward the Right Bank).*

On the corner is the site of the city's oldest public clock. The mechanism of the present clock is from 1334, and the case is 16th-century Renaissance—and it keeps on ticking.

Turn left onto quai de l'Horloge and walk along the river. The round medieval tower just ahead marks the entrance to the Conciergerie. Even if you don't pay to see the Conciergerie, you can visit the courtyard and lobby. Step past the serious-looking guard into the courtyard.

Conciergerie

The Conciergerie is a complex of governmental buildings named for the concierge who managed these offices when the king moved his palace to the Louvre. Next to the courthouse was the gloomy prison famous as the last stop for victims of the guillotine. Kings used it to torture and execute failed assassins. The tower next to the entrance, called "the babbler," was named for the painful sounds that leaked from it. The leaders of the Revolution also used the prison—but without torture, which they had outlawed. The guillotine was considered the modern and humane way to execute people. And,

in good Revolutionary style, it treated people of every class equally.

Look at the stark printing above the doorways. This was a no-nonsense revolutionary time. Everything, including lettering, was subjected to the test of reason. No frills, or we chop 'em off.

Marie-Antoinette was imprisoned here. During a busy eight-month period in the Revolution, she was one of 2,600 prisoners kept here on their way to the guillotine.

The interior (covered by museum pass), with its huge vaulted and pillared rooms, echoes with history but is pretty barren. You can see Marie-Antoinette's cell, with a few mementos. In another room, a thought-provoking list of those made "a foot shorter at the top" by the guillotine includes ex-King Louis XVI, Charlotte Corday (who murdered Marat in his bathtub), and Maximilien Robespierre, the chief Revolutionary who got a taste of his own medicine.

• *Back outside, wink at the flak-vested guard, turn left, and continue your walk along the river. Across the river, you can see the rooftop observatory of the Samaritaine department store, where we'll end this walk. At the first corner, veer left into a sleepy triangular square called "place Dauphine."*

Place Dauphine

It's amazing to find such coziness in the heart of Paris. This city of two million is still a city of neighborhoods, a collection of villages. The French Supreme Court building looms behind like a giant marble gavel. Enjoy the village-Paris feeling in the park. You may see lawyers on their lunch break playing *boules*.

• *Walk through the park to the statue of Henry IV, who in 1607 inaugurated the pont Neuf. (If you need a romantic hideaway in the midst of this mega-city, take the steps down into the park on the island's tip and dangle your legs over the prow of this concrete boat.) From the statue, turn right onto the old bridge. Walk to the little nook halfway across.*

Pont Neuf

The pont Neuf, or "new bridge," is Paris' oldest standing bridge. Its 12 arches span the widest part of the river. The fine view includes the park on the tip of the island (note Seine boats), the Orsay, and the Louvre. These turrets were originally for vendors and street entertainers. In the days of Henry, who originated the promise of "a chicken in every pot," this would have been a lively scene.

• *The first building you'll hit on the Right Bank is the venerable old department store, Samaritaine. Go through the door, veer left, and catch elevator #3 to the ninth floor. Climb two sets of stairs to the panorama level (€2, daily 9:30–19:00). Don't confuse the free 10th-floor terrace level (where light meals and drinks are served) with the higher, better €2* *panorama level—worth the cost of admission. (Public WCs are on the fifth and ninth floors.)*

THE REST OF PARIS

From the circular little crow's nest of the building (with the help of a diorama painted in 1929), ponder the greatest skyline in Europe. Retrace the walk you just made, starting with Notre-Dame and the Sainte-Chapelle. Then spin counterclockwise (or run down the stairs to hop on the Métro) and check out the rest of Paris:

The **Pompidou Center,** the wild and colorful rectangular tangle of blue and white pipes and tubes, is filled with art that makes this building's exterior look tame. ★ See tour on page 148.

Sacré-Coeur is a neo-Romanesque church topping Montmartre. This is an atmospheric quarter after dark, its streets filled with strolling tourists avoiding strolling artists. ⭐ See Montmartre Walk, page 92.

The **Louvre** is the largest building in Paris, the largest palace in Europe, and the largest museum in the Western world. ⭐ See Louvre Tour, page 100.

Stretching away from the Louvre, the **Tuileries Garden,** place de la Concorde, and the Champs-Elysées lead to the Arc de Triomphe. The gardens are Paris' Central Park, filled with families at play, cellists in the shade, carousels, pony rides, and the ghost of Maurice Chevalier.

The gardens overlook the grand **place de la Concorde,** marked by an ancient obelisk, where all of France seems to converge. It was guillotine central during the Revolution and continues to be a place of much festivity.

Europe's grandest boulevard, the **Champs-Elysées,** runs uphill from place de la Concorde about 1.5 kilometers to the Arc de Triomphe. While pretty globalized (and short on rich-and-single aristocrats), it's still the place you're most likely to see Sylvester Stallone. ⭐ See Champs-Elysées Walk, page 69.

Napoleon began constructing the magnificent **Arc de Triomphe** in 1806 to commemorate his victory at the battle of Austerlitz. It was finished in 1836, just in time for the emperor's funeral parade. Today, it commemorates heroes of past wars. There's no triumphal arch bigger (50 meters/165 feet high, 40 meters/130 feet wide). And, with 12 converging boulevards, there's no traffic circle more thrilling, either on foot or behind the wheel. See page 69.

Paris, the capital of Europe, is built on an appropriately monumental plan, with an axis that stretches from the Louvre, up the Champs-Elysées, past the Arc de Triomphe, all the way to the modern Grande Arche among the skyscrapers at **La Défense.** (Find the faint shadow of this arch, just above the Arc de Triomphe.)

The **Orsay Museum,** the train-station-turned-art-museum, is just beyond the Louvre on the Left Bank. See tour on page 121.

The **Eiffel Tower** is a thousand-foot exclamation point built as a temporary engineering stunt to celebrate the 100th anniversary of the French Revolution. Paris decided to let it be an exception to a downtown building code that allows the skyline to be broken only by a few prestigious domes and spires. See page 33.

The body of Napoleon lies under the gilded dome to the left of the Eiffel Tower. The giant building is **Les Invalides,** designed to house France's wounded soldiers. Today, it houses a fine military museum. ✪ See tour on page 194. The **Rodin Museum** is nearby. ✪ See tour on page 178.

The 52-story **Montparnasse Tower,** a city in itself (5,000 workers, 210 meters/700 feet high) reminds us that, while tourists look for hints of Louis and Napoleon, workaday Paris looks to the future.

CHAMPS-
ELYSÉES
WALK

Don't leave Paris without strolling the Champs-Elysées. This is
Paris at its most Parisian: monumental sidewalks, stylish shops,
grand cafés, and glimmering showrooms. This walk covers about
five kilometers/three miles and takes three hours if done completely.
It's a great stroll day or night. Métro stops are located every three
blocks on the Champs-Elysées (pron. shahn-zay-lee-zay).

Start by taking the Métro to the Arc de Triomphe. At the
Métro stop Charles de Gaulle Etoile, follow *sortie* Champs-Elysées/
Avenue Friedland signs to "access Arc de Triomphe" signs. Exit
at the top of the Champs-Elysées and face the Arc de Triomphe.
The tourist information office and underground WCs are on the
other (left) side of Champs-Elysées, and an underground walkway
leading to the arch should be in front of you on the right side of
the Champs-Elysées. Get to that arch (worthwhile even if you
don't climb it; there's no charge to wander around the base).

Ascend the **Arc de Triomphe** via the 284 steps (€7, covered
by museum pass, elevator to top only for disabled, daily April–
Sept 10:00–23:00, Oct–March 10:00–22:30, skip the ticket line if
you have a museum pass, Mo: Etoile, tel. 01 43 80 31 31). A wall
mural by the ticket booth gives a sneak preview for the lazy (or
those wondering if it's worth the climb).

Those hiking to the top find a small museum (explaining
the history of the arch in French) and a great rooftop viewing
terrace complete with circular orientation tables. (The next para-
graphs, while written for those viewing Paris from the top of the
arch, also are helpful at street level.)

Begun in 1806, the arch was intended to honor Napoleon's
soldiers, who, in spite of being vastly outnumbered by the Aus-
trians, scored a remarkable victory at the battle of Austerlitz.
Napoleon died prior to its completion. But it was finished in

Champs-Elysées Walk

1 Arc de Triomphe
2 Lido
3 Fouquet's Café
4 Ladurée Tea Salon
5 Sephora Perfume
6 English Pharmacy
7 Virgin Music
8 Grand & Petit Palais
9 Obelisk of Luxor
10 Pont de la Concorde
11 Hôtel de Crillon
12 Tuileries Garden

time for his 1840 funeral procession to pass underneath, carrying his remains (19 years dead) from exile in St. Helena to Paris. The Arc de Triomphe is dedicated to the glory of all French armies.

Follow the huge axis that stretches all the way from the Louvre, up the Champs-Elysées, straight down the avenue de la Grande Armée to a forest of skyscrapers in La Défense. Notice the contrast between the skyscrapers and the uniform heights of the buildings closer to the arch. Former French President François Mitterand had the huge, white **Grande Arche de la Défense** (see page 42), built as a centerpiece of this mini-Manhattan. The wide boulevard lined with grass and trees a little to your left is avenue Foch (named after a WW I hero) and is the best address to have in Paris (the Shah of Iran and Aristotle Onassis had homes here). The huge park at the end of avenue Foch is the Bois de Boulogne.

From the Champs-Elysées side, scan the cityscape of downtown Paris. Notice the symmetry. The beauty of Paris—basically a flat basin with a river running through it—is man-made. The key to this beauty is the relationship between the width of its grand boulevards and the uniformity in the height and design of the buildings. To the right, the rude **Montparnasse Tower** looks lonely out there, standing like the box the Eiffel Tower came in. It served as a wake-up call in the early 1970s to preserve the building height restriction and strengthen urban design standards.

The 12 boulevards that radiate from the Arc de Triomphe were part of Baron Haussmann's master plan for Paris: the creation of a series of major boulevards, intersecting at diagonals with monuments (such as the Arc de Triomphe) as centerpieces of those intersections. His plan did not anticipate the automobile—obvious when you watch the traffic scene below. Gaze down at what appears to be a chaotic traffic mess. But watch how smoothly it really functions. Cars entering the circle have the right of way (the only one in France this way); those in the circle must yield. Still, there are plenty of accidents, often caused by tourists oblivious to the rules. Tired of disputes, insurance companies split the fault and damages of any Arc de Triomphe accident 50–50. The trick is to make a parabola—get to the center ASAP and then begin working your way out two avenues before you want to exit.

Look straight down the **Champs-Elysées.** Louis XIV opened the lower end—a short extension of the Tuileries Garden—in 1667. This date is a considered the birth of Paris as a grand city. The Champs-Elysées soon became *the* place to cruise in your carriage. (It still is today—traffic can be jammed up even at midnight.) One hundred years later, the café scene arrived.

Like its Roman ancestors, this arch has served as a parade gateway for triumphal armies (French or foe) and important ceremonies. From 1941 to 1944, a large swastika flew from here as Nazis goose-stepped down the Champs-Elysées. Allied troops marched triumphantly under this arch in August 1944.

Descend the arch and stand on the worn eagle directly underneath. You're surrounded by the names of French victories since the Revolution—19th century on the arch, 20th century in the pavement. On the columns you'll see lists of generals (with a line under the names of those who died in battle). Then walk around and stand on the bronze plaque at the foot of the **Tomb of the Unknown Soldier** (from World War I). Every day at 18:30 since just after WW I, the flame has been rekindled and new flowers set in place. National parades start and end here with one minute of silence.

Walk out to the traffic circle on the Champs-Elysées side and study the arch. On your right, the arch's massive column is decorated by its most famous sculpture. *The Departure of the Volunteers,* or *La Marseillaise,* was a rousing effort to rally the troops with what looks like an ugly reincarnation of Joan of Arc. On the left, Napoleon poses confidently, while an overcome-with-awe Paris—crowned by her city walls—kneels at his imperial feet.

Look down the Champs-Elysées. The Louvre is the building at the very end of the avenue through the Tuileries Garden. This guided walk goes straight down the Champs-Elysées to the Tuileries. Notice how the left sidewalk is sunnier and more popular with pedestrians. We'll start on the more interesting left side but cross over later for the exhilarating view from the center of the avenue's 10 lanes and a peek at two fancy cafés.

Cross back under the tunnel to the top of the Champs-Elysées. The *nouveau* Champs-Elysées, revitalized in 1994, has new street benches, lamps, broader sidewalks, and an army of green-suited workers armed with high-tech pooper-scoopers. The plane trees (a kind of sycamore that does well in big-city pollution) are reminiscent of the big push Napoleon III made, planting 600,000 trees to green up the city.

Until the 1960s, this boulevard was pure elegance. Locals actually dressed up to come here. From the 1920s through the 1960s, this was a street of top-end hotels, cafés, and residences; the McDonald's would have been unthinkable back then.

Then, in 1963, the government pumped up the neighborhood's commercial metabolism by bringing in the RER (commuter underground). Suburbanites had easy access, and bam—there went the neighborhood.

In 1985, a law prohibited the demolition of the old elegant building fronts that once gave the boulevard a uniform grace. As a consequence, many of today's modern businesses hide behind preserved facades. Imagine the boulevard pre-1963, with only the finest structures lining both sides all the way to the palace gardens.

Start your descent. The first tiny street you cross, rue de Tilsitt, is part of a shadow ring road—an option for drivers who'd like to avoid the chaos of the arch, complete with stoplights. Pop around the corner (left) to one of a dozen uniformly U-shaped pavilions that were part of the original 1853 grand design. Peek into the foyer—of what is currently the Dresden Bank office— for a glimpse of 19th-century Champs-Elysées elegance.

Back on the main drag, begin your downhill stroll. The coming of McDonald's was a shock to the boulevard. At first, it was allowed only white arches painted on the window. Today, it spills out onto the sidewalk—provided it has café-quality chairs and flower boxes. (There's a public WC nearby.)

At the fancy car dealerships—Peugeot at #136 (showing off its futuristic concept cars next to the classic models) or the flashy Mercedes showrooms at #118 (like an English-language car show)—you can pick up your new sedan and a leather jacket and purse to match. In the 19th century, this was an area for horse stables; today, it's the district of garages, limo companies, and car dealerships.

Next to Mercedes is the famous **Lido,** Paris' largest cabaret— check out the photos, perky R-rated videos, and prices. Movie-going on the Champs-Elysées is also popular. Check to see if there are films you recognize, then look for the showings *(séances);* a "v.o." *(version originale)* next to the time indicates the film will be in its original language.

Now cross the boulevard. Spend one traffic light cycle at the island mid-stream enjoying the view. Look up at the arch with its rooftop bristling with tourists. Notice the architecture—old and elegant, new, and new behind old facades.

Fouquet's café-restaurant, under the red awning, serves very expensive coffee. The setting is stuffy but tops. Since the early 1900s, Fouquet's has been a favorite of French actors and actresses. The golden plaques in the pavement honor winners of France's Oscar-like film awards, the Césars (see "Les Grands Cafés de Paris," page 302).

A block downhill is **Ladurée** (green and purple awning), a classic 19th-century tea salon/restaurant/*patissier*. Its interior is right out of the 1860s. Wander around . . . even peeking into the cozy rooms upstairs. A coffee here is *très élégant.* The bakery makes traditional macaroons, cute little cakes, and gift-wrapped finger sandwiches.

Cross back to the lively side. At #92, a wall plaque marks the place Thomas Jefferson lived while minister to France (1785–1789). A plaque just below marks the spot where Robert Birlinger died fighting the Germans during the liberation of Paris in August 1944.

The nearby Club Med is a reminder of the French commitment to the vacation. Since 1936 the French, by law, have enjoyed one month of paid vacation. In the swinging '60s, Club Med made hedonism accessible to the middle-class French masses.

The Gallerie des Champs, at #76, is a faint reminder of the *années folles* (the "crazy years," as the roaring '20s were called in France). In 1921, this was the first 20th-century mall in Paris. Wander in. Next door, the Arcades du Lido was the original location of the Lido (named for the Venice beach and famed for its elegant public swimming pool). The Galerie du Claridge, down the street, is a fine example of an old facade fronting a new building.

At #74, glide down Sephora's ramp into a vast hall of cosmetics and **perfumes** (daily 10:00–24:00). It's thoughtfully laid out:

The entry hall is lined with the new products—all open and ready (with disposable white sniff strips) to sample. Women's perfumes line the left wall and men's line the (shorter) right wall—organized alphabetically by company from Armani to Versace. Stop first at the central "wheel of scents." The woman here helps shoppers explore their needs. She dishes up samples until you find the scent of your dreams and then assembles a list of products to match. The wheel of scents is organized like a wheel of color (clockwise from fresh to strong). Follow the labeled progression: fresh, sea, flower, fruit, herb, wood, spicy, amber, and leather. Lemon is freshest. *Civette*—eau de cow pie—is strongest. (I'm not kidding... give it a whiff. Now you can mark your territory.) The best-seller in 2002: chocolate. Worst seller? Guess. Grab a basket and follow your nose. The mesmerizing music, chosen just for Sephora, actually made me crave cosmetics. Halfway down on your left in red, flashing numbers are the current prices of perfumes *(cours des parfums)* in cities throughout the world—allowing jet-setters to comparison shop.

The English **pharmacy** is open until midnight at the corner of rue la Boétie, and map-lovers can detour one block down this street to the Espace IGN (Institut Géographique National), France's version of the National Geographic Society (Mon–Fri 9:30–19:00, Sat 11:00–12:30 & 14:00–18:30, closed Sun).

Virgin Megastore sells a world of **music** one block farther down the Champs-Elysées. The Disney, Gap, and Quicksilver stores are reminders of global economics—the French seem to love these stores as much as Americans do. Renault, opposite Sephora, also has a cool concept-car exhibit, worth crossing the boulevard for.

At the Rond Point des Champs-Elysées, the shopping ends and the park begins. This leafy circle is always colorful, lined with flowers or seasonal decorations (thousands of pumpkins at Halloween, hundreds of decorated trees at Christmas).

A block past the Rond Point, at the next intersection, you find a new statue of Charles de Gaulle—striding out as he did the day Paris was liberated in 1944. Cross the street halfway. On the pedestrian island look right (and consider a side-trip) to see the glass- and steel-domed **Grand and Petit Palais** exhibition halls, built for the 1900 World's Fair. Today, these examples of the "can do" spirit of the early 20th century host a variety of exhibits (details at TIs or in *Pariscope*). Impressive temporary exhibits fill the huge Grand Palais (on right, €8, not covered by museum pass), while the Petit Palais (left side) houses a permanent collection of 19th-century paintings by Delacroix, Cézanne, Monet, Picasso, and other masters (free, described on page 41).

Beyond the two palaces, the Alexander III Bridge leads over the Seine to the golden dome of Les Invalides. This exquisite bridge, spiked with golden statues and ironwork lamps, was built to celebrate a turn-of-the-20th-century treaty between France and Russia. Like the Grand and Petit Palais, it's a fine example of belle-époque exuberance.

Les Invalides was built by Louis XIV as a veteran's hospital for his battle-weary troops (see Napoleon's Tomb Tour on page 194). The esplanade leading up to Les Invalides—possibly the largest patch of accessible grass in Paris—gives soccer balls and Frisbees a rare-in-Paris welcome.

From here, it's a straight shot down the last stretch of the Champs Elysées to **place de la Concorde,** the 21-acre square with the obelisk. Walk to the island in the center from the crosswalk on the far side of the square. During the Revolution, this was the place de la Révolution. About 2,000 heads lost their bodies here during the Reign of Terror. The guillotine sat here. A bronze plaque in the ground in front of the obelisk memorializes the place where Louis XVI and Marie-Antoinette, among many others, were made "a foot shorter on top." Three people worked the guillotine: One managed the blade, one held the blood bucket, and one caught the head, raising it high to the roaring crowd.

The 2,300-year-old **obelisk of Luxor** now forms the center-piece of place de la Concorde. It was carted here from Egypt in 1829, a gift to the French king. The gold pictures on the obelisk tell the story of its incredible journey.

The obelisk also forms a center point along a line locals call the "royal perspective." From this straight line (Louvre–obelisk–Arc de Triomphe–Grande Arche de la Défense) you can hang a lot of history. The Louvre symbolizes the old regime (divine-right rule by kings and queens). The obelisk and place de la Concorde symbolize the people's revolution (cutting off the king's head). The Arc de Triomphe calls to mind the triumph of nationalism (victorious armies carrying national flags under the arch). And the huge modern arch in the distance, surrounded by the head-quarters of multinational corporations, heralds a future in which business entities are more powerful than nations.

Your guided walk is over. From here you can go three ways: over the river towards the Orsay, away from the river towards the fancy shopping (from place de la Madeleine; see page 314 of Shopping chapter), or into the park towards the Louvre (read on).

Across the river stands the French National Assembly building. If you walk to the river, you'll cross a freeway underpass similar to the one at the pont de l'Alma, three bridges downstream, where

Princess Diana lost her life in the tragic 1997 car accident. The **pont de la Concorde,** built of stones from the Bastille prison (which was demolished by the Revolu-tion in 1789), symbolizes that, with good government, *concorde* (harmony) can come from chaos. Stand mid-bridge and gaze upriver. If you use a clock as a compass, the Impression-ist art museum L'Orangerie (due to reopen in 2004) hides behind the trees at 10:00, and the tall building with the skinny chimneys at 11:00 is the architectural caboose of the sprawling Louvre Palace. The park between is the Tuileries Garden. The thin spire of the Sainte-Chapelle is dead center at 12:00, with the twin towers of Notre-Dame to its right. The Orsay Museum is closer on the right and connected with the Tuileries Garden by a fine pedestrian bridge (the next bridge upriver).

On the far (north) side of place de la Concorde is the **Hôtel de Crillon,** Paris' most exclusive hotel. It's just left of the twin buildings that guard the entrance to rue Royale (which leads to the Greek-style church of the Madeleine). This hotel is so fancy that one of its belle-époque rooms is displayed in New York's Metropolitan museum. Eleven years before the king lost his head on this square, Louis XVI met with Benjamin Franklin in this hotel to sign a treaty recognizing the United States as an independent country. (Today's heavily fortified American embassy is located next door.) For a memorable splurge, consider high tea at Le Crillon; see "Les Grands Cafés de Paris," page 302.

And from the base of the Champs-Elysées, the beautiful **Tuileries Garden** leads through the iron gates to the Louvre (with a public WC just inside on the right). Pull up a chair next to the pond or find one of the cafés in the gardens.

MARAIS
WALK

This walk takes you through one of Paris' most characteristic quar-
ters, the Marais, and finishes in the artsy Beaubourg neighborhood.
When in Paris, you naturally want to see the big sights, but to experience the city you need to visit a vital neighborhood—like the Marais.

The **Marais** neighborhood, containing more pre-Revolutionary
lanes and buildings than anywhere else in town, is more atmospheric
than touristy. It's medieval Paris and the haunt of the old nobility.
After the aristocrats left, the Marais became a dumpy bohemian
quarter so sordid it was nearly slated for destruction. But today, this
thriving, trendy, real community is a joy to explore. It looks the way
much of the city did until the mid-1800s, when Napoleon III had
Baron Haussmann blast out the narrow streets to construct broad
boulevards (wide enough for the guns and ranks of the army, too
wide for revolutionary barricades), creating modern Paris. (A big
Haussmann-type boulevard was planned to slice efficiently through
the Marais, but its construction was interrupted by World War I
and never restarted.)

The Marais walk is about three kilometers/two miles long.
Allow two hours, and add another hour for each of these museums
you might visit en route: Carnavalet (closed Mon), Picasso (closed
Tue), Jewish Art and History (closed Sat), and the Pompidou Center (closed Tue). The Jewish Quarter is quiet on Saturday.

Paris Walks offers guided tours of this area (see page 26).

Orientation
Carnavalet Museum: Free, Tue–Sun 10:00–18:00, closed Mon,
23 rue de Sévigné.
Picasso Museum: €5.50, covered by museum pass, April–Sept
Wed–Mon 9:30–18:00, Oct–March closes at 17:30, closed Tue,
5 rue Thorigny.

Marais Walk

① Place de la Bastille   **③** Place des Vosges   **⑤** Jewish Quarter
② Hotel de Sully   **④** Carnavalet Museum   **⑥** Pompidou Center

Jewish Art and History Museum: €6.50, ages 18–25-€4, under
18 free, not covered by museum pass, Mon–Fri 11:00–18:00,
Sun 10:00–18:00, closed Sat, 71 rue du Temple.
Pompidou Center: €5.50, covered by museum pass, Wed–Mon
11:00–21:00, closed Tue.

THE TOUR

*Start by riding the Métro to the Bastille stop. Exit the Métro, following
signs to rue St. Antoine (not the signs to rue du Faubourg St. Antoine).
Ascend onto a noisy square dominated by the bronze Colonne de Juillet
(July Column).*

1. Place de la Bastille: There are more revolutionary

images in the Métro station murals than on the square. While the
Bastille is famous for its part in the French Revolution of 1789,
the monument on the square—with its gilded statue of liberty—
commemorates the revolutions of 1830 and 1848. (In 1830, the

Bastille Day in France

Bastille Day—July 14th, the symbolic kickoff date of the French Revolution—was made the French national holiday in 1880. Traditionally, Parisians party at place de la Bastille starting at 20:00 on July 13th (but the best parties are on the numerous smaller squares where firefighter units sponsor dances). At 10:00 on the morning of the 14th, a grand military parade fills the Champs-Elysées. Then, near midnight on the 14th, there's a fireworks display at the Eiffel Tower. *Vive la France!*

conservative King Charles X—who forgot all about the Revolution of the previous generation—needed to be tossed out. In 1848, a time of social unrest throughout Europe, the streets of Paris were barricaded by the working class, as dramatized in *Les Misérables.*)

The actual Bastille, a royal fortress-turned-prison that once symbolized old-regime tyranny and now symbolizes the Parisian emancipation, is long gone. While only a brick outline of the fortress' round turrets survives (under the traffic where rue St. Antoine hits the square), the story of the Bastille is indelibly etched into the city's psyche.

For centuries, the Bastille was used to defend the city (mostly from its own people). On July 14, 1789, the people of Paris stormed the prison, releasing its seven prisoners and hoping to find arms. They demolished the stone fortress and decorated their pikes with the heads of a few bigwigs. By shedding blood, the leaders of the gang made sure it would be tough to turn back the tides of revolution. Ever since, the French have celebrated July 14 as their independence day—Bastille Day.

The flashy, glassy-gray, and controversial **Opéra-Bastille** dominates (some say overwhelms) the square. In a symbolic attempt to bring high culture to the masses, former French President François Mitterand chose this square for the opera that would replace Paris' earlier "palace of the rich," the Garnier-designed opera house (see page 40). Designed by the Canadian architect Carlos Ott, this grand Parisian project was opened with fanfare by Mitterrand on the

200th Bastille Day, July 14, 1989. While tickets are heavily subsidized to encourage the unwashed masses to attend, how much high culture they have actually enjoyed here is a subject of debate. (For opera ticket information, see page 321.)

You'll now turn your back on this Haussmann-style grandeur and walk down what was—before the Revolution—the grandest street in Paris, rue St. Antoine. In 1350, there was a gate to the city here, Porte St. Antoine, defended by a drawbridge and fortress—a "bastille."

• *Passing the Banque de France on your right (opposite a fine map of the area on the curb), head down rue St. Antoine about four blocks into the Marais. Leave rue Saint Antoine at #62 and walk through two elegant courtyards of the Hôtel de Sully (open until 19:00, fine bookstore inside).*

2. Hôtel de Sully: Originally a swamp *(marais)*, during the reign of Henry IV, this area became the hometown of the French aristocracy. In the 17th century, big shots built their private mansions *(hôtels)* like this one, close to Henry's ritzy place des Vosges. Typically, they would have a carriage-friendly, finely decorated courtyard separating the mansion from the noisy and very public street. Walking through the passageway to the back, notice the skillfully carved and painted ceilings in the bookshop and stairway. The peaceful backyard often came with an *orangerie* or greenhouse for homegrown fruits and veggies through the winter (as you'll see here). The bit of Gothic window tracery (on the right) is fun for a framed photo of your travel partner. *Hôtels* that survived the Revolution now house museums, libraries, and national institutions.

• *Continue through the Hôtel de Sully to the place des Vosges; the small door on the far right corner of the second courtyard pops you out into one of Paris' finest squares—a romantic place for dinner; see page 296. Before leaving the arcade, check out the ceiling 10 meters/30 feet to the right—broken stucco exposing strips of wood and plaster masking the fake stone vaulting. Much of this fine square was done on the cheap. (If the Hôtel's entrance is closed, backtrack to rue de Biraque to reach place des Vosges.)*

3. Place des Vosges: Study the architecture: Nine pavilions per side. The two highest—at the front and back—were for the king and queen (but never used). Note that some of the brickwork is real, some is fake. Walk to the center, where Louis XIII sits on a horse, surrounded by locals enjoying their community park. Children frolic in the sandbox, lovers warm benches, and pigeons guard their fountains while trees shade this retreat from the glare of the big city.

Henry IV built this centerpiece of the Marais in 1605 and called it "place Royal." As hoped, it turned the Marais into Paris' most exclusive neighborhood. Just like Versailles 80 years later, this was a magnet for the rich and powerful of France. With the Revolution, the aristocratic elegance of this quarter passed.

To encourage the country to pay its taxes, Napoleon promised to honor the district that paid first by renaming this square in its honor. The Vosges region (near Germany) paid first, and place Royal became place des Vosges.

In the 19th century, the Marais became a working-class quarter, filled with gritty shops, artisans, immigrants, and Jews. **Victor Hugo** lived at #6 when he wrote *Les Misérables*. You can visit his house (free, Tue–Sun 10:00–17:40, closed Mon, marked by the French flag in the corner closest to the Bastille; see page 44).

• *Walk behind Louis' horse, cross the street, turning left in the arcade, exit the place des Vosges, and follow rue des Francs Bourgeois to the Carnavalet Museum and then on to the Jewish Quarter.*

4. Carnavalet Muesum: In two blocks, you'll come to the **Carnavalet Museum,** which focuses on the history of Paris and is housed inside another Marais mansion (closed Mon, 23 rue de Sévigné). As this is the best possible look at the elegance of place des Vosges back when it was place Royal—and the museum is free—any good student of Paris will interrupt this walk and splice in the Carnavalet Tour (page 162) at this point.

• *From the Carnavalet, continue down rue des Francs Bourgeois. Turn left at the post office onto rue Pavée. Picasso fans will want to detour to the **Picasso Museum**, described on page 44, located one block to the right (closed Tue, 5 rue Thorigny).*

From rue Pavée, turn right onto rue des Rosiers (named for the roses that once lined the city wall), which runs straight for three blocks through Paris' Jewish Quarter, lively every day except Saturday.

5. Jewish Quarter: Once considered the largest in Western Europe, Paris' Jewish quarter grew in three waves. First, with Jews escaping 19th-century East European pogroms (surprise attacks on villages). Next, with Jews fleeing Nazi Germany (before 75 percent of the Jewish population was taken to concentration

camps). And, most recently, with Algerian exiles (both Jewish and Muslim—living together peacefully here in Paris).

Today, while rue des Rosiers, the main drag, is lined with colorful Jewish shops and kosher eateries, the district is being squeezed by the trendy boutiques of modern Paris. Notice the old bath, or hamam, at #4—while the sign above it says Hamam, it's now a furniture showroom. Also at #4, the Ecole de Travail (trade school) has a bar at knee-level—an attempt to keep out a terrorist's car. The plaque on the wall remembers the headmaster, staff, and students arrested and killed in Auschwitz in 1943 and 1944.

Jo Goldenberg's delicatessen/restaurant (first corner on left, #7 rue des Rosiers) serves typical—but not kosher—East European Jewish cuisine. A plaque on the wall reminds locals of the 1982 terrorist bombing here, which left six people dead. The nearby rue des Ecouffes (named for a bird of prey) is a derogatory reminder of the moneychangers' shops that once lined this lane.

This is a fine place for a lunch break. You'll be tempted by kosher pizza and plenty of €4-falafel-to-go joints (*emporter* = to go). The best falafels (sit-down or to go) are at #34. The Sacha Finkelsztajn Yiddish bakery (#27) is also good. Vegetarians appreciate the excellent cuisine at the popular **Picolo Teatro** (closed Mon, near rue des Rosiers, 6 rue des Ecouffes, tel. 01 42 72 17 79).

• *Rue des Rosiers dead-ends into rue Vieille du Temple (where the Jewish Quarter's main drag meets Paris' gay district—generally to the left and along nearby rue Ste. Croix de la Bretonnerie). Turn right. Frank Bourgeois is waiting at the corner postcard/print shop. Turn left on rue des Francs Bourgeois, which leads past the national archives (peek inside the courtyard) and turns into rue Rambuteau, then continue for several blocks on rue Rambuteau. As you approach the Pompidou Center, you'll pass within a few doors of the* **Jewish Art and History Museum**—*to the right on rue du Temple (closed Sat, 71 rue du Temple, see page 43). The pipes and glass of the Pompidou Center mark your exit from the Marais and reintroduce you to the 21st century. Pass that huge building on your left to join the fray in front of the center.*

6. Pompidou Center: Survey this popular spot from the

top of the sloping square. Tubular escalators lead up to a great view and the modern art museum (closed Tue, to use escalator must pay €5.50 for museum or show museum pass). ⬛ See Pompidou Center Tour on page 148. The Pompidou Center follows with gusto the 20th-century architectural axiom, "form follows function." To get a more spacious and functional interior, the guts of this exoskeletal building are draped on the outside and color coded: vibrant red for people lifts, cool blue for air-conditioning, eco-green for plumbing, don't-touch-it yellow for electrical stuff, and white for bones (compare the Pompidou Center to another exoskeletal building, Notre-Dame). Enjoy the adjacent ***Homage to Stravinsky*** fountains. Jean Tingley designed these as a tribute to the composer: Every fountain represents one of his hard-to-hum scores.

For low-stress meals, try **Le Mélodine,** a self-service cafeteria at the Rambuteau Métro stop, or the fun **Dame Tartine,** which overlooks the *Homage to Stravinsky* fountains and serves a young clientele good, inexpensive meals. Just behind the Pompidou Center,

the **Studio** serves popular Tex-Mex. It's wonderfully located on a 17th-century courtyard below a dance school (daily, tasty salads, €12 plats du jour, 41 rue de Temple, tel. 01 42 74 10 38).

• *With your back to the Pompidou Center's escalators, walk the cobbled pedestrian mall, crossing the busy boulevard de Sebastopol to the ivy-covered pavilions of* **Les Halles.** *Paris' down-and-dirty central produce market of 800 years was replaced by a glitzy but soulless shopping center in the late 1970s. The mall's most endearing layer is its grassy rooftop park. The Gothic St. Eustache church overlooking this contemporary scene has a famous 8,000-pipe organ. For a more soulful (rue Cler–like) shopping experience, find your way behind St. Eustache church and cross rue Montmartre onto the delightfully traffic-free rue Montorgueil.*

RUE CLER
WALK

The Art of Parisian Living

Paris is changing fast, but a stroll down this street puts you into a thriving, traditional Parisian neighborhood.

Shopping for groceries is an integral part of daily life here. Parisians shop almost daily for three good reasons: Refrigerators are small (tiny kitchens), produce must be fresh, and it's an important social event. Shopping is a chance to hear about the butcher's vacation plans, see photos of the florist's new grandchild, relax over *un café*, and kiss the cheeks of friends (the French standard is twice for regular acquaintances, three times for friends you haven't seen in a while).

Rue Cler—traffic-free since 1984—offers plenty of space for tiny stores and their patrons to spill into the street. It's an ideal environment for this ritual to survive and for you to explore. The street is lined with all the necessary shops—wine, cheese, chocolate, bread—as well as a bank and a post office. And the shops of this community are run by people who've found their niche: boys who grew up on quiche, girls who know a good wine. If you see anyone in uniform, they're likely from the Ecole Militaire (military school, Napoleon's alma mater, two blocks away).

If you wish to learn the fine art of living Parisian-style, rue Cler provides an excellent classroom. And if you wish to assemble the ultimate French picnic, there's no better place. This is the only walking tour in this guidebook you should start hungry.

Do this walk at the start of your Paris visit—as it provides a helpful orientation to the local culture. And visit when the market is open and lively (Tue–Sat 8:30–13:00 or 17:00–19:00, Sun 8:30–12:00, dead on Mon). Remember that these shops are busy serving regular customers. Be polite (say *Bonjour, Madame/Monsieur* as you enter and *Au revoir, Madame/Monsieur* when you leave) and be careful not to get in the way. Start your walk where the pedestrian

Rue Cler Walk

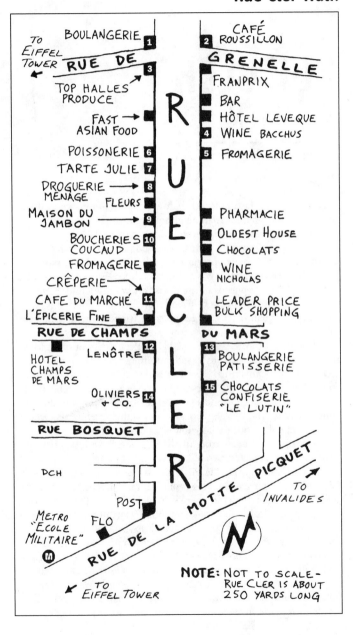

BOULANGERIE 1

TO EIFFEL TOWER ←

RUE DE

CAFÉ ROUSSILLON 2

GRENELLE

3

TOP HALLES PRODUCE

FRANPRIX

FAST → ASIAN FOOD

BAR

HÔTEL LEVEQUE

WINE BACCHUS 4

POISSONERIE 6

FROMAGERIE 5

TARTE JULIE 7

DROGUERIE → 8
MENAGE

FLEURS

MAISON DU → 9
JAMBON

PHARMACIE

BOUCHERIES 10
COUCAUD

OLDEST HOUSE

CHOCOLATS

FROMAGERIE

WINE NICHOLAS

CRÊPERIE →

CAFE DU MARCHÉ 11

L'EPICERIE FINE

LEADER PRICE BULK SHOPPING

RUE DE CHAMPS

DU MARS

LENÔTRE 12

HOTEL CHAMPS DE MARS

13 BOULANGERIE PATISSERIE

OLIVIERS + CO. 14

15 CHOCOLATS CONFISERIE "LE LUTIN"

RUE BOSQUET

DCH

POST

TO INVALIDES →

METRO "ECOLE MILITAIRE"

FLO

RUE DE LA MOTTE PICQUET

Ⓜ

← TO EIFFEL TOWER

NOTE: NOT TO SCALE— RUE CLER IS ABOUT 250 YARDS LONG

section of rue Cler does, at rue de Grenelle (Mo: Ecole Militaire or bus #69 stop).

1. Boulangerie:
The corner bakery is typical of a newer breed of bakeries, with space in the corner for coffee drinkers and fast-fooders (good breakfast deals). The almond croissants here are famous among locals. Since the French Revolution, the government has regulated the cost of a basic baguette. The *Prix du Pain* sign in the window tells you the going rate.

2. Café Roussillon:
This café across the street is a neighborhood fixture. This place recently dumped its old-fashioned, characteristic look for the latest café style—warm, natural wood tones, easy lighting, and music. The *tickets restaurant* and *cheque déjeuner* decals on the door advertise that this café accepts lunch "checks." In France, an employee lunch subsidy program is an expected perk. Employers issue a voucher check (worth about €5) for each day an employee works in a month. Sack lunches are rare. A good lunch is sacred. Inside, drinks at the always-active bar (*comptoir*) are about half the price of drinks at the tables. Notice the list of wines sold by the little (7-centiliter) glass on the blackboard. Kitty-corner from the café, find...

3. Top Halles Fruits and Vegetables:
Each morning, fresh produce is trucked in from farmers to Paris' huge Rungis market—Europe's largest, near Orly Airport—and then dispatched

to merchants with FedEx speed and precision. Locals generally shop with a trolley rather than use bags needlessly. Notice how the French resist excessive packaging and go with what's in season.

Parisians shop with their noses. Try it. Smell the cheap foreign strawberries. Then smell the torpedo-shaped French ones (*garriguettes*). Find the herbs in the back. Is today's delivery in? Look at the price of those melons. What's the country of origin? It must be posted. If they're out of season, they come from Guadeloupe. Many people buy only local products.

The Franprix across the street is a small Safeway-type store. Opposite Hôtel Leveque is Asie Traiteur. Fast Asian food to go is popular in Paris. These shops—about as common as bakeries now—are making an impact on Parisian eating habits. Just past Hôtel Leveque is...

4. Wine Bacchus:

Shoppers often visit the neighborhood wine shop last—once they've assembled their meal and are able to pick the appropriate wine. The wine is classified by region. Most "Parisians" have an affinity to their home region, which affects their choice of wine. Notice the great prices. Wines of the month—in the center—sell for about €5. You can get a fine bottle for €10. The salesperson is a counselor who works with your needs and budget. And notice the beer. Since this is a quality shop, there's nothing French—only Belgian specialty beers. Next door, smell the...

5. Fromagerie:

A long, narrow, canopied cheese table brings the *fromagerie* into the street. Wedges, cylinders, balls, and miniature hockey pucks all powdered white, gray, and burnt marshmallow—it's a festival of mold. Much of the street cart is devoted only to the goat cheeses. *Ooh la la* means you're impressed. If you like cheese, show greater excitement with more *la*s. *Ooh la la la la*. My local friend held the stinkiest glob close to her nose, took an orgasmic breath, and exhaled, "Yes, it smells like zee feet of angels." Try it.

Step inside and browse through some of the 400 different types of French cheese. A cheese shop (like a section at the supermarket) is known as "BOF" *(beurre, oeuf, fromage)*, and is where people go for butter, egg, and cheese products. In the back room are *les meules*, the big, 170-pound wheels of cheese (250 gallons of milk go into each wheel). The "hard" cheeses are cut from these. Don't eat the skin of these big ones... they roll them on the floor. But the skin on most smaller cheeses—the Brie, the Camembert—is part of the taste. "It completes the package," says my local friend.

At dinner tonight, you can take the cheese course just before or instead of dessert. On a good cheese plate, you have a hard cheese (like Emmentaler—a.k.a. "Swiss cheese"), a flowery cheese (maybe Brie or Camembert), a blue, and a goat—ideally from different regions. Because it's strongest, the goat cheese is usually eaten last.

Across the street, find the fish shop, or *poissonerie*.

6. Fish:

Fresh fish is brought into Paris daily from ports on the English Channel, 160 kilometers/1,100 miles away. In fact, fish here is likely fresher than in many towns closer to the sea because Paris is a commerce hub (from here, it's shipped to outlying towns). Anything wiggling? This place, like all such shops, has been recently upgraded to meet the new Europe-wide hygiene standards.

Next door is a particularly tempting storefront on rue Cler...

7. Tarte Julie:
The front windows are filled with various pies, but the shop's classy old storefront is a work of art that survives from the previous occupant. The inset stones and glass advertise horse meat: *Boucherie Chevaline*. The decorated front, from the 1930s and signed by the artist, would fit in a museum. But it belongs right here. And everyone knows this is a place for a fine tart, not horse meat. Next door is...

8. Droguerie Ménage and More:
This French drugstore sells everything but drugs. It's the classic kitchen/hardware store where you buy corkscrews, brooms, knives, and so on.

Wander on past the flower shop and pharmacy (in France, the first diagnosis and prescription are made by the pharmacist—if it's out of his league, he'll recommend a doctor). Next to the pharmacy, notice the oldest and shortest building. It's from the early 1800s, when this street was part of a village near Paris and lined with buildings like this. Of course, over the years Paris engulfed these surrounding villages—and the street is a mishmash of architectural styles.

Across the street from this oldest house is...

9. La Maison du Jambon:
A *charcuterie* sells mouthwatering deli food to go. Because kitchens are so small, these gourmet delis are handy, allowing hosts to concentrate on the main course and buy beautifully prepared side dishes to complete a fine dinner. Notice the system: Order, take your ticket to the cashier to pay, and return with the receipt to pick up your food. Next door is...

10. Boucheries Coucaud:
Sort through pigeons, quail, and rabbit. Look for things you may want to avoid in restaurants: *rognons* (kidneys), *foie* (liver), *coeur de boeuf* (heart of beef). Hoist a duck and check the feet; they should be rough and calloused—an indication that they weren't stuck in an industrial kennel but ran wild on a farm. While Americans prefer beef, pork, and chicken, the French eat just as much rabbit *(lapin)*, quail *(caille)*, lamb *(agneau)*, and duck *(canard)*. The head of a calf is a delight

for its many tasty bits. Horse has gone out of fashion only in the last decade. (The meat came from Eastern Europe and was of questionable quality.) The meat is seasonal. In the winter, game swings from the ceiling.

11. Crêperie and More: Almost

next door, you'll find the smallest business on rue Cler, the *crêperie*. Savory crêpes come with ingredients we'd put in an omelet (cheese, ham, mushrooms, and so on). They're called *galettes*, and the pancake is made from buckwheat flour. Request yours with "no salt" (*pas de sel*, pron. pah duh sehl), as the ingredients are already salty enough. Dessert

crêpes are made of wheat flour and come with everything you might enjoy on your ice-cream sundae. The Café du Marché, on the corner, is *the* place to sit and enjoy the rue Cler action. For a reasonable meal, grab a chair and check the chalk menu listing the plat du jour (special of the day).

The shiny, sterile Leader Price grocery store (across the street) is a French Costco, selling bulk items. Because storage space is so limited in most Parisian apartments, bulk purchases are unlikely to become a big deal here. The trend for Parisians lately is to stock up on non-perishables by shopping online, pick up produce three times a week, and buy fresh bread daily. Across rue du Champ de Mars from the Café du Marché is...

12. Lenôtre: This specialty store is famous among locals as

the deluxe place to buy a gift when invited to someone's home for dinner. When you're invited to dinner in France, it's polite to bring some small gift: flowers, chocolates, wine, or an extra dessert. Parisians enjoy consuming very elegant treats from an over-the-top place like this. While expensive, a little delight from this place would send your host into orbit. Notice the proud little edible nametags. (A short side-trip to 8 rue du Champ de Mars takes you to L'Epicerie Fine, where English-speaking and very helpful Pascal tempts visitors with fine gourmet treats and is generous with tastes.) Across the street, look for the...

13. Boulangerie: Locals debate the merits of rue Cler's rival

boulangeries. It's said that a baker cannot be both good at bread and good at pastry. At cooking school, they major in one or the other, and locals say that when you do good bread, you have no time to do good pastry. The baker at the rue de Grenelle bakery (stop #1) specializes in pastry. The bread suffers. Here, the baker does good bread. He has a man who does the tasty little pastries for him. A bit farther along and across the street is...

14. Oliviers & Co. Olive Oils: This shop, typical of a ritzy neighborhood like this, sells fine gourmet goodies from the South of France and olive oil from around the Mediterranean. They are happy to give visitors a taste test—with tiny spoons—of three distinct oils. Across the street, you'll find...

15. Le Lutin Gourmand Chocolats Confiseries:

Corinne recently took over this shop from a woman who kept this neighborhood in fine chocolates for 30 years. The wholesalers want her to take the new products, but she keeps the old traditional candies, too: "The old ladies, they want the same sweets that made them so happy 80 years ago."

Corinne dips and decorates her chocolates in the back, where the merchants used to live. As was the tradition in rue Cler shops, the merchants lived and produced in the back and sold in the front. She promises readers of the book an assortment of five delightful handmade pieces (your choice) for €3.

Rue Cler ends at the post office. The Ecole Militaire Métro stop is just around the corner. If you bought a rue Cler picnic, you'll find benches and gardens nearby. From the post office, avenue de la Motte Picquet leads to two fine parks: Turn left for Les Invalides or right for the Eiffel Tower. *Bon appétit!*

MONTMARTRE
WALK

While tourists usually make the almost obligatory trek to the top of Paris' Montmartre, eat an overpriced crêpe, and marvel at the view, most miss out on the neighborhood's overlooked charm and history—both uncovered by this short walk. To avoid the crowds, arrive by 9:30 in the morning. If crowds don't get you down, come for the sunset and stay for dinner. I've included several restaurants on this tour. This walk is best done under clear skies—the views can be sensational. There are four sights you can enter on this tour: the Basilica of Sacré-Coeur (daily until 23:00), the church of St. Pierre, the Dalí Museum (daily 10:00–18:30), and the Montmartre Museum (Tue–Sun 11:00–18:00, closed Mon).

You'll walk about 3 kilometers/2 miles up and down on this 90-minute, 12-stop tour. To avoid the climb, either take the funicular (described below) or catch a taxi (about €10 from the Seine River or Bastille to Sacré-Coeur) and begin the tour at the church on top.

To reach Sacré-Coeur by Métro, get off at Anvers. The peeling and neglected Elysées Montmartre theater across the street is the oldest cancan dance hall in Paris, and it sets the stage for this area in transition (it's a rowdy dance club and concert hall today). Historically, people have always moved to this neighborhood for cheap rent. While it still feels neglected, urban gentrification is underway as young professionals restore neglected apartments, hotels renovate for a more upscale clientele, and rents go up.

Walk two blocks up rue de Steinkerque (the street to the right of Elysées Montmartre), through waves of tourists and past cheap clothing and souvenir shops (inexpensive postcards) to the grassy park way below the white Sacré-Coeur church. The dips in the landscapes are from old gypsum quarries. Hike toward the church or ride the funicular (costs 1 Métro ticket, to the left, past the merry-go-round). The best view is just below the top flight of stairs.

Montmartre Walk

● 1 Sacre-Coeur
● 2 St. Pierre, Bus & Taxi stop
● 3 Place du Tertre
● 4 Dali Museum
● 5 Montmarte Museum
● 6 Vineyard
● 7 Lapin Agile
● 8 Bateau-Lavoir
● 9 Moulin de la Galette
● 10 Van Gogh's house
● 11 Moulin Rouge
● 12 Pig Alley
● 13 Renior's house
● 14 Toulouse-Latrec's house

1. Sacré-Coeur Church and View: From Paris' highest point (130 meters/430 feet), the City of Lights fans out at your feet. The big triangular roof on your left is the Gare du Nord train station; the golden dome out there on the right is Les Invalides. The blue-and-red Pompidou Center is straight ahead, and the domed Panthéon lies just beyond to the right, on Paris' other (and far smaller) butte. The Montparnasse Tower is farther off to the right, and the skyscrapers beyond define the southern limit of central Paris. Now face the church.

The Sacré-Coeur ("Sacred Heart") **church,** with its onion domes and bleached-bone pallor, looks ancient but was built only a century ago by Parisians humiliated by German invaders. Otto von Bismarck's Prussian army laid siege to Paris for more than four months in 1870. Things got so bad for residents that urban hunting for dinner (to cook up dogs, cats, and finally rats) became accepted behavior. The church was erected as a "praise the Lord anyway" gesture after France's shocking loss to Germany.

The five-domed, Roman-Byzantine basilica took 40 years to build. The church is dedicated to the sacred heart of Jesus, which enables Him to understand human needs and feelings. The contrast between the brilliant white exterior and the sooty interior is jarring.

Inside, a small plaque (located on the first column, across from the statue of Mary) shows where the 13 WW II bombs that hit Paris fell—all near the church—killing no one. This fueled local devotion to the Sacred Heart and to this church. Explore the impressive mosaics, especially of Christ with his sacred heart, above the altar. Walk clockwise around the ambulatory behind the altar. Notice the colorful mosaic stations of the cross as you walk behind the altar on your right. Between stations VII and VIII, rub St. Peter's bronze foot and look up to the ceiling.

For an unobstructed panoramic view of Paris, climb 80 meters/ 260 feet up the tight and claustrophobic spiral stairs to the top of the **dome** (€5, daily June–Sept 9:00–19:00, Oct–May 10:00–18:00, access outside church and downstairs to the right, especially worthwhile if you have kids with excess energy). The crypt is just a big empty basement.

• *WC is 50 meters from the front of the church (down the stairs on left as you leave). Leaving the church, turn right and follow the tree-lined street with the view on your left. At rue St. Eleuthère, turn right and walk uphill to the Church of St. Pierre (at top on right).*

2. Church of St. Pierre: Originally a headquarters for nuns, this church is one of Paris' oldest—some say Dante prayed here. Older still are the four gray columns inside that may have stood in a temple of Mercury or Mars in Roman times (2 flank the entrance and 2 are behind the altar.) The name "Montmartre" comes from the Roman "Mount of Mars," though later generations, thinking of their beheaded patron St. Denis, preferred a less pagan version, "Mount of Martyrs."

In front of the church, the Café and Cabaret La Bohème remind visitors that the community was a haunt of the bohemian crowd in the late 19th and early 20th centuries. (This is a convenient taxi stand and stop for the electro-bus to Pigalle—1 Métro ticket.) The artist-filled place du Tertre awaits.

3. Bohemian Montmartre—Place du Tertre: In 1800,
a wall separated Paris from this hilltop village. You had to pass toll-booths (which taxed anything for sale) to enter Paris. Montmartre was a mining community (the local gypsum was the original plaster of Paris) where the wine flowed cheap (tax-free) and easy. Life here was a working-class festival of cafés, bistros, and dance halls. Painters came here for the ruddy charm, the light, and the low rents. In 1860, Montmartre was annexed into the growing city of Paris. The "bohemian" ambience survived, and it attracted sophisticated Parisians ready to get down and dirty in the belle époque of cancan.

Lined with cafés and filled with artists, hucksters, and tourists, the scene mixes charm and kitsch in ever-changing proportions. The place du Tertre artists, who at times outnumber the tourists, are the great-great-grandkids of the Renoirs, van Goghs, and Picassos who once roamed here—poor, carefree, seeking inspiration, and occasionally cursing a world too selfish to bankroll their dreams.

• *The Syndicat d'Initiative across the square is a tourist office (daily 10:00–19:00). Escape from place du Tertre via its downhill corner. At the top of the stairs, check out the view, and turn right into the tiny place du Calvaire. Past the café Chez Plumeau (a decent place to eat) is the . . .*

4. Dalí Museum: This museum—a beautifully lit black
gallery—offers a walk through statues, etchings, and paintings by Dalí. Don't miss the printed interview on the exit stairs (€7, not covered by museum pass, daily 10:00–18:30, July–Aug until 21:30, well-described in English, 11 rue Poulbot).

From the museum, curvy rue Poulbot leads to rue Norvins, the spine and main tourist drag of the community (you'll pass the Butte en Vigne restaurant at #5 rue Poulbot—inexpensive and decent plats du jour and menus). Turn left down rue Norvins and walk 20 steps to the crossroads with rue des Saules. The venerable *boulangerie* on the left (dating from 1900) is one of the last surviving bits of the old-time community. From here, we'll side-trip three blocks down the backside of the *mont*, then return to carry on past the *boulangerie*.

From the boulangerie, walk to Auberge de la Bonne Franquette on rue des Saules (allow €15 for lunch, €25 for dinner; fun Montmartre ambience and good French onion soup). At its doorway, notice the dome of Sacré-Coeur rising above the rooftops. Painters such as Maurice Utrillo (1883–1955) captured views like this, making the neighborhood famous. Utrillo, the son of a free-spirited single mom, grew up in Montmartre's streets. He fought, broke street lamps, and haunted the cafés and bars, buying drinks with masterpieces. A very free spirit, he's said to have exposed himself to strangers on the street, yelling, "I paint with this!"

5. Montmartre Museum:
Follow rue des Saules downhill into the less-touristed backside of Montmartre. A right up rue Cortot (just before Maison Rose restaurant) leads up an exclusive street with vine-covered homes to the Montmartre Museum, at #12. Utrillo once lived here with his mom. (Composer Erik Satie lived at #16.) The museum fills eight rooms in this creaky 17th-century manor house with paintings, posters, old photos, music, and memorabilia re-creating the traditional cancan and cabaret Montmartre scene (€4, not covered by museum pass, Tue–Sun 11:00–18:00, closed Mon, reasonably well-described in English).
• *Return to the rue des Saules and walk downhill past the Maison Rose restaurant one block to Paris' last remaining vineyard.*

6. Clos Montmartre Vineyard:
What originally drew artists to Montmartre was its country charm. With vineyards, wheat fields, windmills, animals, and a village tempo of life, it was the perfect escape from grimy Paris. Today's vineyard is off-limits to tourists except during the annual grape-harvest fest (first Sat in Oct), when a thousand costumed locals bring back the boisterous old days and the vineyard's annual production of 300 liters is auctioned off to support local charities.
• *Continue downhill to the foot of the vineyard.*

7. Lapin Agile Cabaret:
The faded poster above the door gives the place its name. A rabbit *(lapin)* makes an agile leap out of the pot while balancing the bottle of wine which he can now drink—rather than be cooked in. This was the village's hot spot. Picasso and other artists and writers would gather for "performances" that ranged from serious poetry, dirty limericks, sing-alongs, and parodies of the famous to anarchist manifestos. Once, to play a practical joke on the avant-garde art community, patrons tied a paintbrush to the tail of the owner's donkey and entered the "abstract painting" that resulted in the Salon. Called *Sunset over the Adriatic*, it won critical acclaim and sold for a nice price.

You now have two options. Most will want to walk back up the rue des Saules to the bakery at the top of the hill, where we'll continue our walk. If you have a reserve of energy and 15 extra minutes, and want to see more of Montmartre (including Renoir's home), walk up the rue des Saules and turn right at Maison Rose restaurant. Follow rue de l'Abreuvoir onto the small walkway at the curve, and you'll pass Renoir's home (at #6). Walk down the steps at the walkway's end, then stroll up through the small park (notice the formal *boules* court overseen by a fascinated St. Denis). Turn left at the top of the park onto rue Junot, which turns into rue Norvins. The bakery is at the top of rue Norvins.

• *Once reunited at the bakery, we all go downhill (along place Jean-Baptiste Clément), hugging the buildings on our left—don't curve right on rue Lepic. Turn right on rue Ravignan and follow it to the "TIM Hôtel." Next door, at 13 place Emile-Goudeau, is Bâteau-Lavoir.*

8. Bâteau-Lavoir, Picasso's Studio: A humble window display marks the place where modern art was born. Here, in a lowly artists' abode (destroyed by fire in 1970), as many as 10 artists lived and worked. The fading photos in the window show Picasso and the studio where he and his friends Georges Braque and Juan Gris revolutionized art. Sharing paints, ideas, and girl-friends, they created art, such as Picasso's *Demoiselles d'Avignon*, that shocked the world. Modigliani and the poet Apollinaire also lived here. Later (when he was one of France's richest men), Picasso wrote, "I know one day we'll return to Bâteau-Lavoir. It was there that we were really happy—where they thought of us as painters, not strange animals."

• *Backtrack uphill to the corner (where you'll see the only surviving bit of the burned studio—complete with artist-pleasing skylights), turn left on rue d'Orchampt, squirt out the end, and (at rue Lepic and rue d'Orchampt) come face-to-face with a wooden windmill. (If you're hungry, detour to Le Montagnard restaurant, uphill 1 block at 102 rue Lepic, offering cozy, country-elegant dining at fair prices.)*

9. Moulin de la Galette: Only two windmills (*moulins*) remain on a hill that was once dotted with 30 of them. Originally, they pressed grapes and crushed stones. When the gypsum mines closed and the vineyards sprouted apartments, this windmill turned into a popular outdoor dance hall. Renoir's *Bal du Moulin de la Galette* (in the Orsay) shows it in its heyday—a sunny Sunday afternoon in the leafy gardens, with ordinary folk dancing, eating, and laughing. Some consider it the quintessential Impressionist painting.

• *Rue Lepic winds down the hill. The green-latticed building to your right was part of the Moulin de la Galette. Continue past the main entrance of Moulin de la Galette down rue Lepic to the rue Durantin. At this intersection, look down rue Tourlaque one block to the building with the tall, brick-framed art studio windows on the corner under the heavy mansard roof. Toulouse-Lautrec lived here. Continue down rue Lepic and, at #54, find...*

10. Van Gogh's House:
Vincent van Gogh lived here with his brother, enjoying a grand city view from his top-floor window from 1886 to 1888. In those two short years, Vincent van Gogh transformed from a gloomy Dutch painter of brown and gray peasant scenes into an inspired visionary with wild ideas and Impressionist colors.

• *Follow the rue Lepic downhill as it makes a hard right at #36 and continue to place Blanche; check out the horse butcher at #30 as you descend. Notice the happy horses on the price stickers. This market street leg of the rue Lepic (lively only in the morning) has an energy not unlike the days when Vincent lived here. Enjoy that notion for the delightful last stretch of rue Lepic before it hits the big street and a big change. On busy place Blanche is the...*

11. Moulin Rouge:
Ooh la la! The new Eiffel Tower at the 1889 World's Fair was nothing compared to the sight of pretty cancan girls spreading their legs at the newly opened "Red Windmill." The nightclub seemed to sum up the belle époque—

the age of elegance, opulence, sophistication, and worldliness. On most nights, you'd see a small man in a sleek black coat, checked pants, a green scarf, and a bowler hat peering through his pince-nez glasses at the dancers and making sketches of them— Henri de Toulouse-Lautrec. Perhaps he'd order an absinthe, the dense green liqueur that was the toxic muse for so many great (and so many forgotten) artists. Toulouse-Lautrec's sketches of dancer Jane Avril and comic La Goulue hang in the Orsay. Walk in and mull over the photos, show options, and prices.

12. Pig Alley:
The stretch of the boulevard de Clichy from place Blanche eastward (toward Sacré-Coeur) to place Pigalle is the den mother of all iniquities. Plaster of Paris from the gypsum

found on this mount was loaded sloppily at place Blanche...the white square. Today, sex shops, peep shows, live sex shows, and hotdog stands line the busy boulevard de Clichy. Dildos abound.

Although raunchy now, the area has always been the place where bistros had tax-free status, wine was cheap, and prostitutes roamed freely. WW II GIs nicknamed Pigalle "Pig Alley."

End your tour at the place Blanche Métro stop (if you want to skip the raunchiness). Or, hike through Pigalle (bars lining the streets downhill from the square are lively with working girls eager to share a drink with anyone passing by). Escape home from the fine Art Nouveau Métro stop, Pigalle.

LOUVRE TOUR

Paris walks you through history in three world-class museums—
the Louvre (ancient world to 1850), the Orsay (1850–1914, including Impressionism), and the Pompidou (20th century to today).
Start your "art-yssey" at the Louvre. With more than 30,000 works
of art, the Louvre is a full inventory of Western civilization. To cover
it all in one visit is in-Seine. Let's focus on the Louvre's specialties—
Greek sculpture, Italian painting, and French painting.

Orientation

Cost: €7.50, €5 after 15:00 and on Sun, free on first Sun of month
and for those under 18, covered by museum pass. Tickets good all
day; reentry allowed.

Hours: Wed–Mon 9:00–18:00, closed Tue. All wings open Wed
until 21:45. On Mon, only the Denon wing is open until 21:45
(but it contains the biggies—*Mona Lisa*, Venus de Milo, and more).
Galleries start closing 30 minutes early. Closed Jan 1, Easter, May
1, Nov 1, and Dec 25. Crowds are worst on Sun, Mon, Wed, and
mornings. Save money by visiting after 15:00.

Getting There: The Métro stop Palais Royal/Musée du Louvre
is closer to the entrance than the stop called Louvre Rivoli.

There is no grander entry than through the pyramid, but metal
detectors create a long line at times. There are several ways to avoid
the line. Museum passholders can use the group entrance in the
pedestrian passageway between the pyramid and rue de Rivoli (facing the pyramid with your back to the Tuileries Garden, go to your
left, which is north; under the arches, you'll find the entrance and
escalator down). Otherwise, you can enter the Louvre underground
directly from the Métro stop Palais Royal/Musée du Louvre (exit
following signs to *Musée du Louvre*) or from the Carrousel shopping mall, which is connected to the museum. Enter the mall at

The Louvre—A Bird's-Eye View

99 rue de Rivoli (the door with the red awning, daily 8:30–23:00).
The taxi stand is across rue de Rivoli next to the Métro station.
Information: Pick up the free *Louvre Handbook* in English at the
information desk under the pyramid as you enter. Tel. 01 40 20
51 51, recorded info tel. 01 40 20 53 17, www.louvre.fr.
Louvre Tours: The 90-minute English-language tours leave
three times daily except Sun (normally at 11:00, 14:00, and 15:45,
€3 plus your entry ticket, tour tel. 01 40 20 52 63). Clever €5
digital audioguides (after ticket booths, at top of stairs) give
you a directory of about 130 masterpieces, allowing you to dial
a rather dull commentary on included works as you stumble
upon them. I prefer the free, self-guided tour described below.
Length of Our Tour: Two hours.
Checkrooms: The coatcheck—which can have a torturously
slow line (drop in the morning, pick up in the afternoon)—does
not take bags. The baggage check (which doesn't take coats that
are not stuffed into bags) is separate from the coatcheck and
generally has almost no line.
Cuisine Art: The underground shopping mall has a dizzying
assortment of good-value, smoke-free eateries (up the escalator
near the inverted pyramid). You'll also find a post office, handy

TI, SNCF train office, glittering boutiques, and the Palais-Royal Métro entrance. Stairs at the far end take you right into the Tuileries Garden, a perfect antidote to the stuffy, crowded rooms of the Louvre. For a fine but more expensive light lunch, cross rue de Rivoli to the venerable Café le Nemours (adjacent to the Comédie Française; see the Eating chapter).

Photography: Photography without a flash is allowed.

Starring: Venus de Milo, Winged Victory, *Mona Lisa*, Raphael, Michelangelo, and the French painters.

Surviving the Louvre

Pick up the map at the information desk under the pyramid as you enter. The Louvre, the largest museum in the Western world, fills three wings in this immense U-shaped palace. The north wing (Richelieu) houses French, Dutch, and Northern art. The east wing (Sully) houses the extensive French painting collection.

For this tour, we'll concentrate on the Louvre's south wing (Denon), which houses the superstars: ancient Greek sculpture, Italian Renaissance painting, and French neoclassical and Romantic painting.

Expect changes. The Louvre is in flux for several years as they shuffle the deck. If you can't find a particular painting, ask a guard where it is. Point to the photo in your book and ask, *"Où est?"* (pron. oo ay).

THE TOUR BEGINS—GREEK STATUES (600 B.C.–A.D. 1)

Every generation defines beauty differently. For Golden Age Greeks, beauty was balance, combining opposites in just the right proportions. They thought that the human body—especially the female form—embodied the order they saw in the universe. In the Louvre, we'll see a series of "Venuses" throughout history. Their different poses and gestures tell us about the people who made them. We'll see how the idea of beauty (as balance) began in ancient Greece, how it evolved into Hellenism (tipping the balance from stability to movement), and then how it resurfaced in the Renaissance, 2,000 years later.

Pre-Classical Greece

• *From inside the big glass pyramid, you'll see signs to the three wings. Head for the Denon wing.*

Escalate up one floor. After showing your ticket, take the first left you can, follow signs to Antiquités Grecques, climb a set of stairs to the brick-ceilinged Salle (Room) 1: La Grèce préclassique. Enter prehistory.

Pre-Classical Greece

These statues are noble but crude. The Greek Barbie dolls (3000 B.C.) are older than the pyramids, as old as writing itself. These prerational voodoo dolls whittle women down to their life-giving traits. Farther along, a woman (*Dame d'Auxerre*) pledges allegiance to stability. Another (*Core*) is essentially a column with breasts. A young, naked man (*Couros*) seems to have a gun to his back—his hands at his sides, facing front, with sketchy muscles and a mask-like face. "Don't move."

The early Greeks, who admired such statues, found stability more attractive than movement. Like their legendary hero, Odysseus, the Greek people had spent generations wandering, war-weary, and longing for the comforts of a secure home.

The noble strength and sturdiness of these works looked beautiful.

• *Exit Salle 1 at the far end and climb the stairs one flight. At the top, veer 10 o'clock left, where you'll soon see Venus de Milo rising above a sea of heads. As you approach her, you'll pass the ornate Antiquités Romaines Hall (we'll return here later). Next, turn right into Salle 7 (Salle du Parthénon), where you'll find two carved panels from the Parthenon on the wall.*

Golden Age Greece

The great Greek cultural explosion that changed the course of history happened in a 50-year stretch (around 450 B.C.) in Athens, a Greek town smaller than Muncie, Indiana. The Greeks dominated the ancient world through brain, not brawn, and the art shows their love of rationality and order.

In a sense, we're all Greek. Democracy, mathematics, theater, philosophy, literature, and science were practically invented in ancient Greece. Most of the art that we'll see in the Louvre either came from Greece or was inspired by it.

Parthenon Frieze (*Fragment de la Frise des Panathénées*), c. 440 B.C.

These stone fragments once decorated the exterior of the greatest Athenian temple, the Parthenon. The right panel shows a half-man/half-horse creature sexually harassing a woman. It tells the story of how these rude centaurs crashed a party of humans. But the Greeks fought back and threw the brutes out, just as Athens (metaphorically) conquered its barbarian neighbors and became civilized.

The other relief shows the sacred procession of young girls who marched up the hill every four years with an embroidered veil for the 12-meter-high (40 feet) statue of Athena, the goddess of wisdom. The maidens, carved in only a few centimeters of stone, are amazingly realistic—more so than anything we saw in the pre-Classical period. They glide along horizontally (their belts and shoulders all in a line), while the folds of their dresses drape down vertically. The man in the center is relaxed and realistic. Notice the veins in his arm.

Greek Statues

1 Parthenon Frieze
2 Venus de Milo
3 Borghese Gladiator
4 Melpomene, Muse of Tragedy
5 Roman detour
6 Winged Victory

WINGED VICTORY

DCH

Greeks of the Golden Age valued the golden mean—that is, balance. The ideal person was well-rounded—an athlete and a bookworm, a lover and a philosopher, a realtor who plays the piano, a warrior and a poet. In art, the balance between timeless stability and fleeting movement made beauty. The maidens' pleated dresses make them look as stable as fluted columns, but their arms and legs step out naturally—the human form is emerging from the stone.

• *Now seek the Goddess of Love. You'll find her floating above a sea of worshiping tourists. It's been said that, among the warlike Greeks, this was the first statue to unilaterally disarm.*

Venus de Milo *(Aphrodite)*, c. 100 B.C.

The Venus de Milo (or goddess of love, from the Greek island of Milos) created a sensation when it was discovered in 1820. Europe was already in the grip of a classical fad, and this statue seemed to sum up all that ancient Greece stood for. The Greeks pictured their gods in human form, telling us they had an optimistic view of the human race.

Most "Greek" statues are actually later Roman copies. This is a rare Greek original. This "epitome of the Golden Age" was actually sculpted three centuries later, though in the style of the earlier.

Venus de Milo is a harmonious balance of opposites. Venus is stable, resting her weight on one leg (called *contrapposto*, or "counterpose"), yet her other leg is slightly raised, ready to take a step. This slight movement sets her whole body in motion, though she remains perfectly still.

Split Venus down the middle (left and right) and see how the two halves balance each other. As she lifts her left leg, her right shoulder droops down. And as her knee points one way, her head turns the other. The twisting pose gives an S-curve to her body (especially noticeable from the back view) that the Greeks and succeeding generations found beautiful.

Other opposites balance as well, like the rough-cut texture of her dress (size 14) that sets off the smooth skin of her upper half. She's actually made from two different pieces of stone plugged together at the hips (the seam is visible). The face is realistic and anatomically accurate, but it's also idealized, a goddess, too generic and too perfect. This isn't any particular woman, but Everywoman—all the idealized features that the Greeks found beautiful.

What were her missing arms doing? Some say her right arm held her dress while her left arm was raised. Others say she was hugging a man statue or leaning on a column. I say she was picking her navel.

• *This statue is interesting and different from every angle. Remember the view from the back—we'll see it again later. Orbit Venus. Make your reentry to Earth as you wander among Greek statues. Try to find even one that's not* contrapposto. *Retracing your steps, find the Antiquités Romaines hall and take a loop . . .*

Roman Detour

The Romans were great conquerors, but bad artists. Fortunately for us, they had a huge appetite for Greek statues and made countless copies. They took the Greek style and wrote it in capital letters—like the huge statue of Melpomene, holding the frowning mask of tragic plays.

One area in which the Romans excelled was realistic portrait busts, especially of their emperors, who were worshiped as gods on earth. Stroll among the Caesars and try to see the person behind the public persona—Augustus, the first emperor, and his wily wife, Livia; Nero ("Neron"), who burned part of his own city; Hadrian, who popular- ized the beard; crazy Caligula; the stoic Marcus Aurelius; Claudius of "I" fame; and the many faces of the ubiquitous Emperor Inconnu.

The Roman rooms also contain sarcophagi and an impressive mosaic floor. Weary? Relax with the statues in the Etruscan Lounge.
• *This Roman detour deposits you at the base of stairs leading up to the dramatic Victory of Samothrace. We'll be there momentarily, but first— to continue the evolution of Greek art from Golden Age balance to the more exuberant Hellenistic Age, find the...*

Borghese Gladiator *(Guerrier Combattant, dit Gladiateur Borghese)*

We see a fighting gladiator at the peak of action. He blocks a blow with the shield that used to be attached to his left arm, while his right hand, weighted with an early version of brass knuckles, prepares to deliver the counterpunch. His striding motion makes a diagonal line from his left foot up his leg, along the body and out the extended arm. It's a dramatic, precariously balanced pose.

This is the motion and emotion of Greece's Hellenistic Age, the time after the culture of Athens was spread around the Mediterranean by Alexander the Great (c. 325 B.C.).

The earlier Golden Age Greeks might have considered this statue ugly. His rippling, knotted muscles are a far cry from the more restrained Parthenon sculptures and the soft-focus beauty of Venus. And the statue's off-balance pose leaves you hanging, like an unfinished melody. But Hellenistic Greeks loved these cliff- hanging scenes of real-life humans struggling to make their mark. The artist himself made his mark, signing the work proudly on the tree trunk: "Agasias of Ephesus, son of Dositheos, did this."
• *Now ascend the staircase, to the...*

Winged Victory of Samothrace *(Victoire de Samothrace)*

This woman with wings, poised on the prow of a ship, once stood on a hilltop to commemorate a great naval victory. Her clothes are windblown and sea-sprayed, clinging to her body like the winner of a wet T-shirt contest. (Notice the detail in the folds of her dress around the navel, curving down to her hips.) Originally, her right arm was stretched high, celebrating the victory like a Super Bowl champion, waving a "we're-number-one" finger.

This is the Venus de Milo gone Hellenistic—a balance of opposites that produces excitement, not grace. As Victory strides forward, the wind blows her and her wings back. Her feet are firmly on the ground, but her wings (and missing arms) stretch upward. She is a pillar of vertical strength while the clothes curve and whip around her. These opposing forces create a feeling of great energy, making her the lightest two-ton piece of rock in captivity.

In the glass case nearby is Victory's open right hand with an outstretched finger, discovered in 1950, a century after the statue itself was unearthed. When the French discovered this was in Turkey, they negotiated with the Turkish government for the rights to it. Considering all the other ancient treasures the French had looted from Turkey in the past, the Turks thought it only appropriate to give France the finger.

• *Enter the octagonal room to the left as you face the Winged Victory, with Icarus bungee-jumping from the ceiling. Bench yourself under a window and look out toward the pyramid.*

FRENCH HISTORY
The Louvre as a Palace

The Louvre, a former palace, was built in stages over several centuries. On your right (the east wing) was the original medieval fortress. Next, another palace, the Tuileries, was built 500 meters to the west—in the open area past the pyramid and past the triumphal arch. Succeeding kings tried to connect these two palaces, each one adding another section onto the long, skinny north and south wings. Finally, in 1852, after three centuries of building, the two palaces were connected, creating a rectangular Louvre. Soon after that, the Tuileries Palace burned down during a riot, leaving the U-shaped Louvre we see today.

The glass pyramid was designed by the American architect I. M. Pei. Many Parisians hated the pyramid, like they used to hate another new and controversial structure 100 years ago— the Eiffel Tower.

The doorway leads to the Apollo Gallery, or Galerie d'Apollon (although the gallery is closed for renovation for several years, the jewels are on display in the Sully wing). The plaque above the

doorway explains that France's
Revolutionary National Assembly
(the same people who brought
you the guillotine) founded this
museum in 1793. What could be
more logical? You behead the king,
inherit his palace and art collection,
open the doors to the masses, and,

Voilà! You have Europe's first public museum. Major supporters of
the museum are listed on the walls—notice all the Rothschilds.

• *The Italian collection ("Peintures Italiennes") is on the other side of the
Winged Victory. Cross in front of the Victory to the other side and pause
at the two fresco paintings on the wall to the left.*

ITALIAN RENAISSANCE

A thousand years after Rome fell, plunging Europe into the Dark
Ages, the Greek ideal of beauty was "reborn" in 15th-century
Italy. This was the Renaissance, the cultural revival of ancient art.

In these two frescoes by the Italian Renaissance artist Botticelli, we see echoes of ancient Greece. The maidens, with their

poses, clear sculptural lines, and
idealized beauty, are virtual
Venus de Milos with clothes.
The Renaissance was a time of
great optimism, exploration, and
liberation, and here we see it in its
fresh-faced springtime.

The key to Renaissance
painting was realism, and for the
Italians "realism" was spelled "3-D." Painters were inspired by
the realism and balanced beauty of Greek sculpture.

• *The Italian collection—including* Mona Lisa—*is scattered throughout the next few rooms (Salles 3 & 4), in the long Grand Gallery,
and in adjoining rooms. To see the paintings in chronological order
may require a little extra shoe leather. When in doubt, show the photo
to a guard and ask,* "Où est, s'il vous plaît?" *(It rhymes.)*

Medieval and Early
Italian Renaissance (1200–1500)

Painting a 3-D world on a 2-D surface is tough, and after a
millennium of Dark Ages, artists were rusty. Living in a religious age, they painted mostly altarpieces full of saints, angels,
Madonnas-and-bambinos, and crucifixes floating in an ethereal
gold-leaf heaven. Gradually, though, they brought these otherworldly scenes down to earth.

Cimabue—*The Madonna of the Angels*

During the Age of Faith (1200s), most
every church in Europe had a painting
like this one. Mary was a cult figure—
bigger than even the 20th-century
Madonna—adored and prayed to by
the faithful for bringing baby Jesus
into the world.

And most every painting followed
the same "Byzantine" style: Somber
iconic faces, stiff poses, elegant folds
in the robes, and generic angels, all
laid flat on a gold background like
cardboard cutouts. Violating 3-D
space, the angels at the "back" of Mary's throne are the same size
as those holding the front.

Still, Cimabue (c. 1240–1302; pron. chee-MAH-bway) is
considered the first painter to experiment with Renaissance techniques. He uses the throne to give some sense of foreground and
background, and puts shading ("modeling") around the edge of
figures to make them look rounded. The work has Renaissance
symmetry, three angels on each side, with the top ones bending
in to frame the Virgin.

Cimabue was the first "name" artist in a world of anonymous
craftsmen. His proud personality was legendary (Cimabue is a nickname meaning "bullheaded"). And the legend grew when, one day, he
came across a shepherd boy sketching his sheep. Cimabue took young
Giotto in, and raised him to shatter the icons of the medieval style.

Giotto—*St. Francis of Assisi Receiving the Stigmata (and Francis Preaching to the Birds)*

Francis of Assisi (1181–1226), a wandering Italian monk of renowned goodness,
breathed the spirit of the Renaissance into
medieval Europe. His humble love of man
and nature inspired artists to portray real
human beings with real emotions living
in a physical world of beauty.

Here, Francis kneels on a rocky Italian
hillside, pondering the pain of Christ's torture and execution. Suddenly he looks up,
startled, to see Christ himself, with six wings,
hovering above. Christ shoots lasers from
his wounds to burn marks on the hands,
feet, and side of the empathetic monk.

Like a good filmmaker, the artist Giotto (1266–1337; pron. JOT-toh) doesn't just *tell* us what happened in the past, he *shows* us in present tense, freezing the scene at the most dramatic moment. Though the perspective is crude—Francis' hut is smaller than he is, and Christ is somehow shooting at Francis while facing us—Giotto gives a glimpse of the 3-D world of the coming Renaissance.

In the predella (the panel of paintings below the altarpiece), birds gather at Francis' feet to hear him talk about God. Giotto catches the late arrivals in mid-flight, an astonishing technical feat for an artist more than a century before the Renaissance. The simple gesture of Francis' companion speaks volumes about his amazement. Breaking the stiff, iconic mold for saints, Francis bends forward at the waist to talk to his fellow creatures, while the tree bends down symmetrically to catch a few words from the beloved hippie of Assisi.

Painters such as Giotto, Fra Angelico, and Uccello broke Renaissance ground by learning to paint realistic, 3-D humans. They placed them in a painted scene with a definite foreground, background, and middle ground to create the illusion of depth. Composition was simple but symmetrically balanced in the Greek style. Art was a visual sermon, appreciated for its moral message, not its beauty.

• *The long Grand Gallery displays Italian Renaissance painting, some masterpieces, some not.*

The Grand Gallery

The Grand Gallery was built in the late 1500s to connect the old palace with the Tuileries Palace. From the doorway, look to the far end and consider this challenge: I hold the world's record for the Grand Gallery Heel-Toe-Fun-Walk-Tourist-Slalom, going end to end in one minute 58 seconds, two injured. Time yourself. Along the way, notice some of the . . .

The Grand Gallery

● BOTTICELLI frescoes
❷ CIMABUE Madonna of the Angels
❸ GIOTTO St. Francis of Assisi
❹ High Renaissance:
   LEONARDO, RAPHAEL
❺ LEONARDO Mona Lisa (if not in this room follow Mona signs
❻ High Renaissance: TITIAN, RAPHAEL, etc.
❼ VERONESE: Marriage at Cana
❽ DAVID Coronation of Napoleon
❾ INGRES La Grande Odalisque
❿ GERICAULT The Raft of the Medusa
⓫ DELACROIX Liberty Leading the People

Features of Italian Renaissance Painting

1. **Religious:** Lots of Madonnas, children, martyrs, and saints.
2. **Symmetrical:** The Madonnas are flanked by saints, two to the left, two to the right, and so on.
3. **Realistic:** Real-life human features are especially obvious in the occasional portrait.
4. **Three-Dimensional:** Every scene gets a spacious setting with a distant horizon.
5. **Classical:** You'll see some Greek gods and classical nudes, but even Christian saints pose like Greek statues, and Mary is a Venus whose face and gestures embody all that was good in the Christian world.

Mantegna—*St. Sebastian*

This isn't the patron saint of acupuncture. St. Sebastian was a Christian martyr, although here he looks more like a classical Greek statue. Notice the *contrapposto* stance (all of his weight resting on one leg) and the Greek ruins scattered around him.

His executioners look like ignorant medieval brutes bewildered by this enlightened Renaissance man. Italian artists were beginning to learn how to create human realism and earthly beauty on the canvas. Let the Renaissance begin.

Italian High Renaissance (1500–1600)

The two masters of Renaissance grace and balance were Raphael and Leonardo da Vinci.

Leonardo was the consummate Renaissance man. Musician, sculptor, engineer, scientist, and sometimes painter, he combined knowledge from all areas to create beauty. If he were alive today, he'd create a Unified Field Theory in physics—and set it to music.

• *Look for the following masterpieces by Leonardo and Raphael in the Grand Gallery.*

Leonardo da Vinci—*Virgin, Child, and St. Anne* (*La Vierge, l'Enfant Jésus, et Sainte Anne*)

Three generations—grandmother, mother, and child—are arranged in a pyramid with Anne's face as the peak and the lamb as the lower-right corner. Within this balanced structure, Leonardo sets the figures in motion. Anne's legs are pointed to our left. (Is Anne *Mona*? Hmm.) Her daughter Mary, sitting on her lap, reaches to the right. Jesus looks at her playfully while turning away. The lamb pulls away from him. But even with all the twisting and turning, this is still a placid scene. It's as orderly as the geometrically perfect universe created by the Renaissance god.

There's a psychological kidney punch in this happy painting. Jesus, the picture of childish joy, is innocently playing with a lamb—the symbol of his inevitable sacrificial death.

The Louvre has the greatest collection of Leonardos in the

world—all five of them. Look for the neighboring *Madonna of the Rocks* and his androgynous *John the Baptist.*

Raphael—*La Belle Jardinière*

Raphael (pron. roff-eye-ELL) perfected the style Leonardo pioneered. This Madonna, Child, and John the Baptist is also a balanced pyramid with hazy grace and beauty. Mary is a mountain of maternal tenderness (the title translates as "The Beautiful Kindergarten Teacher"), eyeing her son with a knowing look. Jesus looks up innocently, standing *contrapposto* like a chubby Greek statue.

With Raphael, the Greek ideal of beauty reborn in the Renaissance reached its peak. His work spawned so many imitators who cranked out sickly sweet, generic Madonnas that we often take him for granted. Don't. This is the real thing.

• *The* Mona Lisa *may be at the end of the Grand Gallery or in the Salle des Etats, midway down the Grand Gallery. Wherever she is, you can't miss her. Just follow the signs and crowds.*

Leonardo da Vinci—*Mona Lisa*

Leonardo was already an old man when François I invited him to France. Determined to pack light, he took only a few paintings with him. One was a portrait of a Lisa del Giocondo, the wife of a wealthy Florentine merchant. When Leonardo arrived, François immediately fell in love with the painting, making it the centerpiece of the small collection of Italian masterpieces that would, in three centuries, become the Louvre museum. He called it *La Gioconda.* We know it as a contraction of the Italian for "my lady Lisa"—*Mona Lisa.*

Advance warning: *Mona* may disappoint you. She's smaller than you'd expect, darker, engulfed in a huge room, and hidden behind a glaring pane of glass. So, you ask, "Why all the hubbub?" Let's take a closer look. Like any lover, you've got to take her for what she is, not what you'd like her to be.

The famous smile attracts you first. Leonardo used a hazy technique called *sfumato,* blurring the edges of *Mona*'s mysterious smile. Try as you might, you can never quite see the corners of her mouth. Is she happy? Sad? Tender? Or is it a cynical supermodel's smirk? Every viewer reads it differently, projecting his own mood onto *Lisa*'s enigmatic face. *Mona* is a Rorschach inkblot...so how are you feeling?

Now look past the smile and the eyes that really do follow you (most eyes in portraits do) to some of the subtle Renaissance elements that make this work work. The body is surprisingly massive and statue-like, a perfectly balanced pyramid turned at an angle so that we can see its mass. Her arm is resting lightly on the chair's armrest almost on the level of the frame itself, like she's sitting in a window looking out at us. The folds of her sleeves and her gently folded hands are remarkably realistic and relaxed. The typical Leonardo landscape shows distance by getting hazier and hazier.

The overall mood is one of balance and serenity, but there's also an element of mystery. Her smile and long-distance beauty are subtle and elusive, tempting but always just out of reach, like strands of a street singer's melody drifting through the Métro tunnel. *Mona* doesn't knock your socks off, but she winks at the patient viewer.

• *Look in the Salle des Etats to find...*

Titian—*Pastoral Symphony (Le Concert Champêtre)*

Venus enters the Renaissance in this colorful work by Titian the Venetian (they rhyme). The nymph turning toward the well at left

is like a Titian reconstruction of the Venus de Milo, but what a difference! The Greek Venus was cold and virginal, but these babes are hot, voluptuous, sensual. The two couples are "making music," if you catch my drift.

The three figures on the grass form a pyramid, giving the scene a balanced, classical beauty, but this appeals more to the senses than to the mind. The golden glow of the skin, the ample flesh, and the hazy outlines became the standard of female nudes for centuries. French painters, especially, learned from Titian's rich colors and sensual beauty.

• *The huge canvas at the far end of the Salle des Etats is...*

Veronese—*Marriage at Cana*

Stand 10 steps away from this enormous canvas to where it just fills your field of vision, and suddenly... you're in a party! Pull up a glass of wine. This is the Renaissance love of beautiful things gone hog-wild. Venetian artists like Veronese painted the good life of

rich, happy-go-lucky Venetian merchants.

In a spacious setting of Renaissance architecture, we see colorful lords and ladies decked out in their fanciest duds, feasting on a great spread of food and drink while the musi-

cians fuel the fires of good fun. Servants prepare and serve the food, jesters play, and animals roam. In the upper left, a dog and his master look on. A sturdy linebacker in yellow pours wine out of a jug, while nearby a ferocious cat battles a lion. The man in white samples some wine and thinks, "Hmm, not bad." The wedding couple at the far left is almost forgotten.

Believe it or not, this is a religious work showing the wedding celebration where Jesus turned water into wine. And there's Jesus in the dead center of 130 frolicking figures, wondering if maybe wine coolers might not have been a better choice. With true Renaissance optimism, Venetians pictured Christ as a party animal, someone who loved the created world as much as they did.

Now, let's hear it for the band! On bass—the bad cat with the funny hat—Titian the Venetian! And joining him on viola—Crazy Veronese!

• *Exit behind the* Marriage at Cana *into the Salle Denon. The dramatic Romantic room is to your left, and the grand neoclassical room is to your right. They feature the most exciting French canvases in the Louvre. In the neoclassical room, kneel before the largest canvas in the Louvre.*

FRENCH PAINTING— NEOCLASSICAL (1780–1850)

J. L. David—*The Coronation of Napoleon*

France's 18th-century kings lived in a fantasy world, far out of touch with the hard lives of their subjects. Then the people revolted, and this decadent world was decapitated—along with the head of state, Louis XVI. Then, after a decade of floundering under an inefficient revolutionary government, France was united by a charismatic,

brilliant, temperamental upstart general who kept his feet on
the ground, his eyes on the horizon, and his hand in his coat—
Napoleon Bonaparte.

Napoleon quickly conquered most of Europe and insisted
on being made emperor (not merely king) of this "New Rome."
He staged an elaborate coronation ceremony in Paris. The painter
David (pron. dah-veed) recorded it for posterity.

We see Napoleon holding aloft the crown—the one we saw
in the Apollo Gallery. He has just made his wife, Josephine,

the empress, and she
kneels at his feet. Seated
behind Napoleon is the
pope, who journeyed
from Rome to place the
imperial crown on his
head. But Napoleon felt
that no one was worthy
of the task. At the last
moment, he shrugged
the pope aside, grabbed the crown, held it up for all to see... and
crowned himself. The pope looks p.o.'d.

The radiant woman in the gallery in the background center
wasn't actually there. Napoleon's mother couldn't make it to see
her boy become the most powerful man in Europe, but he had her
painted in anyway. (There's a key on the frame telling who's who
in the picture.)

The traditional place of French coronations was the ultra-
Gothic Notre-Dame cathedral. But Napoleon wanted a setting
that would reflect the glories of Greece and the grandeur of Rome.
So interior decorators erected stage sets of Greek columns and
Roman arches to give the cathedral the architectural political cor-
rectness you see in this painting. (The *Pietà* statue on the right
edge of the painting is still in Notre-Dame today.)

David was the new emperor's official painter and propagan-
dist, in charge of costumes, flags, and so on for all public ceremonies and spectacles. (Find his self-portrait with curly gray hair
in the *Coronation*, way up in the second balcony, peeking around
the tassel directly above Napoleon's crown.) His "neoclassical"
style influenced French fashion. Take a look at his *Madame Juliet
Récamier* portrait on the opposite wall, showing a modern Parisian woman in ancient garb and Pompeii hairstyle reclining on
a Roman couch. Nearby paintings, such as *The Death of Socrates*
and the *Oath of the Horatii (Le Serment des Horaces)*, are fine
examples of neoclassicism, with Greek subjects, patriotic senti-
ment, and a clean, simple style.

Ingres—*La Grande Odalisque*

Take Venus de Milo, turn her around, lay her down, and stick a
hash pipe next to her and you have the *Grande Odalisque*. OK,
maybe you'd have to add a vertebra or two.

Using clean, polished, sculptural lines, Ingres (pron. ang-
gruh, with a soft "gruh") exaggerates the S-curve of a standing

Greek nude. As in the
Venus de Milo, rough
folds of cloth set off
her smooth skin.
The face, too, has
a touch of Venus'
idealized features (or
like Raphael's kinder-
garten teacher), tak-
ing nature and improving on it. Contrast the cool colors of this
statuelike nude with Titian's golden girls. Ingres preserves
Venus' backside for posterior—I mean, posterity.

• *Cross back through the Salle Denon and into a room gushing with . . .*

ROMANTICISM (1800–1850)

Géricault—*The Raft of the Medusa* (*Le Radeau de la Méduse*)

Not every artist was content to copy the simple, unemotional
style of the Golden Age Greeks. Like the ancient Hellenists, they
wanted to express motion and emotion. In the artistic war between
hearts and minds, the heart style was known as Romanticism.
It was the complete flip side of neoclassicism, though they both
flourished in the early 1800s.

What better setting for an emotional work than a shipwreck?
This painting was based on the actual sinking of the ship *Medusa*
off the coast of Africa. The survivors barely did, floating in open
seas on a raft, suffering hardship and hunger, even resorting to
cannibalism— all the exotic elements for a painter determined to
shock the public and arouse
its emotions.

That painter was young
Géricault (pron. zhair-ee-
ko). He'd honed his craft
sketching dead bodies in
the morgue and the twisted
faces of lunatics in asylums.
Here he paints a tangle of
bodies and lunatics sprawled

over each other. The scene writhes with agitated, ominous motion—the ripple of muscles, churning clouds, and choppy seas. On the right is a deathly green corpse sprawled overboard. In the face of the man at left cradling a dead body, we see the despair of spending weeks stranded in the middle of nowhere.

But wait. There's a stir in the crowd. Someone has spotted something. The bodies rise up in a pyramid of hope culminating in a waving flag. They wave frantically, trying to catch the attention of the tiny ship on the horizon, their last desperate hope... which did finally save them. Géricault uses rippling movement and powerful colors to catch us up in the excitement. If art controls your heartbeat, this is a masterpiece.

Delacroix—*Liberty Leading the People* (*La Liberté Guidant le Peuple*)

France is the symbol of modern democracy. The French weren't the first to adopt it (Americans were), nor are they the best working example of it, but they've had to work harder to achieve it than any other country. No sooner would they throw one king or dictator out than they'd get another. They're now working on their fifth republic.

In this painting, the year is 1830. The Parisians have taken to the streets once again to fight royalist oppressors. There's a hard-bitten proletarian with a sword (far left), an intellectual with

a top hat and a sawed-off shotgun, and even a little boy brandishing pistols.

Leading them on through the smoke and over the dead and dying is the figure of Liberty, a strong woman waving the French flag. Does this symbol of victory look familiar? It's the Winged Victory, wingless and topless.

To stir our emotions, Delacroix (pron. del-ah-kwah) uses only three major colors—the red, white, and blue of the French flag.

This symbol of freedom is a fitting tribute to the Louvre, the first museum ever opened to the common rabble of humanity. The good things in life don't belong only to a small wealthy part of society, but to everyone. The motto of France is *Liberté, Egalité, Fraternité*—liberty, equality, and the brotherhood of all.

• *Exit the room at the far end (past the café) and go downstairs, where you'll bump into the bum of a large, twisting male nude looking like he's just waking up after a thousand-year nap.*

Michelangelo Buonarotti—*Slaves*, c. 1513

These two statues by earth's great-est sculptor are a fitting end to this museum—works that bridge the ancient and modern worlds. Michelangelo, like his fellow Renaissance artists, learned from the Greeks. The perfect anatomy, twisting poses, and idealized faces look like they could have been done 2,000 years earlier.

The so-called Dying Slave (also called the Sleeping Slave, he looks like he should be stretched out on a sofa) twists listlessly against his T-shirt-like bonds, revealing his smooth skin. Compare the polished detail of the rippling, bulging left arm with the sketchy details of the face and neck. With Michelangelo, the body does the talking. This is probably the most sensual nude ever done by the master of the male body.

The *Rebellious Slave* fights against his bondage. His shoulders turn one way while his head and leg turn the other, straining to get free. He even seems to be trying to free himself from the rock he's made of. Michelangelo said that his purpose was to carve away the marble to reveal the figures God put inside. This slave shows the agony of that process and the ecstasy of the result.

• *Finished? I am.* Où est la sortie?

ORSAY MUSEUM
TOUR

The Musée d'Orsay (pron. mew-zay dor-say) houses French art of the 1800s (specifically, 1848–1914), picking up where the Louvre leaves off. For us, that means Impressionism, the art of sun-dappled fields, bright colors, and crowded Parisian cafés. The Orsay houses the best general collection of Manet, Monet, Renoir, Degas, van Gogh, Cézanne, and Gauguin anywhere. If you like Impressionism, visit this museum. If you don't like Impressionism, visit this museum. I personally find it a more enjoyable and rewarding place than the Louvre. Sure, ya gotta see *Mona* and Venus de Milo, but after you get your gottas out of the way, enjoy the Orsay.

Orientation
In the summer of 2003, the main entrance to the Orsay will re-open after renovation. Until then, visitors are admitted through a temporary entrance facing the river. Because of this renovation, some paintings described in this tour (generally only those on the ground floor) may be moved to a new location. If you can't find a particular painting, ask a room guard or simply skip ahead.

Cost: €7; €5 after 16:15, on Sun, and for ages 18 to 25; free for youth under 18 and for anyone first Sun of month; covered by museum pass. Tickets are good all day. Museum passholders can enter to the left of the main entrance (during the renovation, they can walk to the front of the line and show their passes).

Hours: June 20–Sept 20 Tue–Sun 9:00–18:00, Sept 21–June 19 Tue–Sat 10:00–18:00, Sun 9:00–18:00, Thu until 21:45 all year, always closed Mon. Last entrance is 45 minutes before closing. The Impressionist Galleries start closing at 17:15, frustrating many unwary visitors. Note: The Orsay is crowded on Tue, when the Louvre is closed.

Getting There: Above the RER-C stop called Musée d'Orsay.

The nearest Métro stop is Solferino, three blocks south of the Orsay. Bus #69 from the Marais and the rue Cler neighborhoods stops at the museum on the river side (quai Anatole France). From the Louvre, it's a lovely 15-minute walk through the Tuileries and across the river on the pedestrian bridge to the Orsay. Taxis wait in front of the museum on quai Anatole France.

Information: The booth near the entrance gives free floor plans in English (tel. 01 40 49 48 48).

Orsay Tours: English-language tours usually run daily (except Sun) at 11:30. The 90-minute tours cost €6 and are available on audioguide (€5). Tours in English focusing on the Impressionists are offered Tuesdays at 14:30 and Thursdays at 18:30 (sometimes also on other days, €6). I recommend the free, self-guided tour described below.

Length of Our Tour: Two hours.

Cuisine Art: The elegant second-floor restaurant has a pricey but fine buffet and salad bar. A simple fourth-floor café is sandwiched between the Impressionists.

Photography: Photography without a flash is allowed.

Starring: Manet, Monet, Renoir, Degas, van Gogh, Cézanne, and Gauguin.

Gare d'Orsay: The Old Train Station

• *Pick up a free English map upon entering, buy your ticket, and check your bag. Belly up to the stone balustrade overlooking the main floor and orient yourself.*

Trains used to run right under our feet down the center of the gallery. This former train station, or *gare*, barely escaped the wrecking ball in the 1970s, when the French realized it'd be a great place to house their enormous collections of 19th-century art scattered throughout the city.

The main floor has early 19th-century art (as usual, Conservative on the right, Realism on the left). Upstairs (not visible from here) is the core of the collection—the Impressionist rooms (if you are pressed for time, go directly here, for directions, see below after "Opera Exhibit"). Finally, we'll end the tour with "the other Orsay" on the mezzanine level. Clear as Seine water? *Bien.*

THE ORSAY'S 19TH "CENTURY" (1848–1914)

Einstein and Geronimo. Abraham Lincoln and Karl Marx. The train, the bicycle, the horse and buggy, the automobile, and the balloon. Freud and Dickens. Darwin's *Origin of Species* and the

1< 1<

Orsay Ground Floor—Overview

Church's Immaculate Conception. Louis Pasteur and Billy the Kid. V. I. Lenin and Ty Cobb.

The 19th century was a mix of old and new side by side. Europe was entering the modern Industrial Age, with cities, factories, rapid transit, instant communication, and global networks. At the same time, it clung to the past with traditional, rural—almost medieval—attitudes and morals.

According to the Orsay, the "19th century" began in 1848 with the socialist and democratic revolutions (Marx's *Communist Manifesto*). It ended in 1914 with the pull of an assassin's trigger, igniting World War I and ushering in the modern world.

The museum shows art that is also both old and new, conservative and revolutionary. We'll start with the Conservatives and early rebels on the ground floor, then head upstairs to see how a few visionary young artists bucked the system and revolutionized the art world, paving the way for the 20th century.

• *Walk down the steps to the main floor, a gallery filled with statues.*

Conservative Art

No, this isn't ancient Greece. These statues are from the same era as the Theory of Relativity. It's the Conservative art of the French schools that was so popular throughout the 19th century. It was popular because it's beautiful. The balanced poses, the perfect anatomy and sweet faces, the curving lines, the gleaming white stone—all this is very beautiful. (I'll be bad-mouthing it later, but for now appreciate the exquisite craftsmanship of this "perfect" art.)

• *Take your first right into the small Room 1, marked "Ingres." Look for a nude woman with a pitcher of water.*

Ingres—*The Source (La Source)*

Let's start where the Louvre left off. Ingres (pron. ang-gruh, with a soft "gruh"), who helped cap the Louvre collection, championed a neo-classical style. *The Source* is virtually a Greek statue on canvas. Like Venus de Milo, she's a balance of opposite motions—her hips tilt one way, her breasts the other; one arm goes up, the other down; the fluid curve of her body is matched by the water falling from the pitcher.

Ingres worked on this over the course of 35 years and considered it his "image of perfection." Famous in its day, *The Source* influenced many artists whose classical statues and paintings are in the Orsay gallery.

In this and the next few rooms, you'll see more of these visions of idealized beauty—nude women in languid poses, Greek myths, and so on. The "Romantics," like Delacroix, added bright colors, movement, and emotion to the classical coolness of Ingres.

• *Walk uphill (quickly, this is background stuff) to the last room, with a pastel blue-green painting.*

Cabanel—*Birth of Venus (Naissance de Venus)*

This goddess is a perfect fantasy, an orgasm of beauty. The Love Queen stretches back seductively, recently birthed from the ephemeral foam of the wave. This is art of a pre-Freudian society, when sex was dirty and mysterious and had to be exalted into a more pure and divine form. The sex drive was channeled into an acute sense of beauty. French folk would literally swoon in ecstasy before these works of art.

Get a feel for the ideal beauty and refined emotion of these Greek-style works. (Out in the gallery, you'll find another statue with its back posed like Venus'.) Go ahead, swoon. If it feels good, enjoy it.

• *Now, take a mental cold shower, grab a bench in the main gallery of statues, and read on.*

Academy and Salon

Who liked this stuff? The art world was dominated by two conservative institutions: The Academy (the state art school) and the Salon, where works were exhibited to the buying public.

Now let's cross over to the "wrong side of the tracks," to the art of the early rebels.

• *Head back toward the entrance and turn right into Room 4, marked "Daumier" (opposite the Ingres room).*

REALISM—EARLY REBELS

Daumier—36 Caricature Busts *(Ventre Legislatif)*

This is a liberal's look at the stuffy bourgeois establishment that controlled the Academy and the Salon. In these 36 bustlets,

Daumier, trained as a political cartoonist, exaggerates each subject's most distinct characteristic to capture with vicious precision the pomposity and self-righteousness of these self-appointed arbiters of taste. The labels next to the busts give the name of the person being caricatured, his title or job (most were members of the French parliament), and an insulting nickname (like "gross, fat, and satisfied" and Monsieur "Platehead"). Give a few nicknames yourself. Can you find Reagan, Clinton, Yeltsin, Thatcher, and Gingrich?

These people hated what you're about to see. Their prudish faces tightened as their fantasy world was shattered by the Realists.

• *Go uphill four steps and through a few Romantic and pastoral rooms to the final room, #6.*

Millet—*The Gleaners (Les Glaneuses)*

Millet (pron. mee-yay) shows us three gleaners, the poor women who pick up the meager leavings after a field has already been harvested by the wealthy. Millet grew up on a humble farm. He didn't attend the Academy and hated the uppity Paris art scene. Instead of idealized gods, goddesses, nymphs, and winged

Conservative Art & Early Realism

ESCALATOR UP TO IMPRESSIONISM

CONSERVATIVE ART
1. INGRES The Source
2. CABANEL Birth of Venus

REALISM
3. DAUMIER 36 Caricature Busts
4. MILLET The Gleaners
5. COURBET The Painter's Studio
6. COUTURE The Romans of the Fall
7. MANET Olympia
8. Opera Exhibit

babies, he painted simple rural scenes. He was strongly affected by the revolution of 1848, with its affirmation of the working class. Here he captures the innate dignity of these stocky, tanned women who work quietly in a large field for their small reward.

This is "Realism" in two senses. It's painted "realistically," unlike the prettified pastels of Cabanel's *Birth of Venus*. And it's the "real" world—not the fantasy world of Greek myth, but the harsh life of the working poor.

• *Swoon briefly back out into the main gallery and hang a left, climbing the steps to a large alcove with two huge canvases. On the left...*

Courbet—*The Painter's Studio (L'Atelier du Peintre)*

In an age when "Realist painter" was equated with "bomb-throwing Socialist," it took great courage to buck the system. Rejected by the so-called experts, Courbet (pron. coor-bay) held his own one-man exhibit. He built a shed in the middle of Paris, defiantly hung his art out, and basically "mooned" the shocked public.

Here we see Courbet himself in his studio, working diligently on a Realistic landscape, oblivious to the confusion around him. Looking on are ordinary citizens (not Greek heroes), a nude model (not a goddess, but a real woman), and a little boy with an adoring look on his face. Perhaps it's Courbet's inner child admiring the artist who sticks to his guns, whether it's popular or not.

• *Return to the main gallery. Back across the tracks, the huge canvas you see is . . .*

Couture—*The Romans of the Fall (Les Romains de la Décadence)*

We see a fin de siècle (end-of-century) society as if filling a big hot tub. It's stuffed with too much luxury, too much classical beauty, too much pleasure; it's wasted, burned-out, and in decay. The old, backward-looking order was about to be slapped in the face.

• *Continue up the gallery, then left into Room 14 ("Manet, avant 1870"). Find the reclining nude.*

Manet—*Olympia*

"This brunette is thoroughly ugly. Her face is stupid, her skin cadaverous. All this clash of colors is stupefying." So wrote a critic when Edouard Manet's nude hung in the Salon. The public hated it, attacking Manet (pron. mah-nay) in print and literally attacking the canvas.

Think back on Cabanel's painting, *The Birth of Venus*—an idealized, pastel, Vaseline-on-the-lens beauty. Cabanel's nude was soft-core pornography, the kind you see selling lingerie and perfume. The public lapped it up (and Napoleon III purchased it).

Manet's nude doesn't gloss over anything. The pose is classic, used by Titian, Goya, and countless others. But the sharp outlines and harsh, contrasting colors are new and shocking. Her hand is a clamp, and her stare is shockingly defiant, with not a hint of the seductive, hey-sailor look of most nudes. This prostitute, ignoring the flowers sent by her last customer, looks out to us as if to say, "Next." Manet replaced soft-core porn with hard-core art.

Manet had an upper-class upbringing and some formal art training, and he had been accepted by the Salon. He could have cranked out pretty nudes and been a successful painter. Instead, he surrounded himself with a group of young artists experimenting with new techniques. With his reputation and strong personality, he was their master, though he learned equally from them. Let the Impressionist revolution begin.

• *Continue to the end of the gallery, where you'll walk on a glass floor over a model of the city, ending up in front of a model of the Opéra.*

Opera Exhibit

Expand to 100 times your size and hover over a scale model section of the city. There's the 19th-century Garnier Opéra, with its green roof in a diamond-shaped block in the center.

You'll also see a cross-section model of the Opéra. You'd enter from the right end, buy your ticket in the foyer, then move into the entrance hall with its grand staircase, where you could see and be seen by *tout* Paris. At curtain time, you'd find your seat in the golden auditorium, topped by a glorious painted ceiling. (The current ceiling, done by Marc Chagall, is even more wonderful than the one in the model; for information on visiting the actual opera house, see page 40). Notice that the stage is as big as the seating area, with elaborate riggings to raise and lower scenery. Nearby, there are models of set designs from some famous productions. These days, Parisians enjoy their Verdi and Gounod at the modern opera house at place de la Bastille.

• *Behind the Opéra model (go left around model), a covered escalator leads to the often-crowded Impressionist rooms. To take a break and read ahead, consider wandering to the quiet far-left corner of the ground floor, where you'll find a huge painting of a hot-air balloonist's-eye view of pre–Eiffel Tower Paris (c. 1855).*

Ride the escalator to the top floor. Take your first left for a commanding view of the Orsay. The second left takes you between a bookshop and a giant "backwards" clock to the art.

The Impressionist collection is scattered somewhat randomly through the next 10 or so rooms. Shadows dance and the displays mingle. You'll find nearly all of these paintings, but exactly where they're hung is a lot like their brushwork...delightfully sloppy. (If you don't see a described painting, move on. It's either hanging farther down or on vacation.) Now, let there be light.

IMPRESSIONISM

The camera threatened to make artists obsolete. A painter's original function was to record reality faithfully, like a journalist. Now a machine could capture a better likeness faster than you could say Etch-a-Sketch.

But true art is more than just painting reality. It gives us reality from the artist's point of view, putting a personal stamp on the work. It records not only the scene—a camera can do that—but the artist's impressions of the scene. Impressions are often fleeting, so you have to work quickly.

The Impressionist painters rejected camera-like detail for a quick style more suited to capturing the passing moment. Feeling stifled by the rigid rules and stuffy atmosphere of the Academy, the Impressionists took as their motto, "out of the studio, into the open air." They grabbed their berets and scarves and took excursions to the country, setting up their easels on riverbanks and hillsides or sketching in cafés and dance halls. Gods, goddesses, nymphs, and fantasy scenes were out; common people and rural landscapes were in.

The quick style and simple subjects were ridiculed and called childish by the "experts." Rejected by the Salon, the Impressionists staged their own exhibition in 1874. They brashly took their name from an insult thrown at them by a critic who laughed at one of Monet's "impressions" of a sunrise. During the next decade, they exhibited their own work independently. The public, opposed at first, was slowly drawn in by the simplicity, the color, and the vibrancy of Impressionist art.

Impressionism—Manet, Degas, Monet, Renoir

Light! Color! Vibrations! You don't hang an Impressionist canvas— you tether it. Impressionism features light colors, easygoing open-air scenes, spontaneity, broad brushstrokes, and the play of light.

Early Impressionism

The Impressionists made their canvases shimmer by a simple but revolutionary technique. If you mix, say, red, yellow, and blue together, you'll get brown, right? But Impressionists didn't bother to mix them. They'd slap a thick brushstroke of yellow down, then a stroke of green next to it, then red next to that. Up close, all you see are the three messy strokes, but as you back up... *voilà!* Brown! The colors blend in the eye at a distance. But while your eye is saying "bland brown," your subconscious is shouting, "Red! Yellow! Blue! Yes!"

There are no lines in nature. Yet someone in the classical tradition (Ingres, for example) would draw an outline of his subject, then fill it in with color. But the Impressionists built a figure with dabs of paint... a snowman of color.

Manet—*Luncheon on the Grass (Le Déjeuner sur l'Herbe)*

Manet really got a rise out of people with this one. Once again, the public judged the painting on moral terms rather than artistic ones. What are these scantily clad women doing with these fully

clothed men, they wondered? Or rather, what will they be doing after the last baguette is eaten?

A new revolutionary movement is budding: Impressionism. Notice the messy brushwork of the trees and leaves in the background,

and the play of light on the pond in back and filtering through the trees onto the hazy woman stooping behind. And the strong contrasting colors (white skin, black clothes, green grass). And the fact that this is a true out-of-doors painting, not a studio production. The first shot had been fired.

Whistler—*Whistler's Mother (Portrait de la Mère de l'Auteur)*

Why so famous? I don't know either. It shouldn't be, of course, but it is. Perhaps because it's by an American, and we see in his mother some of the monumental solidity of our own ancestral moms made tough by pioneering the American wilderness.

Or perhaps because it was so starkly different in its day. In a roomful of golden goddesses, it'd stand out like a fish in a tree. The experts hated it and didn't understand it. (If music is the fear of silence, is art the fear of reality?) The subtitle is "Arrangement in Gray and Black," and the whole point is the subtle variations on dark shades softened by the rosy tint of her cheeks, but the critics kept waiting for it to come out in Colorization.

Degas—*The Dance Class (La Classe de Danse)*

Clearly, Degas loved dance and the theater. (Also catch his statue, *Tiny Dancer, 14 Years Old*, in the glass case.) The play of stage lights off his dancers, especially the halos of ballet skirts, is made to order for an Impressionist.

Edgar Degas (pron. day-gah) was a rich kid from a family of bankers who got the best classical-style art training. Adoring Ingres' pure lines and cool colors, he painted in the Conservative

style. His work was exhibited in the Salon. He gained
success and a good reputation, and then...he met
the Impressionists.

Degas blends classical
lines with Impressionist
color and spontaneity. His
dancers have outlines, and

he's got them in a classic 3-D setting—with the floor lines slanting
to the upper right.

So, why is Degas an Impressionist? First off, he's captured a
candid, fleeting moment, a momentary "impression"—the dancers
are tired and bored, at the tail end of a long rehearsal. Look at the
girl on the left scratching her back restlessly, and the cuddly little
bundle of dog in the foreground. Degas loved the unposed "snapshot" effect, catching his models off guard.

Finally, he's got that Impressionistic "fury" of the brush. In *The
Dance Class*, look at the bright green bow on the girl with her back
to us. Not only are the outlines sketchy, but see how he slopped
green paint onto her dress and didn't even say, "*Excusez-moi.*"

Degas—*The Glass of Absinthe (Au Café, dit L'Absinthe)*

Degas hung out with low-life Impressionists discussing art, love,
and life in the cheap cafés and bars in Montmartre (the original

Bohemia-ville). He painted Impressionistic snapshots of everyday people. Here a
weary lady of the evening meets morning
with a last lonely coffin-nail drink in the
glaring light of a four-in-the-morning
café. The pale-green drink forming the
center of the composition is that toxic
substance, absinthe, that fueled many
artists and burned out many more.

Look across the room at some later
works by Manet. The old dog was learning
new tricks from his former disciples.

• *The next rooms feature works by two Impressionist masters at their peak,
Monet and Renoir. You're looking at the quintessence of Impressionism.*

Monet—*La Gare St. Lazare*

Claude Monet (pron. mo-nay) is the father of Impressionism.
He learned from Manet (*a* before *o*) but quickly went beyond
even Manet's shocking slabs of colors. Monet fully explored the
possibilities of open-air painting and lighter, brighter colors.

He could even make this drab train station glow with reflected light. The sun diffuses through the skylight and mingles with the steam from the engine. The yellow buildings in the background merge with the blue smoke in the foreground to illuminate an otherwise colorless scene.

Stand a good six feet from the canvas and look at the tall building with the slanted mansard roof behind the station. Looks fine? Now get close up. At six inches, it's a confusing pile of color blobs. And the smoke is truly "thick." Light on!

Monet—*The Cathedral of Rouen (La Cathédrale de Rouen)*

Monet went to Rouen, rented a room across from the cathedral, set up his easel...and waited. He wanted to catch "a series of differing impressions" of the cathedral facade at different times of day and year. He often had several canvases going at once. In all, he did 30 canvases, and each is unique. The time-lapse series shows the sun passing slowly across the sky, creating different-colored light and shadows. These four are labeled right to left: in gray weather, in the morning, morning sun, and full sunlight.

As Monet zeroes in on the play of colors and light, the physical subject—the cathedral—is dissolving. It has become only a rack upon which to hang the light and color. Later artists would boldly throw away the rack, leaving purely abstract modern art in its place.

Monet—Paintings from Monet's Garden at Giverny

One of Monet's favorite places to paint was the garden of his home in Giverny, west of Paris (and worth a visit if you like Monet more than you hate crowds; see page 253). You will find several different views of it, along with the painter's self-portrait. The *Blue Water Lilies* is similar to the large and famous water lily paintings in the nearby Orangerie Museum (scheduled to reopen sometime in 2004, see page 31), across the river in the Tuileries Garden.

Renoir—*Dance at the Moulin de la Galette (Bal du Moulin de la Galette)*

On Sunday afternoons, working-class folk would dress up and head for the fields on butte Montmartre (near Sacré-Coeur church) to dance, drink, and eat little cakes *(galettes)* till dark. Renoir (pron. ren-wah) liked to go there to paint the common Parisians living and loving in the afternoon sun. The sunlight filtering through the trees creates a kaleidoscope of colors, like a 19th-century mirrored ball throwing darts of light on the dancers.

This dappled light is the "impression" that Renoir came away with. He captures it with quick blobs of yellow. Look at the sun-dappled straw hat (right of center) and the glasses (lower right). Smell the powder on the ladies' faces. The painting glows with bright colors. Even the shadows on the ground, which should be gray or black, are colored a warm blue. As if having a good time were required, even the shadows are caught up in the mood, dancing. Like a photographer who uses a slow shutter speed to show motion, Renoir paints a waltzing blur.

Renoir—*The City Dance/The Country Dance (La Danse à la Ville/La Danse à la Campagne)*

In contrast to Monet's haze of colors, Renoir clung to the more traditional technique of drawing a clear outline, then filling it in.

This two-panel "series" by Renoir shows us his exquisite draftsmanship, sense of beauty, and smoother brushwork. Like Degas, Renoir had classical training and exhibited at the Salon.

Renoir's work is lighthearted, with light colors, almost pastels. He seems to be searching for an ideal, the pure beauty we saw on the ground floor. In later years, he used more and more red tones, as if trying for even more warmth.

Pissarro and Others

We've neglected many of the founders of the Impressionist style. Browse around and discover your own favorites. Pissarro is one of mine. His grainy landscapes are more subtle and subdued than the flashy Monet and Renoir, but, as someone said, "He did for the earth what Monet did for the water."

You may find the painting *Young Girl in the Garden (Jeune Fille en Jardin)* with a pastel style as pretty as Renoir's. It's by Mary Cassatt, an American who was attracted to the strong art magnet that was, and still is, Paris.

• *Take a break. Look at the Impressionist effect of the weather on the Paris skyline. Notice the skylight above you—these Impressionist rooms are appropriately lit by ever-changing natural light. Then carry on...*

POST-IMPRESSIONISM

Take a word, put "-ism" on the end, and you've become an intellectual. Commune-ism, sex-ism, cube-ism, computer-ism... Post-Impression-ism.

"Post-Impressionism" is an artificial and clumsy concept to describe those painters who used Impressionist techniques after Monet and Renoir. It might just as well be called something like "Pre-Modernism," because it bridged Impressionism with the 20th century... or you could call it bridge-ism.

• *The Orsay's Post-Impressionist collection (we'll see van Gogh, Cézanne, Gauguin, Rousseau, Seurat, and Toulouse-Lautrec) flip-flops back and forth between here and the end of this gallery. Be prepared to skip around.*

Van Gogh

Impressionists have been accused of being "light"-weights. The colorful style lends itself to bright country scenes, gardens, sunlight on the water, and happy crowds of simple people. It took a remarkable genius to add profound emotion to the Impressionist style.

Vincent van Gogh (pron. van-go; or van-HOCK by the Dutch and the snooty) was the son of a Dutch minister. He too felt a religious calling, and he spread the gospel among the poorest of the poor—peasants and miners. When he turned to painting, he channeled this same spiritual intensity into his work. Like Michelangelo, Beethoven, Rembrandt, Wayne Newton, and a select handful of others, he put so much of himself into his work that art and life became one. In this room, you'll see both van Gogh's painting style and his life unfold.

Van Gogh—*Peasant (Paysanne près de l'Atre)*

As a young man, van Gogh left his steady clerking job to work with poor working people in overcast Belgium and Holland. He painted

Post-Impressionism

these hardworking, dignified folks in a crude, dark style reflecting the oppressiveness of their lives... and the loneliness of his own as he roamed northern Europe in search of a calling.

Van Gogh—*Self-Portrait, Paris (Portrait de l'Artiste),* 1887

Encouraged by his art-dealer brother, van Gogh moves to Paris and, *voilà*! The color! He meets Monet and hobnobs with Gauguin and Toulouse-Lautrec. He rents a room in Montmartre, learning the Impressionist style. (See how he builds a bristling brown beard using thick strokes of reds and greens side by side.)

At first, he paints like the others, but soon he develops his own style. By using thick, swirling brush strokes, he infuses life into even inanimate objects. Van Gogh's brush strokes curve and thrash around like a garden hose pumped with wine.

Van Gogh—*Midday (La Méridienne),* 1890, based on a painting by Millet

The social life of Paris becomes too much for the solitary van Gogh. He moves to the South of France. At first, in the glow of the bright spring sunshine, he has a period of incredible creativity and happiness, overwhelmed by the bright colors—an Impressionist's dream. Here again we see his love of the common people taking a glowing siesta in the noon sun.

Van Gogh—*Van Gogh's Room at Arles (La Chambre de Van Gogh à Arles)*, 1889

But being alone in a strange country begins to wear on him. An ugly man, he finds it hard to get a date. The close-up perspective of this painting makes his tiny rented room look even more cramped. He invites his friend Gauguin to join him, but after two months together arguing passionately about art, nerves get raw. Van Gogh threatens Gauguin with a knife, driving him back to Paris. In crazed despair, van Gogh mutilates his own ear.

The people of Arles realize they have a madman on their hands and convince van Gogh to seek help. He enters a mental hospital.

Van Gogh—*The Church at Auvers-sur-Oise (L'Eglise d'Auvers-sur-Oise)*, 1890

Van Gogh's paintings done in the peace of the mental hospital are more meditative—fewer bright landscapes, more closed-in scenes with deeper and almost surreal colors.

There's also a strong sense of mystery. What's behind this church? The sky is cobalt blue and the church's windows are also blue, like we're looking right through the church to an infinite sky. There's something mysterious lurking on the other side. You can't see it, but you feel its presence like the cold air from an approaching Métro train still hidden in the tunnel. There's a road that leads from us to the church, then splits to go behind. A choice must be made. Which way? You can actually visit this church (see Auvers-sur-Oise, page 254).

Van Gogh—*Self-Portrait, St. Remy,* 1889

Van Gogh wavered between happiness and madness. He despaired of ever being sane enough to continue painting.

This self-portrait shows a man engulfed in a confused but beautiful world. The background brush strokes swirl and rave, setting in motion the waves of the jacket. He's caught in the current, out of control. But in the midst of this rippling sea of mystery floats a still, detached island of a face with probing, questioning, wise eyes.

Do his troubled eyes know that only a few months on, he will take a pistol and put a bullet through his chest?

Cézanne

Cézanne's art brought Impressionism into the 20th century. There's less color here, less swirling brushwork, less passion. It's cleaner, chunkier, more intellectual. Cézanne (pron. say-zahn) can be difficult to appreciate after the warmth of Renoir, and he won't give you the fireworks of van Gogh. But he's worth the effort.

Cézanne—*Self-Portrait* (*Portrait de l'Artiste*)

Cézanne was virtually unknown and unappreciated in his lifetime. He worked alone, lived alone, and died alone, ignored by all but a few revolutionary young artists who understood his efforts.

And Cézanne couldn't draw. His brush was a blunt instrument. With it, he'd bludgeon reality into submission, drag it across a canvas, and leave it there to dry. But Cézanne the mediocre painter was a great innovator. His works are not perfected, finished products but revolutionary works-in-progress—gutter balls with wonderful spin. His work spoke for itself—which is good because, as you can see here, he had no mouth.

Cézanne—*Landscape* (*Rochers près des Grottes au dessus de Château-Noir*)

Cézanne used chunks of color as blocks to build three-dimensional forms. The rocky brown cliffs here consist of cubes of green, tan, and blue that blend at a distance to create a solid 3-D structure. It only makes sense from a distance. Try this: Start at six inches and fade back. At some point the messy slabs become reality on the rocks.

Why is this revolutionary? Past artists created the illusion of 3-D with lines (like when we draw receding lines to turn a square into a cube). The Impressionists pioneered the technique of using blobs of color, not lines, to capture a subject. But most Impressionist art is flat and two-dimensional, a wall of color like Monet's *Cathedral of Rouen* series. Cézanne went 3-D with chunks.

These chunks are like little "cubes." No coincidence that his experiments in reducing forms to their geometric basics influenced the...Cubists.

Cézanne—*The Card Players* (*Les Joueurs de Cartes*)

These aren't people. They're studies in color and pattern. The subject matter—two guys playing cards—is less important than the

pleasingly balanced pattern they make on the canvas, two sloping forms framing a cylin-der (a bottle) in the center. Later, abstract artists would focus solely on the shapes and colors.

Again, notice how the figures are built with chunks of color. The jacket of the player to the right consists of tans, greens, and browns. As one art scholar put it: "Cézanne confused intermingled forms and colors, achieving an extraordinarily luminous density in which lyricism is controlled by a rigorously constructed rhythm." Just what I said—chunks of color.

Cézanne—*A Modern Olympia* (*Une Moderne Olympia*)

Is this Cézanne himself paying homage to Manet? And dreaming up a new, more radical style of painting? We've come a long way since Manet's *Olympia*, which seems tame now.

• *Exit to the café and consider a well-deserved break. From the café, continue ahead, walking under the large green beam, following signs saying "suite de la visite."*

A hallway leads past WCs to a dark room in the right corner...

Redon

Now flip out the lights and step into his mysterious world. If the Orsay's a zoo, this is the nocturnal house. Prowl around. This is wild, wild stuff. It's intense—imagine Richard Nixon on mushrooms playing sax.

• *Coming out of the darkness, pass into the gallery lined with metal columns containing the primitive art of Rousseau and Gauguin. Start in the first alcove to the left.*

PRIMITIVISM

Henri Rousseau—*War*
(La Guerre, ou La Chevauchée de la Discorde)

Some artists, rejecting the harried, scientific, and rational world, remembered a time before "-isms," when works of art weren't scholarly "studies in form and color" but voodoo dolls full of mys-

tery and magic power. They learned from the art of primitive tribes in Africa and the South Seas, trying to recreate a primal Garden of Eden of peace and wholeness. In doing so, they created another "ism": Primitivism.

One such artist was Rousseau, a man who painted like a child. He was an amateur artist who palled around with all the great painters, but they never took his naive style of art seriously.

This looks like a child's drawing of a nightmare. The images are primitive—flat and simple, with unreal colors—but the effect is both beautiful and terrifying. War in the form of a woman with a sword flies on horseback across the battlefield, leaving destruction in her wake—broken bare trees, burning clouds in the background, and heaps of corpses picked at by the birds.

Gauguin—*The Beautiful Angela*
(La Belle Angèle)

A woman in peasant dress sits in a bubble, like the halos in a medieval religious painting. Next to it is a pagan idol. This isn't a scene but an ordered collage of images with symbolic overtones. It's left to us to make the connection.

Paul Gauguin (pron. go-gan) learned the bright clashing colors from the Impressionists, but diverged from this path about the time van Gogh waved a knife in his face.

Gauguin simplifies. His figures are two-dimensional, with thick dark outlines filled in with basic blocks of color. He turned his back on the entire Western tradition of realism begun in the Renaissance, which tried to recreate the 3-D world on a 2-D canvas. Instead he returns to an age where figures become symbols.

Gauguin—*Arearea (Pleasantries) (Joyeusetes)*

Gauguin got the travel bug early in childhood and grew up wanting to be a sailor. Instead, he became a stockbroker. In his spare time, he painted and was introduced to the Impressionist circle. At the age of 35, he got fed up with it all, quit his job, abandoned his wife (see her stern portrait bust) and family, and took refuge in his art. He traveled to the South Seas in search of the exotic, finally settling on Tahiti.

In Tahiti, Gauguin found his Garden of Eden. He simplified his life to the routine of eating, sleeping, and painting. He simplified his painting still more, to flat images with heavy black outlines filled in with bright, pure colors. He painted the native girls in their naked innocence (so different from Cabanel's seductive *Venus*). But this simple style had a deep undercurrent of symbolic meaning.

Arearea shows native women and a dog. In the "distance" (there's no attempt at traditional 3-D here), a procession goes by with a large pagan idol. What's the connection between the idol and the foreground figures who are apparently unaware of it? Gauguin makes us dig deep down into our medulla oblongatae to make a mystical connection between the beautiful women, the dog, and religion. In primitive societies, religion permeates life. Idols, dogs, and women are holy.

Seurat—*The Circus (Le Cirque)*

With pointillism, Impressionism is brought to its logical conclusion—little dabs of different colors placed side by side to blend in the viewer's eye. Using only red, yellow, blue, and green points of paint, Seurat (pron. sur-rah) creates a mosaic of colors that shimmers at a distance, capturing the wonder of the dawn of electric lights.

Toulouse-Lautrec—
The Clownesse Cha-U-Kao

Henri de Toulouse-Lautrec was the black sheep of a noble family. At age 15, he broke both legs, which left him a cripple. Shunned by his family, a freak to society, he felt more at home in the under-

world of other outcasts—prostitutes, drunks, thieves, dancers, and actors. He painted the lowlife in the bars, cafés, dance halls, and brothels he frequented. Toulouse-Lautrec died young of alcoholism.

The Clownesse Cha-U-Kao is one of his fellow freaks, a fat lady clown who made her living being laughed at. She slumps wearily after a performance, indifferent to the applause, and adjusts her dress to pre-pare for the curtain call.

Toulouse-Lautrec was a true impression-ist, catching his models in candid poses.

He worked spontaneously, never correcting his mistakes, as you can see from the blotches on her dark skirt and the unintentional yellow sash hanging down. Can you see a bit of Degas here, in the subject matter, snapshot pose, and colors?

Toulouse-Lautrec—
Jane Avril Dancing

Toulouse-Lautrec hung out at the Moulin Rouge dance hall in Montmartre. One of the most popular dancers was this slim, graceful, elegant, and melancholy woman who stood out above the rabble of the Moulin Rouge. Her legs keep dancing while her mind is far away. Toulouse-Lautrec the artistocrat might have identi-fied with her noble face—sad and weary of the nightlife, but stuck in it.

• *You've seen the essential Orsay and are permitted to cut out (the exit is straight below you). But there's an "Other Orsay" I think you'll find entertaining.*

To reach the mezzanine ("niveau median"), cross to the other side of the gallery at this level and go down three flights. In front of you is the restaurant, behind you (at the foot of the escalator) are a grand ballroom and the mezzanine (which overlooks the main floor).

Peek into the restaurant Le Salon de Thé du Musée (or enjoy a cup of coffee and/or the €9 salad bar—available any time; if it's not

*on the menu, ask). This was part
of the original hotel that adjoined
the station (built in 1900, abandoned after 1939, condemned,
and restored to the elegance you
see today). Then, find the pala-
tial room of mirrors and chandeliers, marked "Salle des Fêtes" or
"Arts et Decors de la IIIème
République" (Room 52).*

THE "OTHER" ORSAY—MEZZANINE

The beauty of the Orsay is that it combines all the art of the
1800s (1848–1914), both modern and classical, in one building.
The classical art, so popular in its own day, has been maligned
and was forgotten in the 20th century. It's time for a reassessment.
Is it as gaudy and gawd-awful as we've been led to believe? From
our next-century perspective, let's take a look at the opulent, fin
de siècle, French high society and its luxurious art.

The Grand Ballroom
(Arts et Décors de la IIIème République)

This was one of France's most luxurious nightspots when the
Orsay hotel was here. You can easily imagine gowned debutantes
and white-gloved dandies waltzing the night away to the music
of a chamber orchestra.

Notice:

1) The interior decorating:
raspberry marble-ripple ice-cream
columns, pastel ceiling painting,
gold work, mirrors, and leafy
strands of chandeliers.

2) The statue *Bacchante Couchée*
sprawled in the middle of the room.
Familiar pose? If not, you flunk
this tour.

3) The statue *Aurore*, with her
canopy of hair, hide-and-seek face,
and silver-dollar nipples.

4) The large painting *The Birth of Venus (La Naissance de
Venus)* by William Bouguereau. Van Gogh once said: "If I
painted like Bouguereau, I could hope to make money. The
public will never change—they love only sweet things."

5) *La Nature*, with the only see-through veil of marble
I've ever seen through.

The "Other" Orsay

1. Grand Ballroom
2. Art worth a second look
3. Art NOT worth a second look
4. Art Nouveau
5. RODIN The Walking Man
6. CLAUDEL L'Age Mur
7. RODIN The Gates of Hell
8. RODIN Balzac

DCH

So here's the question: Is this stuff beautiful or merely gaudy? Divine or decadent?

• *Return to the mezzanine overlooking the main gallery. Head toward the far end. Enter the first room on the left (#55).*

Art Worth a Second Look

We've seen some great art; now let's see some not-so-great art—at least, that's what modern critics tell us. This is realistic art with a subconscious kick, art from a neurotic society before Freud articulated its demons.

• *Working clockwise, you'll see . . .*

Cain

The world's first murderer, with the murder weapon still in his belt, is exiled with his family. Archaeologists had recently discovered a Neanderthal skull, so the artist shows them as a prehistoric hunter/gatherer tribe.

The Dream (Le Rêve)
Soldiers sleep, while visions of Gatling guns dance in their heads.

Payday (La Paye des Moissonneurs)
Peasants getting paid, painted by the man called "the grandson of Courbet and Millet." The subtitle of the work should be, "Is this all there is to life?"

The Excommunication of Robert le Pieux
The bishops exit after performing the rite. The king and queen are stunned, the scepter dropped. The ritual candle has been snuffed out; it falls, fuming, echoing through the huge hall.... Again, is this art or only cheap theatrics?
• *Return to the mezzanine. Skip the next room, then go left into Room 59, labeled "Symbolisme."*

Art Not Worth a Second Look
The Orsay's director said: "Certainly, we have bad paintings. But we have only the greatest bad paintings." And here they are.

Serenity
An idyll in the woods. Three nymphs with harps waft off to the right. These people are stoned on something.

The School of Plato (L'Ecole de Platon)
Subtitled "The Athens YMCA." A Christlike Plato surrounded by adoring, half-naked nubile youths gives new meaning to the term "Platonic relationship."

Will the pendulum shift so that one day art like *The School of Plato* becomes the new, radical avant-garde style?
• *Return to the mezzanine and continue to the far end. Enter the last room on the left (#65) and head for the far corner.*

ART NOUVEAU
The Industrial Age brought factories, row houses, machines, train stations, geometrical precision—and ugliness. At the turn of the century, some artists reacted against the unrelieved geo-metry of harsh, pragmatic, iron-and-steel Eiffel Tower art with a "new art"—Art Nouveau. Hmm. I think I had a driver's-ed teacher by that name.

Charpentier—*Dining Room of Adrien Benard (Boiserie de la Salle à Mangé de la Propriété Benard)*

Like nature, which also abhors a straight line, Art Nouveau artists used the curves of flowers and vines as their pattern. They were convinced that "practical" didn't have to mean "ugly" as well. They turned everyday household objects into art.

This wood-paneled dining room, with its organic shapes, is one of the finest examples of the Art Nouveau style (called *Jugendstil* in Germanic countries). Another is the curvy, wrought-iron work of some of Paris' early Métro entrances (few survive), built by the same man who commissioned this dining room for his home.

• *Browse through the Art Nouveau rooms to the left. You'll spill out back onto the mezzanine. Grab a seat in front of the Rodin statue of a man missing everything but his legs.*

Auguste Rodin

Rodin completes the tour—from classical sculpture to Impressionist painting to an artist who brought them both together. Rodin combined classical solidity with Impressionist surfaces to become the greatest sculptor since Michelangelo.

Rodin—*The Walking Man (L'Homme Qui Marche)*

This muscular, forcefully striding man could be a symbol of the Renaissance Man with his classical power. With no mouth or hands, he speaks with his body. But Rodin also learned a thing or two from the comparatively light-weight Impressionist painters. Get close and look at the statue's surface. This rough, "unfinished" look reflects light like the rough Impressionist brushwork, making the statue come alive, never quite at rest in the viewer's eye.

• *Near the far end of the mezzanine you'll see a small bronze couple* (L'Age Mur) *by Camille Claudel, a student of Rodin's.*

Claudel—*Maturity (L'Age Mur)*

Camille Claudel, Rodin's student and mistress, may have portrayed their doomed love affair here. A young girl desperately reaches out to an older man, who is led away reluctantly by an older woman. The center of the composition is the empty space left when their hands separate. In real life, Rodin refused to leave his wife, and Camille (see her head sticking up from a block of marble nearby) ended up in an insane asylum.

Rodin—*The Gates of Hell (Porte de l'Enfer)*

Rodin worked for decades on these doors depicting Dante's Hell, and they contain some of his greatest hits, small statues that he later executed in full size. Find *The Thinker* squatting above the doorway, contemplating Man's fate. And in the lower left is the same kneeling man eating his children *(Ugolin)* that you'll see in full size nearby. Rodin paid models to run, squat, leap, and spin around his studio however they wanted. When he saw an interesting pose, he'd yell, "freeze" (or "statue maker") and get out his sketch pad.

Rodin—*Balzac*

The great French novelist is given a heroic, monumental ugliness. Wrapped in a long cloak, he thrusts his head out at a defiant angle, showing the strong individualism and egoism of the 19th-century Romantic movement. Balzac is proud and snooty—but his body forms a question mark, and underneath the twisted features we can see a touch of personal pain and self-doubt. This is hardly camera-eye realism—Balzac wasn't that grotesque—but it captures a personality that strikes us even if we don't know the man.

From this perch, look over the main floor at all the classical statues between you and the big clock and realize how far we've come—not in years but in style changes. Many of the statues below—beautiful, smooth, balanced, and idealized—were done at the same time as Rodin's powerful, haunting works. Rodin is a good place to end the tour. With a stable base of 19th-century stone, he launched art into the 20th century.

POMPIDOU CENTER TOUR

The Pompidou Center contains possibly Europe's best museum of 20th-century art. After the super-serious Louvre and Orsay, finish things off with this artistic kick in the pants. You won't find classical beauty here, no dreamy Madonnas-and-Children—just a stimulating, offbeat, and, if you like, instructive walk through nearly every art style of the wild and crazy last century.

Orientation

Cost: Several admissions are possible. You want the *Musée National d'Art Moderne* (€5.50, covered by museum pass, ages 18–25-€3.50, under 18 and "job seekers" enter free). It's free on the first Sun of the month. Buy tickets on ground floor. If lines are long, use the red ticket machines (CC only, follow English instructions). Other temporary exhibits require separate admission (or an all-day pass).

Hours: Wed–Mon 11:00–21:00, closed Tue and May 1.

Getting There: Métro stop Rambuteau or, a few blocks farther away, Hôtel de Ville. Bus #69 from Marais and rue Cler also stops at Hôtel de Ville. The wild, color-coded exterior makes it about as hard to locate as the Eiffel Tower. To use the escalator to reach the museum (fourth floor), you need a ticket for the museum or a museum pass.

Information: Tel. 01 44 78 12 33, www.centrepompidou.fr. Parisians call the complex the "Centre Beaubourg" (pron. sahn-truh boh-boor), but official publications call it the "Centre Pompidou."

Museum Tours: Audioguides cost €4 and are available on the fourth floor. They include explanations of selected works of art, but are not always up to date with the current collection.

Length of Our Tour: One hour.

Coatcheck: Ground floor.

Cuisine Art: You'll find a snobby view restaurant on the sixth

floor, a cool café on the mezzanine level, and a library cafeteria on second floor. Across from the entrance/exit, on rue Rambuteau, is the efficient and cheap Flunch self-service cafeteria—though my favorite places line the playful fountain, *l'Hommage à Stravinsky* (Dame Tartine and Crêperie Beaubourg, above and to the right as you face the museum entrance, are both reasonable).
Starring: Matisse, Picasso, Chagall, Dalí, Warhol, and contemporary art.

MODERN ART COLLECTION

The *Musée National d'Art Moderne: Collection Permanente* (what we'll see) is on the fourth floor, reached by the escalator to the left as you enter. But there's plenty more art scattered all over the building, some free, some requiring a separate ticket. Ask at the ground floor information booth or just wander.

The "permanent" collection...isn't. It changes so often that this chapter is intentionally general—to give you an overview. Pick up a *plan du musée* (museum layout) as you enter the fourth floor to locate the artists described below, and don't hesitate to ask, *"Où est Kandinsky?"* Some rooms have informative, handheld English explanations available in wall slots.

• *Buy your ticket on the ground floor, then ride up the escalator (or run up the down escalator to get in the proper mood) to the fourth floor. When you see the view, your opinion of the Pompidou's exterior should improve a good 15 percent. Enter on the fourth floor, show your ticket, and ask for the museum layout* (plan du musée). *Past the ticket-checkers, hike the stairs to the fifth floor, which covers roughly 1900–1970. (You'll finish back here on the fourth floor, which brings us up to today.)*

The Exterior

That slight tremor you may feel comes from Italy, where Michelangelo has been spinning in his grave ever since 1977, when the Pompidou Center first revolted Paris. Still, it's an appropriate modern temple for the controversial art it houses.

The building is "exoskeletal" (like Notre-Dame or a crab), with its functional parts—the pipes, heating ducts, and escalator—on the outside, and the meaty art inside. It's the epitome of modern architecture where "form follows function."

MODERN ART FROM 1900 TO 1970 (FIFTH FLOOR)

A.D. 1900: A new century dawns. War is a thing of the past. Science will wipe out poverty and disease. Rational Man is poised at a new era of peace and prosperity....

Right. This cozy Victorian dream was soon shattered by

Pompidou—Fifth Floor

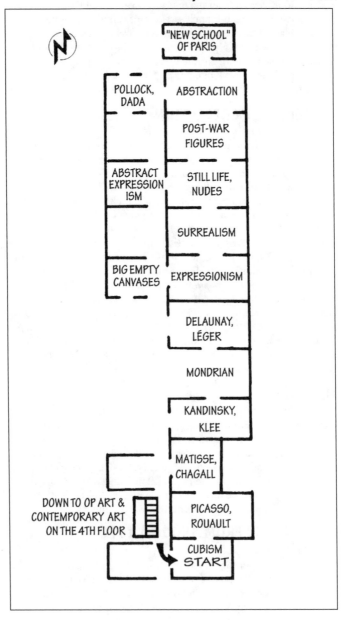

"NEW SCHOOL" OF PARIS

POLLOCK, DADA

ABSTRACTION

POST-WAR FIGURES

ABSTRACT EXPRESSIONISM

STILL LIFE, NUDES

SURREALISM

BIG EMPTY CANVASES

EXPRESSIONISM

DELAUNAY, LÉGER

MONDRIAN

KANDINSKY, KLEE

MATISSE, CHAGALL

DOWN TO OP ART & CONTEMPORARY ART ON THE 4TH FLOOR

PICASSO, ROUAULT

CUBISM START

two world wars and rapid technological change. Nietzsche murdered God. Freud washed ashore on the beach of a vast new continent inside each of us. Einstein made everything merely "relative." Even the fundamental building blocks of the universe, atoms, were behaving erratically.

The 20th century—accelerated by technology and fragmented by war—was exciting and chaotic, and the art reflects the turbulence of that century of change.

• *Twentieth-century art resents being put in chronological order. I've described major modern art trends in a linear way, even though you'll find the rooms less orderly. Read and wander generally counterclockwise around this floor. If you don't see what you're looking for, it'll pop up later.*

Cubism: Reality Shattered (1907–1912)

I throw a rock at a glass statue, shatter it, pick up the pieces, and glue them onto a canvas. I'm a Cubist.

Pablo Picasso (1881–1973) and Georges Braque (1882–1963)

Born in Spain, Picasso moved to Paris as a young man, settling into a studio (the Bâteau-Lavoir) on Montmartre. He worked with next-door neighbor Georges Braque in poverty so dire they often didn't know where their next bottle of wine was coming from. They corrected each other's paintings (it's hard to tell whose is whose without the titles) and shared ideas, meals, and girlfriends while inventing a whole new way to look at the world.

They show the world through a kaleidoscope of brown and gray. The subjects are somewhat recognizable (with the help of the titles), but they are broken into geometric shards (let's call them "cubes," though there are many different shapes), then pieced back together.

Cubism gives us several different angles of the subject at once—say, a woman seen from the front and side angles simultaneously, resulting in two eyes on the same side of the nose. This involves showing three dimensions, plus Einstein's new fourth dimension, the time it takes to walk around the subject to see other angles. Newfangled motion pictures could capture this moving, 4-D world, but how to do it on a 2-D canvas? The Cubist "solution" is a kind of Mercator projection, where the round world is sliced up like an orange peel and laid as flat as possible.

Notice how the "cubes" often overlap. A single cube might contain both an arm (in the foreground) and the window behind (in the background), both painted the same color. The foreground and background are woven together, so that the subject dissolves into a pattern.

Pablo Picasso:
Synthetic Cubism (1912–1915) and Beyond

If the Cubists were as smart as Einstein, why couldn't they draw a picture to save their lives? Picasso was one modern artist who could draw exceptionally well (see his partly finished *Harlequin*). But he constantly explored and adapted his style to new trends, becoming the most famous painter of the century. Scattered throughout the museum are works from the many periods of Picasso's life.

Picasso soon began to use more colorful "cubes" (1912–1915). Eventually, he used curved shapes to build the subject, rather than the straight-line shards of early Cubism.

Picasso married and had children. Works from this period (the 1920s) are more realistic, with full-bodied (and big-nosed) women and children. He tries to capture the solidity, serenity, and volume of classical statues.

As his relationships with women deteriorated, he vented his sexual demons by twisting the female body into grotesque balloon-animal shapes (1925–1931).

All through his life, Picasso was exploring new materials. He made collages, tried his hand at making "statues" out of wood, wire, or whatever, and even made statues out of everyday household objects. These "multimedia" works, so revolutionary at the time, have become stock-in-trade today.

Marc Chagall (1887–1985)

Marc Chagall, at age 22, arrived in Paris with the wide-eyed wonder of a country boy. Lovers are weightless with bliss. Animals smile and wink at us. Musicians, poets, peasants, and dreamers ignore gravity, tumbling in slow-motion circles high above the rooftops. The colors are deep, dark, and earthy—a pool of mystery with figures bleeding through below the surface. (Chagall claimed his early poverty forced him to paint over used canvases, inspiring the overlapping images.)

Chagall's very personal style fuses many influences. He was raised in a small

Russian village, which explains his "naive" outlook and fiddler-on-the-roof motifs. His simple figures are like Russian Orthodox icons. And his Jewish roots produce Old Testament themes. Stylistically, he's thoroughly modern—Cubist shards, bright Fauve colors, and Primitive simplification. This otherworldly style was a natural for religious works, and his murals and stained glass, with both Jewish and Christian motifs, decorate buildings around the world—including the ceiling of Paris' Garnier Opéra (Mo: Opéra).

Georges Rouault (1871–1958)

Young Georges Rouault was apprenticed to a stained-glass window maker. Enough said?

The paintings have the same thick, glowing colors, heavy black outlines, simple subjects, and (mostly) religious themes. The style is modern, but the mood is medieval, solemn, and melancholy. Rouault captures the tragic spirit of those people—clowns, prostitutes, and sons of God—who have been made outcasts by society.

Henri Matisse (1869–1954)

Matisse's colorful "wallpaper" works are not realistic. A man is a few black lines and blocks of paint. The colors are unnaturally bright. There's no illusion of the distance and 3-D that were so important to Renaissance Italians. The "distant" landscape is as bright as things close up, and the slanted lines meant to suggest depth are crudely done.

Traditionally, the canvas was like a window that you looked "through" to see a slice of the real world stretching off into the distance. Now, a camera could do that better. With Matisse, you look "at" the canvas, like wallpaper. *Voilà!* What was a crudely drawn scene now becomes a sophisticated and decorative pattern of colors and shapes.

Though fully "modern," Matisse built on 19th-century art—the bright colors of van Gogh, the primitive figures of Gauguin, the colorful designs of Japanese prints, and the Impressionist patches of paint that only blend together at a distance.

Primitive Masks and Statues

Matisse was one of the Fauves ("wild beasts") who, inspired by African and Oceanic masks and voodoo dolls, tried to inject a bit of the jungle into bored French society. The result? Modern art that looked primitive: long, mask-like faces with almond eyes; bright, clashing colors; simple figures; and "flat," two-dimensional scenes.

Abstract Art

Abstract art simplifies. A man becomes a stick figure. A squiggle is a wave. A streak of red expresses anger. Arches make you want a cheeseburger. These are universal symbols that everyone from a caveman to a banker understands. Abstract artists capture the essence of reality in a few lines and colors, even things a camera can't—emotions, abstract concepts, musical rhythms, and spiritual states of mind. With abstract art, you don't look "through" the canvas to see the visual world, but "at" it to read the symbolism of lines, shapes, and colors.

Wassily Kandinsky (1866–1944)

The bright colors, bent lines, and lack of symmetry tell us that Kandinsky's world was passionate and intense.

Notice titles like *Improvisation* and *Composition*. Kandinsky was inspired by music, an art form that's also "abstract," though it still packs a punch. Like a jazz musician improvising a new pattern of notes from a set scale, Kandinsky plays with new patterns of related colors, looking for just the right combination. Using lines and color, Kandinsky translates the unseen reality into a new medium...like lightning crackling over the radio. Go, man, go.

Piet Mondrian (1872–1944)

Like blueprints for modernism, Mondrian's T-square style boils painting down to its basic building blocks (black lines, white canvas) and the three primary colors (red, yellow, and blue) arranged in orderly patterns.

(When you come right down to it, that's all painting ever has been. A schematic drawing of, say, the *Mona Lisa*, shows that it's less about a woman than about the triangles and rectangles she's composed of.)

Mondrian started out painting realistic landscapes of the orderly fields in his native Holland. Increasingly, he simplified them into horizontal and vertical patterns. For Mondrian, heavy into Eastern mysticism, "up vs. down" and "left vs. right" were the perfect metaphors for life's dualities: "good vs. evil," "body vs. spirit," "man vs. woman." The canvas is a bird's-eye view of Mondrian's personal landscape.

Constantin Brancusi (1876–1957)

Brancusi's curved, shiny statues reduce things to their essence. A bird is a single stylized wing, the one feature that sets it apart from other animals. He rounds off to the closest geometrical form, so a woman's head is a perfect oval on a cubic pedestal.

Humans love symmetry (maybe because our own bodies are roughly symmetrical), finding geometric shapes restful, even worthy of meditation. Brancusi follows the instinct for order that has driven art from earliest times, from circular Stonehenge and Egyptian pyramids to Greek columns and Roman arches to Renaissance symmetry and the American Indian "medicine wheel."

Paul Klee (1879–1940)

Paul Klee's small and playful canvases are deceptively simple, containing shapes so basic they could be read like universal symbols. Klee thought a wavy line, for example, would always suggest motion, and a stick figure would always mean a human (like the psychologist Carl Jung's universal dream symbols, part of our "collective unconscious").

Klee saw these universals in the art of children, who express themselves without censoring or cluttering things up with learning. His art has a childlike playfulness and simple figures, painted in an uninhibited frame of mind.

Klee also turned to nature. The same forces that cause the wave to draw a line of foam on the beach can cause a meditative artist to draw a squiggly line of paint on a canvas. The result is a universal shape. The true artist doesn't just paint nature, he becomes Nature.

Design: Chairs by Rietveld and Alvar Aalto

Hey, if you can't handle modern art, sit on it! (Actually, don't.) The applied arts—chairs, tables, lamps, and vases—are as much a part of the art world as the fine ones. (Some say the first art object was the pot.) As machines became as talented as humans, artists embraced new technology and mass production to bring beauty to the masses.

Fernand Léger (1881–1955)

Fernand Léger's style has been called "Tubism"—breaking the world down into cylinder shapes, rather than cubes. (He supposedly got his inspiration during World War I from the gleaming barrel of a cannon.) Léger captures the feel of the encroaching Age of Machines, with all the world looking like an internal-combustion engine.

Robert and Sonia Delaunay

This husband-and-wife team's colorful, fragmented canvases (including a psychedelic Eiffel Tower) prove that the modern style doesn't have to be ugly or puzzling.

World War I: The Death of Values

Ankle-deep in mud, a soldier shivers in a trench, waiting to be ordered "over the top." He'll have to run through barbed wire, over fallen comrades, and into a hail of machine-gun fire, only to capture a few hundred yards of meaningless territory that will be lost the next day. This soldier was not thinking about art.

World War I left nine million dead. (During the war, France often lost more men in a single day than America lost in all of Vietnam.) The war also killed the optimism and faith in mankind that had guided Europe since the Renaissance. Now, rationality just meant scheming, technology meant machines of death, and morality meant giving your life for an empty cause.

Expressionism: Kirchner, Beckmann, Grosz, Soutine, Dix, and Kokoschka

Cynicism and decadence settled over postwar Europe. Artists "expressed" their disgust by showing a distorted reality that emphasized the ugly. Using the lurid colors and simplified figures of the Fauves, they slapped paint on in thick brushstrokes, depicting a hypocritical, hard-edged, dog-eat-dog world that had lost its bearings. The people have a haunted look in their eyes, the fixed stare of corpses and of those who have to bury them.

Dada: Duchamp's Urinal (1917)

When people could grieve no longer, they turned
to grief's giddy twin, laughter. The war made all
old values a joke, including artistic ones. The
Dada movement, choosing a purposely childish name, made art that was intentionally
outrageous: a moustache on the *Mona
Lisa*, a shovel hung on a wall, or a modern
version of a Renaissance "fountain"—
a urinal (by either Marcel Duchamp or I. P.
Freeley, 1917). It was a dig at all the pompous prewar artistic theo-
ries based on the noble intellect of Rational Women and Men.
While the experts ranted on, Dadaists sat in the back of the class
and made cultural fart noises.

Hey, I love this stuff. My mind says it's sophomoric, but my
heart belongs to Dada.

Surrealism: Dalí, Ernst, and Magritte (1920–1940)

Greek statues with sunglasses, a man as a spinning top, shoes becoming feet, and black ants as musical notes—Surrealism. The world
was moving fast, and Surrealists caught the jumble of images. The
artist scatters seemingly unrelated things on the canvas, leaving us to
trace the connections in a kind of connect-the-dots without numbers.
If it comes together, the synergy of unrelated things can be pretty
startling. But even if the juxtaposed images don't ultimately connect,
the artist has made you think, rerouting your thoughts through new
neural paths. If you don't "get" it . . . you got it.

Complicating the modern world was Freud's discovery of the
"unconscious" mind that thinks dirty thoughts while we sleep. Many
a Surrealist canvas is an uncensored, stream-of-consciousness "landscape" of these deep urges, revealed in the bizarre images of dreams.

In dreams, sometimes one object can be two things at once.
"I dreamt that you walked in with a cat . . . no, wait, maybe you
were the cat . . . no . . . . " Surrealists paint opposites like these and
let them speak for themselves.

Salvador Dalí (1904–1989)

Salvador Dalí could draw
exceptionally well. He painted
"unreal" scenes with photo-
graphic realism, making us
believe they could really happen. Seeing familiar objects in
an unfamiliar setting—like a
grand piano adorned with

disembodied heads of Lenin—creates an air of mystery, the feeling that anything can happen. That's both exciting and unsettling.
Dalí's images—crucifixes, political and religious figures, and naked
bodies—pack an emotional punch. Take one mixed bag of reality,
jumble in a blender, and serve on a canvas . . . Surrealism.

Abstract Surrealists: Miró, Calder, and Arp

Abstract artists described their subconscious urges using color
and shapes alone—Rorschach inkblots in reverse.

The thin-line scrawl of Joan Miró's work is like the doodling
of a three-year-old. You'll recognize crudely drawn birds, stars,
animals, and strange cell-like creatures with whiskers ("Biological
Cubism"). Miró was trying to express the most basic of human
emotions using the most basic of techniques.

Alexander Calder's mobiles hang like Mirós in the sky, waiting for a gust of wind to bring them to life.

And talk about a primal image! Jean Arp builds human beings
out of amoeba-like shapes.

Decorative Art:
Bonnard, Balthus, and Later Picasso and Braque

Most 20th-century paintings are a mix of the real world ("repre-
sentation") and the colorful patterns of "abstract" art. Artists
purposely distort camera-eye reality to make the resulting canvas
more decorative. So, Picasso flattens a woman into a pattern of
colored shapes, Bonnard makes a man a shimmer of golden paint,
and Balthus turns a boudoir scene into colorful wallpaper.

Patterns and Textures:
Jean Dubuffet, Lucio Fontana, and Karel Appel

Increasingly, you'll have to focus your eyes to look "at" the canvases, not "through" them.

Enjoy the lines and colors, but also a new element: texture.
Some works have very thick paint piled on, where you can see the
brush stroke clearly. Some have substances besides paint applied
to the canvas, like Dubuffet's brown, earthy rectangles of real dirt
and organic wastes. Fontana punctures the canvas so the fabric
itself (and the hole) becomes the subject. Artists show their skill
by mastering new materials. The canvas is a tray, serving up a
delightful array of different substances with interesting colors,
patterns, shapes, and textures.

Alberto Giacometti (1901–1966)

Giacometti's skinny statues have the emaciated, haunted, and
faceless look of concentration camp survivors. Their simplicity

of the figures is "primitive," but these aren't stately, sturdy, Easter Island heads. Man is weak in the face of technology and the winds of history.

• *Now you're at the end of the floor. Circle across the main aisle and work your way back to where you started.*

Abstract Expressionism: Pollock and Rothko

America emerged from World War II as the globe's superpower. With Europe in ruins, New York replaced Paris as the art capital. The trend was toward bigger canvases, abstract designs, and experimentation with new materials and techniques. It was called "Abstract Expressionism"—expressing emotions and ideas using color and form alone.

Jackson Pollock (1912–1956)

"Jack the Dripper" attacks convention with a can of paint, dripping and splashing a dense web onto the canvas. Picture Pollock in his studio, jiving to the hi-fi, bouncing off the walls, throwing paint in a moment of enlightenment. Of course, the artist loses some control this way—over the paint flying in mid-air and over himself in an ecstatic trance. Painting becomes a whole-body activity, a "dance" between the artist and his materials.

The act of creating is what's important, not the final product. The canvas is only a record of that moment of ecstasy.

Big, Empty Canvases: Newman and Rauschenberg

All those big, empty canvases with just a few lines or colors— what reality are they trying to show?

In the modern world, we find ourselves insignificant specks in a vast and indifferent universe. Every morning, each of us must confront that big, blank, Existentialist canvas and decide how we're going to make our mark on it. Like, wow.

Another influence was the simplicity of Japanese landscape painting. A Zen master studies and meditates for years to achieve the state of mind where he can draw one pure line. These canvases, again, are only a record of that state of enlightenment. (What is the sound of one brush painting?)

On more familiar ground, postwar painters were following in the footsteps of artists such as Mondrian, Klee, and Kandinsky (whose work they must have considered "busy"). The geometrical forms here reflect the same search for order, but these artists painted to the 5/4 symmetry of "Take Five."

• *Descend to the fourth floor, which houses more current works.*

Pop Art:
Andy Warhol (1930–1987)

America's postwar wealth made the consumer king. Pop art is created from the "pop"-ular objects of that throw-away society—a soup can, a car fender, mannequins, tacky plastic statues, movie icons, advertising posters. Take something out of Sears and hang it in a museum, and you have to think about it in a whole different way.

Is this art? Are all these mass-produced objects beautiful? Or crap? If they're not art, why do we work so hard to acquire them? Pop art, like Dada, questions our society's values.

Andy Warhol (who coined the expression "15 minutes of fame" and became a pop star) concentrated on another mass-produced phenomenon: celebrities. He took publicity photos of famous people and repeated them. The repetition—like the con-stant bombardment we get from repeated images on television—cheapens even the most beautiful things.

THE CONTEMPORARY COLLECTION
(FOURTH FLOOR)

The modern world is history. Picasso and his ilk are now gather-ing dust and boring art students everywhere. Enter the "post-modern" world as seen through the eyes of current artists.

You'll see very few traditional canvases or sculptures. Artists have traded paintbrushes for blowtorches, exploring new materials and new media. (Miró said he was out to "murder" painting.) Mixed media work is the norm, combining painting, sculpture, photogra-phy, welding, film/slides/video, and lighting and sound systems.

Here are some of the trends from the turn-of-the-20th-century odometer:

Op Art: "Op"-tical illusions play tricks with your eyes (like the way a spiral starts to spin when you stare at it).

Found Art: Artists raid dumpsters, recycling junk into the building blocks for larger "assemblages."

Deconstruction: Modern artists critique (or "deconstruct") society by examining things so familiar we take them for granted. A familiar object loaded with meaning (a crucifix), removed from its usual circumstances (a church), and put it in a new setting (in a jar of urine, to cite one notorious art project), makes you see it in a different way.

Video and Film: Clips of inane, ordinary events, repeated ad nauseam.

Words: Plaques of inane slogans or ad copy, repeated ad nauseam.

The Occasional Sculpture: This is usually an abstract, unrecognizable form that emphasizes the material it's made from.

The Occasional Canvas: This comes as a familiar relief.

Natural Objects: A rock in an urban setting is inherently interesting.

New Realism: Hyper-realistic canvases try to recreate the "look" of a photo or video image.

Installations: An entire room is given to an artist to prepare. Like entering an art funhouse, you walk in without quite knowing what to expect (I'm always thinking, "Is this safe?"). Using the latest technology, the artist engages all your senses, controlling the lights, sounds, and sometimes even smells.

Contraptions: Weird, useless, Rube Goldberg machines make fun of technology.

Interaction: Some exhibits require your participation, whether it's pushing a button to get the contraption going, just walking around the room, or touching something. In some cases, the viewer "does" art rather than just stares at it. If art is really meant to change, it has to move you, literally.

Performance Art: A kind of mixed media of live performance. Many artists that in another day would have painted canvases have turned to music, dance, theater, and performance art. This art form is often interactive, dropping the illusion of a performance and encouraging audience participation. When you finish with the Pompidou Center, go outside for some of the street theater.

Playful Art: Children love the art being produced today. If it doesn't put a smile on your face, well, then you must be a jaded grump like me, who's seen the same repetitious s#%t passed off as "daring" since Warhol stole it from Duchamp. I mean, it's *so* 20th century.

VIEW ART

Before leaving, escalate up to the sixth floor, consider the *très* snobby Chez Georges restaurant (where just looking is not OK), then walk the tube as far as you can for great Paris cityscapes.

CARNAVALET MUSEUM TOUR

At the Carnavalet Museum (Musée Carnavalet—Histoire de Paris), French history unfolds in a series of stills—like a Ken Burns documentary, except you have to walk. The Revolution is the highlight, but you get a good overview of everything, from Louis XIV–period rooms (from the place Royal, now the place des Vosges), to Napoleon, to the belle époque.

Orientation

Cost: Free.
Hours: Tue–Sun 10:00–18:00, closed Mon.
Getting There: It's in the heart of the Marais district at 23 rue de Sévigné (Mo: St. Paul), and on the Marais Walk (page 78).
Information: Get the free (necessary) map. Tel. 01 44 59 58 58.
Length of Our Tour: 90 minutes.
Starring: François I, Louis XIV, Louis XV, Louis XVI, the Bastille, Robespierre, the guillotine, Napoleon, Napoleon III, the Paris Commune, and la belle époque.

Overview

The museum, which opened in 1880, is housed in a Marais mansion built for a 16th-century aristocrat (it later expanded to fill an adjoining mansion). It's frustrating for three reasons: There are no English descriptions, the rooms are numbered out of order and out of historical sequence, and sections are closed at different times due to understaffing. Still, it's Paris' top history museum, nestled enjoyably in the charming Marais neighborhood near many recommended hotels and restaurants. To avoid running out of patience and steam, cover the pre-Revolution section in a random wander through the out-of-sequence rooms (ground floor and first floor in main building), with the help of the general commentary below.

Then become a serious student when you move into the adjoining mansion for the heart and soul of the museum: The 1789–1920 exhibits (which flow in easy, logical order as described below).

MAIN BUILDING GROUND FLOOR AND FIRST FLOOR

Grab a bench and read the following. Then wander whichever way room closures dictate through the ground floor (1500s and Reformation) and the first floor (17th and 18th centuries) of the main building. As you wander, you'll get a feel for the luxurious life of France's kings and nobles before the Revolution. In fact, several rooms are straight out of mansions lining the nearby place des Vosges.

Courtyard

You're surrounded by the in-your-face richness of the *ancien régime*—back when people generally accepted the notion that some were born to rule and most were born to be ruled. And the embodiment of that age stands atop the statue in the center: Louis XIV, the ultimate divine monarch. Notice the date: July 14, 1689, exactly 100 years before the French Revolution ended all that. This statue is a rare surviving pre-Revolutionary bronze. In 1792, nearly all of them were melted down to make weapons, as Revolutionary France took on the rest of Europe in an all-out war. Notice the relief below—a great piece of counter-Reformation propaganda. France (the angel with the royal shield) and heaven (portrayed by the angel protecting the Communion Host) are literally stomping the snakes and reformers of Protestantism (Hus, Calvin, Wyclif, and Luther).

Ground Floor, Rooms 7–10: 1500s— Renaissance and Reformation

In Room 7, a **model of Ile de la Cité** (made by a monk around 1900) shows the medieval city before France became a world power—crowded, narrow-laned, and steeple-dotted, with houses piled even on top of bridges. There's Notre-Dame on the east end, and the Sainte-Chapelle, with its royal palace and gardens, on the west. The only straight road in town was the old Roman road that splits the island north-south (and is still used today).

   King François I (1494–1547, Room 7) brought Paris into the modern world. Handsome, athletic François—a writer of poems, leader of knights, and lover of women—embodied the optimism of the Italian Renaissance. *"Le grand roi François"*

(if your French is any good, it rhymes: luh grahn rwah frahn-
swah) centralized the government around his charismatic self and
made a rebuilt Louvre his home. His absolute right to rule was
affirmed every time he ordered something done—"For such is
our pleasure!"

Renaissance open-mindedness brought religious debate,
even leading to open warfare between Catholics and Protestants
(called Huguenots in France). The Catholic **King Charles IX**
and his mother, **Catherine de Medicis** (both depicted in
room 8), plotted to assassinate several prominent Protestants,
but it quickly snowballed into the slaughter of thousands of Parisian Huguenots on St. Bartholomew's Day in 1572. Paintings
show events organized by the **Catholic League:** parades, Bible
studies, and the occasional Protestant barbecue to keep the faithful in good spirits.

Upstairs, passing some pieces of the old Henry IV statue,
continue straight until you reach the following rooms.

FIRST FLOOR
Rooms 13–20 *(Paris au XVII siècle)*: 1600s—Louis XIII and XIV Modernize Paris

In Room 13, notice the wedding party for **Louis XIII,** the 1612
bash that filled the new place Royal (before it was renamed place
des Vosges) and inaugurated it as *the* place in town. Jousting remained a favorite sport of the elite even though just 50 years
earlier, King Henry II died in a jousting accident. Many of the
grand monuments that made Paris a world capital—the pont
Neuf, the expanded Louvre, place Royale, and the Invalides
dome—were begun or completed by Louis XIII (Room 14, rear-
ing on his horse, with angels trumpeting his works) and his more
glorious son, Louis XIV, the Sun King. They financed the arts
and artists (Le Brun, etc., in Room 15), shifting Europe's cultural
axis from Italy to Paris.

Rooms 16 through 20 show off the lifestyles of Paris' rich
and fabulous. Many of these rooms are taken directly from mansions fronting the place Royal. The corner room (near Room 16)
is typical of this Louis XIII period (as are Rooms 19 and 20).

Their flowery walls, Greek-myth ceiling paintings, and
powdered-wig portraits give a tiny glimpse of the opulence of
Louis XIV's greatest monument, the palace at Versailles. Versailles was the physical symbol of Louis' absolute power, ruling
over the largest, most populous, and richest nation in Europe.
Whenever the nobles got uppity, the larger-than-life Sun King
wouldn't hesitate to put his foot down (Room 20).

Rooms 24–48: Louis XV (ruled 1715–1774)

The next 40 or so rooms show off 18th-century Paris—the generations leading up to the Revolution—with furniture and paintings.
Louis XV (portrait in Room 25) ascended the throne of Europe's
most powerful nation when his great-grandfather, the Sun King,
died after reigning for 72 years. Only five years old at the time, he
was for many years a figurehead, while the government was run by
his mentors—a regent during his childhood, his teacher in youth,
one of his many mistresses (Madame de Pompadour) in middle age,
and bureaucrats at the end. Louis was intelligent and educated,
and he personally embraced the budding democratic ideals of the
Enlightenment, but he spent his time at Versailles, gaming and
consorting with Europe's most cultured and beautiful people.
Meanwhile, France's money was spent on costly wars with Austria
and England (including the American "French and Indian War").
Louis, basking in the lap of luxury and the glow of the Enlightenment, looked to the horizon and uttered his prophetic phrase:
 "Après moi—le déluge!" ("After me—the flood!")

Rooms 49–64: Louis XVI (ruled 1774–1792)

As you stroll through the first-floor rooms, you'll see luxurious
wallpaper, tables, chairs, parquet floors, clocks, gaming tables,
statues, paintings, and even a doghouse costing more than a peasant hut (Room 53). Look for subtle differences in decoration
and furnishings:

   Louis XIV Style: Baroque. In these gilded rooms, ceilings
are decorated with curved ornamental frames (cartouches) holding
paintings of Greek myths. The heavy tables and chairs have thick,
curved legs, animal feet, and bronze-corner protectors.

   Louis XV Style: Rococo. The rooms are decorated in pastel
colors, with lighter decoration and exotic landscapes. The chairs
are made of highly polished, rare woods, with delicate curved legs
and padded seats and backs. Note the Chinese decor and objects
(Ming vase).

   Louis XVI Style: Neoclassical. Influenced by recently
excavated Pompeii, the rooms are simpler—with classical motifs—
and the furniture is straighter. The chairs' straight legs taper
to a point.

   Imagine these rooms during the *ancien régime* (the traditional
chessboard society with king on top, pawns on bottom, and the
bishops that walk diagonally), lit by chandeliers glimmering off
mirrors, the sound of a string quartet, exotic foods from newly
colonized lands, billiards in one room and high-stakes card games
in another, a Molière comedy downstairs, dangerous talk by rad-
icals like Voltaire and Rousseau in Room 48, and dangerous liaisons

among social butterflies—male and female—dressed in high heels, makeup, wigs, and perfume.

• *From Room 45, follow signs to "Revolution, 19th and 20th centuries." A long, orange corridor—a gallery of Parisian cityscapes—leads to the next building. Hike up the hardwood stairs to the second floor and* La Révolution Française.

SECOND FLOOR
The Revolution: 1789–1799

No period of history is as charged with the full range of human emotions as the French Revolution. Bloodshed, martyrdom, daring speeches, lasting bonds of friendship, tolerance, murdering priests, emancipating women, feeding the starving, back-stabbing former friends—all done in the name of government "by, for, and of the people." Common people, with their everyday concerns, were driving the engine of history. Or, perhaps they were only foam bubbles swept along in the shifting tides of vast socioeconomic trends.

Room 101: The Estates General

It's 1789, France is bankrupt from wars and corruption, and the people want change. The large **allegorical painting by Dubois** shows King Louis XVI in the boat of France, navigating stormy seas. Lady Truth is trying to light the way, but the winged demon of tyranny keeps nag-

ging at the king. Above shines the fleur-de-lis, whose petals—labeled with the three social groups that held all power in France: clergy, king, and nobles—are now laced together by the new power . . . the people.

In May, the king called each sector of society together at Versailles to solve the financial crisis. But in a bold and unheard-of move, the Third Estate (the people), tired of being outvoted by the clergy and nobility, split and formed their own National Assembly. Amid the chaos of speeches, debate, and deal-making, they raised their hands, bravely pledging to stick together until a new constitution was written (see *The Oath of the Jeu-de-Paume*, a preparatory sketch by David for a huge canvas which was never painted, on wall opposite allegorical painting). **Louis XVI** (see his pink-faced portrait to the left), who seemed to vacillate between democratic change and royalist repression, ordered the Assembly to dissolve (they refused), sent 25,000 Swiss mercenary soldiers to Paris, and fired his most popular, liberal minister.

Room 102: The Bastille (July 14, 1789)

The Bastille (see the **model**) was a medieval fortress turned prison. With its eight towers and 30-meter-high (100 feet) walls, it dominated the Parisian skyline, a symbol of oppression. On the hot, muggy morning of July 14, Paris' citizens waited on edge for a rumored attack by the king's Swiss guards. A crowd formed and marched on the Invalides armory (see series of **paintings**, left to right) and seized 30,000 rifles... but no gunpowder. Word spread it was stored across town at the Bastille.

The mob grew bigger and angrier as it went. By noon, they stood at the foot of the walls of the Bastille, demanding gunpowder. The fort's governor stalled, but two citizens managed to scale the wall and cut the chains. The drawbridge crashed down, and the mob poured through. Terrified guards opened fire, killing dozens and wounding hundreds. At the battle's peak, French soldiers in red and blue appeared on the horizon... but whose side were they on? A loud cheer went up as they pointed their cannons at the Bastille, and soon the governor had no choice but to surrender. The mob trashed the Bastille, opened the dark dungeons, and brought seven prisoners into the light of day. They dragged the governor to City Hall (Hôtel de Ville) where he was literally torn apart by the hysterical crowd. His head was stuck on a stick and carried through the city. The Revolution had begun.

Today, the events of July 14 are celebrated with equally colorful festivities every Bastille Day. The Bastille itself was soon dismantled stone by stone (nothing remains but the open space of place de la Bastille), but the memory became a rallying cry throughout the Revolution: *"Vive le quatorze juillet!"* ("Long live July 14th!").

Room 103 (La Fête de la Fédération): The Celebration (1789)

Imagine the jubilation! To finally be able to shout out loud things formerly whispered in fear.

The large painting of *La Fête de la Fédération* shows the joy and exuberance of the newly freed people, celebrating the first Bastille Day (July 14, 1790). Liberty! Equality! Fraternity!

Members of every social class (even including, it appears, three women) hugged, kissed, and mingled on the Champ de Mars, where the Eiffel Tower stands today. An artificial mound was built for heroes of the Revolution to ascend while a choir sang. Women, dressed up to symbolize Truth, Freedom, Justice, and other capital-letter virtues, were worshiped in a new kind of secular religion. Public demonstrations like these must have infuriated the king, queen, bishops, and nobles, who were now quarantined in their palaces, fuming impotently.

The *Declaration of the Rights of Man and the Citizen* (see 2 different versions) made freedom the law. The preamble makes clear that "Le Peuple Français" (the French people)—not the king—were the ultimate authority. "Men are born free and equal," it states, possessing "freedom of the individual, freedom of conscience, freedom of speech."

Room 104 *(de la Monarchie à la République)*: Louis XVI Quietly Responds (1789–1792)

Louis XVI (1754–1793, see the bust)— studious, shy, aloof, and easily dominated—was stunned by the ferocious summer of 1789. The Bastille's violence spread to the countryside, where uppity peasants tenderized their masters with pitchforks. The Assembly was changing France with lightning speed, abolishing Church privileges, nationalizing nobles' land, and declaring the king irrelevant.

Louis accepted his role as a rubber-stamp monarch, hoping the furor would pass, trying to appear idealistic and optimistic. But looming on the horizon was...*Le docteur Joseph-Ignace Guillotin* (1738–1814, see portrait, opposite window).

The progressive Assembly abolished brutal medieval-style torture and executions. In their place, Dr. Guillotin proposed a kinder, gentler execution device that would make France a model of compassion. The guillotine—also known as "the national razor," or, simply, "The Machine"—could nearly instantly make someone "a head shorter at the top." (In 1977, it claimed its last victim; now capital punishment is abolished.)

Room 105 (*La famille royale*): Royalty Loses Its Head (1793)

Louis' wife, **Queen Marie-Antoinette** (several portraits), became the focus of the citizens' disgust. Reports flew that she spent extravagantly, plunging France into debt. More decisive than her husband, she steered him toward repressive measures to snuff out the Revolution. And worst of all, she was foreign-born, known simply as "The Austrian," and Austria was soon making war on the French, trying to preserve the monarchy. When Marie was informed that the Parisians had no bread to eat, a rumor spread that she sneered, "Let them eat cake!" ("Cake" was the term for the burnt crusts peeled off the oven and generally fed only to the cattle.)

Enraged and hungry, 6,000 Parisian women (backed by armed men) marched through the rain to Versailles to demand lower bread prices. On the night of October 5, 1789, a small band infiltrated the palace, burst into the Queen's room, killed her bodyguards, and chased her down the hall. The royal family was kidnapped and taken to Paris, where—though still monarchs—they were virtual prisoners in the Tuileries Palace (which once stood where, today, the Louvre meets the Tuileries Garden).

Three years later, the royal family became actual prisoners (see the reconstructed and rather cushy **Prison du Temple** in Room 106) after trying to escape to Austria to begin a counter-revolution. One of their servants pretended to be a German baroness, while Louis dressed up as her servant (the irony must have been killing him). When a citizen recognized Louis from his portrait on a franc note, the family was captured, thrown into prison, and soon put on trial as traitors to France. The National Convention (the Assembly's successor) declared the monarchy abolished.

On January 21, 1793 (see **painting** in Room 105), King Louis XVI—excuse me, "Citizen Capet"—was led to the place de la Concorde, laid face down on a slab, and—shoop!—a thousand years of monarchy dating back before Charlemagne was decapitated.

A few months later, Marie-Antoinette was tearfully torn (see **painting**) from her eight-year-old son (Louis XVII) and moved to a prison in the Conciergerie. On October 16, 1793 (see **painting**), she too met her fate on place de la Concorde. Genteel to the end, she apologized to the executioner for stepping on his foot. The blade fell, the blood gushed, and her head was shown to the crowd on a stick—an exclamation point for the new rallying cry: *Vive la nation!* Louis XVII died in prison at age 10. Notice his cute portrait in the corner next to his mother portrayed as a widow in prison. Rumors spread that the boy-king had escaped, fueled by Elvis-type sightings and impersonators. But recent DNA evidence confirms that the *dauphin* (heir to the throne) did indeed die in prison in 1795.

Room 108 *(La Convention–La Terreur)*: The Reign of Terror (1793–1794)

Here are **portraits** of key players in the Revolutionary spectacle. Some were moderate reformers, some radical priest-killers. They all lived in fear that, with Europe ganging up on the Revolution, any backward step could tip the delicate balance of power back to the *ancien régime*. Enemies of the Revolution were everywhere—even in their own ranks.

By the summer of 1793, the left-of-center Jacobin party took control of France's fledgling democracy. Pug-faced but silver-tongued **Georges Danton** (see portrait of a Newt Gingrich lookalike) drove the Revolution with his personal charisma and bold speeches: "To conquer the enemies of the fatherland, we need daring, more daring, daring now, always daring." He led the "Committee of Public Safety" to root out and execute those enemies, even guillotining moderates opposed to the Jacobins.

More radical still, **Jean-Paul Marat** (the "Friend of the People," portrait next to Danton) dressed and burped like a man of the street, but he wrote eloquently against all forms of authority. Wildly popular with the commoners, he was seen by others as a loose cannon. A beautiful 25-year-old noblewoman named **Charlotte Corday** decided it was her mission in life to save France by silencing him. On July 11, 1793, she entered his home under the pretext of giving him names of counter-revolutionaries. Marat, seated in a bathtub to nurse a skin condition, wrote the names down and said, "Good. I'll have them all guillotined." Corday stood up, whipped a knife out from under her dress, and stabbed him through the heart. Corday was guillotined, and Marat was hailed a martyr to the cause.

Marat's death was further "proof" that counter-revolutionaries were everywhere. For the next year (summer of 1793 to summer of 1794, see **paintings of guillotine scenes**), the Jacobin government arrested, briefly tried, then guillotined everyone suspected of being "enemies of the Revolution"—nobles, priests, and the

rich, as well as many true Revolutionaries who simply belonged to the wrong political party. More than 2,500 Parisians were beheaded, 18,000 were executed by other means, and tens of thousands died in similar violence around the country. The violence begun at the **Bastille** in July 1789 would climax in July 1794.

Master of the Reign of Terror was **Maximilien Robespierre** (the portrait opposite Danton's), a 35-year-old lawyer who promoted the Revolution with a religious fervor. By July 1794, the guillotine was slicing 30 necks a day. In Paris' main squares, grim executions alternated with politically correct public spectacles honoring "Liberty," "Truth," and the heroes of France. As the death toll rose, so did public cynicism. Finally, Robespierre even sentenced to death his old friend Danton, when he spoke out against the bloodshed. As Danton knelt under the blade, he joked—"My turn." The people had had enough.

Room 109 *(Thermidor—Le Directoire)*: Terror Ends (July 1794)

Engravings show Robespierre's meteoric fall from power. Food shortages, inflation, and Robespierre's own self-righteousness made him an easy target. On July 27, 1794, as Robespierre prepared to name the daily list of victims, his fellow committee members started yelling "Tyrant!" and shouted him down. Robespierre, stunned by the sudden fall from grace, tried to commit suicide by shooting himself in the mouth.

The next day, he walked the walk he'd ordered thousands to take. Hands tied behind his back, he was carried through the streets on a two-wheeled cart, while citizens jeered and spat on him. At the guillotine, the broken-down demagogue had no last words, thanks to his wounded jaw. When the executioner yanked off the bandage, Robespierre let out a horrible cry, the blade fell, and the Reign of Terror came to an end.

From 1795 to 1799, France caught its breath, ruled by the Directory, a government so intentionally weak and decentralized (2 houses of parliament and 5 executives, with no funding) that it could never create another Robespierre.

Room 110 *(La Guerre)*: France vs. Europe

The blade that dropped on Louis XVI rattled royal teacups throughout Europe. Even as early as 1792, France had to defend its young democracy against Austria and Prussia. Surprisingly, France's new army—ordinary citizens from a universal draft, led by daring young citizen-officers, singing a stirring, bloodthirsty new song, "La Marseillaise"—quickly defeated the apathetic mercenaries they faced. France vowed to liberate all Europe from tyranny. Europe feared that, by "exporting Revolution," France would export democracy...plus senseless violence and chaos.

French National Anthem: "La Marseillaise"

The genteel French have a gory past.

Allons enfants de la Patrie, (Let's go, children of
    the fatherland,)
Le jour de gloire est arrivé. (The day of glory has arrived.)
Contre nous de la tyrannie (The blood-covered flag
    of tyranny)
L'étendard sanglant est levé. (Is raised against us.)
L'étendard sanglant est levé. (Is raised against us.)
Entendez-vous dans les campagnes (Do you hear these
    ferocious soldiers)
Mugir ces féroces soldats? (Howling in the countryside?)
Qui viennent jusque dans nos bras (They're coming nearly
    into our grasp)
Egorger vos fils et vos compagnes. (To slit the throats of
    your sons and your women.)
Aux armes citoyens, (Grab your weapons, citizens,)
Formez vos bataillons, (Form your battalions,)
Marchons, marchons, (March on, march on,)
Qu'un sang impur (So that their impure blood)
Abreuve nos sillons. (Will fill our trenches.)

A young Corsican named **Napoleon Bonaparte** (see the bust) rose quickly through the ranks, proving himself by fighting royalists in Italy, Egypt, and on the streets of Paris. In 1799, the 29-year-old general returned to Paris a conquering hero. Backed by an adoring public, he dissolved the Directory, established order, and gave himself the Roman-style title of "first consul."

Room 111 *(Vandalisme et Conservation)*: The Revolution vs. Religion

Three-fourths of France's churches were destroyed or vandalized during the Revolution, a backlash against the wealthy and politically repressive Catholic Church. In Notre-Dame, Christ was mothballed and a woman dressed as "Dame Reason" was worshiped on the altar.

Room 113: Souvenirs of Revolution

After the Reign of Terror, *Liberté, Egalité, Fraternité* was just a slogan, remembered fondly on commemorative **plates and knickknacks.** The Revolution was over.

- *The visit continues down four flights of stairs—or down the elevator— to the ground floor.*

Room 115 *(Le Premier Empire)*: Napoleon Conquers Europe (1799–1815)

Here's **Napoleon** (see portrait, also breastplate and death mask in glass case) at the peak of power, master of Western Europe. Dressed in his general's uniform, he's checking the maps to see who's left to conquer. Behind him is a throne with his imperial seal. This Corsican-born commoner, educated in Paris' military schools, became a young Revolutionary and a daring general, rising to prominence as a champion of democracy. Once in power, he preached revolution but in fact became a dictator and crowned himself emperor (1804).

During the Empire, bishops such as **Talleyrand** and wealthy socialites such as **Juliette Recamier** (see painting) could bring their fine clothes out of mothballs without fear of the guillotine. Paris was rebuilt (Room 117) with neoclassical monuments such as the Arc de Triomphe to make it the "New Rome."

In 1812, Napoleon foolishly invaded Russia, starting a downward spiral that ended in defeat by allied Europe at the Battle of Waterloo in Belgium (1815). Napoleon was exiled, and died (1822) on the island of St. Helena, off the coast of Africa.

Room 118 *(La Restauration)*: The Monarchy Restored (1815–1830)

After 25 years in exile, **Louis XVIII**—younger brother of headless Louis XVI—returned to Paris with the backing of Europe's royalty and reclaimed the crown as a constitutional monarch (see the otherworldly painted crowd scene of *3 mai 1814*).

The next king, retro-looking **Charles X** (youngest brother of Louis XVI), in glorious coronation robes, revived the fashion and oppression of the *ancien régime*, plotting to dissolve the people's Assembly. But the French people were not about to turn the clock back.

Room 119 *(Juillet 1830)*: Revolution of 1830

Parisians again blocked off the narrow streets with barricades to fight the king's soldiers. They **stormed the Louvre** (biggest painting) and the king's palace, and slaughtered the mercenary Swiss Guards. After "Three Glorious Days" of fighting, order was restored by Louis-Philippe (see **model**), an unassuming nobleman who appeared on the balcony of the Hôtel de Ville and was cheered by royalists, the middle class, and peasants alike.

Room 120 (La Monarchie de Juillet): Constitutional Monarchy (1830–1848)

King Louis-Philippe (see black bust)—a former lieutenant turned banker, with a few drops of royal blood—was a true constitutional monarch, harmlessly presiding over an era of middle-class progress fueled by the Industrial Revolution. Still, liberal reforms came too slowly. New factories brought division between wealthy employers and poor workers, and only 200,000 out of 30 million French citizens (1:150) could vote.

Room 121 (La Deuxième République): Revolution of 1848

In February 1848—a time of Europe-wide depression and social-ist strikes—Parisians took to the streets again **(battle scenes)**, battling at the Bastille, Palais-Royal, Panthéon, and place de la Concorde, and toppling the king. Even prosperous accountants and shoe salesmen caught the spirit of revolution. After five dec-ades of dictators (Napoleon), retread Bourbons (the Restoration), and self-proclaimed monarchs (Louis-Philippe), France was back in the hands of the people—the Second Republic.

Room 122 (Le Romantisme): Romanticism

Freedom of expression, the uniqueness of each person, the glories of the human spirit and the natural world—these values from the 1789 Revolution were continued by artists of the 1800s known as Romantics. Working clockwise, you'll see **caricature busts** of many famous Frenchmen and visitors to the center of European culture, Paris: Victor Hugo (author of *Les Misérables* and *The Hunchback of Notre-Dame*), Johann Strauss, Sr. (inventor of the scandalous waltz craze), Paganini (touring violinist who played like a man possessed), Chopin (Polish pianist who charmed Par-isian society), Adolphe Sax (-ophone), Giuseppe Verdi (composer of stirring operas—*Aida*, etc.), and Rossini (*Lone Ranger* theme). There are also **paintings** of Romantic painter Delacroix and of glamorous pianist Franz Liszt and his mistress Marie d'Agoult—the ultimate Romantic. She left her husband and children to follow the dynamic Liszt on a journey of self-discovery in Italy and Switzerland—"the years of pilgrimage."

• *Journey upstairs and to the left toward* "Paris: Du Second Empire à nos jours"—*From the Second Empire to Today.*

Room 128 *(Le Second Empire)*: Napoleon III and the Second Empire (1852–1870)

Louis-Napoleon Bonaparte (in the big painting, with red pants and sash, waxed moustache, and goatee) was the nephew of the famous Emperor Napoleon I. He used his famous name to get elected president by a landslide in 1848, then combined democracy with monarchy to

be voted "Emperor Napoleon III." He suppressed opposition but promoted liberal reforms and economic and colonial expansion.

Here he hands an order to **Baron Georges Haussmann** (mutton-chop sideburns) to modernize Paris. Haussmann cut the wide, straight boulevards of today to move goods, open up the crowded city…and prevent barricades for future revolutions. Parks, railroad stations, and the Garnier Opéra made Paris the model for world capitals. (Room 129 shows building projects.)

The **boat-like cradle** (Room 128) is a copy of the famous cradle of Napoleon II (1811–1832, known to history as the King of Rome), the only son of Napoleon I, who died at 21 of tuberculosis before ever ruling anything.

Napoleon III pursued popular wars (the **model** in Room 129 celebrates Crimean War vets, 1855) and unpopular ones (backing Austrian Emperor Maximilian in Mexico). In the summer of 1870, he personally led a jubilant French Army to crush upstart Prussia— "On to Berlin!" Uh-oh.

Room 130 *(Le siège de Paris)*: The Franco-Prussian War (1870–1871)

Within weeks, the overconfident French were surrounded, Napoleon III himself was captured, and he surrendered. Paris was stunned. (See **painting of crowd** hearing the news on the legislature steps.) The Germans quickly put a stranglehold on Paris, and a long, especially cold winter settled in.

Some would not give up. Without an emperor, they proclaimed yet another democratic republic (France's third in a century) and sent minister Leon Gambetta in a newfangled balloon **(painting)** over the Germans' heads to rally the countryside to come save Paris. The Parisians themselves held out bravely **(painting** of Tuileries as army camp), but German efficiency and modern technology simply overwhelmed the French.

Room 131 *(La Commune)*:
The Paris Commune (Spring 1871)

The Republic finally agreed to a humiliating surrender. Paris'
liberals—enraged at the capitulation after such a brave winter
and fearing a return of monarchy—rejected the surrender and
proclaimed their own government, the Paris Commune. **Portraits**
honor the proud idealists who barricaded themselves inside Paris'
neighborhoods, refusing to bow to the German emperor.

Then, in one "bloody week" in May **(battle scenes)**, French
troops backing the Republic stormed through Paris, leaving 15,000
dead, 5,000 jailed, and 8,000 deported. The Commune was snuffed
out, but the memory was treasured by generations of liberals in
popular **souvenirs:** a jar of bread from the hungry winter, a carrier
pigeon's feather, a box reading "*Vive la Commune!*"

The church of Sacré-Coeur **(painting)** was built after the war
as a form of national penance.

Rooms 132–142 *(La Belle Epoque)*:
The Beautiful Age (1871–1914)

The Third Republic restored peace to a prosperous middle-
class society. The **Eiffel Tower** (Room 132) marked the
1889 centennial of the Revolution, and the **Statue of Liberty**
(Room 133) honored America's revolution.

Paris was a capital of world culture, a city of **Impressionist
painters** (Room 135); of the actress **Sarah Bernhardt** (Room 136),
called the world's first international star ("a force of nature, a fiery
soul, a marvelous intelligence, a magnificent creature of the highest
order," raved one of the smitten); of **Georges Bizet** (Room 136),
composer of *Carmen;* of balls, carriages, cafés, and parks **(paintings,** Rooms 137–140); and the city of Art Nouveau.

Two delightful turn-of-the-century Parisian shops—spliced
into this old-regime mansion—illustrate the curvy, decorative
Art Nouveau style: the *très chic* **Café de Paris** (Room 141) and
the **Boutique Fouquet** (Room 142). Imagine browsing through
jewelry in the spindly splendor of this Alfons Mucha–created
world of peacocks peering through stained glass and nubile
nymphs shinnying up lampposts.

Room 145: World War I (1914–1918)

Three costly wars with Germany—Franco-Prussian, World
War I, and World War II—drained France. Although **Marshal
Foch** (big painting) is hailed as the man who coordinated the
Allied armies to defeat Germany in World War I, France was
hardly a winner. More than 1.5 million Frenchmen died, a
generation was lost, and the country would be a pushover

when Hitler invaded in 1940. France's long history as a global superpower was over.

Room 147 *(La vie littéraire du XXe siècle)*: Remembrance of Things Past

The last room is filled with portraits of Paris' 20th-century literary greats. By producing such figures as the writer **Marcel Proust** (see his reconstructed bedroom) and the dreamy writer/filmmaker **Jean Cocteau,** France has remained a cultural superpower.

RODIN MUSEUM TOUR

Auguste Rodin (1840–1917) was a modern Michelangelo, sculpting human figures on an epic scale, revealing through the body their deepest thoughts and feelings. Like many of Michelangelo's unfinished works, Rodin's statues rise from the raw stone around them, driven by the life force. With missing limbs and scarred skin, these are prefab classics, making ugliness noble. Rodin's people are always moving restlessly. Even the famous *Thinker* is moving. While he's plopped down solidly, his mind is a million miles away. The museum presents a full range of Rodin's work, housed in a historic mansion where he once lived and worked. The gardens are picnic-perfect (BYO), but there's also a pleasant, if pricey, café.

Orientation

Cost: €5, €3 on Sun and for students, free for youth under 18 and for anyone on the first Sun of month; €1 for garden only; all covered by museum pass.

Hours: April–Sept Tue–Sun 9:30–17:45, garden closes at 18:45. Oct–March Tue–Sun 9:30–17:00, garden closes at 16:45. Closed Mon. Last entrance 30 minutes before closing.

Getting There: It's at 77 rue de Varennes, near Napoleon's Tomb (Mo: Varennes).

Information: Tel. 01 44 18 61 10, www.musee-rodin.fr.

Museum Tours: Audioguides covering the museum and gardens cost €4.

Length of Our Tour: One hour.

THE TOUR BEGINS

• *As you enter the mansion, pick up a museum plan with room numbers (this tour is keyed to that plan), turn left, and walk through the shop to the room in the museum's far corner to start a circular tour of the ground floor.*

Rodin Museum

TO GARDENS

Room 3 | Room 4 | Room 5 | Room 6 | Room 7

Room 2 | SHOP | Room 8

Room 1 | STAIRS | Room 9

ENTER | UP

GROUND FLOOR

Room 13 | Room 14 | Room 15 | Room 16 | Room 17

Room 12 | Room 11 | Room 10 | DOWN

BURGHERS | STAIRS

FIRST FLOOR

Room 1: Rodin's early works match the style of the time—pretty portrait busts and classical themes. Born of working-class roots, Rodin taught himself art by sketching statues at the Louvre and then sculpting copies.

The Man with the Broken Nose (L'Homme au nez cassé)—a deliberately ugly work—was 23-year-old Rodin's first break from the norm. He meticulously sculpted this deformed man (one of the few models the struggling sculptor could afford), but then the clay statue froze in his unheated studio, and the back of the head fell off. Rodin loved it! The Salon hated it. Rodin persevered.

See the painting of Rodin's future wife, Rose Beuret

(Portrait de Madame Rodin), who suffered with him through obscurity and celebrity.

Room 2: To feed his new family, Rodin cranked out small works with his boss' name on them—portraits, ornamental vases, nymphs, and knickknacks to decorate buildings. Still, the series of mother-and-childs (Rose and baby Auguste?) allowed him to experiment on a small scale with the intertwined twosomes he'd do later.

His job gave him enough money to visit Italy, where he was inspired by Michelangelo's boldness, monumental scale, restless figures, and "unfinished" look. Rapidly approaching middle age, Rodin was ready to rock.

Room 3: Rodin moved to Brussels, where his first major work, *The Bronze Age (L'âge d'airain)*, brought controversy and the fame that surrounds it. This nude youth, perhaps inspired by Michelangelo's "Dying Slave" in the Louvre, awakens to a new world. It was so lifelike that Rodin was accused of not sculpting it himself but simply casting it directly from a live body. The boy's left hand looks like he should be leaning on a spear, but it's just that missing element that makes the pose more tenuous and interesting.

The art establishment still snubbed Rodin the outsider, and no wonder. Look at his ultra-intense take on the symbol of France *(La Défense)*—this Marseillaise screams, "Off with their heads!" at the top of her lungs. Rodin was a slave to his muses, and some inspired monsters.

Room 4: Like the hand of a sculptor, *The Hand of God (La main de Dieu)* shapes Adam and Eve from the mud of the earth to which they will return. Rodin himself worked in "mud," using his hands to model clay figures, which were then reproduced in marble or bronze, usually by his assistants. Spin this masterpiece on its turntable. Rodin wants you to see it from every angle. He first worked from the front view, then checked the back and side profiles, then filled in the in-between.

In *The Kiss*, a passionate woman twines around a solid man for their first, spontaneous kiss. In their bodies, we can almost read the thoughts, words, and movements that led up to this meeting of lips. *The Kiss* was the first Rodin work the public loved. Rodin despised it, thinking it simple and sentimental.

Other works in this room show embracing couples who seem to emerge from the stone just long enough to love. Rodin left many works "unfinished," reminding us that all creation is a difficult process of dragging a form out of chaos.

Room 5: The two hands that form the arch of *The Cathedral (La Cathédrale)* are actually two right hands (a man's and a woman's?).

In the room's center, two bronze men stride forward, as bold as the often-controversial Rodin. *The Walking Man (L'Homme Qui Marche)* plants his back foot forcefully, as though he's about to step, while his front foot already has stepped. Rodin, who himself had one foot in the past, one in the future, captures two poses at once.

Rodin worked with many materials—he chiseled marble, modeled clay, cast bronze, worked plaster, painted, and sketched. He often created different versions of the same subject in different media.

Room 6: This room displays works by Camille Claudel, mostly in the style of her master. The 44-year-old Rodin took 18-year-old Camille as his pupil, muse, colleague, and lover. We can follow the arc of their relationship:

Rodin was inspired by young Camille's beauty and spirit, and he often used her as a model. You'll see her head emerging from a block of marble.

As his student, "Mademoiselle C" learned from Rodin, doing portrait busts in his lumpy style. Her bronze bust of Rodin (by the door) shows the steely-eyed sculptor with strong front and side profiles, barely emerging from the materials he worked with.

Soon they were lovers. *The Waltz (La Valse)* captures the spinning exuberance the two must have felt as they embarked together on a new life. The couple twirls in a delicate balance.

But Rodin was devoted as well to his lifelong companion, Rose. *Maturity (L'Age Mûr)* shows the breakup. A young girl on her knees begs the man not to leave her, as he's led away reluctantly by an older woman. The center of the composition is the hole left when their hands drift apart.

Rodin did leave Camille. Overwhelmed by grief and jealousy, she went crazy and had to be institutionalized until she died. *The Wave (La Vague)*, carved in onyx in a very un-Rodin style, shows sensitive—perhaps fragile—women huddled under a wave about to engulf them.

Rooms 7 and 8: What did Rodin think of women? Here are many different images from which you can draw conclusions.

Eve buries her head in shame, hiding her nakedness. But she can't hide the consequences of that first sin—she's pregnant.

Rodin became famous, wealthy, and respected, and society ladies all wanted him to do their portraits. In Room 8, you'll also see his last mistress *(La Duchesse de Choiseul)*, who lived with him here in this mansion.

Room 9: This dimly lit room is filled with Rodin's sketches (temporary exhibits occasionally occupy this space). The first flash of inspiration for a huge statue might be a single line sketched on notepaper. Rodin wanted nude models in his studio at all times—walking, dancing, and squatting—in case they struck some new and interesting pose. Rodin thought of sculpture as simply "drawing in all dimensions."

• *Upstairs, you'll find a glass display case that tries hard to explain how...*

Rodin made his bronze statues by pouring molten bronze into the narrow space between an original clay model and the mold around it. Once you had a mold, you could produce other copies, which is why there are famous Rodin bronzes all over the world.

As the display case clearly fails to make clear, the classic "lost wax" technique works like this:

1) The artist sculpts a clay model.

2) It is covered with materials that harden to make a shell that's hard on the outside, flexible inside. The shell is removed by cutting it into two halves that can be pieced back together—this is your mold.

3) Cement is poured into the mold to make a durable, rough copy. The mold is removed.

4) The surface of the copy is sanded down slightly.

5) The mold is put back over it, using pins to keep a one-centimeter space between the mold and the rough copy. Hot wax is poured into the

RODIN'S "THE QUACKER"

PINS   WAX

ROUGH COPY

OUTER MOLD

TUBES (TO DRAIN THE WAX)

DCH

space, it cools, and the mold is removed. The artist touches up the wax "skin" of the rough copy into its final form.

6) The waxy piece of art is covered with materials that harden into a new mold. Ventilation tubes are added.

7) The whole contraption is coated with heat-resistant materials.

8) The wax is heated—it melts and drains away (gets "lost"), leaving a centimeter of open space between the rough copy and the mold. Molten bronze is poured in to fill the space. As the bronze cools, it takes the shape of the mold.

9) The mold and the tubing are removed, and the bronze halves are lifted off the rough copy. After the halves are soldered together, you have a hollow bronze statue ready to be polished and varnished.

Rooms 10 and 11:
For decades, Rodin wrestled with a massive project—a doorway encrusted with characters from Dante's *Inferno.* These *Gates of Hell* were never completed (see unfinished piece in the garden), but studies for it are some of Rodin's masterpieces—including *The Thinker,* who was to be the centerpiece.

Rodin's figures struggle to come into existence. Rodin was fascinated with the theory of evolution—not Darwin's version of the survival of the fittest, but the Frenchman Lamarck's. His figures survive not by the good fortune of random mutation (Darwin), but by their own striving (Lamarck). They are driven by the life force, a restless energy that animates and shapes dead matter (Lamarck and Bergson). Rodin must have felt that force even as a child, when he first squeezed soft clay and saw a worm emerge.

In Room 11, you'll see studies of the female body in all its aspects—open, closed, wrinkled.

Room 12:
A virtual unknown until his mid-30s, Rodin slowly began receiving major commissions for public monuments. *The Burghers of Calais* depicts the actual event in 1347, when, in order to save their people, the city fathers surrendered the keys of the city—and their own lives—to the enemy. Rodin portrays them not in some glorious pose drenched in pomp and allegory, but as a simple example of men sacrificing their lives together. As they head to the gallows, with ropes already around their necks, each shows a distinct emotion, ranging from courage to despair. Compare the small plaster model in the glass case with the final, life-size bronze group out the window in the garden (near the street behind the ticket booth).
• *Double back to the wing overlooking the gardens.*

Room 15:
Rodin's feverish attempts to capture a portrait of the novelist Balzac ranged from a pot-bellied Bacchus to a headless nude

cradling an erection. In a moment of inspiration, Rodin threw a plaster-soaked robe
over the nude and watched it dry into what
would become the final, definitive version.

The museum's film clip shows Rodin
making the marble chips fly. In fact, he
rarely picked up a chisel, leaving that
to assistants.

Room 17: Legendary lovers kiss,
embrace, and intertwine in yin-yang bliss.

Room 14: Rodin's portrait busts of celebrities and some paintings by (yawn, are we through yet?) van Gogh, Monet, and Renoir.
Rodin enjoyed discussions with Monet and other artists and incor-
porated their ideas in his work. Rodin is often considered an
Impressionist because he captured spontaneous "impressions"
of figures and created rough surfaces that catch reflected light.

Room 13: By the end of his life, Rodin was more famous than
his works. Compare Rodin's small plaster "sketches" (in the glass
case) with the final, large-scale marble versions.

THE GARDENS

Rodin lived and worked in this mansion, renting rooms alongside
Matisse, the poet Rilke (Rodin's secretary), and the dancer Isadora
Duncan. He loved placing his creations in the overgrown gardens.
These are his greatest works, Rodin at his most expansive. The epic
human figures are enhanced, not dwarfed, by nature.
• *Leaving the house, there are five more stops: Two on the left and three
on the right. Beyond these stops is a big, breezy garden ornamented with
statues, a cafeteria, and a WC.*

The Thinker: Leaning slightly forward, tense and compact,
every muscle working toward producing that one great thought,
Man contemplates his fate. No constipation jokes, please.

This is not an intellectual, but a
linebacker who's realizing there's
more to life than frat parties. It's the
first man evolving beyond his animal
nature to think the first thought. It's
anyone who's ever worked hard to
reinvent himself or to make something new or better. Said Rodin:
"It is a statue of myself."

Rodin Museum Gardens

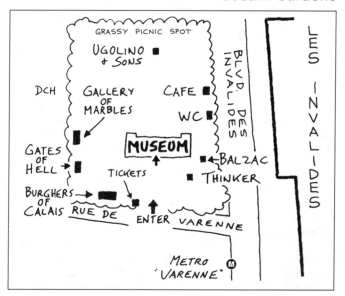

There are 29 other authorized copies of this statue, arguably the most famous in the world.
• *To the left of* The Thinker, *you'll find...*

Balzac: The iconoclastic novelist turns his nose up at the notion he should be honored with a statue. This final version also stands in the Musée d'Orsay and on a street median in Montparnasse. When the statue was unveiled, the crowd booed, a fitting tribute to both the defiant novelist and the bold man who sculpted him.
• *Along the street near the ticket booth are...*

The Burghers of Calais: The six city fathers trudge to their execution, and we can read in their faces and poses what their last thoughts are. They mill about, dazed, as each one deals with the decision he's made to sacrifice himself for his city.
• *Circling counterclockwise...*

The man carrying the key to the city tightens his lips in determination. The bearded man is weighed down with grief. Another buries his head in his hands. One turns, seeking reassurance from his friend, who turns away and gestures helplessly. The final key bearer (in back) raises his hand to his head.

Each is alone in his thoughts, but they're united by their

mutual sacrifice, by the base they stand on, and by their weighty robes—gravity is already dragging them down to their graves.

Pity the poor souls, then salute King Edward III, who, at the last second, pardoned them.

• *Follow* The Thinker*'s gaze to the opposite side of the house. Standing before a tall white backdrop is a big dark door—the* Gates of Hell.

The Gates of Hell: These doors (never meant to actually open) were never finished for a museum that was never built. But the vision of Dante's trip into hell gave Rodin a chance to explore the dark side of human experience. "Abandon hope all ye who enter in," was hell's motto. The three Shades at the top of the door point down—that's where we're going. Beneath the Shades, pondering the whole scene from above, is Dante as the Thinker. Below him, the figures emerge from the darkness just long enough to tell their sad tale of depravity. There's Paolo and Francesca (in the center of the right door), who were driven into an illicit love affair that brought them here. Ugolino (left door, just below center) crouches in prison over his kids. This poor soul was so driven by hunger that he ate the corpses of his own children. On all fours like an animal, he is the dark side of natural selection. Finally, find what some say is Rodin himself (at the very bottom, inside the right doorjamb, where it just starts to jut out), crouching humbly.

You'll find some of these figures writ large in the garden. *The Thinker* is behind you, *The Shades* are 27 meters/90 feet to the right, and *Ugolino* dines in the fountain at the far end.

It's appropriate that the *Gates*—Rodin's "cathedral"—remained unfinished. He was always a restless artist for whom the process of discovery was as important as the finished product.

• *To the right of the* Gates of Hell *is a glassed-in building, the . . .*

Gallery of Marbles: Unfinished, they show human features emerging from the rough stone. Imagine Rodin in his studio, working to give them life.

Victor Hugo (at the far end of the Gallery), the great champion of progress (and author of *Les Misérables*), leans back like Michelangelo's nude *Adam*, waiting for the spark of creation. He tenses his face and cups his ear, straining to hear the call from the blurry Muse above him. Once inspired, he can bring the idea to life (just as Rodin did) with the strength of his powerful arms. It's been said that all of Rodin's work shows the struggle of mind over matter, of brute creatures emerging from the mud and evolving into a species of thinkers.

MARMOTTAN MUSEUM TOUR

The Marmottan (or Musée Marmottan Monet) has the best collection of works by the master Impressionist, Claude Monet. In this mansion on the fringe of urban Paris, you can walk through Monet's life, from black-and-white sketches to colorful open-air paintings to the canvas that gave Impressionism its name. The museum's highlights are scenes of his garden at Giverny, including larger-than-life water lilies.

Orientation

Cost: €6.50, €4 for students under 25 and anyone over 60, free for children under 8. The Marmottan is not covered by the museum pass.

Hours: Tue–Sun 10:00–18:00 (last entrance 17:30), closed Mon, May 1, and Dec 25.

Getting There: It's in northwest Paris at 2 rue Louis Boilly. Métro, RER, and buses all work: Take the Métro to La Muette, then walk six blocks in 10 minutes, following brown signs down chaussée de la Muette through the delightful, kid-filled park to the museum. Or take the RER-C from the rue Cler area (Invalides or Pont de l'Alma), get off at Boulainvilliers stop, follow *sortie* Singer, turn left on rue Singer, turn right up rue Boulainvilliers, and then turn left down chaussée de la Muette to the museum. Bus #63 is handy from the rue Cler area or from the Latin Quarter (buses #32, #22, and #52 also serve the museum).

Information: Tel. 01 44 96 50 33, www.marmottan.com.

Length of Our Tour: One hour.

Photography: Not allowed. Cameras must be checked.

Starring: Claude Monet, including *Impression: Sunrise* (shown above), Rouen Cathedral, Gare St. Lazare, Houses of Parliament, scenes from Giverny, water lilies.

Overview

The museum traces Monet's life chronologically, but in a way that's as rough and fragmented as a Monet canvas. The collection is reorganized about every two to three years, so have patience and keep the big picture.

Basement: Entirely devoted to Monet, with works from throughout his life—mostly from his gardens at Giverny (including water lilies).

Ground floor: Bookstore, some Monet memorabilia, and an eclectic collection of non-Monet objects (including a beautifully displayed series of illuminated manuscript drawings).

First Floor (upstairs): Paintings by Impressionist colleagues (Renoir, Pissarro, Morisot, and more), period furnishings.

GROUND FLOOR

• *Turn left after entering and walk to the end of the hall to the timeline on the wall.*

Monet's Life

Claude Monet was the leading light of the Impressionist movement that revolutionized painting in the 1870s. Fiercely independent and dedicated to his craft, Monet gave courage to Renoir and others in the face of harsh criticism.

A wall chart shows high and low points of Monet's life: his birth in 1840; the first acceptance of two of his paintings by *le jury* in 1865; his draft dodge to London (*Londres*, where M. Daubigny introduced him to an art dealer who provided long-term dividends) to avoid the Franco-Prussian War in 1870; the first Impressionist exhibition he organized with friends in 1874; his move to Giverny in 1883; and his death in 1926. An actual palette hangs nearby.

Monet's Two Families (portraits of son Michel)

Monet's wife, Camille, died in 1879, leaving Monet to raise 12-year-old Jean and babe-in-arms Michel. (Michel would grow up to inherit the family home and many of the paintings that ended up here.) But Monet was also involved with Alice Hoschede, who had recently been abandoned by her husband. Alice moved in with her six kids and took care of the dying Camille, and the two families made a Brady-Bunch merger. Baby Michel became bosom buddies with Alice's baby, Jean-Pierre, and teenage Jean Monet and stepsister Blanche fell in love and later married.

This painting dates from the middle of Monet's life. Now head downstairs to trace the beginning of the artist's career.

• *Drop downstairs and find the black-and-white drawings in a glass case (usually in the center of the first room, but you may need to hunt for these).*

BASEMENT LEVEL, FIRST ROOM
FROM LE HAVRE TO LONDON (1857–1900)

Growing up in Le Havre (1840–1860):
Caricature Drawings (c. 1858)

Teenage Monet's first works—black-and-white, meticulously drawn, humorous sketches of small-town celebrities—are as different as can be from the colorful, messy oils that would make him famous. Still, they show his gift for quickly capturing an overall impression with a few simple strokes.

The son of a grocer, Monet defied his family, insisted he was an artist, and sketched the world around him—beaches, boats, and small-town life. A fellow artist encouraged him to don a scarf, set up his easel outdoors, and paint the scene exactly as he saw it. (Today, we say: Well, duh! But "open-air" painting was unorthodox for artists trained to study their subjects thoroughly in the perfect lighting of a controlled studio setting.)

• *Walk back toward the stairs and find the painting above the glass case to the right of the stairs.*

The 1870s: Pure Impressionism

At 19, Monet went to Paris but refused to enroll in the official art schools. The letters (in the glass case) from Monet asking for survival money from his friends show the price he paid for his bohemian principles throughout his early life.

Monet teamed up with Auguste Renoir and Alfred Sisley, leading them on open-air painting safaris to the countryside. Inspired by the realism of Edouard Manet, they painted everyday things—landscapes, seascapes, street scenes, ladies with parasols, family picnics—in bright, basic colors.

In 1870, Monet married his girlfriend, Camille (the dark-haired woman in many of his paintings), and moved just outside Paris to the resort town of Argenteuil. Playing host to Renoir, Manet, and others, he perfected the Impressionist style—painting nature as a mosaic of short brushstrokes of different colors placed side by side, suggesting shimmering light.

First, he simplified. In *The Beach at Trouville* (1870), a lady's dress is a few thick strokes of paint. Gradually (*Stroll Near Argenteuil*, 1872), Monet broke things down into smaller dots of different colors. If you back up from a Monet canvas, the colors blend into one (for example, red plus green plus yellow equals a brown boat). Still, they never fully resolve, creating the effect of colorful, shimmering light. Monet limited his palette to a few bright colors—cobalt blue, white, yellow, two shades of red, and emerald green abound. But no black—even shadows are a combination of bright colors.

Monet's constant quest was to faithfully reproduce nature in colored blobs of paint. His eye was a camera lens set at a very slow shutter speed to admit maximum light. Then he "developed" the impression made on his retina with an oil-based, pigmented solution. Even as the heartbroken Monet watched Camille die of tuberculosis in 1879, he was (he admitted later) intrigued by the changing colors in her dying face.

• *Move around the room, going clockwise.*

Impression: Sunrise (1873)

Here's the painting that started the revolution—a simple, serene view of boats bobbing under an orange sun. At the first public showing by Monet, Renoir, Degas, and others in Paris in 1874, critics howled at this work and ridiculed the title. "Wallpaper," one called it. The sloppy brushstrokes and ordinary subject looked like a study, not a finished work. The whole group and style got dubbed "Impressionist"—a pretty accurate name.

The misty harbor scene obviously made an "impression" on Monet, who faithfully rendered the fleeting moment in quick strokes of paint. The waves are simple horizontal brushstrokes. The sun's reflection on the water is a few thick, bold strokes of orange tipped with white. They zigzag down the canvas, the way a reflection shifts on moving water.

In search of new light and new scenes, Monet traveled throughout France and Europe. As you enjoy canvases painted in all kinds of weather, picture Monet at work—hiking to a remote spot; carrying an easel, several canvases, brushes (large-size), a palette, tubes of paint (an invention that made open-air painting practical), food and drink, a folding chair, and an umbrella; and wearing his trademark hat, with a cigarette on his lip. He weathered the elements, occasionally putting himself in danger by clambering on cliffs to get the shot.

The key was to work fast, before the weather changed and the light shifted, completely changing the colors. Monet worked "wet-in-wet," applying new paint before the first layer dried, mixing colors on the canvas, and piling them up into a thick paste.

The 1890s: Series

Monet often painted the same subject several times under different light (such as one of Paris' train stations, the *Gare St. Lazare*, 1870s). In the 1890s, he conceived of a series of paintings to be shown as a group, giving a time-lapse view of a single subject.

He rented several rooms offering different angles overlooking the *Cathedral of Rouen* and worked on up to 14 different canvases at a time, shuffling the right one onto the easel as the sun moved across the sky. The cathedral is made of brown stone, but at sunset it becomes gold and pink with blue shadows, softened by thick smudges of paint. The true subject is not the cathedral, but the full spectrum of light that bounces off it.

These series—of the cathedral, of haystacks, poplars, and mornings on the Seine—were very popular. Monet, poverty-stricken until his mid-40s, was slowly becoming famous, first in America, then London, and finally in France.

• *Just before leaving the first room, you'll see...*

The 1900s: London

Turning a hotel room into a studio, Monet—working on nearly a hundred different canvases simultaneously—painted the changing light on the River Thames. The *London Houses of Parliament*, reflected in the Thames, stretch and bend with the tide. *Charing Cross Bridge* is only a few smudgy lines enveloped in fog.

London's fog epitomized Monet's favorite subject—the atmosphere that distorts distant objects. That filtering haze gives even different-colored objects a similar tone, resulting in a more harmonious picture. When the light was just right and the atmosphere glowed, the moment of "instantaneity" had arrived, and Monet worked like a madman.

In truth, many of Monet's canvases were begun quickly in the open air, then painstakingly perfected later in the studio. He composed his scenes with great care—clear horizon lines give a strong horizontal, while diagonal lines (of trees or shorelines) create solid triangles. And he wasn't above airbrushing out details that might spoil the composition—such as Cleopatra's Needle near Charing Cross.

• *Wander into the next room and find a seat in front of the five paintings on the right.*

PAINTINGS OF GIVERNY (1883–1926)

Rose Trellises and the Japanese Bridge
(several versions)

In 1883, Monet's brood settled into a farmhouse in Giverny (80 kilometers west of Paris). Monet would spend the next 40 years here, traveling less with each passing year. Financially stable and domestically blissful, he turned Giverny into a garden paradise—painting nature without the long commute.

These colorful canvases immerse you in Monet's garden at Giverny. He did his own landscaping: flowerbeds of lilies, iris, and clematis, arbors of climbing roses forming a tunnel-like "Grand Alley," and a Japanese garden with an arched footbridge, willows, bamboo, and a pond filled with water lilies. The arched trellises form a natural tunnel effect that leads your eye down the path, "into" the canvas. But the canvas is fully saturated with color, the distant objects as bright as close ones. Monet's mosaic of brushstrokes forms a colorful design that's beautiful even if you just look "at" the canvas like wallpaper. He wanted his paintings to be realistic (3-dimensional), but with a pleasant (2-dimensional) pattern.

In the last half of his life, Monet's world shrank—from the broad vistas of the world traveler to the tranquility of his home, family, and garden. But his artistic vision expanded as he painted smaller details on bigger canvases and helped invent modern abstract art.

In 1890, Monet started work on a Japanese garden, inspired by tranquil scenes from the Japanese prints he collected. He diverted a river to form a pond, planted willows and bamboo on the shores, filled the pond with water lilies, then crossed it with this wooden footbridge. As years passed, the bridge became overgrown with wisteria (compare the early bridge canvas behind you and the later bridge canvases in front of you). He painted it at different times of day and year, exploring different color schemes.

Monet uses the bridge as the symmetrical center of simple, pleasing designs. The water is drawn with horizontal brushstrokes that get shorter as you move up the canvas ("farther away"), creating the illusion of distance. The horizontal water contrasts with the vertical-stroke willows, while the bridge "bridges" the sides of the square canvas, lacing the scene together.

Monet—the greatest visionary, literally, of his generation—began to go blind. Cataracts distorted his perception of depth and color, and sent him into a tailspin of despair. The (angry?) red paintings date from this period.
• *Turn around.*

Early Water Lilies (several versions)

As his vision slowly failed, Monet concentrated on painting close-ups of the surface of the pond and its water lilies (scientific name *Nympheas*), using red, white, yellow, lavender, and various combos. Some lilies are just a few broad strokes on a bare canvas (a study), while others are piles of paint formed with overlapping colors.

The true subject is not the lilies, however, but the changing reflections on the surface of the pond—of the blue sky, white clouds, and green trees that line the shore. Pan slowly around the room and watch the pond go from predawn to bright sunlight to twilight. Monet, assisted by his favorite daughter, Blanche (also a painter—and a widow after Jean died young), worked on several canvases at once, moving with the sun from one to the next.

Early lily paintings (c. 1900) show the shoreline as a reference point. But increasingly, Monet cropped the scene ever closer, until there was no shoreline, no horizon, no sense of what's up or down. Lilies float among clouds. Stepping back from the canvas, you see the lilies just hang there on the museum wall, suspended in space. The surface of the pond and the surface of the canvas are one. Modern, abstract art—a colored design on a flat surface— is just around the corner.

• *Enter the final, round room and find the big tree trunk.*

Big Weeping Willow

Get close—Monet did—and analyze the trunk. Rough "brown" bark is made of thick strokes (an inch wide and 4 inches long) of pink, purple, orange, and green. Impressionism lives. But to get these colors to resolve in your eye, you'd have to back up all the way to Giverny.

Later Water Lilies (1915–1926)

Like Beethoven going deaf, blind Monet wrote his final sympho- nies on a monumental scale. He planned a series of huge canvases (2 meters/6 feet tall) of water lilies to hang in special rooms at L'Orangerie (scheduled to reopen in 2004). He built a special studio with skylights and wheeled easels, and worked on them ob- sessively. A successful eye operation in 1923 gave him new energy. Here at the Marmottan are smaller-scale studies for that series.

Some lilies are patches of thick paint circled by a squiggly "caricature" of a lily pad. Monet simplifies in a way that Matisse and Picasso would envy. But getting close, you see that the lily is made of many brushstrokes, and also that each brushstroke is itself a mix of different colored paints.

Monet is thought of as a light-weight, but he deals with the fundamentals of life, especially in his later work: green lilies float- ing among lavender clouds reflected in the blue water. Staring into Monet's pond, we see the intermingling of the four classical elements, earth (foliage), air (the sky), fire (sunlight), and water— the primordial soup where life begins.

When Monet died in 1926, he was famous. Starting with meticulous line drawings, he evolved into an open-air realist, then Impressionist color-analyst, then serial painter, and finally master of reflections. As the subjects of his work became fuzzier, the colors and patterns predominated. Monet builds a bridge between Impressionism and modern abstract art.

FIRST FLOOR COLLECTION

Check out the fine collection of paintings by Monet's Impression- ist colleagues: Renoir, Gauguin, Pissarro, Morisot (find her portrait by Manet), and others before saying *au revoir* to this museum.

NAPOLEON'S TOMB & LES INVALIDES TOUR

If you've ever considered being absolute dictator of a united Europe, come here first. Hitler did, but still went out and made the same mistakes as his role model. (Hint: Don't invade Russia.)

Napoleon's tomb can be seen where it rests beneath the golden dome of Les Invalides church. Around the church, in a former veterans' hospital built by Louis XIV, are various military museums. The best is the new World War II wing in the Armay Museum (see description and tour information page 199).

Orientation

Cost: €6, students pay €5, free for those under 18, covered by museum pass.

Hours: Daily April–Sept 9:00–17:45, mid-June–mid-Sept until 18:45, Oct–March 10:00–16:45. Closed the first Monday of every month, Jan 1, May 1, Nov 1, and Dec 25.

Getting There: The tomb is at the Hôtel des Invalides at 129 rue de Grenelle (near Rodin Museum, Mo: La Tour Maubourg, Varenne, or Invalides). Bus #69 from the Marais and Rue Cler area is also handy. The museum is a 10-minute walk from rue Cler.

Information: Helpful English handouts at the ticket office (tel. 01 44 42 37 72, www.invalides.org).

Length of Our Tour: Women—two hours, men—three hours, Republican men—all day.

Cuisine Art: A reasonable cafeteria is next to the ticket office, and the rear gardens are picnic-perfect.

• *Start at Napoleon's tomb, underneath the golden dome. It's at the back end (farthest from the Seine) of this vast complex of churches and museums.*

NAPOLEON'S TOMB

Enter the church, gaze up at the dome, then lean over the railing and bow to the emperor lying inside the red, porphyry, scrolled tomb. If the lid were opened, you'd find an oak coffin inside, which holds another ebony coffin, housing two lead ones, then mahogany, then tinplate... until finally you'd find Napoleon himself staring up, with his head closest to the door. When his body was exhumed from the original grave and transported here, it was still perfectly preserved, even after 19 years in the ground.

Born of humble Italian heritage on the French-owned isle of Corsica, Napoleon Bonaparte (1769–1821) went to school at Paris' Ecole Militaire (Military School), then rose quickly through the ranks amid the chaos of the Revolution. The charismatic "Little Corporal" won fans by fighting for democracy at home and abroad. In 1799, he assumed power and, within five short years, conquered most of Europe. The great champion of the Revolution had become a dictator, declaring himself emperor of a new Rome.

Napoleon's red tomb on its green base stands 4.5 meters/ 15 feet high in the center of a marble floor. It's exalted by the dome above (where dead Frenchmen cavort with saints and angels), forming a golden halo over Napoleon.

Napoleon is surrounded by family. After conquering Europe, he installed his big brother, Joseph, as king of Spain (turn around to see Joseph's black-and-white marble tomb in the alcove to the left of the door); his little brother, Jerome, became king of Westphalia (to right of door); and his baby boy, Napoleon Junior (downstairs), sat in diapers on the throne of Rome.

In other alcoves, you'll find more dead war heroes (including World War I's Marshal Foch, his tomb lit with otherwordly blue light) and many painted saints, making this the French Valhalla in the Versailles of churches.

The Crypt

• *The stairs behind the altar (with the corkscrew columns) take you down to crypt level for a closer look at the tomb.*

Wandering clockwise, read the names of Napoleon's battles on the floor. Rivoli marks the battle where the rookie 26-year-old general took a ragtag band of "citizens" and thrashed the professional Austrian troops in Italy, returning to Paris a celebrity. In Egypt (Pyramides), he fought Turks and tribesmen to a standstill, but the exotic expedition caught the public eye, and he returned home a legend.

Napoleon' huge victory over Austria at Austerlitz on the first anniversary of his coronation made him Europe's top dog. At the head of the million-man Great Army, he made a three-month blitz attack through Germany and Austria. As a general, he was daring, relying on top-notch generals and on a mobile force of independent armies. His personal charisma on the battlefield was said to be worth 10,000 additional men.

Pause in the battles to gaze at the grand statue of Napoleon the emperor in the alcove at the head of the tomb—royal scepter and orb of Earth in his hands. By 1804, all of Europe was at his feet. He held an elaborate ceremony in Notre-Dame, where he proclaimed his wife, Josephine, as empress, and himself—the 36-year-old son of humble immigrants—as emperor. The laurel wreath, the robes, and the Roman eagles proclaim him the equal of the Caesars. The floor at the statue's feet marks the grave of his son, Napoleon II (Roi de Rome).

Around the crypt are relief panels showing Napoleon's constructive side. Dressed in toga and laurel leaves, he dispenses justice, charity, and pork-barrel projects to an awed populace.

• *In the first panel to the right of the statue ...*

He establishes an Imperial University to educate naked boys throughout "*tout l'empire*." The roll of great scholars links modern France with those of the past: Plutarch, Homer, Plato, and Aristotle. Three panels later, his various building projects (canals, roads, and so on) are celebrated with a list and his quote, "Everywhere I passed, I left durable benefit."

Hail Napoleon. Then, at his peak, came his fatal mistake.

• *Continue around the tomb to the Battle of Moscow (Moscowa) ...*

Napoleon invaded Russia with 600,000 men and returned to Paris with 60,000 frostbitten survivors. Two years later, the Russians marched into Paris, and Napoleon's days were numbered. After a brief exile on the isle of Elba, he skipped parole, sailed to France, bared his breast, and said, "Strike me down or follow me!" For 100 days, they followed him, finally into Belgium, where the British finished him off at the Battle of Waterloo (conspicuously absent on the floor decor). Exiled again by a war tribunal, he spent his last days in a crude shack on the small South Atlantic island of St. Helena.

LES INVALIDES AND THE ARMY MUSEUM (MUSÉE DE L'ARMÉE)

Your tomb ticket also admits you to several military museums scattered around the complex (listed in free English map/guide in ticket hall). Most of it consists of dummies in uniforms and endless glass cases full of muskets, without historical context. But the wing on World War II is worthwhile.

Les Invalides

GRAND ESPLANADE DES INVALIDES

←TO METRO LA TOUR MAUBOURG

↑ TO SEINE

Tickets & Info   ENTER

N

ARMY MUSEUM (WEST) (WING)

COURT-YARD OF HONOR

ARMY MUSEUM (EAST) (WING)

FRENCH WARS

Ⓜ VARENNE

B L V D.

50 YDS.
50 m

WW I   III WW II

ST. HELENA GRAVE

MUSEÉ DE L'ARCH DE LA LIB.

DCH

WC

INFO & TICKETS

CAFÉ

SOLDIER'S CHURCH (ST. LOUIS)

GILDED DOME CHURCH

←NAPOLEON'S TOMB

ENTER

←TO GARDENS, METRO: ECOLE MILITAIRE & RUE CLER

R. VARENNE

D E S   I N V A L I D E S

RODIN MUSEUM

Exiting the church with Napoleon's tomb, make a U-turn right and march past the ticket hall and café. Halfway down the long hallway, on the right through the glass, you'll see a bare stone slab beside weeping willows that originally marked Napoleon's grave on the island of St. Helena. There was no epitaph, since the French and British wrangled over what to call the hero/tyrant. The stones read simply, "Here lies..."

Continuing on, you'll spill out into the large Courtyard of Honor, where Napoleon honored his troops and de Gaulle once kissed Churchill. The Army Museum flanks both sides of the courtyard.

• *Cross the courtyard, enter under the golden letters, and go up to the second floor (European) to reach the East Wing (elevator available, WC downstairs).*

ARMY MUSEUM: EAST WING

This museum traces uniforms and weapons through French history, from Louis XIV to World War I. This is interesting for Napoleophiles. As you circle this floor, you'll follow the history and art of French warfare from about 1700 to 1850: Pre-Revolution, Revolution, Napoleon, and Restoration. Red banners give an English overview in each room.

The "First Republic: 1793–1804" section has early Napoleonic exhibits. In the Salle Boulogne are the emperor's hat and sword. The tent (behind screen) shows his bivouac equipment—a bed with mosquito netting, a director's chair, and a table that you can imagine his generals hunched over, making battle plans.

Back in the hall, at the Salle Consulat, a glass case displays a French-Breton dictionary *(Grammaire Françoise-Celtique)*, providing soldiers the necessary lingo to survive in the foreign region of Brittany.

In the rooms covering "Napoleon and The Empire 1804–1814" (first room: Salle Austerlitz), you'll find the famous portrait by Ingres of Napoleon at the peak of his power, stretching his right arm to supernatural lengths. Then comes Napoleon's beloved horse, Le Vizir, who weathered many a campaign and grew old with him in exile (stuffed in a glass case, third room: Salle Eylau).

Later, in Salle Montmirail, there's a portrait of a dejected Napoleon after his first abdication in 1814. A glass case is dedicated to Napoleon's son, the "Roi de Rome." His little soldier boots are there, and an engraving shows the child king in a royal carriage. When he grew up (miniature portrait in the center), he looked a lot like his dad—a fact that kept French Royalists wary until his death. Junior's mother (engraving to the left) was Maria-Louise, whom Napoleon married after divorcing barren Josephine.

Napoleon's big white dog (in a glass case after you turn the corner into the long blue Corridor de Tarascon) suffered the same fate as the horse. On the wall to the left of the dog hang proclamations of thanks and good-byes Napoleon sent to his soldiers and the French people, announcing the surrender at Waterloo. Directly behind the dog (other side of the wall), a shining breastplate shows the effectiveness of British artillery in the battle of Waterloo. Several steps further along at the blue drapes, you'll find Napoleon's death mask and a reconstruction of a room in his final home on St. Helena (inside the drapes). Picture a lonely man suffering from ulcers sitting here in his nightcap and slippers, playing chess, not war.

As you leave the Salle Restauration (the mid-1800s, when France brought back the royalty) and enter the green-bordered room, the last display before the exit is an American flag in a glass case, honoring General la Fayette of France, who helped George Washington take Yorktown.

The Musée des Plans Reliefs (top floor of East Wing) has 17th- and 18th-century models of fortified cities used to by the French in developing strategies to thwart enemy attacks (see English flier at the door). Big models of Mont St. Michel and Antibes lie at either end. Other floors of this wing are filled with temporary exhibits.

ARMY MUSEUM: WEST WING

Across the courtyard is a twin museum in the West Wing. The ground floor covers military implements, from stone axes to Axis powers. Near the entrance, two long, interesting rooms of armor and medieval weaponry have good English descriptions.

Upstairs on the second floor, you'll find a small but worthwhile World War I wing (14–18 Gallerie) that makes warfare feel less glorious. Wander clockwise around this room and find (in order): the first machine guns (whose developer thought his invention would end war, assuming that no one would send a soldier into its flurry of bullets), a model of WWI trenches, a "trench-rifle" designed to shoot over a trench, a model of Verdun's battlefields with a case opposite showing various hand-launched bombs, and a glass case displaying art objects created by soldiers while mired in the trenches.

The next floor up displays models of artillery over the years.
• *The World War II Wing is located in the southwest corner of the main courtyard; go upstairs, following signs to "General de Gaulle: Deuxième Guerre Mondiale, 39/45." The museum has two other names as well: "General de Gaulle, Seconde Guerre Mondiale" and "France Libre, France Combattante."*

ARMY MUSEUM: WORLD WAR II WING

World War II was the most destructive of earth's struggles. In this new exhibit, the war unfolds in photos, displays, and newsreels, with special emphasis on the French contribution. You may never have realized that it was Charles de Gaulle who won the war for us.

The free museum map is helpful for locating the displays we'll see. Climb to the top floor and work back down, from Germany's quick domination (third floor) to the Allies turning the tide (second floor) to the final surrender (first floor).

There are fine English descriptions. Make time!

Third Floor: Axis Aggression

Room 1: Treaty of Versailles to 1939 *(Du Traité de Versailles à 1939):* In 1918, the "war to end all wars" ground to a halt, leaving 10 million dead, a defeated Germany, and a devastated (if victorious) France. For the next two decades, Adolf Hitler would feed off German resentment for the Treaty of Versailles, which had humiliated and ruined Germany.

Room 2: The Defeat of 1940 *(La Défaite de 1940):* On September 1, 1939, Hitler invaded Poland, starting World War II. France and Britain mobilized, but Germany did nothing for six months. Then, in the spring of 1940 came the Blitzkrieg ("lightning war"), and Germany's better-trained and better-equipped soldiers and tanks swept west through Belgium. France was immediately overwhelmed, and British troops barely escaped across the Channel from Dunkirk. Within a month, Nazis were goose-stepping down the Champs-Elysées, and Hitler was on his way to Napoleon's tomb.

Room 3: The Appeal of June 18, 1940: Just like that, virtually all of Europe was dominated by fascists. During those darkest days, as France fell and Nazism spread across the Continent, one Frenchman—an obscure military man named Charles de Gaulle—refused to admit defeat. He escaped to London and made inspiring speeches over the radio, slowly convincing a small audience of French expatriates that victory was still possible.

Room 4: Charles de Gaulle (1890–1970): This 20th-century John of Arc had an unshakable belief in his mission to save France. He was born into a literate, upper-class family, raised in military academies, and became a WWI hero and POW. After the

war, he helped administer the occupied Rhineland. When World War II broke out, he was only a minor officer (the title of "Brigadier General" was hastily acquired during the invasion). He had limited political experience, and was virtually unknown to the French public. But he rallied France, became the focus of French patriotism, and later guided the country in the postwar years.

Room 6: The Vichy Government *(La France après l'Armistice, L'Empire colonial: un enjeu):* After the surrender, Germany ruled northern France (including Paris) but allowed the French to administer the south and the colonies (North Africa). This puppet government, centered in the city of Vichy, was right-wing and traditional, bowing to Hitler's demands as he looted France's raw materials and manpower for the war machine. (The movie *Casablanca*, set in Vichy-controlled Morocco, shows French officials following Nazi orders while French citizens defiantly sing "The Marseillaise.")

Room 7: The Battle of Britain—June 1940–June 1941
(La Bataille d'Angleterre, Du Refus de la Défaite à l'Esprit de Résistance): Facing a "New Dark Age" in Europe, British Prime Minister Winston Churchill pledged, "We will fight on the beaches . . . . We will fight in the hills. We will never surrender."

In June 1940, Germany mobilized to invade Britain across the Channel. From June to September, they paved the way, sending bombers—up to 1,500 planes a day—to destroy military and industrial sites. When Britain wouldn't budge, Hitler concentrated on London and civilian targets—this was "The Blitz" of the winter of 1940, which killed 30,000 and left London in ruins. But Britain hung on, armed with newfangled radar, speedy Spitfires, and an iron will.

They also had the Germans' secret "Enigma" code. The "Enigma machine" (in display case), with its set of revolving drums, allowed German commanders to scramble orders in a complex code that could safely be broadcast to their troops. The British captured a machine, broke the code (a project called "Ultra"), then moni-tored German airwaves. For the rest of the war, they had advance knowledge of many top-secret plans. (Occasionally, Britain even let Germany's plans succeed—sacrificing their own people—to avoid suspicion.)

By spring of 1941, Hitler had given up any hope of invading the Isle of Britain. Churchill said of his people: "This was their finest hour."

Room 10: Germany Invades the Soviet Union—June 1941 *(L'Allemagne Envahit l'Union Sovietique):* Perhaps hoping to one-up Napoleon, Hitler sent his state-of-the-art tanks speeding toward Moscow (betraying his former ally, Josef Stalin). By winter, the advance had stalled at the gates of Moscow, bogged down by bad weather and Soviet stubbornness. The Third Reich had reached its peak. From now on, Hitler would have to fight a

two-front war. The French Renault tank (displayed) was downright puny compared to the big, fast, high-caliber German Panzers. This war was often a battle of factories, to see who could produce the latest technology fastest and in the greatest numbers.

Room 12: The United States Enters the War *(Les Etats-Unis Entrent dans la Guerre):* "On December 7, 1941, a date which will live in infamy" (as F.D.R. put it), Japanese planes made a sneak attack on the U.S. base at Pearl Harbor, Hawaii, destroying the pride of the Pacific fleet in two hours. The United States quickly declared war on Japan and her ally, Germany. In two short years, America had gone from isolationist observer to supplier of Britain's arms to full-blown war ally against fascism. The United States now faced a two-front war—in Europe against Hitler, and against Japan's imperialist conquest of China, Southeast Asia, and the South Pacific.

America's first victory came when Japan tried a sneak attack on the U.S. base at Midway Island (June 3, 1942). This time— thanks to the Allies who cracked the "Enigma" code—America had the U.S.S. *Enterprise* (see model) and two of her buddies lying in wait. In five minutes, three of Japan's carriers (with valuable planes) were fatally wounded, their major attack force was sunk, and Japan and the United States were dead even and settling in for a long war of attrition.

Though slow to start, America eventually had an army of 16 million strong, 80,000 planes, the latest technology, $250 million a day, unlimited raw materials, and a population fighting for freedom to a boogie-woogie beat.

• *Continue downstairs to the second floor.*

Second Floor: The Tide Turns
In 1942, the Continent was black with fascism and Japan was secure on a distant island. The Allies had to chip away on the fringes.

Room 13: Battle of the Atlantic *(La Bataille de l'Atlantique):* German U-boats (short for "Unterseeboot," see model) and battleships such as the *Bismarck* patrolled Europe's perimeter, keeping America from aiding Britain. (Until long-range transport planes were invented near war's end, virtually all military transport was by ship.) The Allies traveled in convoys with air cover, used sonar and radar, and dropped depth charges, but for years they endured the loss of up to 60 ships per month.

Room 14: El Alamein, Stalingrad, and Guadalcanal—
The War Turns: Three crucial battles in autumn of 1942 put the first chink in the fascist armor. Off the east coast of Australia, 10,000 marines took an airstrip on Guadalcanal, while 30,000 Japanese held the rest of the tiny, isolated island. For the next six months, the two armies were marooned together, duking it out in thick jungles and malaria-infested swamps while their countries struggled to reinforce or rescue them. By February 1943, America had won and gained a crucial launch pad for bombing raids.

A world away, German tanks under General Erwin Rommel rolled across the vast deserts of North Africa. In October 1942, a well-equipped, well-planned offensive by British General Bernard Montgomery attacked at El Alamein, Libya. "Monty" drove "the Desert Fox" east into Tunisia for the first real Allied victory against the Nazi *Wehrmacht* war machine.

Then came Stalingrad. In August 1942, Germany attacked the Soviet city, an industrial center and gateway to the Caucasus oil fields. By October, the Germans had battled their way into the city center and were fighting house-to-house, but their supplies were running low, the Soviets wouldn't give up, and winter was coming. The snow fell, their tanks had no fuel, and relief efforts failed. Hitler ordered them to fight on through the bitter cold. On the worst days, 50,000 men died. (America lost 58,000 in Vietnam.) Finally, on January 31, 1943, the Germans surrendered, against Hitler's orders. The six-month totals? Eight hundred thousand German and other Axis soldiers dead, 1.1 million Soviets dead. The Russian campaign put hard miles on the German war machine.

Also in 1942, the Allies began long-range bombing of German-held territory, including saturation bombing of civilians. It was global war and total war.

Room 16: The Allies Land in North Africa *(Le Débarquement en Afrique du Nord, La Campagne de Tunisie):*
Winston Churchill and U.S. President Franklin D. Roosevelt (see photo with de Gaulle), two of the century's most dynamic and strong-willed statesmen, decided to attack Hitler indirectly by invading Vichy-controlled Mor-

occo and Algeria. On November 8, 1942, 100,000 Americans and British—under the joint command of an unknown, low-key problem-solver named General Dwight ("Ike") Eisenhower—landed on three separate beaches (including Casablanca). More than 120,000

Vichy French soldiers, ordered by their superiors to defend the
fascist cause, confronted the Allies and . . . gave up.

The Allies moved east, but bad weather, their own inexperience,
and the powerful Afrika Korps under Rommel stopped them in
Tunisia. But with flamboyant General George S. ("Old Blood-and-
Guts") Patton punching from the west and Monty pushing from
the south, they captured the port town of Tunis (May 7, 1943).
The Allies now had a base from which to retake Europe.

Room 17: The French Resistance *(L'Unification de la Résistance, La Lutte Clandestine):* Inside occupied France,
other ordinary heroes fought the Nazis—the "underground," or
Resistance. Bakers hid radios in loaves of bread to secretly contact
London. Barmaids passed along tips from tipsy Nazis. Communists
in black berets cut telephone lines. Farmers hid downed airmen
in haystacks. Housewives spread news from the front with their
gossip. Printers countered Nazi propaganda with pamphlets.

Jean Moulin (see photo in museum), de Gaulle's assistant,
secretly parachuted into France and organized these scattered
heroes into a unified effort. In May 1943, Moulin was elected
chairman of the National Council of the Resistance. A month
later, he was arrested by the Gestapo (Nazi secret police), imprisoned, tortured, and sent to Germany, where he died in transit.
Still, Free France now had a (secret) government again, rallied
around de Gaulle and ready to take over when liberation came.

Room 18: The Red Army *(L'Armée Rouge Reprend l'Initiative):* Monty, Patton, and Ike were certainly heroes, but
the war was won on the Eastern Front by Soviet grunts, who slowly
bled Germany dry.

Room 21: The Allies Land in Italy *(Premiers Débarque-ments Alliés en Europe):* On July 10, 1943, the assault on
Hitler's European fortress began. More than 150,000 Americans
and British sailed from Tunis, landing on the south shore of Sicily.
(See maps showing the campaigns.) Speedy Patton and metho-
dical Monty began a "horse race" to take the city of Messina
(the United States won the friendly competition by a few hours).
They met little resistance from 300,000 Italian soldiers, and were
actually cheered as liberators by the Sicilian people. Their real
enemies were the 50,000 German troops sent by Hitler to bolster
his ally, Benito Mussolini. By September, the island was captured.
On the mainland, Mussolini was arrested by his own people, and
Italy surrendered to the Allies. Hitler quickly poured troops into
Italy (and reinstalled Mussolini) to hold off the Allied onslaught.

In early September, the Allies launched a two-pronged landing onto the beaches of southern Italy. Finally, after four long years of war, free men set foot on the European continent.

Room 22: The Italian Campaign *(La Campagne d'Italie):*
Lieutenant General Mark Clark, leading the slow, bloody push north to liberate Rome, must have been reminded of the French trenches he'd fought in during World War I. As in that bloody war, the fighting in Italy was a war of attrition, fought on the ground by foot soldiers, costing many lives to gain just a few miles.

In January 1944, the Germans dug in between Rome and Naples at Monte Cassino, a rocky hill topped by the monastery of St. Benedict. Thousands died as the Allies tried inching up the hillside. In frustration, the Allies air-bombed the historic monastery, killing hundreds of monks... but no Germans, who dug in deeper. Finally, after four months of vicious, sometimes hand-to-hand combat, the Allies—Americans, Brits, Free French, Poles, Italian partisans, Indians, etc.—stormed the monastery, and the German back was broken.

Meanwhile, 50,000 Allies had landed on Anzio (a beach near Rome), holding the narrow beachhead for months against massive German attacks. When reinforcements arrived, they broke out and joined the two-pronged assault on the capital. Rome fell without a single bomb threatening its historic treasures on June 4, 1944.

Room 23: D-Day—June 6, 1944, "Operation Overlord":
Three million Allies and six million tons of materiel were massed in England in preparation for the biggest fleet-led invasion in history—across the Channel to France, then eastward to Berlin. The Germans, hunkered down in Northern France, knew an invasion was imminent, but the Allies kept it top secret. On the night of June 5, 150,000 soldiers boarded ships and planes, not knowing where they were headed until they were underway. Each one carried a note from General Eisenhower: "The tide has turned. The free men of the world are marching together to victory."

At 6:30 in the morning on June 6, 1944, Americans spilled out of troop transports into the cold waters off a beach in Normandy, code-named Omaha. The weather was bad, seas were rough, and the prep bombing had failed. The soldiers, many seeing their first action, were dazed and confused. Nazi machine guns pinned them against the sea. Slowly, they crawled up the beach on their stomachs. A thousand died. They held on until the next wave of transports arrived.

All day long, Allied confusion did battle with German indecision—the Nazis never really counterattacked, thinking D-Day was just a ruse, not the main invasion. By day's end, the Allies had taken several beaches along the Normandy coast and began building artificial harbors, providing a tiny port-of-entry for the reconquest of Europe. The stage was set for a quick and easy end to the war. Right.

• *Go downstairs to the...*

First Floor: The War Ends... Very Slowly (June 1944–Aug 1945)

Room 24: Battle of Normandy *(La Bataille de Norman-die):* For a month, the Allies (mostly Americans) secured Normandy, taking bigger ports (Cherbourg and Caen) and amassing troops and supplies for the assault on Germany. In July, they broke out and sped eastward across France, Patton's tanks covering up to 65 kilometers/40 miles a day. They had "Jerry" on the run.

Room 25: Landing in Provence, August 1944 *(Le Débarquement de Provence):* On France's Mediterranean coast, American troops under General Alexander Patch landed near Cannes, took Marseilles, and headed north to meet up with Patton.

Room 26: "Les Maquis": French Resistance guerrilla fighters helped reconquer France from behind the lines. (Don't miss the folding motorcycle in its parachute case.) The liberation of Paris was started by a Resistance attack on a German garrison.

Room 27: Liberation of Paris: As the Allies marched on Paris, Hitler ordered his officers to torch the city—but they sanely disobeyed and prepared to surrender. On August 26, General Charles de Gaulle walked ramrod-straight down the Champs-Elysées, followed by Free French troops and U.S. GIs passing out chocolate and Camels. Two million Parisians went ape.

Room 28: On to Berlin—Offensive from the West *(Vers Berlin—Offensives de l'Ouest):* The quick advance through France, Belgium, and Luxembourg bogged down at the German border in autumn of 1944. Patton outstripped supply lines, a parachute invasion of Holland (Battle of Arnhem) was disastrous, and bad weather grounded planes and slowed tanks.

On December 16, the Allies met a deadly surprise. An enormous, well-equipped, energetic German army appeared from nowhere, punched a "bulge" deep into Allied lines, and demanded surrender. General Anthony McAuliffe sent a one-word response—"Nuts!"—and the tide turned. The Battle of the Bulge was Germany's last great offensive.

The Germans retreated across the Rhine River, blowing up bridges behind them. The last bridge, at Remagen, was captured by the Allies just long enough to cross and establish themselves on German soil. Soon U.S. tanks were speeding down the autobahns and Patton could wire the good news back to Ike: "General, I have just pissed in the Rhine."

Soviet soldiers did the dirty work of taking fortified Berlin, launching a final offensive in January 1945, and surrounding the city in April. German citizens fled west to surrender to the more-benevolent Americans and Brits. Hitler, defiant to the end, hunkered in his underground bunker.

On April 28, 1945, Mussolini and his girlfriend were killed and hung by their heels in Milan. Two days later, Adolf Hitler and his new bride, Eva Braun, avoided similar humiliation by committing suicide (pistol in mouth) and having their bodies burned beyond recognition. Germany formally surrendered on May 8, 1945.

In Corridor to the left of Room 28: Concentration Camps: Lest anyone mourn Hitler or doubt this war's purpose, gaze on photos from Germany's concentration camps. Some camps held political enemies and prisoners of war (including 2 million French), others were expressly built to exterminate peoples considered "genetically inferior" to the "Aryan master race"—particularly, Jews, Gypsies, homosexuals, and the mentally ill.

Room 29: War of the Pacific *(Pacifique—Les Grandes Offensives Americaines):* Often treated as an afterthought, the final campaign against Japan was a massive American effort, costing many lives but saving millions from Japanese domination.

Japan was an island bunker surrounded by a vast ring of fortified Pacific islands. America's strategy was to take one island at a time, "island hopping" until close enough for B-29 Superfortress bombers to attack Japan itself. The war spread across thousands of miles. In a new form of warfare, ships carrying planes led the attack, preparing tiny islands for troops to land and build an airbase. While General Douglas MacArthur island-hopped south to retake the Philippines ("I have returned!"), others pushed north toward Japan.

In February 1945, marines landed on Iwo Jima, a city-size island-volcano close enough to Japan (1,300 kilometers/800 miles) to launch air raids. Twenty thousand Japanese had dug in on the volcano-top, picking off the advancing Americans. On February 23, several U.S. soldiers raised the Stars and Stripes on the mountain (that famous photo), inspiring their mates to victory at a cost of nearly 7,000 men.

Japan Surrenders *(Capitulation du Japon):* On March 9, Tokyo was firebombed and 90,000 were killed. Japan was losing, but a land invasion would cost hundreds of thousands of lives. The Japanese had a reputation for choosing death over the shame of surrender—they even sent bomb-laden "kamikaze" planes on suicide missions.

America unleashed its secret weapon, an atomic bomb (originally suggested by German-turned-American Albert Einstein). On August 6, a B-29 dropped one (named "Little Boy") on the city of Hiroshima, instantly vaporizing 100,000 people and 6.5 square kilometers/4 square miles. Three days later, a second bomb fell on Nagasaki. The next day, Emperor Hirohito unofficially surrendered. The long war was over, and U.S. sailors returned home to kiss their girlfriends in public places.

War Totals *(Le Bilan de la Guerre):* The death toll for World War II (Sept 1939–Aug 1945) totaled 80 million soldiers and civilians. The Soviet Union lost 26 million, China 13 million, France 580,000, and the United States 340,000.

World War II changed the world, with America emerging as the dominant political, military, and economic superpower. Europe was split in two. The western half recovered, with American aid. The east remained under Soviet occupation. For 45 years, the United States and the Soviet Union would compete—without ever actually doing battle—in a "Cold War" of espionage, propaganda, and weapons production that stretched from Korea to Cuba, from Vietnam to the moon.

• *Before you leave Les Invalides, go down a long hall between the ticket office and bookshop, near the exit of the WWII wing, to find the ...*

MUSEE DE L'ORDRE DE LA LIBERATION

This museum tells the story of the Resistance in World War II (free, no English descriptions). The French refer to World War II as "The War of '39–40," but this proud collection makes it clear that the French were busy during the Nazi occupation.

CLUNY MUSEUM TOUR

Musée National du Moyen Age

The "National Museum of the Middle Ages" doesn't sound quite so boring as I approach middle age myself. Aside from the solemn religious art, there is some lively stuff here.

Paris emerged on the world stage in the "Middle Ages," the time between ancient Rome and the Renaissance. Europe was awakening from a thousand-year slumber. Trade was booming, people actually owned chairs, and the Renaissance was moving in like a warm front from Italy.

Orientation

Cost and Hours: €7, €5.50 on Sun, free first Sun of month, covered by museum pass, Wed–Mon 9:15–17:45, closed Tue.

Getting There: The entrance is a block above the intersection of boulevards St. Germain and St. Michel at 6 place Paul-Painlevé (Mo: Cluny-La Sorbonne, St. Michel, or Odéon, bus #63 from rue Cler or #86 from the Marais).

Information: Pick up the free and handy museum map guide. Tel. 01 53 73 78 00.

Length of Our Tour: One hour.

Baggage Check: Required and free.

The Tour Begins

The museum hosts frequent special exhibits, slightly affecting the permanent collection described below. You may find the works described in Room 4 on display in Room 2 and temporary exhibits filling Rooms 8 and 9.

Room 2 (first room after the bookshop): The first art you see is not some grim, gray crucifixion but a colorful tapestry depicting grape-stomping peasants during the *vendange* (the annual autumn wine harvest/celebration). A peasant man treads grapes in a vat

Cluny Ground Floor

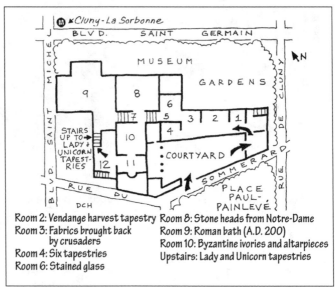

Room 2: Vendange harvest tapestry
Room 3: Fabrics brought back by crusaders
Room 4: Six tapestries
Room 6: Stained glass
Room 8: Stone heads from Notre-Dame
Room 9: Roman bath (A.D. 200)
Room 10: Byzantine ivories and altarpieces
Upstairs: Lady and Unicorn tapestries

while his wife collects the juice. A wealthy man gives orders. Above that, a peasant with a pimple turns a newfangled mechanical press. On the right, you'll see the joy of picking—pawns, knights, and queens all working side by side.

Having survived their Y1K crisis, these people realize the world won't end, and they turn their attention to the beauty of their surroundings.

Room 3: Colorful woven fabrics were brought back to France by crusaders, who went off to conquer barbarian infidels but returned with tales of enlightened peoples on the fringes of Europe.

Room 4: Six tapestries in wool and silk show the rich enjoying the simple, secular pleasures of their estate. The humans mingle harmoniously with the trees, flowers, and animals of the glorious physical world.

Reading clockwise: 1) A lady with a puppy spins wool while her husband relaxes with the morning paper. 2) Out in the garden, the sexes mingle unchaperoned by the Church. A lady takes a

breath mint while a troubadour puts the moves on her servant.
3) A lady embroiders a pillow. 4) The family picks fruit from their
plentiful orchards. 5) A lord goes hunting with his falcon, dog,
and servant. 6) A naked woman takes a chilly bath, enjoying fruits,
jewels, and music—the good things of a material world becoming
increasingly less sinful.

Room 6: Enter the Dark Ages,
when life was harsh and violent,
angels and demons made regular
appearances, and the Church
was your only refuge. This room
offers a rare close-up look at
stained glass, which gave the poor
a glimpse of the glories of heaven

and served as a visual aid for teaching Bible lessons to the illiter-
ate masses. These panels (many from the cathedral of light, the
Sainte-Chapelle) give us a window into the magical, supernatural,
miraculous—and often violent—medieval mind.

Read clockwise around the room following the lowest level
only, and begin with the wall immediately to your left as you enter:
1) The angel Gabriel blasts his horn on Resurrection morning,
rousting the grateful dead from their coffins. Notice that Gabriel's
royal purple robe is made up of several different pieces of glass—
purples, whites, blues—held together with lead. 2) King Herod
seems shocked? pleased? to see the head of John the Baptist presented to him on a plate by Salome, his dancing stepdaughter.
3) A red-faced, horned, horny demon (with his equally lascivious
wolf and henchman) carries off a frightened girl in red to do
unspeakable acts. 4) Blond, pious Joseph is sold into slavery to
camel merchants by his plotting brothers.

Next wall: 5) Samson is about to pull down the temple...
6) Then, he has his eyes gouged out by Philistines. 7) Slaughter
on the battlefield. Men with bloodstained hands and faces hack
at each other with golden swords. 8) Aaron, disobeying God and
Moses, worships a golden calf. 9) A king on a throne closes his
eyes to all this wickedness.

Next wall (with some panels from the first Gothic church, St.
Denis): 10) Two monks with prayer books gaze up as one of their
brothers disappears into heaven. The Latin inscription, *"hec est
via,"* means "This is the way." 11) Seated Jesus, in a royal purple
robe, is consoled by two angels. 12) Theophilus ("Lover of God")
has struck a Faustian deal with the devil and is now feeling buyer's
remorse. 13) Sleeping St. Martin is visited by a heavenly vision.
14) Angels in Rock-and-Roll Heaven.

Last wall: Four apostles—John ("Ioanneus"), James, Peter ("Petrus," with key), and Paul.

Room 8: On the stage, you'll find 21 stone heads (sculpted 1220–1230) of the kings of Judah from the Bible that once decorated the front of Notre-Dame. In 1793, an angry mob of revolutionaries mistook the kings of Judah for the kings of France and abused and decapitated the statues. (Today's heads on the Notre-Dame statues are reconstructions.) Someone gathered up the heads and buried them in his backyard near the present-day Garnier Opéra. There they slept for two centuries, unknown and noseless, until 1977, when some diggers accidentally unearthed them and brought them to an astounded world. Their stoic expressions accept what fate, time, and liberals have done to them.

The statue of Adam (usually on the left, sometimes behind you) is also from Notre-Dame. He's scrawny and flaccid by Renaissance standards. And it will be another 200 years before naked Adam can step out from behind that bush.

Room 9: This echoing cavern was a Roman frigidarium. Pretty cool. The museum is located on the site of a Roman bathhouse, a reminder of the Romans' centuries of occupation. After hot baths and exercise in adjoining rooms, ordinary Romans would take a cold dip in the sunken pool (in the alcove), then relax cheek to cheek with notables such as Emperor Julian the Apostate (see his statue), who lived right next door. The 12-meter/40-foot ceiling is the largest Roman vault in France, and it took the French another 1,000 years to improve on that crisscross-arch technology. The sheer size of this room, constructed in A.D. 200 when Rome was at its peak, gives an idea of the epic scale in which the Romans built, inspiring Europeans to greatness during the less civilized Middle Ages.

The four square columns (Pilier des Nautes) are the oldest man-made objects you'll see from Paris. These pillars once supported a 6-meter-high (20 feet) altar to the king of the gods in the Temple of Jupiter, where Notre-Dame now stands. The carving on one says it was built in the time of the Emperor Tiberius, A.D. 14–37 ("TIB. CAESARE"), and was paid for by the Parisian boatmen's union (see them holding their canoe-shaped boats).

Room 10: Rome lived on after the Fall. The finely carved Byzantine ivories (first glass case) show how pagan gods, emperors, and griffins became Christian saints, gargoyles, and icons. Constantinople—the eastern half of the empire that survived the Fall—preserved Roman tastes and imagery, like the willowy, bare-breasted, dreamy-eyed *Ariadne (Ariane)*, with the sneaky satyr peeking out. In painting, Byzantine gold-background icons inspired medieval altarpieces, like others in the room.

Rome also lived on in the Romanesque grandeur of Christian churches like St. Germain-des-Prés (the 12 column capitals). The central capital shows Christ in robes on a throne, ruling the world like a Roman emperor. These capitals were originally painted, much like the painted wooden statues across the room. Don't leave this room before eyeing the tusk of a narwhal (on the wall), which must have convinced superstitious folk to believe in unicorns.

• *Go upstairs to . . .*

"The Lady and the Unicorn" Tapestries

As Europeans emerged from the Dark Ages, they rediscovered the beauty of the world around them.

These six mysterious tapestries, designed by an unknown (but probably French) artist before 1500 and woven in Belgium out of wool and silk, are loaded with symbols, some serious, some playful. They have been interpreted many ways, but the series deals with each of the five senses (handheld English explanations that you can pick up from slots hanging on the wall add more detail).

• *Moving clockwise around the room . . .*

Taste: A blond lady takes candy from a servant's dish to feed it to her parakeet. A unicorn and a lion look on. At the lady's feet, a monkey also tastes something, while the little white dog behind her wishes he had some. This was the Age of Discovery, when Columbus and Vasco da Gama spiced up Europe's bland gruel with new fruits, herbs, and spices.

The lion (symbol of knighthood?) and unicorn (symbol of "bourgeois nobility," purity, or fertility?) wave flags with the coat of arms of the family that bought the tapestries—three silver crescents in a band of blue.

Hearing: Wearing a stunning dress, the lady plays sweet music on an organ, soothing the savage beasts around her. The pattern and folds of the tablecloth are lovely. Humans and their fellow creatures live in harmony in an enchanted blue garden filled with flowers, set in a red background.

Sight: The unicorn cuddles up and looks at himself in the lady's mirror, pleased with what he sees. The lion turns away and snickers. As the Renaissance dawns, vanity is a less-than-deadly sin.

Admire the great artistic skill in some of the detail work, such as the necklace and the patterns in her dress. This tapestry had quality control in all its stages—drawing the scene, enlarging and transferring it to a cartoon, and weaving it. Still, the design itself is crude by Renaissance 3-D standards. The fox and rabbits, supposedly in the distance, simply float overhead, as big as the animals at the lady's feet.

Smell: The lady picks flowers and weaves them into a sweet-smelling wreath. On a bench behind, the monkey apes her. The flowers, trees, and animals are exotic and varied. Each detail is exquisite alone; but stepping back, they blend together into pleasing patterns.

Touch: This is the most basic and dangerous of the senses. The lady "strokes the unicorn's horn," if you know what I mean, and the lion gets the double-entendre. Unicorns, a species extinct since the Age of Reason, were so wild that only the purest virgins could entice and tame them. Medieval Europeans were exploring the wonders of love and the pleasures of sex. The Renaissance is coming.

Tapestry #6: The most talked-about tapestry gets its name from the words on our lady's tent: *A Mon Seul Désir* ("To My Sole Desire"). What *is* her only desire?

Is it jewelry, as she grabs a necklace from the jewel box? Or is she putting the necklace away, renouncing material things in order to follow her only desire?

Our lady has tried all things sensual and is now prepared to follow the one true impulse. Is it God? Or love? Her friends the unicorn and lion open the tent doors. Flickering flames cover the tent. Perhaps she's going in to meet the object of her desire. Or maybe she's stepping out. An old dark age is ending, and a new Renaissance world dawns.

THE REST OF THE MUSEUM

While the Unicorn tapestry is the Cluny's prize, there's much more: seventh-century Visigoth crowns (Room 16), the chapel (Room 20), and a medieval garden (outside and explained in the museum map guide).

VERSAILLES
TOUR

If you've ever wondered why your American passport has French writing in it, you'll find the answer at Versailles (pron. vehr-sigh). The powerful court of Louis XIV at Versailles set the standard of culture for all of Europe, right up to modern times. Versailles was every king's dream palace. Today, if you're planning to visit just one palace in all of Europe, make it Versailles. And if you have a car, or simply prefer a smaller town base for Paris, see my "Sleeping near Paris, in Versailles" recommendations on page 280.

Orientation

Cost: €7.50 (covered by museum pass); €5.50 after 15:30, under 18 free (the palace is also theoretically free for all teachers, professors, and architecture students). Admission is payable at entrances A, C, and D. Tours cost extra (see "Touring Versailles," below). The Grand and Petit Trianon Palaces cost €5 together, €3 after 15:30 (both covered by museum pass). The gardens, which usually cost €3, are €5.50 on fountain "spray days" on summer weekends (gardens not covered by museum pass, see "Fountain Spectacles," below).

If you don't have a museum pass, consider getting the Versailles Pass, which covers your entrance, gives you priority access (no lines) to everything, and includes an audioguide (€21, sold at Versailles train station, RER stations that serve Versailles, and at FNAC department stores).

Hours: The **palace** is open April–Oct Tue–Sun 9:00–18:30, Nov–March Tue–Sun 9:00–17:30, closed Mon (last entry 30 min before closing). The **Grand and Petit Trianon Palaces** are open daily April–Oct 12:00–18:00, Nov–March 12:00–17:00, closed Mon. The **garden** is open daily from 7:00 to sunset (as late as 21:30).

In summer, Versailles is especially crowded around 10:00 and 13:00, and all day Tue and Sun. Remember, the crowds gave

Versailles

WALKING TIMES

Train Stn to Chateau = 10 min.

Chateau to Grand Trianon = 30 min.

Grand Trianon to Le Hameau = 20 min.

Le Hameau to Chateau = 30 min.

GRAND TRIANON
SUMMER HOUSE
TEMPLE OF LOVE
GRAND CANAL
PETIT TRIANON
APOLLO BASIN
BIKE RENTAL
COLONNADE
LE HAMEAU
GARDENS
LATONA BASIN
NEPTUNE BASIN
ORANGERIE
CHÂTEAU
SATORY
SCEAUX
P
L'EUROPE
PLACE DU VIEUX MARCHÉ
AVE DE GAULLE
TOWN
VERSAILLES R.G. TRAIN STN.
TO PARIS VIA R.E.R. TRAIN
DCH

1 Hotel Le Cheval Rouge

2 Hotel Ibis Versailles

3 Hotel du Palais

4 Hotel d'Angleterre

5 Hotel de France

6 Rest. A la Cote Bretonne

7 Rest. Fenetres sur Cour

8 Rest. La Boeuf a la Mode

Versailles' Entrances

QUEEN'S & NOBLES WING

KING'S WING

HALL OF MIRRORS

D

F

C

B-2

DCH

CAFÉ & WC

EQUESTRIAN STATUE

A

FROM STATION

ENTRANCES

A = Self-guided tours entrance

B-2 = Pass holders entrance

C = Entrance for audioguide tours of private apartments

D = Buy tickets for guided tours here

F = Guided tours begin here

• • • = Tour route

Marie-Antoinette a pain in the neck, too, so relax and let them eat cake. For fewer crowds, go early or late: Either arrive by 9:00 (when the palace opens, touring the palace first, then the gardens) or after 15:30 (you'll get a reduced entry ticket but you'll miss the last guided tours of the day, which generally depart at 15:00). If you arrive midday, see the gardens first and the palace later, at 15:00. The gardens and palace are great late. On my last visit, at 18:00 I was the only tourist in the Hall of Mirrors... even on a Tuesday.

Getting There: Take the **RER-C train** (€5 round-trip, 30 min one-way) from these RER stops: Gare d'Austerlitz, St. Michel, Musée d'Orsay, Invalides, Pont de l'Alma, and Champ de Mars. Trains named "Vick" leave about five times an hour for the palace. Any train named Vick goes to Versailles; don't board other trains. Get off at the last stop (Versailles R.G. or "Rive Gauche"—not Versailles C.H., which is farther from the palace), turn right out of the station, and turn left at the first boulevard. It's a 10-minute walk to the palace.

Your Eurailpass covers this inexpensive trip, but it uses up a valuable "flexi" day. If you really want to use your railpass, consider seeing Versailles on your way into or out of Paris. To get free passage, show your railpass at an SCNF ticket window—for example, at the Invalides or Musée d'Orsay RER stop—and get a *contremarque de passage*. Keep this ticket to exit the system.

When returning from Versailles, look through the windows past the turnstiles for the departure board. Any train leaving Versailles serves all downtown Paris RER line C stops (they're marked on the schedule as stopping at *"toutes les gares jusqu'à Austerlitz,"* meaning "all stations up to Austerlitz").

Taxis for the 30-minute ride between Versailles and Paris cost about €25.

To reach Versailles from Paris by **car,** get on the *périphérique* freeway that circles Paris and take the toll-free autoroute A-13 toward Rouen. Follow signs into Versailles, then look for "*château*" signs and park in the huge lot in front of the palace (pay lot). The drive takes about 30 minutes one-way.

Information: A helpful TI is just past Sofitel Hôtel on your walk from the station to the palace (May–Sept daily 9:00–19:00, Oct–April daily 9:00–18:00, tel. 01 39 24 88 88, www.chateauversailles.fr). You'll also find information booths inside the château (doors A, B-2, and C) and, in peak season, kiosks scattered around the courtyard. The useful brochure "Versailles Orientation Guide" explains your sightseeing options.

Touring Versailles: Versailles' highlights are the State Apartments, the lavish King's Private Apartments, the Opera House,

and the magnificent Hall of Mirrors. Most visitors are satisfied with a spin through the State Apartments (following my self-guided tour, below), the gardens, and the Trianon Palaces. Versailles aficionados should spend the time (and money) to see the King's Private Apartments, which can be visited only with an audioguide or live guide (neither tour covered by museum pass).

Self-guided tour—To tour the palace on your own, join the line at entrance A if you need to pay admission. Those with a museum pass are allowed in through entrance B-2 without a wait. Enter the palace and take a one-way walk through the State Apartments (follow my tour, below) from the King's Wing, through the Hall of Mirrors, and out via the Queen's and Nobles' Wing.

Audioguide tours—There are two informative but dry audioguide tours. One covers the State Apartments (€4, includes Hall of Mirrors and queen's bedchamber; start at entrance A or, if you have a museum pass, entrance B-2). The other includes more of the King's Private Apartments (Louis XIV) and a sampling of nobles' chambers (€4, entrance C). Both audioguide tours are sold until one hour before closing and are available at each entrance.

Guided tours—You may select a one-hour guided tour from a variety of themes, such as the daily life of a king or the lives of such lesser-known nobles as the well-coiffed Madame de Pompadour (€4, join first English tour available). Or consider the 90-minute tour (€6) of the King's Private Apartments (Louis XV, Louis XVI, and Marie-Antoinette) and the chapel. This tour, which is the only way visitors can see the Opera House, can be long depending on the quality of your guide.

For a live tour, make reservations immediately upon arrival, at entrance D, as tours can sell out by 13:00 (first tours generally begin at 10:00, last tours depart usually at 15:00 but as late as 16:00). Guided tours begin at entrance F. The price of any tour is added to the €7.50 entry fee to Versailles (entry covered by museum pass, tours extra).

If you don't have a museum pass or Versailles Pass, and you think you might want to take a guided tour after you've seen the palace on your own, remember to keep your ticket to prove you've already paid for admission.

Length of Our Tour: Allow two hours for the palace and two for the gardens. Including two hours to cover your round-trip transit time, it's a six-hour day trip from Paris.

Baggage Check: Available at door A.

Cuisine Art: The cafeteria and WCs are next to the general entrance (door A). A sandwich kiosk and a decent restaurant are at the canal in the garden.

You'll find restaurants on the street to the right of the parking lot (as you face château), though the best places line the pleasant market square, place du Marché, in the town center (turn right out of the train station, cross avenue de Paris, and continue about 5 blocks to place du Marché). For a list of recommended eateries, see the Eating chapter, page 301. For a shortcut to Versailles' gardens from place du Marché, walk 10 minutes west down rue de la Paroisse. The château is to your left after entering, and the main gardens, Trianon Palaces, and Hameau are straight ahead. The quickest way to the château's front door is along avenue de St. Cloud and rue Colbert.

A handy McDonald's is immediately across from the train station (WC without crowds).

Fountain Spectacles: Classical music fills the king's backyard, and the garden's fountains are in full squirt, on Sat July–Sept and on Sun early April–early Oct (schedule for both days: 11:00–12:00 & 15:30–17:00 & 17:20–17:30). On these "spray days," the gardens cost €5.50 (not covered by museum pass, ask for a map of fountains). Louis had his engineers literally reroute a river to fuel these fountains. Even by today's standards, they are impressive. Pick up the helpful brochure of the fountain show ("Les Grandes Eaux Musicales") at any information booth for a guide to the fountains. Also ask about the impressive *Les Fêtes de Nuit* nighttime spectacle (some Sat, July–mid-Sept).

Getting around the Gardens: It's a 30-minute hike from the palace, down the canal, past the two mini-palaces to the Hamlet. You can rent bikes (€6/hr). The fast-looking, slow-moving tourist train leaves from behind the château and serves the Grand Canal and the Trianon Palaces (€5, 4/hr, 4 stops, you can hop on and off as you like; nearly worthless commentary).

Starring: Louis XIV and the Old Regime.

KINGS AND QUEENS AND GUILLOTINES

• *Read this on the train ride out there. Relax, the palace is the last stop.*

Come the Revolution, when they line us up and make us stick out our hands, will you have enough calluses to keep them from shooting you? A grim thought, but Versailles raises questions like that. It's the symbol of the Old Regime, a time when society was divided into rulers and the ruled, when you were born to be rich or to be poor. To some it's the pinnacle of civilization, to others the sign of a civilization in decay. Either way, it remains one of Europe's most impressive sights.

Versailles was the residence of the king and seat of France's government for a hundred years. Louis XIV (reigned 1643–1715) moved out of the Louvre in Paris, the previous royal residence, and built an elaborate palace in the forests and swamps of Versailles, 19 kilometers/12 miles west. The reasons for the move were partly personal—Louis loved the outdoors and disliked the sniping environs of stuffy Paris—and partly political.

Louis was creating the first modern, centralized state. At Versailles, he consolidated Paris' scattered ministries so he could personally control policy. More important, he invited to Versailles all of France's nobles, so he could control them. Living a life of almost enforced idleness, the "domesticated" aristocracy couldn't interfere with the way Louis ran things. With 18 million people united under one king (England had only

5.5 million), a booming economy, and a powerful military, France was Europe's number-one power.

Around 1700, Versailles was the cultural heartbeat of Europe, and French culture was at its zenith. Throughout Europe, when you said "the king," you were referring to the French king... Louis. Every king wanted a palace like Versailles. Everyone learned French. French taste in clothes, hairstyles, table manners, theater, music, art, and kissing spread across the Continent. That cultural dominance has continued, to some extent, right up to this century.

Louis XIV

At the center of all this was Europe's greatest king. He was a true Renaissance man, a century after the Renaissance—athletic, good-looking, a musician, dancer, horseman, statesman, art-lover, lover. For all his grandeur, he was one of history's most polite and approachable kings, a good listener who could put even commoners at ease in his presence.

Louis called himself the Sun King because he gave life and warmth to all that he touched. He was also thought of as Apollo, the Greek god of the sun. Versailles became the personal temple of this god on earth, decorated with statues and symbols of Apollo, the sun, and Louis himself.

Louis was a hands-on king who personally ran affairs of state. All decisions were made by him. Nobles, who in other countries were the center of power, became virtual slaves dependent on Louis' generosity. For 70 years, he was the perfect embodiment of the absolute monarch. He summed it up best himself with his famous rhyme—"*L'état, c'est moi!*" (pron. lay-tah say-mwah): "The state, that's me!"

Another Louis or Two to Remember

Three kings lived in Versailles during its century of glory. Louis XIV built it and established French dominance. Louis XV, his great-grandson (Louis XIV reigned for 72 years), carried on the tradition and policies, but without the Sun King's flair. During Louis XV's reign, France's power abroad was weakening, and there were rumblings of rebellion from within.

France's monarchy was crumbling, and the time was ripe for a strong leader to reestablish the old feudal order. They didn't get one. Instead, they got Louis XVI, a shy, meek bookworm, the kind of guy who lost sleep over Revolutionary graffiti... because it was misspelled. Louis XVI married a sweet girl from the Austrian royal family, Marie-Antoinette, and together they retreated into the idyllic gardens of Versailles while Revolutionary fires smoldered.

THE TOUR BEGINS

• *Start outside the palace at the equestrian statue of Louis XIV.*

This tour covers the ceremonial center of the palace (the State, or Grand Apartments) and the extensive grounds.

The central palace, the part we'll tour, forms a U around the courtyard in front of you. The right half (King's Wing) is separated from the left half (Queen's and Nobles' Wing) by the Hall of Mirrors ahead of you. Then two long wings shoot out to the right and left (north and south) of this U. In this tour, we'll walk counterclockwise through the U-shaped part on the middle floor.

The Original Château

The part of the palace directly behind the horse statue, at the far end of the courtyard, is the original château. Louis XIV's dad used to come out to the forests of Versailles to escape the worries of kingship. Here, he built this small hunting lodge. His son spent the happiest times of his boyhood at the lodge, hunting and riding.

Louis XIV's three arched bedroom windows (beneath the clock) overlooked the courtyard. Naturally, it faced the rising sun. The palace and grounds are laid out on an east-west axis.

When he became king, Louis XIV spent more and more time here, away from the hubbub of Paris. He expanded the lodge, planted gardens, and entertained guests. The reputation spread about this "Enchanted Island," a kind of Disneyland for dukes and duchesses. As visitors flocked here, Louis expanded around the original hunting château, attaching wings to create the present U-shape. Then, the long north and south wings were built. The total cost of the project has been estimated at half of France's entire GNP for one year.

Think how busy this courtyard must have been 300 years ago. There were as many as 5,000 nobles here at any one time, each with an entourage. They'd buzz from games to parties to amorous rendezvous in sedan-chair taxis. Servants ran about delivering secret messages and roast legs of lamb. Horse-drawn carriages arrived at the fancy gate with their finely dressed passengers, having driven up the broad boulevard that ran direct from Paris. (You can still see the horse stables lining the boulevard.) Incredible as it seems, both the grounds and most of the palace were public territory where even the lowliest peasant could come to gawk. Of course, this meant that there were, then as now, hordes of tourists, pickpockets, and men selling wind-up children's toys.

• *Enter at door A (or at B-2 if you have a museum pass) and buy your ticket. Show your ticket, and you'll be directed immediately upstairs (or sometimes through the 21 rooms of the history museum, with paintings on the background of Versailles and its kings).*

Our tour starts upstairs, in the room that overlooks the lavish Royal Chapel. (Note: As you jostle through the crowded corridors of the palace, pickpockets will be working the tourist crowds.)

The State Apartments

Royal Chapel: In the vast pagan "temple" that is Versailles, built to glorify one man, Louis XIV, this Royal Chapel is a paltry tip of the hat to that "other" god—the Christian one. It's virtually the first, last, and only hint of Christianity you'll see in the entire complex. Versailles celebrates Man, not God, by raising Louis to almost godlike status, the personification of all good human qualities. In a way, Versailles is the last great flowering of Renaissance humanism and revival of the classical world.

Louis attended Mass here every morning. While he sat on the upper level, the lowly nobles below would turn their backs to the altar and look up—worshiping Louis worshiping God. Important religious ceremonies took place here, including the marriage of young Louis XVI to Marie-Antoinette.

• *Take a map flier and enter the next room, a large room with a fireplace and a colorful painting on the ceiling.*

Hercules Drawing Room: Pleasure ruled. The main suppers, balls, and receptions were held in this room. Picture elegant partygoers in fine silks, wigs, rouge, and lipstick (and that's just the men), dancing to the strains of a string quartet.

On the wall opposite the fireplace is an appropriate painting showing Christ in the middle of a Venetian party. The work by Veronese, a gift from the Republic of Venice, was one of Louis' favorites, so they decorated the room around it.

The ceiling painting of Hercules being crowned a god gives the room its name. Hercules (with his club) rides up to heaven on a chariot, where the king of the gods is ready to give him his daughter in marriage. Louis XIV built the room for his own daughter's wedding reception. Except for the ceiling, the room is pure Louis XIV style—pure Baroque. As you wander, the palace feels bare, but remember that entire industries were created to furnish and decorate the palace with carpets, mirrors, furniture, and tapestries.

• *The following rooms are listed in order. The names of the rooms generally come from the paintings on the ceilings. From here on, it's a one-way tour—getting lost is not allowed. Follow the crowds into the small green room with a goddess in pink on the ceiling.*

The King's Wing

Cornucopia Room: If the party in the Hercules Room got too intense, you could always step in here for some refreshments. Silver trays were loaded up with liqueurs, coffee, juice, chocolates, and, on really special occasions, three-bean salad.

The ceiling painting shows the cornucopia of riches poured down on invited guests. Around the edges of the ceiling are painted versions of the king's actual dinnerware and treasures.

Louis himself might be here. He was a gracious host who enjoyed letting his hair down at night. If he took a liking to you, he might sneak you through those doors there (in the middle of the wall) and into his own private study, where he'd show off his collection of dishes, medals, jewels, or . . . the *Mona Lisa*, which hung on his wall.

Venus Room: Love ruled at Versailles. In this room, couples would cavort beneath a canopy of golden garlands (on the ceiling) sent down to earth by the goddess of love to ensnare mortals in love. Notice how a painted garland goes "out" the bottom of the central painting, becomes a gilded wood garland held by a satyr, and then turns back to a painting again. Baroque artists loved to mix their media to fool the eye. Another illusion is in the paintings at both ends of the room, which extend this grand room into mythical courtyards.

Don't let the statue of a confident Louis as a Roman emperor fool you. He started out as a poor little rich kid with a chip on his shoulder. His father died before Louis was old enough to rule, and, during the regency period, the French Parliament treated little Louis and his mother like trash. They were virtual prisoners, humiliated in their home (the Royal Palace in Paris), surviving on bland meals, wearing hand-me-down leotards and pointed shoes. Once Louis attained power and wealth, there was one topic you never discussed in his presence—poverty. Maybe Versailles was his way of saying, "Living well is the best revenge."

Diana Room: This was the billiards room. Men played on a table that stood in the center of the room, while ladies sat surrounding them on Persian-carpet cushions.

The famous bust of Louis by Bernini (now in the center)

shows a handsome, dashing, 27-year-old playboy-king. His gaze is steady amid his windblown cloak and hair. Young Louis loved life. He hunted by day (notice Diana the Huntress on the ceiling) and partied by night.

Games were actually an important part of Louis' political strategy, known as "the domestication of the nobility." By distracting the nobles with the pleasures of courtly life, he was free to run the government his way. Billiards, dancing, and concerts were popular, but the biggest distraction was gambling, usually a card game similar to blackjack. Louis lent money to the losers, making them even more indebted to him. The good life was an addiction, and Louis kept the medicine cabinet well-stocked.

Mars Room: Decorated with a military flair, this was the room for Louis' Swiss bodyguards. On the ceiling, there's Mars, the Greek god of war, in a chariot pulled by wolves. The bronze cupids in the corners are escalating from love arrows to heavier artillery. Notice the fat walls that hid thin servants, who were to be at their master's constant call—but out of sight when not needed. Don't miss the view of the sculpted gardens out the window.

Mercury Room: Louis' life was a work of art, and Versailles was the display case. Everything he did was a public event designed to show his subjects how it should be done. This room served as Louis' official bedroom, where the Sun King would ritually rise each morning to warm his subjects.

From a canopied bed, Louis would rise, dress, and take a seat for morning prayer. Meanwhile, the nobles (on the left) stand behind a balustrade, in awe of his piety, nobility, and clean socks. When Louis went to bed at night, the nobles would fight over who got to hold the candle while he slipped into his royal jammies. Bedtime, wake-up, and meals were all public rituals.

The clock dates from Louis' time. When the cocks crowed at the top of the hour and the temple doors opened, guess who popped out?

Apollo Room: This was the grand throne room. Louis held court from a 3-meter-tall (10 feet) silver-canopied throne on a raised platform placed in the center of the room. (Notice the 6 metal bolts in the ceiling that once supported the canopy.)

Everything in here reminds us that Louis was not just any

ruler, but the Sun King, who lit the whole world with his presence. The ceiling shows Apollo in his chariot, dragging the sun across the heavens every day. Notice the ceiling's beautifully gilded frame and Goldfinger maidens.

In the corners are the four corners of the world—all, of course, warmed by the sun. Counterclockwise from above the exit door are: 1) Europe, with a sword; 2) Asia, with a lion; 3) Africa, with an elephant; and 4) good old America, an Indian maiden with a crocodile.

The famous portrait by Rigaud over the fireplace gives a more human look at Louis. He's shown in a dancer's pose, displaying the legs that made him one of the all-time dancing fools of kingery. At night, they often held parties in this room, actually dancing around the throne.

Louis (who was 63 when this was painted) had more than 300 wigs like this one, and he changed them many times a day. This fashion first started when his hairline began to recede, then sprouted all over Europe, spreading even to the American colonies in the time of George Washington.

Louis may have been treated like a god, but he was not an overly arrogant man. His subjects adored him because he was a symbol of everything a man could be, the fullest expression of the Renaissance Man.

The War Room: Versailles was good propaganda. It showed the rest of the world how rich and powerful Louis was. One look at this eye-saturating view of the gardens sent visitors reeling.

But France's success also made other countries jealous and nervous. The semicircles on the ceiling show Germany (with the double eagle), Holland (with its ships), and Spain (with a red flag and roaring lion) ganging up on Louis. Two guesses who won. Of course, these mere mortals were no match for the Sun King. The stucco relief on the wall shows Louis on horseback, triumphing over his fallen enemies.

But Louis' greatest triumph may be the next room, the one that everybody wrote home about.

The Hall of Mirrors: No one had ever seen anything like this hall when it was opened. Mirrors were still a great luxury at the time, and the number and size of these monsters were astounding. The hall is almost 75 meters/250 feet long. There are 17 arched mirrors matched by 17 windows with that breathtaking view of the gardens. Lining the hall are 24 gilded candelabras, eight busts of Roman emperors, and eight classical-style statues (7 of them ancient). The ceiling decoration chronicles Louis' military accomplishments, topped off by Louis himself in the central panel (with cupids playing cards at his divine feet), doing what he did best—triumphing. Originally, two huge carpets mirrored the action on the ceiling.

This was where the grandest festivities were held for the most important ambassadors and guests. The throne could be moved from the Apollo Room and set up at the far end of the hall. Imagine this place lit by the flames of thousands of candles, filled with guests dressed in silks and powdered wigs. The mirrors are a reflection of an age when beautiful people loved to look at themselves. It was no longer a sin to be proud of good looks or fine clothes, or to enjoy the good things in life: laughing, dancing, eating, drinking, flirting, and enjoying the view.

From the center of the hall, you can fully appreciate the epic scale of Versailles. The huge palace (by architect Le Vau), the fantasy interior (Le Brun), and the endless gardens (Le Nôtre) made Versailles *le* best. In 1871, after the Prussians defeated the French, Bismarck declared the establishment of the German Empire in this room. And in 1918, the Treaty of Versailles was signed, ending World War I (and, some say, starting World War II) here in the Hall of Mirrors.

• *Enter the small Peace Room and grab a bench.*

The Peace Room: "Louis Quatorze was addicted to wars..." but by the end of his life, he was tired of fighting. In this sequel to the War Room, peace is granted to Germany, Holland, and Spain as cupids play with the discarded cannons, armor, and swords.

The oval painting above the fireplace shows 19-year-old Louis XV bestowing an olive branch on Europe. Beside him is his wife, Marie from Poland, cradling their baby twin daughters.

The Peace Room marks the beginning of the queen's

half of the palace. On Sundays, the queen held chamber-music concerts here for family and friends (notice the gilded music motifs).
• *Enter the first room of the Queen's Wing, with its canopied bed.*

The Queen's and Nobles' Wing

The Queen's Bedchamber: This was the queen's official bedroom. It was here that she rendezvoused with her husband. Two queens died here. This is where 19 princes were born. The chandelier is where two of them were conceived. Just kidding.

True, Louis was not the most faithful husband. There was no attempt to hide the fact that the Sun King warmed more than one bed, for he was above the rules of mere mortals. Adultery became acceptable—even fashionable—in court circles. The secret-looking door on the left side of the bed was for Louis' late-night liaisons—it led straight to his rooms.

Some of Louis' mistresses became more famous and powerful than his rather quiet queen, but he was faithful to the show of marriage and had genuine affection for his wife. Their private apartments were connected, and Louis made a point of sleeping with the queen as often as possible, regardless of whose tiara he tickled earlier in the evening.

This room looks like it did in the days of the last queen, Marie-Antoinette. That's her bust over the fireplace, and the double eagle of her native Austria in the corners. The big chest to the left of the bed held her jewels.

The queen's canopied bed is a reconstruction. The bed, chair, and wall coverings switched with the seasons. This was the cheery summer pattern.

Drawing Room of the Nobles: The queen's circle of friends met here, seated on the stools. Discussions ranged from politics to gossip, food to literature, fashion to philosophy. The Versailles kings considered themselves enlightened monarchs who promoted the arts and new ideas. Folks like Voltaire—a political radical—and the playwright Molière participated in the Versailles court. Ironically, these discussions planted the seeds of liberal thought that would grow into the Revolution.

Queen's Antechamber: This is where the royal family dined publicly while servants and nobles fluttered around them, admiring their table manners and laughing at the king's jokes like courtly Paul Shaffers. A typical dinner consisted of four different soups, two whole birds stuffed with truffles, plus mutton, ham slices, fruit, pastries, compotes, and preserves.

The central portrait is of luxury-loving, "Let-them-eat-cake" Marie-Antoinette, who became a symbol of decadence to the peasants. The portrait at the far end is a public-relations attempt to soften her image, showing her with three of her children.

Queen's Guard Room: On October 6, 1789, a mob of revolutionaries—appalled by their queen's taste in wallpaper—stormed the palace. They were fed up with the life of luxury led by the ruling class in the countryside while they were starving in the grimy streets of Paris.

The king and queen locked themselves in. Some of the revolutionaries got access to this upper floor. They burst into this room, where Marie-Antoinette had taken refuge, then overcame her bodyguards and dragged her and her husband off. (Some claim that, as they carried her away, she sang "Louis, Louis, oh-oh... we gotta go now.")

The enraged peasants then proceeded to ransack the place, taking revenge for the years of poverty and oppression they'd suffered. Marie-Antoinette and Louis XVI were later taken to the place de la Concorde in Paris, where they knelt under the guillotine and were made a foot shorter at the top.

Did the king and queen deserve it? Were the revolutionaries destroying civilization or clearing the decks for a new and better one? Was Versailles progress or decadence?

Coronation Room: No sooner did they throw out a king than they got an emperor. The Revolution established democracy, but it was shaky in a country that wasn't used to it. In the midst of the confusion, the upstart general Napoleon Bonaparte took control and soon held dictatorial powers. This room captures the glory of the Napoleon years, when he conquered most of Europe. In the huge canvas on the left-hand wall, we see him crowning himself emperor of a new, revived "Roman" Empire. (While also painted by the master, David, this is a lesser-quality copy of a version hanging in the Louvre.)

Catch the portrait of a dashing, young, charismatic Napoleon (by the window on the right). This shows him in 1796, when he was just a general in command of the Revolution's army in Italy. Compare this with the portrait next to it from 10 years later—looking less like a revolutionary and more like a Louis. Above the young Napoleon is a portrait of Josephine, his wife and France's empress. In David's *Distribution of Eagles* (opposite the *Coronation*), the victorious general (in imperial garb) passes out emblems of victory to his loyal troops. In *The Battle of Aboukir* (opposite the window), Murat—Napoleon's general and brother-in-law—looks bored as he slashes through a tangle of dark-skinned warriors. His horse, though, has a look of "What are we doing in this mob? Let's get out of here!" Let's.

• *Pass through a couple of rooms filled with portraits of Revolutionary and Napoleonic generals to the exit staircase on your left. The long (often closed) Battle Gallery ahead of you shows 120 meters/400 feet of scenes from famous French battles, arranged chronologically clockwise around the gallery. This collection was opened to the public in 1837, when King Louis-Philippe made Versailles a museum. The exit staircase puts you outside on the left (south) side of the palace.*

The Gardens—Controlling Nature

Louis was a divine-right ruler. One way he proved it was by controlling nature like a god. These lavish grounds, elaborately planned out, pruned, and decorated, showed everyone that Louis was in total command.

• *Exiting the palace into the gardens, veer to the left toward the stone railing about 70 meters/ 225 feet away. You'll pass through flowers and cookie-cutter patterns of shrubs and green cones. Stand at the railing overlooking the courtyard below and the Louis-made lake in the distance.*

The Orangerie: The warmth from the Sun King was so great that he could even grow orange trees in chilly France. Louis had a thousand of these to amaze his visitors. In winter, they were kept in the green-houses (beneath your feet) that surround the courtyard. On sunny days, they were wheeled out in their silver planters and scattered around the grounds.

• *From the stone railing, turn about-face and walk back toward the palace, veering left toward the two large pools of water. Sit on the top stair and look away from the palace.*

View down the Royal Drive: This, to me, is the most stunning spot in all of Versailles. In one direction, the palace.

Stretching out in the other, the endless grounds. Versailles was laid out along a 13-kilometer/8-mile axis that included the grounds, the palace, and the town of Versailles itself, one of the first instances of urban planning since Roman times and a model for future capitals such as Washington, D.C., and Brasilia.

Looking down the Royal Drive (also known as "The Green Carpet"), you see the round Apollo fountain way in the distance. Just beyond that is the Grand Canal. The groves on either side of the Royal Drive were planted with trees from all over, laid out in an elaborate grid and dotted with statues and fountains. Of the original 1,500 fountains, 300 remain.

Looking back at the palace, you can see the Hall of Mirrors—it's the middle story, with the arched windows.

• *Stroll down the steps to get a good look at the frogs and lizards that fill the round Latona Basin.*

The Latona Basin: Absolutely everything in the garden has a symbolic meaning. The theme of Versailles is Apollo, the god of the sun, associated with Louis. This round fountain tells the story of the birth of Apollo and his sister, Diana. On top of the fountain are Apollo and Diana as little kids with their mother, Latona (they're facing toward the Apollo fountain). Latona, an unwed mother, was insulted by the local peasants. She called on the king of the gods, Zeus (the children's father), to avenge the insult. Zeus swooped down and turned all the peasants into the frogs and lizards that ring the fountain.

• *As you walk down past the basin toward the Royal Drive, you'll pass by "ancient" statues done by 17th-century French sculptors. The Colonnade is hidden in the woods on the left-hand side of the Royal Drive, about three-fourths of the way to the Apollo Basin.*

The Colonnade: Versailles had no prestigious ancient ruins, so the king built his own. This prefab Roman ruin is a 30-meter/ 100-foot circle of 64 marble columns supporting arches. Beneath the arches are small birdbath fountains. Nobles would picnic in the shade to the tunes of a string quartet, pretending they were the enlightened citizens of the ancient world.

The Apollo Basin: The fountains of Versailles were its most famous attraction, a marvel of both art and engineering. This one was the centerpiece, showing the sun god—Louis—in his sunny chariot, starting his journey across the sky. The horses are half-submerged, giving the impression, when the fountains play, of the sun rising out of the mists of dawn. Most of the fountains were only turned on when the king walked by, but this one played constantly for the benefit of those watching from the palace.

All the fountains are gravity-powered. They work on the same principle as when you block a hose with your finger to make it squirt. Underground streams (pumped into Versailles by Seine River pressure) feed into smaller pipes at the fountains that shoot the water high into the air.

Looking back at the palace from here, realize that the distance you just walked is only a fraction of this vast complex of buildings, gardens, and waterways. Be glad you don't have to mow the lawn.

The Grand Canal: Why visit Venice when you can just build your own? In an era before virtual reality, this was the next best thing to an actual trip. Couples in gondolas would pole along the waters accompanied by barges with orchestras playing "O Sole Mio." The canal is actually cross-shaped, this being the long arm, 1.5 kilometers/1 mile from end to end. Of course, this too is a man-made body of water with no function other than to please. Originally, actual gondoliers, imported with their boats from Venice, lived in a little settlement next to the canal.

The Trianon Area—Retreat from Reality

Versailles began as an escape from the pressures of kingship. In a short time, the palace was as busy as Paris ever was. Louis needed an escape from his escape and built a smaller palace out in the tulies. Later, his successors retreated still farther into the garden, building a fantasy world of simple pleasures from which to ignore the real world, which was crumbling all around them.

• *You can rent a bike or catch the pokey tourist train (4/hr, 4 stops, does not stop at the Hamlet), but the walk is half the fun. It's about a 30-minute walk from here to the end of the tour, plus another 30 minutes to walk back to the palace.*

Grand Trianon: This was the king's private residence away from the main palace. Louis usually spent a couple of nights a week here, but the two later Louis spent more and more time retreating. While the main palace of Versailles was a screen separating French reality from the royal utopia, the Trianon Palaces were engulfed in the royals' fantasy world and therefore favored.

The facade of this one-story building is a charming combination of pink, yellow, and white, a cheery contrast to the imposing Baroque facade of the main palace. Ahead you can see the gardens through the columns. The king's apartments were to the left of the columns.

The flower gardens were changed daily for the king's pleasure—for new color combinations and new "nasal cocktails."

Walk around the palace (to the right), if you'd like, for a view of the gardens and rear facade.

• *Facing the front, do an about-face. The Summer House is not down the driveway but about 180 meters/600 feet away, along the smaller pathway at about 10 o'clock.*

Summer House of the French Garden:
This small white building with four rooms fanning out from the center was

one more step away from the modern world. Here, the queen spent summer evenings with family and a few friends, listening to music or playing parlor games. All avenues of *la douceur de vivre*—"the sweetness of living"—were explored. To the left are the buildings of the Menagerie, where cows, goats, chickens, and ducks were bred.

• *Continue frolicking along the path until you run into the...*

Petit Trianon:
Louis XV developed an interest in botany. He wanted to spend more time near the French Gardens, but the Summer House just wasn't big enough. He built the Petit Trianon (the "small" Trianon), a masterpiece of neoclassical architecture. This gray, cubical building has four distinct facades, each a perfect and harmonious combination of Greek-style columns, windows, and railings. Walk around it and find your favorite.

Louis XVI's wife, Marie-Antoinette, made this her home base. Despite her bad public reputation (see Carnavalet Museum Tour, page 162), Marie-Antoinette was a sweet girl from Vienna who never quite fit in with the fast, sophisticated crowd at Versailles. Here at the Petit Trianon, she could get away and re-create the simple home life she remembered from her childhood. On the lawn outside, she installed a merry-go-round.

• *Five minutes more will bring you to the...*

Temple of Love:
A circle of 12 marble Corinthian columns supporting a dome decorates a path where lovers would stroll. Underneath, there's a statue of Cupid making a bow (to shoot arrows of love) out of the club of Hercules. It's a delightful monument to a society whose rich could afford that ultimate

luxury, romantic love. When the Revolution came, I bet they
wished they'd kept the club.
• *And finally, you'll reach . . .*

The Hamlet (Le Hameau): Marie-Antoinette longed for the
simple life of a peasant. Not the hard labor of real peasants—who

sweated and starved around
her—but the fairy-tale world
of simple country pleasures.
She built this complex of
12 buildings as her own
private village.

This was an actual
working farm with a dairy,
a water mill, and domestic
animals. The harvest was served at Marie's table. Marie didn't do
much work herself, but she "supervised," dressed in a plain white
muslin dress and a straw hat.

The Queen's House is the main building, actually two buildings connected by a wooden gallery. Like any typical peasant farmhouse, it had a billiard room, library, elegant dining hall, and two
living rooms.

Nearby was the small theater. Here, Marie and her friends
acted out plays far from the rude intrusions of the real world . . .
• *The real world and the main palace are a 30-minute walk to the
southeast. Along the way, stop at the Neptune Basin near the palace,
an impressive miniature lake with fountains, and indulge your own
favorite fantasy.*

CHARTRES
TOUR

Many of the children who watched the old church burn to the ground on June 10, 1194, grew up to build Chartres cathedral and attend the dedication Mass in 1260. That's astonishing, considering that other Gothic cathedrals, such as Paris' Notre-Dame, took hundreds of years to build. Having been built so quickly, Chartres is arguably Europe's best example of pure Gothic, with a unity of architecture, statues, and stained glass that captures the spirit of the Age of Faith.

Chartres' pleasing, cobbled old center is overshadowed by its great cathedral. Discover the picnic-friendly park behind the cathedral and wander the quiet alleys and peaceful squares. The helpful TI has a map with a self-guided tour of Chartres. For accommodations, see the end of this chapter.

CHARTRES CATHEDRAL TOUR
Orientation
Cost: Free.

Hours: Daily 7:00–19:00.

Getting There: Chartres is a one-hour train trip from Paris' Gare Montparnasse (about €11.50 one-way, 10/day, last train on Sat departs Chartres about 19:00; figure on a round-trip total of 3 hrs from Paris to cathedral doorstep and back). Upon arrival in Chartres, confirm your return schedule. Leaving the train station and heading uphill, you'll soon see the medieval church rise above the modern city of Chartres.

Bring: Binoculars, if you've got 'em.

Information: The TI is located 100 meters in front of the church (TI hours: Mon–Sat 9:00–19:00, Sun 9:30–17:30, tel. 02 37 18 26 26).

Cathedral Tours by Malcolm Miller: Fine one-hour tours

Chartres

1 Hotel Chatelet
2 Hotel Jehan de Beauce
3 Bistrot de la Cathedrale
4 Le Pichet
5 Access to crypt (through "La Crypt" bookshop)

Mon–Sat at 12:00 and 14:45 cost €10 and are led by either Malcolm Miller or his capable assistant. Tours begin at the gift shop inside the church. Private tours can be arranged (tel. 02 37 28 15 58, fax 02 37 28 33 03).

Length of Our Tour: One hour, but Chartres is an all-day excursion from Paris.

Accommodations and Restaurants: See end of chapter (page 246).

THE CHARTRES GENERATION—THE 1200s

• *Kill train time by reading this.*
From king to bishop and knight to pawn, French society was devoted to the Christian faith. It inspired knights to undertake the formidable Crusades, artists to re-create heaven in statues and stained glass, and architects to build skyscraping cathedrals filled with the mystic light of heaven. They aimed for a golden age, blending faith and reason, though misguided faith often outstripped reason, resulting in very un-Christian intolerance and violence.

Timeline

1194—The old cathedral burns down.

c. 1200—The University of Paris is founded, using human reason to analyze Christian faith. Borrowing from the pagan Greek philosopher Aristotle, scholars described the Christian universe as a series of concentric rings spinning around the Earth in geometrical perfection.

1202—The pope calls on all true Christians to rescue the Holy Land from Muslim "infidels" in the Fourth Crusade (1202–1204). This crusade ends disastrously in the sacking of Constantinople, a Christian city.

1206—Chartres' cornerstone is laid. The style is *opus francigenum* ("French-style work")—which is what the people in Gothic times called Gothic. Chartres is just one of several great cathedrals under construction in Europe.

1207—Francis of Assisi, a rebellious Italian youth, undergoes a conversion to a life of Christian poverty and love. His open spirit inspires many followers, including France's King Louis IX (a generation later).

1209—France's King Phillip Augustus, based in Paris, invades southern France, massacring fellow Christians (the Cathars or Albigensians) as heretics.

1212—Thousands of boys and girls idealistically join the Children's Crusade to save the Holy Land. Most die in transit or are sold into slavery.

1220—The external structure of Chartres cathedral is nearly finished. Work begins on the statues and stained glass.

1226—Eleven-year-old Louis IX is crowned as *rex et sacerdos,* "King and Priest," beginning a 45-year Golden Age combining church and state. His mother, Blanche of Castile (granddaughter of Eleanor of Aquitaine), is his lifelong mentor.

1230—Most of Chartres' stained glass is completed.

1244—At age 30, Louis falls sick and sees a vision in a coma that changes his life. His personal trustworthiness helps unify the nation. He reforms the judicial system along Christian lines, helping the poor.

1245—The last Albigensian heretics are burned at Montsegur, in a crusade ordered by Louis and his mother, Blanche.

1248—Louis personally leads the Seventh Crusade by walking barefoot from Paris to the port of departure. During the fighting, he is captured and ransomed. He later returns home a changed man. Humbled, he adopts the poverty of the Franciscan brotherhood. His devotion earns him the title of Saint Louis.

1260—Chartres cathedral is dedicated. The church is the physical embodiment of the Age of Faith, with architecture as mathematically perfect as God's Creation, sculpture serving as sermons in stone, and stained glass lit by the light of God.

Mary's Church ("Notre-Dame" = "Our Lady" of Chartres)

The church is (at least) the fourth church on this spot dedicated to Mary, the mother of Jesus, who has been venerated here for some 1700 years. There's even speculation that the pagan Romans dedicated a temple to a mother-goddess. In earliest times, Mary was honored next to a natural spring with healing waters (not visible today). In the ninth century, the church acquired Mary's veil (which we'll see) as the focus of devotion. A crude wooden statue of Mary also attracted pilgrims (the statue was destroyed in 1793, but copies remain).

The Book of Chartres

Historian Malcolm Miller calls Chartres a picture book of statues, stained glass, and symbolic architecture, telling the entire Christian story—from Creation to Christ's birth (the north side of the church), from Christ and his followers up to the present (south entrance), to the end of time when Christ returns as judge (west entrance).

The Christian universe is a complex web of heaven and earth, angels and demons, and prophets and martyrs. Much of the medieval symbolism is obscure today. Expect to be overwhelmed by the thousands of things to see, but appreciate the perfect unity of this Gothic masterpiece.

THE TOUR BEGINS

1. The Main Entrance (West Facade), c. 1150:

The two mismatched steeples, three doors, rose window, and various statues are the only survivors of the intense, lead-melting fire that incinerated the rest of the church in 1194. The church of today was rebuilt behind this facade in a single generation (1194–1260).

Towers: The right (south) tower, with a stone steeple, is original Romanesque. The left (north) tower lost its wooden steeple in the 1194 fire. In the 1500s, it was topped by a steeple bigger than the tapered lower half was meant to hold.

The West Doors: Christ, the center of Christian history, sits above the **central door,** surrounded by symbolic animals.

Chartres Cathedral

① Main façade
② Nave
③ Labyrinth
④ View of 3 rose windows
⑤ Blue Virgin window

NORTH
⑬
PORCH

SOUTH
⑫
PORCH

⑥ Choir screen sculptures
⑦ Mary's veil
⑧ Charlemagne window
⑨ Our Lady of Pillar Chapel
⑩ Noah window
⑪ Flying buttresses
⑫ South porch
⑬ North porch

BOOK-SHOP

20 YARDS
20 METERS

WEST ↑ FAÇADE
① MAIN ENTRANCE

DCH

The anorexic statues between the doors are pillars of the faith that foretold the coming of Christ. With solemn gestures and faces, they patiently endure the wait.

History's pivotal event is shown above the **right door,** where Mary (seated) produces baby Jesus from her loins. This Mary-and-baby sculpture is a 12th-century stone version of an older wooden statue (burned 1793). Centuries of pilgrims have visited Chartres to see

Mary's statue, gaze at her veil (which we'll see), and ponder the mystery of how God in Heaven became Man on Earth, passing through immaculate Mary like sunlight through stained glass.

• *Enter the church and wait for your pupils to enlarge.*

2. Nave: The church has a long, tall central nave, flanked by raised side aisles for crowd flow, so pilgrims could circle the church without disturbing worshipers. The 12 pillars lining the nave support pointed crisscrossed arches on the ceiling, which

lace together the heavy stone vaulting. The pillars are supported
by flying buttresses on the outside of the church (which we'll see
later). This skeleton structure was the miracle of Gothic, allowing
tall buildings with ribbed walls and lots of stained-glass windows
(like the big saints in the upper stories of the nave). The floor of
the nave slopes in to the center, for easy drainage when hosing
down dirty pilgrims who camped here.

3. The Labyrinth: The round maze inlaid in black stone on
the floor of the nave is a spiritual journey. Pilgrims enter from the
west rim by foot or on knees and wind inward, meditating. And
300 meters/980 feet later, they hope to meet God in the middle.
(Current world record for reaching enlightenment is 3:42.)
• *Walk up the nave to where the transept crosses. As you face the altar,
north is to the left.*

4. The Rose Windows—North, South, and West:
The three big, round "rose" (floral-shaped) windows over the
entrances open like flowers to receive sunlight at different times
of day. All three are predominantly blue and red, but each has
different "petals," and each tells a different part of the Christian
story in a kaleidoscope of fragmented images.

Having trouble making out the tiny, distant details? As we've
all read, stained glass was a way to teach Bible stories to the illiter-
ate medieval masses... who apparently owned state-of-the-art
binoculars. Yes, the windows tell stories, but obviously, their main
purpose was to light a dark church in a colorful and decorative way.

The **north rose window** charts history from the distant past
up to the birth of Jesus. On the outer rim, murky, ancient (barely
visible) prophets foretell Christ's coming. Then (circling inward),
there's a ring of red squares with kings who are Christ's direct
ancestors. Still closer, a circle of white doves and winged angels
zero in on the central event of history—Mary, the heart of the
flower, with her newborn baby, Jesus.

This window was donated by King Louis IX (who built
Paris' Sainte-Chapelle) and his mom, Blanche of Castile. See
their coats of arms just below the rose—Louis' yellow fleur-
de-lis on a blue background and Blanche's yellow castles on
a red background.

In the **south rose window,** the Old Testament prophecies
are fulfilled. Christ sits in the center (dressed in blue, with a red
background), setting in motion the radiating rings of angels, beasts,
and apocalyptic elders who labor to bring history to its close. The
five lancet windows below show Old Testament prophets lifting
New Testament writers on their shoulders (in first window on left,

"Stained Glass Supreme"

- Melt one part sand with two parts wood ash to make glass.
- Mix in rusty metals to get different colors—iron makes red, cobalt makes blue, copper green, manganese purple, cadmium yellow.
- Blow glass into a cylinder shape, cut lengthwise, and lay flat.
- Cut into pieces with an iron tool, or by heating and cooling a select spot to make it crack.
- Fit pieces together to form a figure, using strips of lead to hold in place.
- Place masterpiece so high on a wall that no one can read it.

see white-robed Luke riding piggyback on dark-robed Jeremiah), demonstrating how the ancients prepared the way for Christ. A dark Christ rings in history's final Day of Judgment at the center of the **west rose window.** Around him, winged angels blow their trumpets and the dead rise, are judged, and are sent to hell or raised to eternal bliss. The frilly edge of this glorious "rose" is flecked with tiny, clover-shaped dewdrops.

God = Light

You can try to examine the details, but a better way to experience the mystery of Chartres is to just sit and stare at these enormous panels, as they float in the dark of empty space like holograms or space stations or the Queen of Heaven's crown jewels. Ponder the medieval concept that God is light.

To the Chartres generation, the church was a metaphor for how God brings his creation to life, like the way light animates stained glass. They were heavy into mysticism, feeling a oneness with all creation in a moment of enlightenment. The Gospel of John (as well as a writer known to historians as the Pseudo-Dionysius) was their favorite. Here are select verses from John 1:1–12 (loosely translated):

In the beginning was The Word.
He [Jesus] was the light of the human race.
The light shines in the darkness, and the darkness
     cannot resist it.
It was the real light coming into the world, the light
     that enlightens everyone.
He was in the world, but the world did not recognize Him.
     But to those who did,
He gave the power to become the children of God.

5. The Blue Virgin Window: Mary, dressed in blue on a rich red background, cradles purple Jesus, while the dove of the Holy Spirit descends on her. This is some of the oldest stained glass (1150), a survivor of the 1194 fire, which was reinserted into this new window frame around 1230. The Blue Virgin was one of the most popular stops for pilgrims—especially pregnant ones—of the cult of the Virgin-about-to-give-birth. Devotees prayed, carried stones to repair the church, or donated to the church coffers—Mary rewarded them with peace of mind, easy births, and occasional miracles.

Below Mary, see **Christ being tempted** by a red-faced, horned, smirking devil.

Hail, maiden, what's your sign? Pick up chicks at the **Zodiac Window** (second window to the left). The 12 signs are in the right half of the window; read from the bottom up—Pisces, Aries, Gemini (in the cloverleaf), Taurus, Cockroach, Leo, Virgo, etc.

6. The Choir Screen—Life of Mary: In the center of the church sits the stone **choir** (the enclosed area behind the altar where church officials sat), ringed with **41 statue groups** illustrating Mary's life (by various sculptors, 1520–1714). Although the Bible says little about the mother of Jesus, legend and lore fleshed out her life.

Scene #1 (south side) shows an angel telling her dad that Mary's on the way. In #4, Anne gives birth to Mary. In #6, Mary marries Joseph. In #10, she gives birth to Jesus in a manger. In #12, the Three Kings arrive. Scenes #15–27 show her famous son's life. In #28, Jesus is crucified. In #34, the resurrected Jesus appears to his mother. In #38, Mary dies . . . in #39, she's raised by angels into heaven . . . and in #41, she's crowned Queen of Heaven by the Father, Son, and the Holy Ghost.

The **plain windows** surrounding the choir date from the 1770s, when the dark mystery of medieval stained glass was replaced by the open light of the French Enlightenment. The plain windows and the choir are some of the only "new" features. Most of the 1200s church has remained, despite style changes, Revolutionary vandals, and war bombs.

7. Mary's Veil: Sitting in a glass case with a gold frame held by angels, this is the torn, 2,000-year-old **veil** supposedly worn by Mary when she gave birth to Jesus. Since the ninth century, this has been the main object of adoration for the cult of the Virgin, and stories abound of its magical powers.

In A.D. 911, with the city surrounded by Vikings, the bishop hoisted the veil like a battle flag and waved it at the invaders.

It scared the bejesus out them with visions of extended labor, and the town was saved.

When the fire of 1194 incinerated the old church, the veil was feared lost. Lo and behold, several days later they found it miraculously unharmed in the crypt (beneath today's choir). The people were so stoked, they worked like madmen to erect this grand cathedral to display it in.

8. Charlemagne Window: The window tells the story of how the veil ended up here. **Charlemagne** (bottom left semicircle), the great king of the Franks (A.D. 768–814) and first Holy Roman Emperor (800–814), sits on his throne between two advisers and plans a great adventure—a crusade to the Holy City of Jerusalem. Next (the semicircle just above), he attacks the Muslim infidels occupying Jerusalem. Charlemagne (heart-shaped shield) stabs a Saracen (round shield) in the neck, driving the Muslims out of the city.

On the way home, Charlemagne stops in the great Christian city of Constantinople (in the diamond directly to the right), where he's welcomed at the gate by the emperor. The emperor rewards him (semicircle directly to the right) with three chests of holy relics . . . including Mary's veil. Charlemagne returns home (the circle above the diamond) to his palace in Aix-la-Chappelle, kneels, and places the relics before the altar. Charlemagne's grandson, Charles the Bald, gave the veil to Chartres in 876.

The fashion-conscious will notice the clothes are from the 1220s, when the window was made.

9. Chapel of Our Lady on the Pillar: A 16th-century **statue of Mary and baby**—draped in cloth, crowned and sceptered—sits on a column in a wonderful carved-wood alcove. This is today's pilgrimage center, built to keep visitors from clogging up the altar area. Modern pilgrims honor the Virgin by leaving flowers, lighting candles, and kissing the column.

10. The Noah Window: Read Chartres' windows from left to right and bottom to top.

Bottom-left is a man making a wheel. He's one of the donors of this window. His colleagues to the right are from the axe- and barrel-maker guilds.

Then comes the story of **Noah** (read from the bottom up): God tells Noah he'll destroy the earth (#1, bottom diamond). Noah hefts an axe to build an ark, while his son hauls wood (diamond #2). He loads horses (cloverleaf, above left), purple elephants (cloverleaf, above right), and other animals. The psychedelic ark sets sail (diamond #3). Waves cover the earth, drowning the wicked (two cloverleaves). The ark survives (diamond #4) and Noah releases a dove. Finally, up near the top (diamond #7), a rainbow arches overhead, God drapes himself over it, and Noah and his family give thanks.

• *Exit the church (through the main entrance or the door in the south transept) to view its south side.*

11. South Exterior—Flying Buttresses: Six flying

buttresses on the south side (the arches that stick out from the upper walls) push against six pillars lining the nave inside, helping to hold up the heavy stone ceiling and sloped, lead-over-wood roof. The ceiling and roof push down onto the pillars, of course, but also outward (north and south) because of the miracle of Gothic, the pointed arch. These flying buttresses push back, channeling the stress outward to the six vertical buttresses, then down to the ground. The result is a tall cathedral held up by slender pillars buttressed from the outside, allowing the walls to be opened up for stained glass.

The church is built from large blocks of limestone. Peasants trod in hamster-wheel contraptions to raise these blocks into place—a testament to their great faith.

12. South Porch: The three doorways of the south

entrance show the world from Christ to the present, as Christianity triumphs over persecution.

Center Door—Christ and Apostles: Jesus stands between the double doors, holding a book and raising his arm in blessing. He's a simple, itinerant, bareheaded, barefoot rabbi, but underneath his feet he tramples symbols of evil, the dragon and lion (which is which?). Christ's face is among the most noble of all Gothic sculpture.

Christ is surrounded by his **apostles,** who spread the good news to a hostile world. **Peter** (to the left as you face Jesus), with curly hair and beard, holds the key to the kingdom of heaven and the slender cross on which he was crucified upside down. **Paul** (to the right of Jesus) fingers the sword of his martyrdom, contemplating the inevitable loss of his head and the hair upon it. In fact, all of the apostles were killed or persecuted, and their faces are humble, with sad eyes. But their message prevailed, and under their feet they crush the squirming emperors who once persecuted them.

The final triumph comes above the door in the **Last Judgment.** Christ sits in judgment, raising his hands, while Mary and John beg him to take it easy on poor humankind. Beneath Christ, the souls are judged—the righteous on our left, the wicked on the right, who are thrown into the fiery jaws of hell. Farther to the right (above the statues of Paul and the apostles), horny demons subject wicked women to an eternity of sexual harassment.

Left Door—Martyrs: Eight martyrs flank the left door. **St. Lawrence** (second from left) cradles the grill on which he was barbecued alive. His last brave words to the Romans actually were: "You can turn me over—I'm done on this side." **St. George** (far right) wears the knightly uniform of the 1200s, when Chartres was built and King Louis IX was crusading. Depicted beneath the martyrs are gruesome **methods of torture** (e.g., George stretched on the wheel), many of which were used in the 1200s against heretics, Muslims, Jews, and Albigensians (the Cathar sect of Southern France).

Right Door—Confessors: Among these eight pillars of the faith, find **Jerome** (third from the right), holding the Bible he translated into everyday Latin; and **Gregory** (second from the right), the pope who organized church hierarchy and wrote Gregorian chants.

• *Reach the north side by circling around the back end of the church (great views) or cutting through the church.*

13. The North Porch: In the Book of Chartres, the north porch is chapter one, from the Creation up to the coming of Christ.

Center Door: Baby Mary (headless), in the arms of **her mother Anne** (the statue between the double doors), marks the culmination of the Old Testament world.

History begins in the tiny details in the concentric arches over the doorway. **God creates Adam** (at the peak of the outer arch) by cradling his head in his lap like a child.

Melchizedek (farthest to the left of Mary and Anne), with cap and cup, is the Biblical model of the *rex et sacerdos* (king-priest), the title bestowed on King Louis IX.

Abraham (second from left) holds his son by the throat and raises a knife to slit him for sacrifice. Just then, he hears something and turns his head up to see God's angel, who stops the bloodshed. The drama of this frozen moment anticipates Renaissance naturalism by 200 years.

John the Baptist (fourth to the right from Mary/Anne), the last Old Testament prophet who prepared the way for Jesus, holds a lamb, the symbol of Christ. John is skinny from his diet of locusts and honey. His body twists and flickers like a flame.

All these **prophets,** with their beards turning down the corners of their mouths, have the sad, wise look of having been around since the beginning of time, and having seen it all—from Creation to Christ to Apocalypse. They are some of the last work done on the church, completing the church's stone-and-glass sermon.

Imagine all this painted and covered with gold leaf in preparation for the dedication ceremonies in 1260, when the Chartres generation could finally stand back and watch as their great-grandchildren, carrying candles, entered the cathedral.

The Rest of the Church

Malcolm Miller's tours and books: This fascinating English scholar illuminates a new detail of the church with each tour (see "Orientation," above). His tours are worthwhile even if you've taken this self-guided tour. For a detailed look at Chartres' windows, sculpture, and history, pick up Malcolm Miller's two guidebooks (sold at the church bookstore).

The crypt: The foundations can be visited only as part of a guided tour in French. You'll see remnants of the earlier churches, a modern copy of the old wooden Mary-and-baby statue, and hints of the old well and Roman wall (30-min tours start in La Crypte bookstore, located outside church near south porch).

Climb the north tower: Three hundred steps lead to a great view (€4, students-€2.50, children free, Mon–Sat 9:00–18:00 in summer, Sun 13:00–18:00, entrance inside church near bookstore).

Sleeping and Eating in Chartres
(€1 = about $1, country code: 33, zip code: 28000)

See page 258 for an explanation of the sleep code.

Chartres, a good getaway from Paris, can also be a first or last overnight stop for those flying to/from Orly airport. These hotels face each other (200 meters straight out of train station, 300 meters below cathedral): **Hôtel Chatelet***** is comfortable, from its welcoming lobby to its spotless, spacious, well-furnished rooms (Sb-€65–75, Db-€72–83, extra person-€10, streetside rooms are cheaper, CC, 6 avenue Jehan de Beauce, tel. 02 37 21 78 00, fax 02 37 36 23 01, e-mail: hchatel@club-internet.fr). **Hôtel Jehan de Beauce**** is basic, clean, and quiet, with some tiny bathrooms (S-€31, D-€40, Ds-€43, Db-€54, Tb-€62, CC, 19 avenue Jehan de Beauce, tel. 02 37 21 01 41, fax 02 37 21 59 10).

Eating: Le Pichet, near the TI, is reasonable, friendly, and homey (19 rue du Cheval Blanc, tel. 02 37 21 08 35). **Le Bistrot de la Cathédrale** is good for salads and basic bistro fare (on south side of cathedral at 1 cloître Notre-Dame, tel. 02 37 36 59 60). **Trois Lys** makes cheap crêpes just across the river on Pont Boujou (3 rue de la Porte Guillaume, tel. 02 37 28 42 02).

MORE DAY TRIPS

Grand Châteaux near Paris • Impressionist Excursions: Giverny and Auvers-sur-Oise • Disneyland Paris

GRAND CHÂTEAUX NEAR PARIS

The region around Paris (the Ile de France) is dotted with sumptuous palaces. Paris' booming upper class made this the heartland of European château-building in the 16th and 17th centuries. Most of these châteaux were lavish hunting lodges—getaways from the big city. The only things they defended were noble and royal egos.

Consider four very different châteaux:

▲▲▲**Versailles**—for its history, grandeur, and accessibility (closed Mon)

▲▲▲**Vaux-le-Vicomte**—for sheer beauty and intimacy (open daily)

▲▲**Fontainebleau**—for its history, fine interior, and pleasant city (closed Tue)

▲**Chantilly**—for its beautiful setting and fine collection of paintings (closed Tue except in summer)

If you only have time for one château, choose between Vaux-le-Vicomte and Versailles (see tour on page 215). Except for Versailles, these châteaux are quiet on weekdays. Versailles, Fontainebleau, and Chantilly are covered by the Paris museum pass.

Vaux-le-Vicomte

While Versailles is most travelers' first choice for its sheer historic weight, Vaux-le-Vicomte (pron. voh luh vee-komt) offers a more intimate interior and a better sense of 17th-century château life. Sitting in a huge forest, with magnificent gardens and no urban sprawl in sight, Vaux-le-Vicomte gave me just a twinge of palace envy.

Day Trips from Paris

Vaux-le-Vicomte was the architectural inspiration of Versailles and set the standard for European châteaux to come. The proud owner, Nicolas Fouquet (Louis XIV's finance minister), threw a château-warming party. Louis was so jealous that he arrested his host, took his architect (Le Vau), artist (Le Brun), and landscaper (Le Nôtre), and proceeded with the construction of the bigger and costlier (but not necessarily more splendid) palace of Versailles. Monsieur Fouquet's party and his later arrest feature prominently in the third Musketeer book by Alexandre Dumas, and at least two versions of *The Man in the Iron Mask* were filmed here.

Vaux-le-Vicomte is more expensive to get to (because of cab fare) but a joy to tour. Most rooms have English explanations. For more information, rent a €2.50 audioguide (with a pro-Fouquet perspective) or get a souvenir booklet at the gift shop. Outside the gift shop is a reasonable café (limited menu, daily

11:30–18:00 and, during candlelit visits, until midnight).

Start your tour with the fine
exhibit of carriages *(équipages)* in
the old stables. Wax figures and
an evocative soundtrack get you
in the proper mood. Next, stroll
like a wide-eyed peasant across
the stone bridge (any fish down
there?) and up the front steps
into the château. Turn around to admire the symmetry and elegance
of the stables; horses lived well here.

As you wander through Fouquet's dream home, you'll understand Louis' jealousy. Versailles was a rather simple hunting lodge
when this was built. The furniture in Vaux-le-Vicomte is not original—Louis confiscated the real thing for Versailles. You'll see
cozy bedrooms upstairs and grand living rooms downstairs (billiards room, library, card room, and dining room; feel free to
fast-forward the 90-min audioguide tour). The kitchen and wine
cellar are in the basement. Climb the cupola for a great view (€2).

Survey the garden from the back steps of the palace. This
was the landscaper Le Nôtre's first claim to fame. This garden was
the cutting edge of sculpted French gardens. He integrated ponds,
shrubbery, and trees in a style that would be copied in palaces all
over Europe. Take the 30-minute walk (one-way) to the Hercules
viewpoint atop the grassy hill way in the distance. Rentable golf
carts (Club Cars, €15/45 min, €125 deposit) make the trip easier,
and the funky Nautilles (pedal boats in the shape of water animals,
€10 for 30 min) are fun for kids. Picnics are not allowed.

Cost and Hours: €10 for gardens, château, and carriage
museum, not covered by museum pass. Open March–early Nov
daily 10:00–18:00, closed in winter, tel. 01 64 14 41 90. The
impressive fountains run 15:00–18:00 the second and last Sat of
each month (April–Oct).

Candlelit Visits: Two thousand candles and piped-in classical music illuminate the palace on Sat and holiday nights (open
20:00–24:00) May–October; call to ask about any upcoming holidays. These *visites aux chandelles* are worth the €13 entry, but remember, it doesn't get really dark until 22:00 in late May, June, and
early July, and the last train to Paris leaves Melun at about 22:00.

Getting to Vaux-le-Vicomte: To reach Vaux-le-Vicomte
by a train-and-taxi combination, you can take the RER-D train
to Melun from Paris' Gare du Nord or Chatelet stations. Much
faster SNCF *banlieue* trains to Melun leave from Paris' Gare de
Lyon (about €7.50 one-way, hourly, 35 min). From Melun's

station, taxis make the 10-minute drive to Vaux-le-Vicomte (€15 weekdays, €18 eves and Sun, taxi tel. 01 64 52 51 50, other numbers posted above taxi stand). Ask a staff person at the château to call a cab for your return or schedule a pick-up time with your driver. In either direction, split the fare with other travelers.

By car from Paris, take the A-6 autoroute toward Lyon, then follow signs to Melun. In Melun, follow signs to Meaux (N-36), then Vaux-le-Vicomte.

Adding Fontainebleau: Vaux-le-Vicomte and Fontainebleau can be combined into a full, though manageable, day trip by car, taxi, or train from Paris (except on Tue, when Fontainebleau is closed). Fontainebleau is 12 minutes by train from Melun (allow €30 by taxi).

Sleeping near Vaux-le-Vicomte: The modern and ugly, but handy and cheap, **Ibis Hôtel** is between Melun and the château, just off N-105 (Db-€49, CC, less on weekends, tel. 01 60 68 42 45, fax 01 64 09 62 00). The bypassed town of Melun has more appealing hotels in its handsome old center. Also consider sleeping in nearby Fontainebleau (see below).

Château of Fontainebleau

Fontainebleau's history rivals that of Versailles. Many French kings have called this glamorous hunting lodge home. Napoleon welcomed the pope here during his coronation celebration, and it was here that he abdicated his rule when exiled to Elba in 1814. General Patton set up headquarters at this château on his way to Berlin.

While Vaux-le-Vicomte and Versailles are French-designed, Fontainebleau was built a century earlier by an Italian. The palace you see today was largely financed by Renaissance King François I. Inspired by his travels through Renaissance Italy, he hired Italian artists to build his palace.

Orient with a quick visit to the château information room and its huge model of the château (first door on your right in the grand courtyard). The palace entry is next door. Your ticket provides access to the Chinese rooms and the main rooms of the château. Napoleon buffs will enjoy the little museum of Napoleonic history, which

requires an additional ticket and a guided tour in French (€2.75, mornings only). The €3 guidebooks give excellent room-by-room descriptions, though basic English explanations are posted throughout.

Start downstairs with the small but impressive

Chinese collection of Napoleon III's empress, then climb to
the main rooms of the palace. Highlights include the stunning
Renaissance hall of François I, the opulent dance hall with piped-
in music *(salle de bal)*, Napoleon's throne room, and Diana's
Gallery (library). The gardens, designed a century later by the
landscaper Le Nôtre, are worth a stroll. Rent a rowboat for the
étang des carpes (carp pond), or walk its path for a good view of
the château complex.

Cost and Hours: €5.50, covered by museum pass, Wed–
Mon 9:30–18:00, closed Tue, last entry 45 minutes before closing.

Getting to Fontainebleau: Catch a train from Paris' Gare
de Lyon in the direction of Montereau (about €8.50 one-way,
40 min) to the Fontainebleau-Avon station, where a bus goes to
the château (Cars Verts, about €1.50, 4/hr; schedules posted in
English). Taxis to the château cost about €6; to nearby Vaux-le-
Vicomte costs about €30 (taxi tel. 01 64 22 00 06).

Town of Fontainebleau: Turn right out of the château
courtyard and keep right to reach the town center, where cafés
and restaurants abound. The helpful **TI** is two blocks up from
the château behind Hôtel Londres and has hiking maps, bike
rental, and hotel listings (Mon–Sat 10:00–18:30, Sun 10:00–
16:00, tel. 01 60 74 99 99).

Sleeping and Eating in Fontainebleau: The **Hôtel Lon-
dres***** offers a helpful staff and very pleasant rooms, many with
point-blank views of the château (small Db-€106, larger Db with
château view-€135–140, CC, 1 place du Général de Gaulle, tel.
01 64 22 20 21, fax 01 60 72 39 16, www.hotellondres.com).
Turn right out of the château entrance and keep right for about
five blocks to reach **Hôtel Legris et Parc*****, a quiet, dreamy
getaway with a pleasant garden, pool, and a country-classy restaurant (small Db-€56, bigger Db-€78–94, suites-€135, CC,
36 rue Paul Seramy, tel. 01 64 22 24 24, fax 01 64 22 22 05,
e-mail: legrisetparc@easynet.fr). To eat well, try one of these
central places: **Croquembouche** *(menus* from €20, closed Wed
and Sun, 43 rue de France, tel. 01 64 22 01 57) or **Chez Arrighi**
(menus from €23, closed Mon, 53 rue de France, 01 64 22 29 43).

Château of Chantilly

Chantilly (pron. shahn-tee-yee), 35 minutes north of Paris, floats
serenely on a reflecting pond amid grand gardens. Unfortunately,
the château interior is disappointing. Its best rooms can be seen
only on a boring French-language guided tour, and the fine works
of art in the picture galleries are poorly displayed. Still, Chantilly
can be a pleasant experience if approached in the right way. Allow
most of a day for Chantilly.

This extravagant hunting palace was destroyed during the Revolution. Today's château was largely rebuilt during the 19th century. It's divided into two parts: the painting gallery, with paintings by Raphael, Titian, Poussin, Delacroix, and others; and the private apartments, which require a French-language tour. The highlight of the otherwise dull apartments is the first stop: the prince's library, lined with more than 13,000 books and beautiful copies of pages from *Les Très Riches Heures du Duc du Berry*, a much-admired 15th-century illuminated manuscript.

The gardens immediately behind the château are formal and austere. With your back to the château, follow the signs to the right to *le Hameau*. This little hamlet, with an enchanting garden café, was the prototype for the more famous *hameau* at Versailles. Just beyond is a small kiosk offering boat trips along the canals (tel. 03 44 57 35 35).

Cost and Hours: €6, €3 for gardens only, covered by museum pass, March–Oct Wed–Mon 10:00–18:00, closed Tue; July–Aug also open Tue 10:00–18:00; Nov–Feb Wed–Fri and Mon 10:30–12:45 & 14:00–17:00, Sat–Sun 10:00–18:00, closed Tue; tel. 03 44 62 62 62.

Live Horse Stables (Les Ecuries Vivant): The Prince de Condé believed he'd be reincarnated as a horse, so he built this opulent horse château for his next go-round. You'd have to have similar beliefs to pay the €8 entry for this horse museum (although it's impressive and thorough). The museum features 40 live horses in their stables, and a daily demonstration, generally at 15:30, more often during summer weekends (April–Oct Wed–Mon 10:30–17:30; May–June also open Tue 10:30–17:30; July–Aug also open Tue 14:00–17:30; Nov–March Mon and Wed–Fri 14:00–18:00, Sat–Sun 10:30–17:30, closed Tue, tel. 03 44 57 13 13).

Getting to Chantilly: Leave from Paris' Gare du Nord for Chantilly-Gouvieux. While the RER serves Chantilly, service is faster on the main lines at Grandes Lignes level. Ask any information desk for the next departure (about €7 one-way, nearly hourly, 35 min). Upon arrival in Chantilly, confirm return times (fewer trips on weekends). To get to the château, catch a rare bus (buses marked "Senlis" meet some trains); walk 30 minutes (follow signs, stay on path, turn right before BP gas station, cross grass field, "château" in distance is stables, real château is beyond that); or take a taxi (allow €6, tel. 06 05 45 37 55).

IMPRESSIONIST EXCURSIONS: GIVERNY AND AUVERS-SUR-OISE

Giverny

From 1883 to 1926, Monet spent 43 of his most creative years at Giverny (pron. zhee-vayr-nee), the Camp David of Impressionism. Monet's gardens and home are, unfortunately, split by a busy road and very popular with tourists. Buy your ticket, walk through the gardens, and take the underpass into the artist's famous lily-pad land. The path leads over the Japanese bridge, under weeping willows, and past countless scenes that leave artists aching for an easel. For Monet fans, it's strangely nostalgic. Back on the other side, continue your visit with a wander through his more robust and structured garden and his mildly interesting home. The jammed gift shop at the exit is the actual skylit studio where Monet painted his water-lily masterpieces. While lines may be long and tour groups may trample the flowers, true fans still find magic in those lily pads. Minimize crowds by arriving before 10:00 (get in line) or after 16:00 (€5.50, €4 for gardens only, April–Oct Tue–Sun 10:00–18:00, closed Mon and Nov–March, tel. 02 32 51 94 65).

Getting to Giverny: Take the Rouen-bound train from Paris' Gare St. Lazare station to Vernon (about €22 round-trip, long gaps in service, know schedule before you go). From the Vernon train station to Monet's garden (4 km/2.5 miles one-way), you have three good options: bus, taxi, and bike. The Vernon-Giverny **bus** is scheduled to meet most trains (4/day, make sure the driver knows you plan to return by bus and on which trip, otherwise he may not make the last Giverny pickup). If you miss the last bus, find others to share a **taxi** (about €11 for up to 3, €12 for 4, tel. 06 07 34 36 68, 06 76 08 50 78, or 02 32 21 31 31). The ticket office at Monet's home in Giverny has bus schedules and can call a taxi if you don't see one waiting by the bus stop (see taxi phone numbers above). The bus stop is on the main road from Vernon, just below Monet's home. You can also rent a **bike** at the bar opposite the train station (€12, tel. 02 32 21 16 01), and follow a paved bike path *(piste cyclable)* that runs along an abandoned railroad right-of-way (the bike path begins across the river from Vernon in Veronnet).

Big tour companies do a Giverny day trip from Paris for around €65. Ask at your hotel.

The **Musée de l'Art Américain** (American Art Museum, turn left when leaving Monet's place and walk 100 meters) is devoted to American artists who followed Claude to Giverny. Giverny had a great influence on American artists of Monet's day. This bright, modern gallery—with a good little Mary Cassatt section—is well-explained in English (same price and hours as Monet's home), though its most appealing feature might be its garden café.

Sleeping and Eating in Giverny: The adorable **Hôtel La Musardiere****, two blocks to the right out of Monet's home, makes an ideal Paris escape or stopover on your way farther into Normandy (Db-€50–66, Tb-€65–75, CC, 132 rue Claude Monet, 27620 Giverny, tel. 02 32 21 03 18, fax 02 32 21 60 00). You'll find a café and sandwich stand near the entrance to Monet's home, but the garden café at the overlooked American Impressionist Museum is better—peaceful and surrounded by gardens Monet would appreciate (€9 salads, picnics possible at the far end).

Auvers-sur-Oise

There's no better place to appreciate life during the Impressionist era than here on the banks of the Oise River, about a 45-minute drive (or 1-hr train ride) northwest of Paris. Auvers-sur-Oise (pron. oh-vay soor wahz) is most famous as the village where Vincent van Gogh committed suicide, though many other artists enjoyed this peaceful rural retreat, including Daubigny, Corot, Pissarro, and Cézanne. Today, this little town offers a handful of interesting sights, posted walking trails leading to scenes painted by the artists, and a tranquil break from the big city. Most sights are closed Mondays and Tuesdays, and from November to Easter (call the TI to confirm which sights are open, a few are open only after lunch).

Stop by the **TI,** which has good information on all village sights and a €0.50 map of Auvers showing the walking routes, with famous art scenes posted. The TI (daily 9:30–12:30 & 14:00–18:00, tel. 01 30 36 10 06) is housed with Musée Daubigny in Manoir des Colombières (below).

The most worthwhile sight in Auvers is **Château d'Auvers.** The entire château has been brilliantly transformed into a re-creation of life during the Impressionist years. Elaborate multi-media displays use headphones, video screens, and lasers to guide you along the Impressionist route that led from Montmartre to the sea, giving you a keen appreciation of life's daily struggles and pleasures during this time (€10, April–Sept Tue–Sun 10:30–18:00, closed Mon; Oct–March Tue–Sun 10:30–16:30, closed Mon; tel. 01 34 48 48 48). The **Musée Daubigny** houses a small but pleasing collection of works from artists who came to work with Monsieur Daubigny, an ardent defender of the Impressionists (€3, Wed–Sun 14:00–18:00, closed Mon–Tue, next to TI in Manoir des Colombières). You can visit **Daubigny's studio** for its serene setting and the murals inside (€4.50, Thu–Sun 14:00–18:30, closed Mon–Wed and Nov–Easter, 61 rue

Daubigny). The little café **Museum of Absinthe** is interesting only for aficionados (€4.50, includes a mini–guided tour, open June–Sept Wed–Sun 11:00–18:00, closed Mon–Tue, Oct–May Sat–Sun only 11:00–18:00, 44 rue Callé).

Van Gogh fans seek out the **Auberge Ravoux** to see the room where Vincent died after shooting himself (€5, daily 10:00–18:00; food connoisseurs skip the room and have a tasty lunch in the *auberge*'s perfectly preserved restaurant, on place de la Mairie). To continue a van Gogh pilgrimage, visit the **Church at Auvers** (see painting at Orsay Museum), above the train station. Vincent and his brother Theo are buried at the cemetery located up rue Bernard from the church. Beginning in 2003, van Goghphiles can visit the home of Vincent's physician, Dr. Gachet (get details at TI).

Sleeping and Eating in Auvers (zip code: 95430): Auvers is a handy first or last stop for drivers using Charles de Gaulle airport. If you want to begin or end your trip with style, sleep luxuriously at the small, friendly, and polished **Hostellerie du Nord*****, with modern, spacious rooms and a seriously good restaurant requiring reservations (Db-€93–124, suites-€185, CC, menus €48-59, a block from train station at 6 rue du Général de Gaulle, tel. 01 30 36 70 74, fax 01 30 36 72 75, www.hostelleriedunord.fr). **Gites aux Ecuries** is a nine-room *chambre d'hôte* at a horse stable run by friendly Dominique (Sb, Db, or Tb-€39, no CC, on river side of main road below TI at 5 bis rue de la Bourgogne, tel. 01 30 36 81 44 or 06 84 81 67 52, fax 01 30 36 87 43). The place to eat in Auvers is **Auberge Ravoux,** unchanged since 1876, when painters would meet here over a good meal (closed Sun eve and all day Mon, below TI on place de la Mairie, tel. 01 30 36 60 60).

Getting to Auvers: Take the *banlieue* **train** from Paris' Gare du Nord to Pontoise (2/hr, 40 min, departs from tracks 30–36), then transfer to Auvers-sur-Oise (2/hr, 10 min; allow 1 hr for entire trip one-way). Turn left on the main road leaving Auvers' station to reach the TI.

By **car,** Auvers is about 45 minutes northwest of Paris, off autoroute A-15 (exit #7, then follow direction: Beauvais).

DISNEYLAND PARIS

Europe's Disneyland is a remake of California's, with most of the same rides and smiles. The main difference is that Mickey Mouse speaks French (and you can buy wine with your lunch). My kids went ducky. It's easy to get to and worth a day if Paris is handier than Florida or California. Saturday, Sunday, Wednesday, public holidays, and July and August are most crowded. After dinner, crowds are gone. Food is fun and not outrageously priced. (Still, many smuggle in a picnic.) The free FASTPASS system is a

worthwhile timesaver (get FASTPASS card at entry, good for
5 most popular rides, at ride insert card in machine to get a window of time to enter—often within about 45 min). You'll also save
time by buying your tickets ahead (at airport TIs, over 100 Métro
stations, or along the Champs-Elysées at the TI, Disney Store, or
Virgin Megastore). Disney brochures are in every Paris hotel. For
Disneyland information and reservations, contact call 01 60 30 60
30 (www.disneylandparis.com).

Walt Disney Studios: The new zone, opened in 2002 next
to the original 10-year-old amusement park, has the same hours,
contact information, and admission prices (but you must pay separately to enjoy both parks; see below). Its Hollywood focus aims
at an older crowd with animation, special effects, and movie magic
"rides." The Aerosmith Rock 'n' Roller Coaster is nothing special.
The highlight is the Stunt Show Spectacular, filling a huge back-
lot stadium five times a day for 45 minutes of car chases and thriller
filming tips. An actual movie sequence is filmed with stunt drivers,
audience bit players, and brash MTV-style hosts.

Cost: Disneyland Paris and Walt Disney Studios each charge
the same and you pay separately. Only the three-day passes (called
"Hopper" tickets) include entry to both parks. From March 31
through Nov 5, adults pay €38 for one day (€72 for 2 days, €99
for 3-day "Hopper" ticket) and kids ages 3–11 pay €29 for one
day (€56 for 2 days, €80 for 3-day "Hopper" ticket). Regular
prices are about 25 percent less off-season. Kids under 3 are always
free. On summer evenings (17:00–23:00) at the Disneyland Park
only, everyone pays €19. The only budget deal (and, I think, the
only way the Walt Disney Studios are worth visiting) is to pay for
a full-price Walt Disney Studios ticket, which gets you into the
Disneyland Park for free during the last three hours of that day.

Hours: Open April–June daily 9:00–20:00, July–Aug
daily 9:00–23:00, Sept–March Mon–Fri 10:00–20:00, Sat–
Sun 9:00–20:00.

Sleeping at Disneyland: Most are better off sleeping in reality (Paris), though with direct buses and freeways to both airports,
Disneyland makes a convenient first- or last-night stop. Seven different Disney-owned hotels offer accommodations at or near the
park in all price ranges. The cheapest is **Davy Crockett,** but you'll
need a car. **Hôtel Sante Fe**** offers the best value, with shuttle service to the park every 12 minutes (Db-€214 includes breakfast and
2-day park pass, CC). The most expensive is **Disneyland Hotel******,
right at the park entry (Db-€427 for the same deal, CC). To reserve any Disneyland hotel, call 01 60 30 60 30, fax 01 60 30 60 65,
or check www.disneylandparis.com. The prices you'll be quoted
include entry to the park.

Transportation Connections—Disneyland Paris

By train: TGV trains connect Disneyland directly with **Charles de Gaulle airport** (10 min), the **Loire Valley** (1.5 hrs, Tours-St. Pierre des Corps station, 15 min from Amboise), **Avignon** (3 hrs, TGV station), **Lyon** (2 hrs, Part Dieu station), and **Nice** (6 hrs, main station).

By RER: The slick one-hour RER trip is the best way to Disneyland from downtown Paris. Take RER line A-4 to Marne-la-Vallée-Chessy (from Etoile, Auber-Opéra, Chatelet, or Gare de Lyon stations, about €7.50 each way, hourly, drops you 1 hour later right in the park). The last train back to Paris leaves shortly after midnight. Be sure to get a ticket that is good on both the RER and Métro; returning, remember to use your RER ticket for your Métro connection in Paris.

By bus: Both airports have direct shuttle buses to Disneyland Paris (€13, daily 8:30–19:45, every 45 min).

By car: Disneyland is about 40 minutes east of Paris on the A-4 autoroute (direction Nancy/Metz, exit #14). Parking is €7 per day at the park.

SLEEPING

I've focused on three safe, handy, and colorful neighborhoods: stately rue Cler, artsy and trendy Marais, and Left Bank Contrescarpe. For each, I list good hotels, helpful hints, and restaurants (see Eating chapter, page 282). Before reserving, read the descriptions of the three neighborhoods closely. Each offers different pros and cons, and your neighborhood is as important as your hotel for the success of your trip. Less expensive and less central accommodations are also listed below for Versailles and in various chapters: Chartres, Day Trips (Fontainebleau, Giverny, Auvers-sur-Oise, and Disneyland Paris), and Shopping (place du Bercy).

Reserve ahead for Paris—the sooner the better. Conventions clog Paris in September (worst), October, May, and June (very tough). In August, when Paris is quiet, some hotels offer lower rates. But August is also a time when paying extra for a place with air-conditioning can be money well spent. Most hotels accept telephone reservations, require a credit-card number and may charge one night's deposit, and prefer a faxed follow-up to be sure everything is in order. For more information, see "Making Reservations," below.

A comfortable hotel in Paris costs less than a comparable hotel in London, Amsterdam, Rome, or in most major U.S. cities. It's a good hotel city. Still, reserve as far as possible in advance for the best values. I like places that are clean, small, central, traditional, friendly, and a good value. Most places I list have at least four of these six virtues.

In this book, the price for a double room will normally range from €40 (very simple, toilet and shower down the hall) to €250 (grand lobbies, maximum plumbing, and more), with most clustering around €80–100.

If you have any trouble finding a room using my listings,

try www.parishotel.com and www.hotelboulevard.com. You can select from various neighborhood areas (e.g., Eiffel Tower area), give the dates of your visit and preferred price range, and presto—they'll list options with rates. You'll find the hotels listed in this book to be better located and more objectively reviewed, though as a last resort, the Web site services are handy.

Hotels

The French have a simple hotel rating system depending on amenities (zero through four stars, indicated in this book by * through ****). One star is simple, two has most of the comforts, and three is generally a two-star with a minibar and fancier lobby. Four stars offer more luxury than you have time to appreciate. One- and two-star hotels are the best budget values, though some three-star hotels (and even a few 4-star hotels) can justify the extra cost. Lately, the star system is less reliable. Unclassified hotels (no stars) can be bargains or depressing dumps. Look before you leap and lay before you pay (upon departure). Hotels in France must charge a daily tax *(taxe du séjour)* that is normally added to the bill. It varies from €0.50 to €1 per day per person depending on the hotel's number of stars. While some hotels include it in the price list, most add it to your bill.

Old, characteristic, budget Parisian hotels have always been cramped. Retrofitted with toilets, private showers, and elevators (as most are today), they are even more cramped. Recommended hotels have an elevator unless otherwise noted.

Most hotels have a few singles, triples, and quads. While groups sleep cheap, traveling alone can be expensive. Singles (except for the rare closet-type rooms that fit only 1 twin bed) are simply doubles used by one person—so they cost about the same as a double. Because rooms with double beds and showers are cheaper than rooms with twin beds and baths, room prices vary within each hotel. A triple and a double are often the same room, with a small double bed and a sliver single, so a third person sleeps very cheaply. Quad rooms usually have two double beds. Hotels cannot legally allow more in the room than what's shown on their price list.

Receptionists often don't mention the cheaper rooms (they assume you want a private bathroom). Study the price list on the Web site or posted at the desk. Understand it. You can save as much as €20–25 by finding the increasingly rare room without a private shower or toilet *(une chambre sans douche* or *sans WC).* You'll save less (about €15) on a room with a toilet but no shower *(une chambre avec cabinet de toilette).* Some hotels charge for down-the-hall showers. A room with a bathtub *(salle de bain)* costs €5–10 more than a room with a shower *(douche)* and is generally larger.

Hotels often have more rooms with tubs than showers and are inclined to give you a room with a tub (which the French prefer).

A double bed *(grand lit)* is €5–10 cheaper than twins *(deux petits lits)*, though rooms with twin beds tend to be larger and French double beds are generally smaller than American double beds. Hotels rarely offer queen-size beds *(un lit de 160, meaning a bed that's 160 centimeters wide—most doubles are 140)*. To see if a hotel has queen-size beds, ask, *"Avez-vous un lit de cent-soixante?,"* (pron. ah-vay-voo uh lee duh sahn-swah-sahnt). Some hotels push two twins together under king-size sheets and blankets.

If you prefer a double bed (instead of twins) and a shower (instead of a tub), you need to ask for it—and you'll save up to €30. If you're willing to take either twins or a double, ask generically for a *chambre pour deux* (room for two) to avoid being needlessly turned away.

You'll almost always have the option of breakfast at your hotel, which is pleasant and convenient—but, at €5–10, it's more than the price of breakfast at the corner café with less ambience (though you get more coffee at your hotel). Some hotels offer only the classic continental breakfast for about €5–7, but others offer buffet breakfasts for about €8–10 (cereal, yogurt, fruit, cheese, croissants, juice, and hard-boiled eggs)—which I usually spring for. While hotels hope you'll buy their breakfast, it's optional unless otherwise noted.

Rooms are safe. Still, keep cameras and money out of sight. Towels aren't routinely replaced every day; drip-dry and conserve. If that French Lincoln-log pillow isn't your idea of comfort, American-style pillows (and extra blankets) are sometimes in the closet or available on request. To get a pillow, ask for *"Un oreiller, s'il vous plaît"* (pron. un oh-ray-yay, see voo play). If you're planning to visit Paris in the summer, the extra expense of an air-conditioned room can be money well spent. (When using the air-conditioner, remember that 20 degrees Celsius = 68 degrees Fahrenheit).

Two- and three-star hotels are required to have an English-speaking staff. Nearly all hotels listed below have someone who speaks English.

Many hotels offer reasonable Internet access.

Get advice from your hotel for safe parking (consider long-term parking at Orly Airport and a taxi in). Meters are free in August. Garages are plentiful (€14–23/day, with special rates through some hotels, see page 336).

Self-serve launderettes are common; ask your hotelier for the nearest one (*Où est un laverie automatique?*; pron. ooh ay uh lah-vay-ree oh-to-mah-teek).

Hostels

Parisian hostels charge about €25 per bed. Some require a hostel membership. Get a hostel card before you go if you need one. Travelers of any age are welcome if they don't mind dorm-style accommodations and meeting other travelers. Travelers without a hostel card can generally spend the night for a small, extra "one-night membership" fee at those places requiring membership. Cheap meals are sometimes available, and kitchen facilities are usually provided for do-it-yourselfers.

Apartments

It's easy, though not necessarily cheaper, to rent a furnished apartment in Paris. Consider this option if you're either traveling with a family or staying two weeks or longer. For listings, see the end of this chapter.

Country Code and Exchange Rate

To phone France, you'll need to know its country code: 33. To call France from the United States or Canada, dial 011 - 33 - local number (without the initial 0). If calling France from another European country, dial 00 - 33 - local number (without the initial 0).

The exchange rate: €1 = about $1.

Making Reservations

Reserve ahead for Paris, the sooner the better. May, June, September, and October are busiest. If you're not sure how long you'll stay, guess long. You can always cancel the last days once there (48 hours advance notice is generally required), but it's very hard to add days at the last minute.

To reserve from home, call, fax, e-mail, or write the hotel. E-mail is preferred (see the reservation form online at www .ricksteves.com/reservation). Phone and fax costs are reasonable. To fax, use the form in the appendix. If you're writing, add the zip code and confirm the need and method for a deposit. Most hotels listed are accustomed to English-only speakers.

A two-night stay in August would be "2 nights, 16/8/03 to 18/8/03"—Europeans write the date day/month/year, and European hotel jargon uses your day of departure.

If you send a reservation request and receive a response with rates stating that rooms are available, this is not a confirmation. You must confirm that the rates are fine and that indeed you want the room. One night's deposit is generally required. A credit card will usually be accepted as a deposit, though you may need to send a signed traveler's check or a bank draft in the local currency. Don't give your credit-card number as a deposit unless you're

Sleep Code

To help you sort easily through these listings, I've divided the rooms into three categories, based on the price for a standard double room with bath:

Higher Priced—Most rooms more than €140.
Moderately Priced—Most rooms €100–140.
Lower Priced—Most rooms €100 or less.

To give maximum information in a minimum of space, I use these codes to describe accommodations listed in this book. Prices listed are per room, not per person.

S = Single room (or price for one person in a double).

D = Double or Twin. French double beds can be very small.

T = Triple (generally a double bed with a single).

Q = Quad (usually two double beds).

b = Private bathroom with toilet and shower or tub.

s = Private shower or tub only. (The toilet is down the hall.)

CC = Accepts credit cards (Visa and MasterCard, rarely American Express).

no CC = Does not accept credit cards; pay in local cash.

* = French hotel rating system, ranging from zero to four stars.

According to this code, a couple staying at a "Db-€90, CC" hotel would pay a total of 90 euros (or about $90) for a double room with a private bathroom. The hotel accepts credit cards or cash in payment.

absolutely sure you want to stay at the hotel on the dates you requested and are clear that they have a room available. If you don't show up, you'll be billed for one night, and if you cancel in advance, you may not receive your entire deposit back.

Reconfirm your reservation a few days in advance for safety. Be sure to honor (or cancel by phone) your reservation.

Rue Cler Orientation

Rue Cler is a safe, tidy, village-like pedestrian street. It's so French that when I step out of my hotel in the morning, I feel like I must have been a poodle in a previous life. How such coziness lodged itself between the high-powered government district and the wealthy Eiffel Tower and Invalides areas, I'll never know. This is a neighborhood of wide, tree-lined boulevards, stately apartment buildings, and lots of Americans. The American Church, American library, American University, and many of my readers call this area home.

Become a local at a rue Cler café for breakfast or join the afternoon crowd for *une bière pression* (a draft beer). On rue Cler, you can eat and browse your way through a street full of tart shops, delis, cheeseries, and colorful outdoor produce stalls. Afternoon *boules* (lawn bowling) on the esplanade des Invalides is a relaxing spectator sport (look for the dirt area to the upper right as you face the Invalides), and the manicured gardens behind the golden dome of Invalides are free, peaceful, and filled with flowers (close at about 19:00).

For an after-dinner cruise on the Seine, it's a 15-minute walk to the river and the Bâteaux-Mouches (see page 26). For a post-dinner cruise on foot, saunter into Champ de Mars park to admire the glowing Eiffel Tower (see also the Nightlife and Paris with Children chapters). Cross the Champ de Mars park to mix it up with bargain-hunters at the twice-weekly open market, **Marché boulevard de Grenelle,** under the Métro a few blocks southwest of Champ de Mars park (Wed and Sun until 12:30, between Mo: Dupleix and Mo: La Motte Picquet-Grenelle).

Your neighborhood **TI** is at the Eiffel Tower (May–Sept daily 11:00–18:42, no kidding, tel. 01 45 51 22 15). There's a **post office** at the end of rue Cler on avenue de la Motte Piquet, and a handy **SNCF office** at 78 rue St. Dominique (Mon–Fri 9:00–19:00, Sat 10:00–12:20 & 14:00–18:00, closed Sun). Rue St. Dominique is the area's boutique-browsing street. The Epicerie de la Tour **grocery** is open until midnight (197 rue de Grenelle). **Cyber World Café** is at 20 rue de l'Exposition (open daily, tel. 01 53 59 96 54).

The **American Church and College** is the community center for Americans living in Paris and should be one of your first stops if you're planning to stay awhile (reception open Mon–Sat 9:00–22:00, Sun 9:00–19:30, 65 quai d'Orsay, tel. 01 40 62 05 00). Pick up copies of the *Paris Voice* for a monthly review of Paris entertainment, and *France-U.S.A. Contacts* for information on housing and employment through the community of 30,000 Americans living in Paris. The interdenominational service at 11:00 on Sunday, the coffee hour after church, and the free Sunday concerts (18:00, not every week, Sept–May only) are a great way to make some friends and get a taste of émigré life in Paris.

Key **Métro** stops are Ecole Militaire, La Tour Maubourg, and Invalides. The **RER-C** line runs along the river, serving Versailles to the west and the Orsay Museum, Latin Quarter

Rue Cler Hotels

T TAXIS
1 Hotel Relais Bosquet
2 Hotel Beaugency
3 Hotel Leveque
4 Hotel du Champ de Mars
5 Hotel la Motte Piquet
6 Hotel le Tourville
7 Hotel Splendid
8 Hotel de la Bourdonnais
9 Hotel Londres Eiffel
10 Mars Hotel
11 Hotel de la Tulipe
12 Hotel de l'Alma

13 Hotel de Turenne
14 Hotel de la Paix
15 Hotel Kensington
16 Hotel Les Jardins Eiffel & Hotel Amelie
17 Hotel de l'Empereur
18 Hotel Muguet
19 Hotel Cadran
20 Hotel de la Tour Eiffel
21 Hotel Prince
22 Hotel le Pavillon
23 Hotel Royal Phare
24 Hotel la Serre

25 SNCF office
26 Bus #69 to Orsay, Louvre & Marais
27 Bus #92 to Arc de Triomphe
28 Bus #87 to Lux. Gardens
29 Bus #28 to Gare St. Lazare

(St. Michel stop), and Austerlitz train station to the east (in rue Cler area, use Pont de l'Alma or Invalides RER stops). Smart travelers take advantage of these helpful **bus routes:** Line #69 runs along rue St. Dominique and serves Les Invalides, Orsay, Louvre, Marais, and Père-Lachaise cemetery. Line #63 runs along the river (the Quai d'Orsay), serving the Latin Quarter along boulevard St. Germain to the east, and the Trocadéro and the Musée Marmottan to the west. Line #92 runs along avenue Bosquet north to the Champs-Elysées and Arc de Triomphe and south to the Montparnasse Tower. Line #87 runs on avenue de la Bourdonnais and serves St. Sulpice, the Luxembourg Garden, and the Sèvres-Babylone shopping area. Line #28 runs on boulevard La Tour Maubourg and serves the St. Lazare station.

Sleeping in the Rue Cler Neighborhood
(7th arrondissement, Mo: Ecole Militaire, zip code: 75007)
Rue Cler is the glue that holds this pleasant neighborhood together. From here you can walk to the Eiffel Tower, Napoleon's Tomb, the Seine, and the Orsay and Rodin Museums. Hotels here are relatively spacious and a great value, considering the elegance of the neighborhood and the high prices of the more cramped hotels of the trendy Marais.

Many of my readers stay in this neighborhood. If you want to disappear into Paris, choose a hotel away from the rue Cler, or in the other neighborhoods I list. And if nightlife matters, sleep elsewhere. The first five hotels listed below are within Camembert-smelling distance of rue Cler; the others are within a 5- to 10-minute stroll.

Sleeping in the Heart of Rue Cler

HIGHER PRICED
Hôtel Relais Bosquet*** is modern, spacious, and a bit upscale, with snazzy, air-conditioned rooms, electric darkness blinds, and big beds. Gerard and his staff are politely formal and friendly (Sb-€125–146, standard Db-€140, spacious Db-€160, extra bed-€30, CC, parking-€14, 19 rue du Champ de Mars, tel. 01 47 05 25 45, fax 01 45 55 08 24, www.relaisbosquet.com).

MODERATELY PRICED
Hôtel Beaugency***, on a quieter street a short block off rue Cler, has 30 small but comfortable rooms, a lobby you can stretch out in, and friendly Chantal in charge. When I have tour groups in Paris, this is my first choice for their home base (Sb-€104,

Db-€111, Tb-€127, CC, buffet breakfast, 21 rue Duvivier, tel. 01 47 05 01 63, fax 01 45 51 04 96, www.hotel-beaugency.com).

LOWER PRICED
Warning: The first two hotels listed here—while the best value— are overrun with my readers (reserve long in advance ... or avoid).

Hôtel Leveque** is ideally located, with a helpful staff (Pascale and Christophe SE), a singing maid, and a Starship *Enterprise* elevator. It's a classic old hotel with well-designed rooms that have all the comforts (S–€53, Db-€84–91, Tb-€114 for 2 adults and 1 child only, breakfast-€7, first breakfast free for readers of this book, CC, air-con, 29 rue Cler, tel. 01 47 05 49 15, fax 01 45 50 49 36, www.hotel-leveque.com, e-mail: info@hotelleveque.com).

Hôtel du Champ de Mars**, with charming pastel rooms and helpful English-speaking owners Françoise and Stephane, is a homier rue Cler option. This plush little hotel has a Provence-style, small-town feel from top to bottom. Rooms are small, but comfortable and a good value. Single rooms can work as tiny doubles (Sb-€66, Db-€72–76, Tb-€92, CC, 30 meters off rue Cler at 7 rue du Champ de Mars, tel. 01 45 51 52 30, fax 01 45 51 64 36, www.hotel-du-champ-de-mars.com, e-mail: stg@club-internet.fr).

Hôtel la Motte Piquet**, at the end of rue Cler, is reasonable and spotless, and comes with a cheery welcome from Daniele. Most of its 18 cozy rooms face a busy street, but the twins are on the quieter rue Cler (Ss-€57, Sb-€60–64, Db-€73–81, CC, 30 avenue de la Motte Piquet, tel. 01 47 05 09 57, fax 01 47 05 74 36).

Sleeping near Rue Cler
The following listings are a 5- to 10-minute walk from rue Cler.

HIGHER PRICED
Hôtel le Tourville**** is the most classy and expensive of my rue Cler listings. This four-star place is surprisingly intimate and friendly, from its designer lobby and vaulted breakfast area to its pretty but small pastel rooms (small standard Db-€145, superior Db-€215, Db with private terrace-€240, junior suite for 3–4 people-€310, extra bed-€17, CC, air-con, 16 avenue de Tourville, Mo: Ecole Militaire, tel. 01 47 05 62 62, fax 01 47 05 43 90, e-mail: hotel@tourville.com).

Hôtel Splendid*** is Art Deco modern, friendly, and worth your while if you land one of its suites with great Eiffel Tower views (Db-€124–146, Db suite-€205-220, CC, 29 avenue Tourville, tel. 01 45 51 24 77, fax 01 44 18 94 60, e-mail: splendid@club-internet.fr).

Hôtel de la Bourdonnais*** is a *très* Parisian place, mixing slightly faded Old World elegance with professional service and mostly spacious rooms (their smaller rooms can be cramped, confirm that room is not small, Sb-€120, Db-€150, Tb-€160, Qb-€180, 5-person suite-€210, CC, air-con, 111 avenue de la Bourdonnais, tel. 01 47 05 45 42, fax 01 45 55 75 54, www .hotellabourdonnais.fr).

MODERATELY PRICED

Hôtel Londres Eiffel*** is my closest listing to the Eiffel Tower and Champ de Mars park. It offers immaculate, warmly decorated rooms, cozy public spaces, and Internet access. The helpful staff take good care of their guests (Sb-€93–102, Db-€105–115, Tb-€137, extra bed-€17, CC, use handy bus #69 or the RER Alma stop, 1 rue Augerau, tel. 01 45 51 63 02, fax 01 47 05 28 96, www.londres-eiffel.com).

Eber-Mars Hôtel**, with helpful owner Jean-Marc, is a good midrange value with larger-than-average rooms and a beam-me-up-Jacques, coffin-sized elevator (small Db-€75, large Db-€90-110, Tb-€130, extra bed-€20, CC, 117 avenue de la Bourdonnais, tel. 01 47 05 42 30, fax 01 47 05 45 91).

Hôtel de la Tulipe*** is a unique place two blocks from rue Cler toward the river, with a seductive wood-beamed lounge and a peaceful, leafy courtyard. Its artistically decorated rooms (each one different) come with small, stylish bathrooms (Db-€105-135, Tb-€160, CC, no elevator, 33 rue Malar, tel. 01 45 51 67 21, fax 01 47 53 96 37, www.hoteldelatulipe.com).

Hôtel de l'Alma*** is well-located on "restaurant row," with good rooms (but small bathrooms) and reasonable rates (Db-€100-115, CC, 32 rue de l'Exposition, tel. 01 47 05 45 70, fax 01 45 51 84 47, e-mail: almahotel@minitel.net, Carine SE).

LOWER PRICED

Hôtel de Turenne**, with sufficiently comfortable, air-conditioned rooms, is a good value when it's hot. It also has five truly single rooms (Sb-€61, Db-€71–81, Tb-€96, extra bed-€9.50, CC, 20 avenue de Tourville, tel. 01 47 05 99 92, fax 01 45 56 06 04, e-mail: hotel.turenne.paris7@wanadoo.fr).

Hôtel de la Paix **, a smart hotel located away from the fray on a quiet little street, offers 23 plush, well-designed rooms and a good value (Sb-€61, Db-€80, big Db-€91, Tb-€11, CC, fine buffet breakfast, Internet access, 19 rue du Gros-Caillou, tel. 01 45 51 86 17, fax 01 45 55 93 28, e-mail: hotel.de.la.paix@wanadoo.fr).

Hôtel Kensington** is impersonal and has teeny rooms, but is a fair value (Sb-€53, Db-€67–82, CC, 79 avenue de la

Bourdonnais, tel. 01 47 05 74 00, fax 01 47 05 25 81, www
.hotel-kensington.com).

Sleeping near Métro: La Tour Maubourg

The next three listings are within two blocks of the intersection of
avenue de la Motte Piquet and boulevard de la Tour Maubourg.

HIGHER PRICED

Hôtel les Jardins Eiffel*** feels like a modern motel, but earns its
three stars with professional service, a spacious lobby, an outdoor
patio, and 80 comfortable, air-conditioned rooms—some with private
balconies (ask for a room *avec petit balcon*). Even better: Readers of
this book get free buffet breakfasts (Db-€130–€160, extra bed-€21
or free for a child, CC, parking-€17/day, 8 rue Amélie, tel. 01 47 05
46 21, fax 01 45 55 28 08, e-mail: eiffel@unimedia.fr, Marie SE).

LOWER PRICED

Hôtel de l'Empereur** lacks personality but is roomy and a fine
value. Its 38 pleasant, woody rooms come with sturdy furniture
and all the comforts except air-conditioning. Streetside rooms
have views but some noise; fifth-floor rooms have small balconies and Napoleonic views (Sb-€70–75, Db-€75–85, Tb-€105,
Qb-€120, CC, 2 rue Chevert, tel. 01 45 55 88 02, fax 01 45 51
88 54, www.hotelempereur.com, Petra SE).

   Hôtel Muguet**, a peaceful and clean hotel, gives you
three-star comfort for a two-star price. The remarkably spacious
hotel offers 48 sharp, air-conditioned rooms and a small garden
courtyard. The hands-on owner, Catherine, gives her guests
a peaceful and secure home in Paris (Sb-€85, Db-€95–103,
Tb-€130, CC, 11 rue Chevert, tel. 01 47 05 05 93, fax 01 45
50 25 37, www.hotelmuguet.com).

Lesser Values

Given this fine area, these are acceptable last choices.

HIGHER PRICED

Hôtel du Cadran***, while perfectly located, has a shiny lobby
but no charm and tight, narrow, overpriced rooms (Db-€148–
165, CC, 10 rue du Champ de Mars, air-con, tel. 01 40 62 67 00,
fax 01 40 62 67 13, www.hotelducadran.com).

LOWER PRICED

Hôtel de la Tour Eiffel** is a modest little place with fairly
priced rooms but cheap furnishings and foam mattresses (Sb-€65,
Db-€80, Tb-€100, CC, 17 rue de l'Exposition, tel. 01 47 05 14 75,

fax 01 47 53 99 46, Muriel SE). **Hôtel Prince****, just across avenue Bosquet from the Ecole Militaire Métro stop, has good-enough rooms, many overlooking a busy street (Sb-€70, Db-€82-105, CC, 66 avenue Bosquet, tel. 01 47 05 40 90, fax 01 47 53 06 62, www.hotel-paris-prince.com). **Hôtel le Pavillon**** is quiet, with basic rooms, no elevator, and cramped halls in a charming location (Sb-€72, Db-€80, Tb, Qb, or Quint/b-€105, CC, 54 rue St. Dominique, tel. 01 45 51 42 87, fax 01 45 51 32 79, e-mail: patrickpavillon@aol.com). **Hôtel Royal Phare**** is very simple (Db-€61-74, CC, facing Ecole Militaire Métro stop, 40 avenue de la Motte Piquet, tel. 01 47 05 57 30, fax 01 45 51 64 41, www .hotel-royalphare-paris.com). **Hôtel Amélie**** is another possibility (Db-€95, CC, 5 rue Amélie, tel. 01 45 51 74 75, fax 01 45 56 93 55). The basic **Hôtel la Serre*** has a good location on rue Cler but generates readers' complaints for its rude staff and bizarre hotel practices—you can't see a room in advance or get a refund (Db-€90, CC, 24 rue Cler, across from Hôtel Leveque, Mo: Ecole Militaire, tel. 01 47 05 52 33, fax 01 40 62 95 66).

Marais Orientation

Those interested in a more Soho/Greenwich Village locale should make the Marais their Parisian home. Only 15 years ago, it was a forgotten Parisian backwater, but now the Marais is one of Paris' most popular residential, tourist, and shopping areas. This is jumbled, medieval Paris at its finest, where elegant stone mansions sit alongside trendy bars, antique shops, and fashion-conscious boutiques. The streets are a fascinating parade of artists, students, tourists, immigrants, and babies in strollers munching baguettes— and the Marais is also known as a hub of the Parisian gay and lesbian scene. This area is *sans* doubt livelier (and louder) than the rue Cler area.

In the Marais, you have these sights at your fingertips: Picasso Museum, Carnavalet Museum, Victor Hugo's house, Jewish Art and History Museum, and the Pompidou Center. You're also a manageable walk from Paris' two islands (Ile St. Louis and Ile de la Cité), where you'll find Notre-Dame and the Sainte-Chapelle. The Opéra de la Bastille, Promenade Plantée park, place des Vosges (Paris' oldest square), Jewish Quarter (rue des Rosiers), and nightlife-packed rue de Lappe are also nearby. (For sight descriptions, see "Northeast Paris," page 52; for the Opéra, see page 40.) Two good open markets lie nearby: the sprawling Marché de la Bastille on place de la Bastille (Thu and Sun until 12:30) and the more intimate Marché de la place d'Aligre (daily 9:00–12:00, a few blocks behind Opéra on place d'Aligre).

The nearest **TIs** are in the Louvre (Wed–Mon 10:00–19:00,

closed Tue) and the Gare de Lyon (daily 8:00–20:00, tel. 08 92 68 31 12, wait for English recording). Most banks and other services are on the main drag, rue de Rivoli/rue St. Antoine. For your Parisian Sears, find the **BHV** next to the Hôtel de Ville. Marais **post offices** are on rue Castex and on the corner of rue Pavée and rue des Francs Bourgeois.

Métro service to the Marais neighborhood is excellent, with direct service to the Louvre, Champs-Elysées, Arc de Triomphe, and four major train stations: Gare de Lyon, Gare du Nord, Gare de l'Est and Gare d'Austerlitz. Key Métro stops in the Marais are, from east to west: Bastille, St. Paul, and Hotel de Ville (Sully Morland, Pont Marie, and Rambuteau stops are also handy). There are also several helpful **bus routes:** Line #69 on rue St. Antoine takes you to the Louvre, Orsay, Rodin, and Napoleon's Tomb and ends at the Eiffel Tower. Line #86 runs down boulevard Henri IV, crossing Ile St. Louis and serving the Latin Quarter along boulevard St. Germain. Line #96 runs on rues Turenne and François Miron and serves the Louvre and boulevard St. Germain (near Luxembourg Garden), ending at the Gare Montparnasse. Line #65 serves the Gare d'Austerlitz, Gare de l'Est, and Gare du Nord train stations from place de la Bastille.

You'll find **taxi stands** on place de la Bastille, on the north side of rue St. Antoine (where it meets rue Castex), and on the south side of rue St. Antoine (in front of St. Paul church).

Sleeping in the Marais Neighborhood
(4th arrondissement, Mo: St. Paul or Bastille, zip code: 75004)
The Marais runs from the Pompidou Center to the Bastille (a 15-min walk), with most hotels located a few blocks north of the main east–west drag, the rue de Rivoli/rue St. Antoine (one street with two names). It's about 15 minutes on foot from any hotel in this area to Notre-Dame, Ile St. Louis, and the Latin Quarter. Strolling home (day or night) from Notre-Dame along the Ile St. Louis is marvelous.

MODERATELY PRICED
Hôtel Castex***, on a quiet street near the place de la Bastille, is completely renovating and upgrading to three stars in early 2003, with the addition of an elevator, air-conditioning, and brand-spanking-new rooms (estimated new prices: Sb-€100, Db-€120, Tb-€140, CC, closed until March, just off place de la Bastille and rue St. Antoine, 5 rue Castex, Mo: Bastille, tel. 01 42 72 31 52, fax 01 42 72 57 91, www.castexhotel.com, e-mail: info@castexhotel.com).

Marais Hotels

1 Hotel Castex
2 Hotel Bastille Speria
3 Hotel de la Place des Vosges
4 Hotel des Chevaliers
5 Hotel St. Louis Marais
6 Grand Hotel Jeanne d'Arc
7 Hotel Lyon-Mulhouse
8 Hotel Sevigne
9 Hotel Pointe Rivoli
10 Hotel de 7eme Art
11 Hotel de la Republique
12 MIJE hostels
13 Hotel Axial & Hotel Sansonnet
14 Hotel de la Bretonnerie
15 Hotel Caron de Beaumarchais
16 Hotel de Vieux Marais
17 Hotel Beaubourg
18 Hotel de Nice
19 Grand Hotel du Loiret
20 Hotel Jeu de Paume
21 Hotels Des Deux Iles & Lutece
22 BHV Department store
23 Bus #69 to Louvre, Orsay & Eiffel Tower
24 Bus #s 86 & 87 to Latin Quarter

T TAXI STANDS   P PARKING

Hôtel Bastille Speria***, a short block off the place de la Bastille, offers business-type service. The 42 plain but cheery rooms have air-conditioning, thin walls, and curiously cheap and sweaty foam mattresses. It's English-language-friendly, from the *Herald Tribune*s in the lobby to the history of the Bastille posted in the elevator (Sb-€95, Db-€112–120, child's bed-€20, CC, 1 rue de la Bastille, Mo: Bastille, tel. 01 42 72 04 01, fax 01 42 72 56 38, www.hotel-bastille-speria.com).

Hôtel de la Place des Vosges** is so well-located—in a medieval building on a quiet street just off place des Vosges—that the staff can take or leave your business. Still, its customers leave happy (Sb-€84, Db-€120, CC, 16 rooms, 1 flight of stairs then elevator, 12 rue de Biraque, Mo: St. Paul, tel. 01 42 72 60 46, fax 01 42 72 02 64, e-mail: hotel.place.des .vosges@gofornet.com).

Hôtel des Chevaliers***, a little boutique hotel one block northwest of place des Vosges, offers small, pleasant rooms with modern comforts. Eight of its 24 rooms are off the street and quiet—worth requesting (Db-€110–130, prices depend on season, CC, 30 rue de Turenne, Mo: St. Paul, tel. 01 42 72 73 47, fax 01 42 72 54 10, e-mail: info @hoteldeschevaliers.com, Christele SE).

Hôtel St. Louis Marais** is a tiny place, well situated on a quiet residential street between the river and rue St. Antoine, with a cute lobby and 16 cozy, if pricey, rooms (Sb-€90, small Db-€105, standard Db-€120, CC, no elevator but only 2 floors, 1 rue Charles V, tel. 01 48 87 87 04, fax 01 48 87 33 26, www .saintlouismarais.com).

LOWER PRICED
Grand Hôtel Jeanne d'Arc**, a warm, welcoming place with thoughtfully appointed rooms, is ideally located for (and very popular with) connoisseurs of the Marais. Rooms on the street can be noisy until the bars close. Sixth-floor rooms have a view, and corner rooms are wonderfully bright in the City of Lights. Reserve this place way ahead (Sb-€53, Db-€73, larger twin Db-€92, Tb-€109, good Qb-€125, CC, 3 rue de Jarente, Mo: St. Paul, tel. 01 48 87 62 11, fax 01 48 87 37 31, e-mail: hoteljeannedarc@wanadoo.fr, Gail SE).

Hôtel Lyon-Mulhouse**, with half of its 40 pleasant rooms on a busy street just off place de la Bastille, is a good value. Its bigger and quieter rooms on the back are worth the extra euros (Sb-€55, Db-€64, twin Db-€75, Tb-€88–92, Qb-€100, CC, 8 boulevard Beaumarchais, tel. 01 47 00 91 50, fax 01 47 00 06 31, e-mail: hotelyonmulhouse@wanadoo.fr).

Hôtel Sévigné**, less personal with dreary halls, rents 30 well-worn but sleepable rooms at fair prices, with the cheapest breakfast in Paris at €3.50 (Sb-€56, Db-€63, Tb-€83, CC, 2 rue Malher, Mo: St. Paul, tel. 01 42 72 76 17, fax 01 42 78 68 26, www.le-sevigne.com).

Hotel Pointe Rivoli*, across from the St. Paul Métro stop, is in the thick of the Marais, with Paris' steepest stairs (no elevator) and modest, though pleasant, rooms at fair rates (Sb-€60, Db-€70, Tb-€100, CC, 125 rue St. Antoine, tel. 01 42 72 14 23, fax 01 42 72 51 11, e-mail: pointerivoli@libertysurf.fr).

Hôtel de 7ème Art**, two blocks south of rue St. Antoine toward the river, is a relaxed, Hollywood-nostalgia place, run by young, friendly Marais types, with a full-service café/bar and Charlie Chaplin murals. Its 23 rooms lack imagination, but are comfortable and a fair value. The large rooms are American-spacious (small Db-€72, standard Db-€82–92, large Db-€107–122, extra bed-€20, CC, 20 rue St. Paul, Mo: St. Paul, tel. 01 44 54 85 00, fax 01 42 77 69 10, e-mail: hotel7art@wanadoo.fr).

Hôtel de la République**, owned by the people who run the Castex (see above), is in a less appealing, out-of-the-way location than other listed Marais hotels, but often has rooms when others don't (Sb-€53, Db-€61, CC, near place de la République, 31 rue Albert Thomas, 75010 Paris, Mo: République, tel. 01 42 39 19 03, fax 01 42 39 22 66, www.republiquehotel.com).

MIJE Youth Hostels: The Maison Internationale de la Jeunesse et des Etudiants (MIJE) runs three classy old residences clustered a few blocks south of rue St. Antoine. Each offers simple, clean, single-sex, one- to four-bed rooms for travelers under the age of 30 (exceptions are made for families). None has an elevator or double beds, each has an Internet station, and all rooms have showers. Prices are per person and favor single travelers (2 people can find a double in a simple hotel for similar rates). You can pay more to have your own room, or pay less and room with as many as three others (Sb-€37, Db-€27, Tb-€24, Qb-€22, no CC, includes breakfast but not towels, which you can get from a machine; required membership card-€2.50 extra/person; rooms locked 12:00–15:00 and at 1:00).

The hostels are: **MIJE Fourcy** (€9 dinners available to anyone with a membership card, 6 rue de Fourcy, just south of rue de Rivoli), **MIJE Fauconnier** (11 rue du Fauconnier), and the best, **MIJE Maubisson** (12 rue des Barres). They all share the same contact information (tel. 01 42 74 23 45, fax 01 40 27 81 64, www.mije.com) and Métro stop (St. Paul). Reservations are accepted, though you must arrive by noon.

Sleeping near the Pompidou Center
These hotels are farther west and closer to the Pompidou Center
than to place Bastille.

HIGHER PRICED
Hôtel Axial Beaubourg***, a block from the Hôtel de Ville
toward the Pompidou Center, has a minimalist lobby and
28 nicely decorated, plush rooms, many with wood beams
(standard Db-€134–142, big Db-€165, CC, air-con, 11 rue
du Temple, tel. 01 42 72 72 22, fax 02 42 72 03 53, www
.axialbeaubourg.com).

MODERATELY PRICED
Hôtel de la Bretonnerie***, three blocks from the Hôtel de
Ville, is a fine Marais splurge. It has an on-the-ball staff, a big,
welcoming lobby, elegant decor, and tastefully appointed rooms
with an antique, open-beam warmth (perfectly good standard
"classic" Db-€108, bigger "charming" Db-€140, Db suite-€180,
Tb suite-€205, Qb suite-€230, CC, closed Aug, between rue
Vielle du Temple and rue des Archives at 22 rue Sainte Croix
de la Bretonnerie, Mo: Hôtel de Ville, tel. 01 48 87 77 63,
fax 01 42 77 26 78, www.bretonnerie.com).

    Hôtel Caron de Beaumarchais***, feels like a dollhouse,
with its 20 sweet little rooms and a lobby cluttered with bits
from an elegant 18th-century Marais house. Short antique col-
lectors love this place (small back-side Db-€130, larger Db on
the front–€145, CC, air-con, 12 rue Vielle du Temple, Mo:
Hôtel de Ville, tel. 01 42 72 34 12, fax 01 42 72 34 63, www
.carondebeaumarchais.com).

    Hôtel de Vieux Marais** is tucked away on a quiet street
two blocks east of the Pompidou Center. It offers bright, spacious, well-maintained rooms, simple decor, and we-try-harder
owners. Marie-Hélène, the in-love-with-her-work owner, gives
this place its charm. Greet Leeloo, the hotel hound (Db-€125,
extra bed-€23, CC, air-con, just off rue des Archives at 8 rue
du Plâtre, Mo: Rambuteau/Hôtel de Ville, tel. 01 42 78 47 22,
fax 01 42 78 34 32, www.vieuxmarais.com).

    Hôtel Beaubourg*** is a good three-star value on a
quiet street in the menacing shadow of the Pompidou Center.
Its 28 rooms are wood-beam comfy, and the inviting lounge is
warm and pleasant (Db-€93–122 depending on the size, some
with balconies-€122, twins are considerably larger than doubles,
includes breakfast, CC, 11 rue Simon Lefranc, Mo: Rambuteau,
tel. 01 42 74 34 24, fax 01 42 78 68 11, e-mail: htlbeaubourg
@hotellerie.net).

LOWER PRICED

Hôtel de Nice**, on the Marais' busy main drag, is a turquoise-and-rose "Marie-Antoinette does tie-dye" place. Its narrow halls are littered with paintings, and its 23 rooms are filled with thoughtful touches and include tight bathrooms. Twin rooms, which cost the same as doubles, are larger and on the street side—but have effective double-paned windows (Sb-€62, Db-€97, Tb-€117, Qb-€135, CC, 42 bis rue de Rivoli, Mo: Hôtel de Ville, tel. 01 42 78 55 29, fax 01 42 78 36 07).

At **Grand Hôtel du Loiret****, you get what you pay for in an inexpensive and basic, laid-back place (S-€37, Sb-€47–62, D-€42, Db-€56–72, Tb-€72–84, CC, just north of rue de Rivoli, 8 rue des Mauvais Garçons, Mo: Hôtel de Ville, tel. 01 48 87 77 00, fax 01 48 04 96 56, e-mail: hoteloiret@aol.com).

Hotel Sansonnet**, a block from the Hôtel de Ville toward the Pompidou Center, is a homey, unassuming place with no elevator but with 26 comfortable, well-maintained, and good-value rooms (Sb-€46-55, Db-€58–78, CC, 48 rue de la Verrerie, Mo: Hôtel de Ville, tel. 01 48 87 96 14, fax 01 48 87 30 46, www.hotel-sansonnet.com, e-mail: info@hotel-sansonnet.com).

Sleeping near the Marais on Ile St. Louis

The peaceful, residential character of this river-wrapped island, its brilliant location, and homemade ice cream have drawn Americans for decades, allowing hotels to charge top euro for their rooms. There are no budget values here, but the island's coziness and proximity to the Marais, Notre-Dame, and the Latin Quarter compensate for higher rates. These hotels are on the island's main drag, the rue St. Louis en l'Ile, where I list several restaurants (see Eating chapter, page 282).

HIGHER PRICED

Hôtel Jeu de Paume****, located in a 17th-century tennis center, is the most expensive hotel I list in Paris. When you enter its magnificent lobby, you'll understand why. Ride the glass elevator for a half-timbered-tree-house experience, and marvel at the cozy lounges. The 30 quite comfortable rooms have muted tones and feel more three-plus than four-star (you're paying for the location and public spaces). Most face a small garden and all are peaceful (Sb-€152, standard Db-€210, larger Db-€220–250, Db suite-€450, CC, 54 rue St. Louis en l'Ile, tel. 01 43 26 14 18, fax 01 40 46 02 76, www.jeudepaumehotel.com).

The following two hotels are owned by the same person. For both, if you must cancel, do so a week in advance or pay fees: **Hôtel de Lutèce***** is the best value on the island, with a sit-a-while wood-paneled lobby, a fireplace, and appealing air-conditioned rooms. Twin rooms are larger and the same price as double rooms (Sb-€125, Db-€149, Tb-€165, CC, 65 rue St. Louis en l'Ile, tel. 01 43 26 23 52, fax 01 43 29 60 25, www.hotel-ile-saintlouis.com). **Hôtel des Deux Iles***** is a *très* similar value, with marginally smaller rooms (Sb-€125, Db-€149, CC, air-con, 59 rue St. Louis en l'Ile, tel. 01 43 26 13 35, fax 01 43 29 60 25, www.hotel-ile-saintlouis.com).

Contrescarpe Orientation

I've patched together several neighborhoods to construct this diverse hotel neighborhood whose strength is its central location and proximity to the Luxembourg Garden. The Latin Quarter, Luxembourg Garden, boulevard St. Germain, and Jardin des Plantes are all easily reachable by foot. Hotel listings are concentrated near the monumental Panthéon and along the more colorful rue Mouffetard. Perfectly Parisian place de la Contrescarpe ties these distinctly different areas together.

The rue Mouffetard is the spine of this area, running south from place de la Contrescarpe to rue de Bazeilles. Two thousand years ago, it was the principal Roman road south to Italy. Today, this small, meandering street has a split personality. The lower part thrives in the daytime as a pedestrian market street. The upper part sleeps during the day but comes alive after dark, teeming with bars, restaurants, and nightlife.

The flowery Jardin des Plantes park is just east, and the sublime Luxembourg Garden is just west. Both are ideal for afternoon walks, picnics, naps, and kids. The doorway at 49 rue Monge leads to a hidden **Roman arena** (Arènes de Lutèce). Today, *boules* players occupy the stage while couples cuddle on the seats. Admire the Panthéon from the outside (it's not worth paying to enter), and peek inside the exquisitely beautiful St. Etienne-du-Mont church.

The nearest **TI** is at the Louvre Museum. The **post offices** (PTT) are between rue Mouffetard and rue Monge at 10 rue de l'Epée de Bois, and at the corner of rue des Ecoles and rue du Cardinal Lemoine. Place Monge hosts a good **outdoor market** on Wednesday, Friday, and Sunday mornings until 13:00. The **street market** at the bottom of rue Mouffetard bustles daily except Monday (Tue–Sat 8:00–12:00 & 15:30–19:00, Sun 8:00–12:00, 5 blocks south of place de la Contrescarpe). Lively cafés at place de la Contrescarpe hop with action from the afternoon into the wee hours. **Bus #47** runs along rue Monge north to Notre-Dame, the Pompidou Center, Gare de l'Est, and Gare du Nord.

Sleeping in the Contrescarpe Neighborhood
(5th arrondissement, Mo: Monge, zip code: 75005)

The first six hotels here are a 10–15 minute walk from Notre-Dame, Ile de la Cité, and Ile St. Louis, and a 5–10 minute walk from the Luxembourg Garden, St. Sulpice, and the grand boulevards St. Germain and St. Michel. Add 10 minutes for the last five hotels to reach the same places.

Sleeping near the Seine

MODERATELY PRICED

Hôtel des Grandes Ecoles* is simply idyllic. A short alley leads to three buildings protecting a flower-filled garden courtyard, preserving a sense of tranquility that is rare in a city this size. Its 51 rooms are reasonably spacious and comfortable, with large beds. This romantic place is deservedly popular, so call well in advance (reservations not accepted more than 4 months ahead, Db-€95–110, a few bigger rooms-€120, extra bed-€15, parking-€25, CC, 75 rue du Cardinal Lemoine, Mo: Cardinal Lemoine, tel. 01 43 26 79 23, fax 01 43 25 28 15, www.hotel-grandes-ecoles.com, mellow Marie speaks some English, Maman does not).

LOWER PRICED

Hôtel Central* defines unpretentiousness, with a charming location, smoky reception area, steep, slippery, castle-like stairway, so-so beds, and basic-but-cheery rooms (all with showers, though toilets are down the hall). It's a fine budget value (Ss-€29–37, Ds-€39–45, no CC, no elevator, 6 rue Descartes, Mo: Cardinal Lemoine, tel. 01 46 33 57 93, sweet Pilar NSE).

Sleeping between the Panthéon and Luxembourg Garden

The following four hotels are a five-minute walk from place Contrescarpe. For these listings, the RER stop Luxembourg (with direct connections to the airports) is closer than the nearest Métro stop, Maubert Mutualité.

HIGHER PRICED

Both of these hotels face the Panthéon's right transept and are owned by the same family (ask about their low-season promotional rates).

Hôtel du Panthéon* welcomes you with a melt-in-your-chair lobby and 32 country-French-cute rooms with air-conditioning and every possible comfort. Fifth-floor rooms have skinny balconies, but sixth-floor rooms have the best views (standard Db-€188, larger Db-€218, Tb-€235, CC, 19 place du Panthéon, tel. 01 43 54 32 95, fax 01 43 26 64 65, www.hoteldupantheon.com).

Contrescarpe Hotels and Restaurants

- ❶ Hotel Elysa-Luxembourg
- ❷ Hotel Central & Gaudeamus rest.
- ❸ Hotel des Grandes Ecoles
- ❹ Y & H Hostel
- ❺ Hotel de l'Esperance
- ❻ Hotel de France
- ❼ Hotel Port Royal
- ❽ Le Jardin d'Artemis rest.
- ❾ Hotel Bresil
- ❿ Comfort Hotel Cardinal
- ⓫ Le Jardin des Pates rest.
- ⓬ Les Vignes du Pantheon rest.
- ⓭ Café le Mouffetard
- ⓮ Cave de la Bourgogne
- ⓯ Café de la Mosque
- ⓰ Hotel des Grandes Hommes & Hotel du Pantheon
- ⓱ Hotel Senlis
- ⓲ Hotel Medicis
- ⓳ Le Bistro des Cigales
- ⓴ Café Delmas

Hôtel des Grandes Hommes*** was designed to look good—and it does. The lobby is to be admired but not enjoyed, and the 31 rooms are design-magazine perfect. They're generally tight but adorable, with great attention to detail and little expense spared. Fifth- and sixth-floor rooms have balconies (sixth-floor balconies, with grand views, are big enough to enjoy). For more luxury, splurge for a suite (standard Db-€218, Db suite-€250, CC, air-con, 17 place du Panthéon, tel. 01 46 34 19 60, fax 01 43 26 67 32, www.hoteldesgrandshommes.com).

LOWER PRICED

Hôtel Senlis** hides quietly two blocks from Luxembourg Garden, with modest rooms, carpeted walls, and metal closets. Most rooms have beamed ceilings, and all could use a facelift (Sb-€67, Db-€72–87, Tb-€95, Qb-€110, CC, 7 rue Malebranche, tel. 01 43 29 93 10, fax 01 43 29 00 24, www.hoteldesenlis.fr).

Hôtel Medicis is as cheap, stripped-down, and basic as it gets, with a soiled linoleum charm, a happy owner, and a great location (S-€16, D-€31, 214 rue St. Jacques, tel. 01 43 54 14 66, Denis speaks English).

Sleeping at the Bottom of rue Mouffetard

Of my recommended accommodations in the Contrescarpe, these are farthest from the Seine and other tourists, in an appealing workaday area. They may have rooms when others don't.

HIGHER PRICED

Comfort Hôtel Cardinal*** is a well-designed hotel with less character but agreeable décor and modern comforts (ask about off-season promotional rates, Sb-€100, standard Db-€138, large Db-€185, CC, air-con, 20 rue Pascal, tel. 01 47 07 41 92, fax 01 47 07 43 80, e-mail: hotelcardinal@aol.com).

LOWER PRICED

Don't let **Hôtel Port Royal*'**s lone star fool you—this 46-room place is polished bottom to top and has been well-run by the same proud family for 66 years. You could eat off the floors of its spotless, comfy rooms. Ask for a room off the street (S-€37–48, D-€64, big hall showers-€2.50, Db-€73, deluxe Db-€84, no CC, requires cash deposit, climb stairs from rue Pascal to busy boulevard de Port Royal, 8 boulevard de Port Royal, Mo: Gobelins, tel. 01 43 31 70 06, fax 01 43 31 33 67, www.portroyal.fr.st).

Hôtel de l'Esperance** is a solid two-star value. It's quiet, pink, fluffy, and comfortable, with thoughtfully appointed rooms complete with canopy beds and a flamboyant owner (Sb-€70,

Db-€73–86, small Tb-€101, CC, 15 rue Pascal, Mo: Censier-Daubenton, tel. 01 47 07 10 99, fax 01 43 37 56 19, e-mail: hotel.esperance@wanadoo.fr).

Hôtel de France** is set on a busy street, with adequately comfortable rooms, fair prices, and less welcoming owners. The best and quietest rooms are *sur le cour* (on the courtyard), though streetside rooms are OK (Sb-€64, Db-€76–80, CC, requires 1 night non-refundable deposit, 108 rue Monge, Mo: Censier-Daubenton, tel. 01 47 07 19 04, fax 01 43 36 62 34, e-mail: hotel.de.fce@wanadoo.fr).

Y&H Hostel is easygoing and English-speaking, with Internet access, kitchen facilities, and basic but acceptable hostel conditions (beds in 4-bed rooms-€22, beds in double rooms-€25, sheets-€2.50, no CC, rooms closed 11:00–16:00 but reception stays open, 2:00 curfew, reservations require deposit, 80 rue Mouffetard, Mo: Cardinal Lemoine, tel. 01 47 07 47 07, fax 01 47 07 22 24, e-mail: smile@youngandhappy.fr).

Lesser Values

MODERATELY PRICED

Hôtel Elysa-Luxembourg*** sits on a busy street at the Luxembourg Garden and charges top euro for its plush, air-conditioned rooms (Db-€138, CC, 6 rue Gay Lussac, tel. 01 43 25 31 74, fax 01 46 34 56 27, www.elysa-luxembourg.fr).

LOWER PRICED

Hôtel Brésil** lies one block from the Luxembourg Garden and offers little character, some smoky rooms, and reasonable rates (Sb-€64, Db-€68–85, CC, 10 rue le Goff, tel. 01 43 54 76 11, fax 01 46 33 45 78, e-mail: hoteldubresil@wanadoo.fr).

Sleeping near Paris, in Versailles

For a laid-back alternative to Paris within easy reach of the big city by RER train (5/hr, 30 min), Versailles, with easy, safe parking and reasonably priced hotels, can be a good overnight stop (see map on page 216). Park in the château's main lot while looking for a hotel, or leave your car there overnight (free 19:30–8:00). Get a map of Versailles at your hotel or at the TI. For restaurant recommendations, see page 301.

MODERATELY PRICED

Hôtel de France***, in an 18th-century townhouse, offers four-star value, with air-conditioned, appropriately royal rooms, a pleasant courtyard, comfy public spaces, a bar, and a restaurant (Db-€125–130, Tb-€168, CC, just off parking lot across from château, 5 rue Colbert, tel. 01 30 83 92 23, fax 01 30 83 92 24, www.hotelfrance-versailles.com).

LOWER PRICED
Hôtel le Cheval Rouge**, built in 1676 as Louis XIV's stables, now houses tourists. It's a block behind the place du Marché in a quaint corner of town on a large, quiet courtyard with free, safe parking and sufficiently comfortable rooms (Ds-€49, Db-€58–72, Tb-€86, Qb-€90, CC, 18 rue André Chenier, tel. 01 39 50 03 03, fax 01 39 50 61 27).

Ibis Versailles** offers fair value and modern comfort, but no air-conditioning (Db-€71, cheaper weekend rates can't be reserved ahead, CC, across from RER station, 4 avenue du Général de Gaulle, tel. 01 39 53 03 30, fax 01 39 50 06 31).

Hôtel du Palais, facing the RER station, has clean, sharp rooms—the cheapest I list in this area. Ask for a quiet room off the street (Ds-€43, Db-€49, extra person-€11, CC, piles of stairs, 6 place Lyautey, tel. 01 39 50 39 29, fax 01 39 50 80 41).

Hôtel d'Angleterre**, away from the frenzy, is a tranquil old place with comfortable and spacious rooms. Park nearby in the château lot (Db-€56–72, extra bed-€15, CC, just below palace to the right as you exit, 2 rue de Fontenay, tel. 01 39 51 43 50, fax 01 39 51 45 63).

For Longer Stays

Staying a week or longer? Consider the advantages that come with renting a furnished apartment. Complete with a small, equipped kitchen and living room, this option is great for families. Among the many English-speaking organizations ready to help, the following have proven most reliable. Their Web sites are generally excellent and essential to understanding your options.

Paris Appartements Services rents studios and one-bedroom apartments in the Opéra, Louvre, and Marais neighborhoods (2 rue d'Argout, 75002 Paris, tel. 01 40 28 01 28, fax 01 40 28 92 01, www.paris-appartements-services.fr).

Apalachee Bay is British-owned and offers an extensive range of carefully selected, furnished apartments (21 rue de Madrid, 75008 Paris, tel. 01 42 94 13 13, fax 01 42 94 83 01, www.apalachee.com).

Locaflat offers accommodations ranging from studios to five-room apartments (tel. 01 43 06 78 79, fax 01 40 56 99 69, www.locaflat.com).

EATING

The Parisian eating scene is kept at a rolling boil. Entire books (and lives) are dedicated to the subject. Paris is France's wine and cuisine melting pot. While it lacks a style of its own (only French onion soup is truly Parisian), it draws from the best of France. Paris could hold a gourmet's Olympics and import nothing.

Parisians eat long and well. Relaxed lunches, three-hour dinners, and endless hours sitting in outdoor cafés are the norm. They have a legislated 35-hour workweek and a self-imposed 36-hour eat-week. Local cafés, cuisine, and wines become a highlight of any Parisian adventure—sightseeing for your palate. Even if the rest of you is sleeping in a cheap hotel, let your taste buds travel first-class in Paris. (They can go coach in London.)

You can eat well without going broke, but choose carefully—you're just as likely to blow a small fortune on a mediocre meal as you are to dine wonderfully for €20. By following the suggestions offered below, you'll have a more positive dining experience.

Breakfast

Petit déjeuner (pron. puh-tee day-zhu-nay) is typically *café au lait*, hot chocolate, or tea; a roll with butter and marmalade; and a croissant, though more hotels are starting to provide breakfast buffets with fruit, cereal, yogurt, and cheese (usually for a few extra euros and well worth it). While breakfasts are available at your hotel (about €5–10), they're cheaper at corner cafés (but no coffee refills; see also "Café Culture," below). It's fine to buy a croissant or roll at a bakery and eat it with your cup of coffee at a café. Better still, some bakeries offer worthwhile breakfast deals with juice, croissant, and coffee or tea for about €3 (the chain of bakeries called La Brioche Dorée is one example). If the urge for an egg in the morning gets the best of you, drop into a café and order *une omelette* or *oeufs sur le plat* (fried eggs). You could also buy or bring plastic bowls and spoons from home, buy a box of cereal and a small box of milk, and eat in your room before heading out for coffee.

Picnics

Great for lunch or dinner, Parisian picnics can be first-class affairs and adventures in high cuisine. Be daring. Try the smelly cheeses, ugly pâtés, sissy quiches, and minuscule (usually drinkable) yogurts. Local shopkeepers are accustomed to selling small quantities of produce. Try the tasty salads to go and ask for *une fourchette en plastique* (a plastic fork).

Gather supplies early for a picnic lunch; you'll probably visit several small stores to assemble a complete meal, and many close at noon. Look for a *boulangerie* (bakery), a *crémerie* (cheeses), a *charcuterie* (deli items, meats, and pâtés), an *épicerie* or *alimentation* (small grocery store with veggies, drinks, and so on), and a *pâtisserie* (delicious pastries). For fine picnic shopping, check out our street market recommendations in the Shopping chapter. While wine is taboo in public places in the United States, it's *pas de problème* in France.

Supermarchés offer less color and cost, more efficiency, and adequate quality. Department stores often have supermarkets in the basement and top-floor cafeterias offering not really cheap but low-risk, low-stress, what-you-see-is-what-you-get meals. For a quick meal to go, look for food stands and bakeries selling take-out sandwiches and drinks. For an affordable sit-down meal, try a *crêperie* or café.

In stores, unrefrigerated soft drinks and beer are one-half the price of cold drinks. Milk and boxed fruit juice are the cheapest drinks. Avoid buying drinks to go at streetside stands; you'll find them far cheaper in a shop. Try to keep a water bottle with you. Water quenches your thirst better and cheaper than anything you'll find in a store or café. I drink tap water in Paris.

For good lunch picnic sites, consider these suggestions. The Palais Royal (across the street from the Louvre) is a good spot for a peaceful, royal picnic, as is the little triangular Henry IV Park on the west tip of Ile de la Cité. The pedestrian Pont des Arts bridge, across from the Louvre, has unmatched views and plentiful benches. For great people-watching, try the Pompidou Center (by the *Homage to Stravinsky* fountains), the elegant place des Vosges (closes at dusk), the gardens at the Rodin Museum, and the Luxembourg Garden.

Café Culture

French cafés (or *brasseries*) provide reasonable light meals and a refuge from museum and church overload. Feel free to order only a bowl of soup or a salad for lunch or dinner at a café.

Cafés generally open by 7:00, but closing varies wildly. Food is served throughout the day, so if you want a late lunch or an early dinner—find a café.

It's easier for the novice to sit and feel comfortable when you know the system. Check the price list first. Prices, which must be posted prominently, vary wildly between cafés. Cafés charge different prices for the same drink depending upon where you want to be seated. Prices are posted: *comptoir* (counter/bar) or the more expensive *salle* (seated).

Your waiter probably won't overwhelm you with friendliness. Notice how hard they work. They almost never stop. Cozying up to clients (French or foreign) is probably the last thing on their minds.

The **standard menu items** (generally served day and night) are the Croque Monsieur (grilled cheese sandwich) and Croque Madame (Monsieur with a fried egg on top). The *salade composée* (pron. com-po-zay) is a hearty chef's salad. Sandwiches are least expensive but plain unless you buy them at the *boulangerie* (bakery). To get more than a piece of ham *(jambon)* on a baguette, order a sandwich *jambon-crudité* (pron. zhahm-bohn crew-dee-tay), which means garnished with lettuce, tomatoes, cucumbers, and so on. Omelets come lonely on a plate with a basket of bread. The **daily special**—*plat du jour* (pron. plah dew zhoor)—is your fast, hearty hot plate for €10–14. At most cafés (though never at a restaurant), feel free to order only appetizers—which many find lighter, more fun, and more interesting than entrées. Regardless of what you order, bread is free; to get more, just hold up your breadbasket and ask, "*Encore, s'il vous plaît.*"

House **wine** at the bar is cheap (about €2 per glass, cheapest by the *pichet*, or pitcher), and the local beer is cheaper on tap (*une pression*) than in the bottle (*bouteille*). France's best **beer** is Alsatian; try Krônenburg or the heavier Pelfort. *Une panaché* (pron. pan-a-shay) is a refreshing French shandy (7-Up and beer). For a fun, bright, nonalcoholic drink, order *un diablo menthe* (pron. dee-ah-bloh mahnt; 7-Up with mint syrup). Kids love the local lemonade (*citron pressé*; pron. see-trohn preh-say) and the flavored syrups mixed with bottled water (*sirops à l'eau*; pron. see-roh ah loh). The ice cubes melted after the last Yankee tour group left.

If you order **coffee,** here's the lingo:

- *un express* (pron. uh nex-press) = shot of espresso
- *une noisette* (pron. oon nwah-zette) = espresso with a shot of milk
- *café au lait* (pron. kah-fay oh leh) = coffee with lots of milk. Also called *un grand crème* (large size; pron. uh grahn krehm) or *un petit crème* (average size; pron. uh puh-tee krehm)

- *un grand café noir* (pron. uh grahn kah-fay nwahr) = cup of black coffee, closest to American style
- *un décaffiné* (pron. uh day-kah-fee-nay) = decaf; can modify any of the above drinks

By law, the waiter must give you a glass of tap water with your coffee if you request it; ask for *un verre d'eau, s'il vous plaît* (pron. uh vayr doh, see voo play).

Tipping

Virtually all cafés and restaurants include a service charge in the bill (usually 15 percent), but it's polite to round up for a drink or meal well-served. This bonus tip is usually about 5 percent of the bill (e.g., if your bill is €19, leave €20). For exceptional service, tip up to 10 percent. In the rare instance that service is not included (the menu states *service non compris*), tip 15 percent. When you hand your payment plus a tip to your waiter, you can say, "*C'est bon*" (pron. say bohn), meaning, "It's good."

If you order your food at a counter, don't tip.

Restaurants

Choose restaurants filled with locals, not places with big neon signs boasting, We Speak English. Consider your hotelier's opinion. If a restaurant doesn't post its menu *(la carte)* outside, move along.

If you want the menu, ask for *la carte* (and order à la carte like the locals do); if you ask for the *menu* (pron. muh-noo), you'll get a fixed-price meal. *Menus*, which offer three or four courses, are generally a good value: You get your choice of soup, appetizer, or salad; your choice of three or four main courses with vegetables; plus a cheese course and/or a choice of desserts. Service is included, but wine and other drinks are generally extra. Restaurants that offer a *menu* for lunch often charge about €6 more for the same *menu* at dinner.

If you'd rather dine à la carte, ask the waiter for help deciphering the French. Go with his or her recommendations and anything *de la maison* (of the house), as long as it's not an organ meat (*tripes, rognons, andouillette*—yuck). Galloping gourmets should bring a menu translator; the *Marling Menu Master* is excellent. The *Rick Steves' French Phrase Book*, with a Menu Decoder, works well for most travelers. The wines are often listed in a separate *carte des vins*.

In France, an entrée is the first course and *le plat* is the main course. *Le plat* or *le plat du jour* (plate of the day) is the main course with vegetables (usually €10–14). If all you want is a salad, find a café instead. By American standards, the French undercook meats:

rare or *saignant* (pron. seh-nyahn) is close to raw; medium, or *à point* (pron. ah pwahn) is rare; and well-done, or *bien cuit* (pron. bee-yehn kwee), is medium.

Parisians are willing to pay for bottled water with their meal (*eau minérale*; pron. oh mee-nay-rahl) because they prefer the taste over tap water. If you prefer a free pitcher of tap water, ask for *une carafe d'eau* (pron. oon kah-rahf doh). Otherwise, you may unwittingly buy bottled water. To get inexpensive wine at a restaurant, order table wine in a pitcher (*un pichet*; pron. pee-shay), rather than a bottle (though finer restaurants usually offer only bottles of wine). If all you want is a glass of wine, ask for *un verre de vin* (pron. uh vehr duh van). A half carafe of wine is *un demi-pichet* (pron. uh duh-mee pee-shay), a quarter carafe (ideal for one) is *un quart* (pron. uh car).

To get a waiter's attention, simply say, "*S'il vous plaît*" (pron. see voo play)—please.

PARISIAN CUISINE

There is no Parisian cuisine to speak of. The principal advantage of dining in Paris is that you can sample fine cuisine from throughout France. Many restaurants specialize in a particular region's cuisine (in this book, I list restaurants specializing in food from Provence, Burgundy, Alsace, Normandy, Dordogne, Languedoc, and the Basque region). So be a galloping gourmet and try a few of these regional restaurants (see the note on "French Specialities by Region," page 288). For general, classic, anywhere-in-France dishes, consider these suggestions:

First Course *(Entrée)*

Soupe à l'oignon: Hot, salty, and filling, French onion soup is a beef broth served with cheesy bread croutons floating on top.
Salade au chèvre chaud: A mixed green salad topped with warmed goat cheese and toasted bread croutons.
Salade Niçoise: While famous as a specialty from Nice, this classic salad is served throughout France. There are many versions, though most include a base of green salad topped with green beans, boiled potatoes (sometimes rice), tomatoes, anchovies, lots of tuna, and hard-boiled eggs.
Crudités: A mix of raw and lightly-cooked, fresh vegetables usually including grated carrots, celery root, tomatoes, and beets, often with a hefty dose of vinaigrette dressing. If you want the dressing on the side, say, "*La sauce à côté, s'il vous plaît*" (pron. lah sohss ah co-tay see voo play).
Escargots: Snails cooked in parsley-garlic butter. You don't even have to like the snail itself. Just dipping your bread in

garlic butter is more than satisfying. Prepared a variety of ways, the classic is *à la bourguignonne* (served in their shells).

Huîtres: Oysters served raw any month and delivered fresh from nearby Brittany. This food is particularly popular at Christmas and New Year's, when every café seems to have overflowing baskets lining the storefront.

Pâtés and *Terrines:* Slowly cooked ground meat (usually pork, though chicken and rabbit are also common) that is highly seasoned and served in slices with mustard and *cornichons* (little pickles). Pâtés are smoother than the similarly prepared, but more chunky *terrines.*

Foie gras: Rich and buttery in consistency, it's made from the swollen livers of force-fed geese (or ducks, in *foie de canard*). Spread it on bread with your knife, and do not add mustard to this pâté dish.

Main Course *(Plat Principal)*

Coq au vin: This Burgundian dish is chicken marinated ever so slowly in red wine, then cooked until it melts in your mouth. It's served (often family-style) with vegetables.

Boeuf bourguignon: Another Burgundian specialty, this classy beef stew is cooked slowly in red wine, then served with onions, potatoes, and mushrooms.

Steak: Referred to as *pavé, bavette,* or *entrecôte,* French steak is usually thinner than American steak and is always served with sauces (*au poivre* is a pepper sauce, *une sauce roquefort* is a cheese sauce).

Steak tartare: This wonderfully French dish is for adventurous types only. It's very lean, raw hamburger served with spices (usually tabasco, onions, salt, and pepper on the side) and topped with a raw egg.

Gigot d'agneau: Leg of lamb served in many styles, often with white beans. The best lamb is *pré salé,* which means the lamb has been raised in salt marsh lands (like at Mont St. Michel).

Confit de canard: This Southwest favorite is duck that has been preserved in its own fat, then cooked in its fat, and often served with potatoes cooked in the same fat. Not for dieters.

Saumon: You'll see salmon dishes served in various styles. The salmon usually comes from the North Sea and is always served with sauce, most commonly a sorel sauce.

Cheese Course *(Le Fromage)*

In France, the cheese course is served just before (or instead of) dessert. It not only helps with digestion, it gives you a great opportunity to sample the tasty regional cheeses. There are more

French Specialties by Region

Alsace: The German influence is obvious: sausages, potatoes, onions, and sauerkraut. Look for *choucroute garni* (sauerkraut and sausage—although it seems a shame to eat it in a fancy restaurant), the more traditionally Alsatian *baeckeanoffe* (potato, meat, and onion stew), *rösti* (an oven-baked potato-and-cheese dish), fresh trout, and foie gras.

Burgundy: Considered by many to be France's best, Burgundian cuisine is peasant cooking elevated to an art. This wine region excels in *coq au vin* (chicken with wine sauce), *boeuf Bourguignon* (beef stew cooked with wine, bacon, onions, and mushrooms), *oeufs en meurette* (eggs poached in red wine), *escargots* (snails), and *jambon persillé* (ham with garlic and parsley).

Basque: Mixing influences from the mountains, sea, Spain, and France, it's dominated by seafood, tomatoes, and red peppers. Look for anything *basquaise* (cooked with tomatoes, eggplant, red peppers, and garlic), such as *thon* (tuna) or *poulet* (chicken). Try *piperade*, a dish combining peppers, tomatoes, garlic, and eggs (ham optional), and *ttoro*, a seafood stew that is the Basque answer to bouillabaisse.

Languedoc and Périgord: The cuisine of these regions is referred to in Paris as Southwest cuisine *(cuisine du sudouest)*. It's hearty peasant cooking using full-bodied red wines and lots of duck. Try the hearty *cassoulet* (white bean, duck, and sausage stew), *canard* (duck), *pâté de foie gras* (goose liver pâté), *pommes sar-*

than 400 different French cheeses to try. Most restaurants will offer a cheese platter from which you select a few different cheeses (3 is average). Those most commonly served in Paris are *brie de Meaux* (mild and creamy, from just outside Paris), camembert (semi-creamy and pungent, from Normandy), *chèvre* (goat cheeses with a sharp taste, usually from the Loire), and roquefort (strong and blue-veined, from South-central France).

If you'd like a little of each type of cheese from the cheese plate, say, *"Un peu de chaque, s'il vous plaît"* (pron. uh puh duh shahk, see voo play). If you serve yourself from the cheese plate, observe French etiquette and keep the shape of the cheese. To avoid being gauche, politely shave off a slice from the side or cut small wedges.

Dessert *(Le Dessert)*
Crème brulée: A rich, creamy, dense, and carmelized custard.

ladaise (potatoes fried in duck fat), *truffes* (truffles, earthy mush-rooms), and anything with *noix* (walnuts).

Normandy and Brittany: Normandy specializes in cream sauces, organ meats (sweetbreads, tripe, and kidneys—the "gizzard salads" are great), and seafood *(fruits de mer)*. Dairy products are big here. Munch some *moules* (mussels) and *escalope normande* (veal in cream sauce). Brittany is famous for its oysters and crêpes. Both regions use lots of *cidre* (hard apple cider) in their cuisine.

Provence: The almost extravagant use of garlic, olive oil, herbs, and tomatoes makes Provence cuisine France's liveliest. To sample it, order anything *à la provençale*. Among the area's spicy specialties are *ratatouille* (a thick mixture of vegetables in an herb-flavored tomato sauce), *brandade* (a salt cod, garlic, and cream mousse), *aioli* (a garlicky mayonnaise often served atop fresh veg-etables), *tapenade* (a paste of puréed olives, capers, anchovies, herbs, and sometimes tuna), *soupe au pistou* (vegetable soup with basil, garlic, and cheese), and *soupe à l'ail* (garlic soup).

Riviera: The Côte d'Azur gives Provence's cuisine a Mediter-ranean flair. Local specialties are *bouillabaisse* (the spicy seafood stew/soup that seems worth the cost only for those with a seafood fetish), *bourride* (a creamy fish soup thickened with aioli garlic sauce), and *salade niçoise* (pron. nee-swaz; a tasty tomato, potato, olive, anchovy, and tuna salad).

Tarte tatin: This is apple pie like grandma never made, with caramelized apples cooked upside down, but served upright.
Mousse au chocolat: Chocolate mousse.
Ile flottante: This lighter dessert consists of islands of meringue floating on a pond of custard sauce.
Profiteroles: Cream puffs filled with vanilla ice cream, smothered in warm chocolate sauce.
Tartes: Narrow strips of fresh fruit, baked in a crust and served in thin slices (without ice cream).
Sorbets: Known to us as sherbets, these light, flavorful, and fruity ices are sometimes laced with brandy.

Coffee *(Café)*
If you order espresso, it will always come after dessert. To have coffee with dessert, ask for *"café avec le dessert"* (pron. kah-fay ah-vehk luh day-sayr).

EATING IN PARIS

My recommendations are centered around the same three great neighborhoods listed in the Sleeping chapter; you can come home exhausted after a busy day of sightseeing and find a good selection of restaurants right around the corner. And evening is a fine time to explore any of these delightful neighborhoods, even if you're sleeping elsewhere.

To save piles of euros, review the budget eating tips above and restaurant recommendations below, and consider dinner picnics (great take-out dishes available at *charcuteries*).

Restaurants open for dinner around 19:00, and small local favorites get crowded after 21:00. When lunch is served, it generally begins at 11:30 and goes until 14:00, with last orders taken at about 13:30. Beware: Many restaurants close Sunday and Monday. Most of the restaurants listed below accept credit cards.

Eating in the Rue Cler Neighborhood

The rue Cler neighborhood caters to its residents. Its eateries, while not destination places, have an intimate charm. My favorites are small mom-and-pop places that love to serve good French food at good prices to a local clientele. You'll generally find great dinner *menus* for €15–23 and *plats du jour* for around €12. My first two recommendations are easygoing cafés, ideal if you want a light dinner (good dinner salads) or a more substantial but simple meal. Eat early with tourists or late with locals.

Café du Marché, with the best seats, coffee, and prices on rue Cler, serves hearty €7 salads and good €9 *plats du jour* for lunch or dinner to a trendy, smoky, mainly French crowd (Mon–Sat 11:00–23:00, closed Sun, at the corner of rue Cler and rue du Champ de Mars, tel. 01 47 05 51 27, well-run by Frank, Jack, and Bruno). Arrive before 19:30. It's packed at 21:00. A chalkboard lists the plates of the day—each a meal. You'll find the same dishes and prices with better (but smoky) indoor seating at their other restaurant, **Le Comptoir du Septième,** two blocks away at the Ecole Militaire Métro stop (39 avenue de la Motte Piquet, tel. 01 45 55 90 20).

Café le Bosquet is a vintage Parisian brasserie with dressy waiters and classic indoor or sidewalk tables on a busy street. Come here for a bowl of French onion soup, a salad, or a three-course set *menu* for €16 (closed Sun, many choices from a fun menu, the house red wine is plenty good, corner of rue du Champs de Mars and avenue Bosquet, tel. 01 45 51 38 13).

Leo le Lion, a warm, charming souvenir of old Paris, is popular with locals. Expect to spend €23 per person for fine à la carte choices (closed Sun, 23 rue Duvivier, tel. 01 45 51 41 77).

Rue Cler Restaurants

1. Café du Marche
2. Le Comptoir du Septieme
3. Café le Bosquet
4. Leo le Lion
5. L'Ami de Jean & L'Affriole
6. Au Petit Tonneau
7. Brasserie Thoumieux
8. P'tit Troquet & Casa Sergio
9. Restaurant la Serre
10. La Fontaine de Mars
11. La Varangue
12. Chez Agnes
13. Le Bourdonnais
14. Café de l'Esplanade
15. Tarte Julie
16. Flo Prestige
17. Real McCoy
18. Pourjauran bakery
19. Petite Brasserie PTT
20. To Le Sancerre
21. Maison Altmayer
22. Café la Roussillon
23. O'Brien's Pub
24. Café Thoumieux

L'Ami de Jean celebrates the rustic joys of Basque living—and that includes fine peasant-pleasing food. Beginners should trust the €15 *menu Basque.* For a full red wine, try the Spanish Rioja. Stepping into the jumbled little room is like leaving Paris. Wear your beret (closed Sun, 27 rue Malar, tel. 01 47 05 86 89).

At **L'Affriole,** you'll compete with young professionals for a table. This small and trendy place is well-deserving of its rave reviews. Item selections change daily and the wine list is extensive, with some good bargains (€32 *menu,* closed Sun, 17 rue Malar, tel. 01 44 18 31 33).

Au Petit Tonneau is a purely Parisian experience. Fun-loving owner-chef Madame Boyer prepares everything herself, wearing her tall chef's hat like a crown as she rules from her family-style kitchen. The small dining room is plain and a bit smoky (allow €30/person with wine, open daily, 20 rue Surcouf, tel. 01 47 05 09 01).

Thoumieux, the neighborhood's classy, traditional Parisian brasserie, is a local institution and deservedly popular. It's big and dressy, with formal but good-natured waiters (daily, €14 lunch *menu,* 3-course with wine dinner *menu* for €31, really good *crème brulée,* 79 rue St. Dominique, tel. 01 47 05 49 75).

Le P'tit Troquet is a petite place taking you back to Paris in the 1920s, gracefully and earnestly run by Dominique. The delicious three-course €27 *menu* comes with fun, traditional choices (closed Sun, 28 rue de l'Exposition, tel. 01 47 05 80 39).

Restaurant la Serre, across the street at #29, is also worth considering (*plats du jour* €11–15, daily, good onion soup and duck specialties, tel. 01 45 55 20 96, Margot).

La Casa di Sergio is *the* place for gourmet Italian cuisine served family-style. Only Sergio could make me enthusiastic about Italian food in Paris. Sergio, a people-loving Sicilian, says he's waited his entire life to open a restaurant like this. Eating here involves a little trust...just sit down and let Sergio spoil you (€26–34 *menus,* closed Wed, 20 rue de l'Exposition, tel. 01 45 51 37 71).

La Fontaine de Mars is a longtime favorite for locals, charmingly situated on a classic tiny Parisian street and jumbled square. It's a happening scene, with tables jammed together for the serious business of good eating. Reserve in advance or risk eating upstairs without the fun street-level ambience (allow €40/person with wine, nightly, where rue de l'Exposition and rue St. Dominique meet, tel. 01 47 05 46 44).

La Varangue is an entertaining one-man show featuring English-speaking Phillipe, who ran a French catering shop in Pennsylvania for three years, then returned to Paris to open his own place. He lives upstairs, and clearly has found his niche serving a Franco-American clientele who are all on a first-name basis. The food is cheap and good (try his snails and chocolate cake—but not together), the tables are few, and he opens at 18:00. Norman Rockwell would dig his tiny dining room (€9–10 *plats du jour* and a €13.50 *menu*, always a veggie option, 27 rue Augereau, tel. 01 47 05 51 22).

Chez Agnes is the smallest restaurant listed in this book. Eccentric and flowery, it's truly a family-style place where engaging Agnes (with dog Gypsy at her side) does it all—working wonders in her minuscule kitchen, and serving, too, without a word of English. Don't come for a quick dinner; she expects to get to know you (€23 *menu*, closed Mon, 1 rue Augereau, tel. 01 45 51 06 04).

Le Bourdonnais, boasting one Michelin star, is the neighborhood's intimate gourmet splurge. You'll find friendly but formal service in a plush and very subdued 10-table room. Micheline Coat, your hostess, will take good care of you (€42 lunch *menu*, €64 dinner *menu*, 113 avenue de la Bourdonnais, tel. 01 47 05 47 96).

Café de l'Esplanade, the latest buzz, is your opportunity to be surrounded by chic, yet older and sophisticated, Parisians enjoying top-notch traditional cuisine as foreplay. There's not a tourist in sight. It's a sprawling place—half its tables with well-stuffed chairs fill a plush, living room–like interior, and the other half are lined up outside under its elegant awning facing the street, valet boys, and park. Dress competitively, as this is *the* place to be seen in the 7th *arrondissement* (€20 *plats du jour*, plan on €40 plus wine for dinner, open daily, reserve—especially if you want a curbside table, smoke-free room in the back, bordering les Invalides at 52 rue Fabert, tel. 01 47 05 38 80).

Picnicking: The rue Cler is a moveable feast that gives "fast food" a good name. The entire street is clogged with connoisseurs of good eating. Only the health-food store goes unnoticed. A festival of food, the street is lined with people whose lives seem to be devoted to their specialty: polished produce, rotisserie chicken, crêpes, or cheese.

For a magical picnic dinner at the Eiffel Tower, assemble it in no fewer than five shops on rue Cler and lounge on the best grass in Paris (the police don't mind after dusk), with the dogs, Frisbees, a floodlit tower, and a cool breeze in the Parc du Champ de Mars.

The **crêpe stand** next to Café du Marché does a wonderful top-end dinner crêpe for €4. **Asian delis** (generically called *Traiteur Asie*) provide tasty, low-stress, low-price, take-out treats (€6 dinner plates, 2 delis have tables on the rue Cler—one across from Hôtel Leveque, and the other near the rue du Champ de Mars). For a variety of savory quiches or a tasty pear-and-chocolate tart, try **Tarte Julie** (take-out or stools, 28 rue Cler). The elegant **Flo Prestige** *charcuterie* is open until 23:00 and offers mouthwatering meals to go (at the Ecole Militaire Métro stop). **Real McCoy** is a little shop selling American food and sandwiches (194 rue de Grenelle). A good, small, **late-night grocery** is at 197 rue de Grenelle.

The **bakery** *(boulangerie)* on the corner of rue Cler and rue de Grenelle is the place for sandwiches, *pain au chocolat*, or almond croissants. And the **Pourjauran** bakery, offering great baguettes, hasn't changed in 70 years (20 rue Jean Nicot). The **bakery** at 112 rue St. Dominique is worth the detour, with classic decor and tables where you can enjoy your *café au lait* and croissant.

Cafés and Bars: If you want to linger over coffee or a drink at a sidewalk café, try **Café du Marché** (see above), **Petite Brasserie PTT** (local workers eat here, opposite 53 rue Cler), or **Café le Bosquet** (46 avenue Bosquet, tel. 01 45 51 38 13). **Le Sancerre** wine bar/café is wood-beam warm and ideal for a light lunch or dinner, or just a glass of wine after a long day of sightseeing. The owner's cheeks are the same color as his wine (open until 21:30, great omelets, 22 avenue Rapp, tel. 01 45 51 75 91). **Maison Altmayer** is a hole-in-the-wall place good for a quiet drink (9:00–19:30, next to Hôtel Eiffel Rive Gauche, 6 rue du Gros Caillou). Cafés like this originated (and this one still functions) as a place where locals enjoyed a drink while their heating wood, coal, or gas was prepared for delivery.

Nightlife: This sleepy neighborhood is not the place for night owls, but there are a few notable exceptions. **Café du Marché** and its brother, **Le Comptoir du Septième** (both listed above), hop with a Franco-American crowd until about midnight, as does the flashier **Café la Roussillon** (at corner of rue de Grenelle and rue Cler). **O'Brien's Pub** is a relaxed, Parisian rendition of an Irish pub (77 avenue St. Dominique). **Café Thoumieux** (younger brother of the brasserie listed above) has big-screen sports and a trendy young crowd (4 rue de la Comète, Mo: Latour Maubourg).

Eating in the Marais Neighborhood

The trendy Marais is filled with locals enjoying good food in colorful and atmospheric eateries. The scene is competitive and changes all the time. Here is an assortment of places—all handy to recommended hotels—that offer good food at reasonable prices, plus a memorable experience.

Eating at place du Marché Ste. Catherine: This tiny square just off rue St. Antoine is an international food festival cloaked in extremely Parisian, leafy-square ambience. On a balmy evening, this is clearly a neighborhood favorite, with five popular restaurants offering €20–25 meals. Survey the square and you'll find two French-style bistros (**Le Marché** and **Au Bistrot de la Place**), a fun Italian place, a popular Japanese/Korean restaurant, and a

Marais Restaurants

1. Le Marché & De la Place
2. Auberge de Jarente
3. Nectarine
4. Ma Bourgogne
5. L'Impasse (Chez Robert)
6. Chez Janou
7. Bofinger
8. L'Excuse
9. L'Enoteca
10. Picolo Teatro
11. L'As du Falafel
12. Au Bourguignon du Marais
13. Les Sans Culottes
14. Studio
15. Camille
16. Au Petit Fer a Cheval
17. Café de la Poste & Delizie Italiane
18. Petite Gavroche
19. Au Temps des Cerises
20. Flo Prestige
21. Le Vieux Comptoir
22. La Perla
23. The Quiet Man

Russian eatery with an easy but adventurous menu. You'll eat under the trees surrounded by a futuristic-in-1800 planned residential quarter. Just around the corner with none of the ambience is **L'Auberge de Jarente,** a reliable, rainy-day, budget option, where a hard-working father-and-son team serve good Basque food (€18 3-course *menu* with wine, closed Sun–Mon, just off the square at 7 rue de Jarente, tel. 01 42 77 49 35).

Eating at place des Vosges: This elegant square, built by King Henry IV in 1605, put the Marais on the aristocratic map. And today, the posh ambience survives, with several good places offering romantic meals under its venerable arches, overlooking one of Paris' most elegant little parks. And prices are reasonable. The mod and pastel **Nectarine** at #16 is a teahouse serving healthy salads, quiches, and inexpensive *plats du jour* both day and night. Its fun menu lets you mix and match omelets and crêpes (tel. 01 42 77 23 78). **Café Hugo,** next door (named for the square's most famous resident), is a typical bistro serving good traditional favorites such as onion soup (€5) and crêpes (€4). **Ma Bourgogne** has the snob appeal—bigger, darker, and more traditional. You'll sit under arcades in a whirlpool of Frenchness as bow-tied and black-aproned waiters serve traditional Burgundian specialties: steak, *coq au vin,* lots of French fries, escargot, and great red wine. Service at this institution comes with food but no smiles (allow €38/person with wine, open daily, dinner reservations smart, no CC, at northwest corner, tel. 01 42 78 44 64).

Eating elsewhere in the Marais: **L'Impasse,** a cozy, neighborhood bistro on a quiet alley, serves an enthusiastically French, €24 three-course *menu* (very good escargot). Françoise, a former dancer and artist, runs the place *con brio* and, judging by the clientele, she's a fixture in the neighborhood. It's a spacious place with great ambience indoors and out (closed Sun, 4 impasse Guéménée, tel. 01 42 72 08 45). Françoise promises anyone with this book a free glass of *byrrh*—a French port-like drink (pron. beer). It's next to a self-serve laundry (open nightly until 21:30—clean your clothes while you dine).

Chez Janou, a Provençal bistro, tumbles out of its corner building, filling its broad sidewalk with keen eaters. At first glance, you know this is a find. It's relaxed and charming, yet youthful and bustling with energy. The style is French Mediterranean, with an emphasis on vegetables (€13 *plats du jour* and a €26 3-course *menu* that changes with the season, a block beyond place des Vosges at 2 rue Roger-Verlomme, tel. 01 42 72 28 41).

Brasserie Bofinger, an institution for over 100 years, is famous for fish and traditional cuisine with an Alsatian flair. You're surrounded by brisk, black-and-white attired waiters in plush rooms reminiscent of the Roaring Twenties. The nonsmoking room is best—under the grand 1919 *coupole*. Watch the boys shucking and stacking seafood platters out front before going in. Their €31 three-course (with wine) *menu* is a good value (daily and nightly, reservations smart, 5 rue de la Bastille, don't be confused by the lesser "Petite" Bofinger across the street, tel. 01 42 72 87 82).

L'Excuse, one of the neighborhood's top restaurants, is a good splurge for a romantic, dressy evening in a hushed atmosphere, with lounge-lizard music and elegant Mediterranean nouveau cuisine. The plates are petite but creative and presented with panache (€36 *menu*, closed Sun, reserve ahead, request downstairs—ideally by the window, 14 rue Charles V, tel. 01 42 77 98 97).

L'Enoteca is a high-energy, half-timbered Italian wine bar/restaurant serving reasonable Italian cuisine (no pizza) with a tempting antipasti bar. It's a relaxed, open setting with busy, blue-aproned waiters serving two floors of local eaters (€25 meals with wine, daily, across from L'Excuse at rue St. Paul and rue Charles V, tel. 01 42 78 91 44).

Vegetarians will appreciate the excellent cuisine at the popular **Picolo Teatro** (closed Mon, near rue des Rosiers, 6 rue des Ecouffes, tel. 01 42 72 17 79) or **L'As du Falafel**, which serves the best falafel on rue des Rosiers (at #34).

Au Bourguignon du Marais, a small wine bar on the other side of rue de Rivoli, is a place that wine-lovers shouldn't miss. The excellent Burgundy wines blend well with a fine, though limited, selection of *plats du jour* (closed Sat–Sun, call by 19:00 to reserve, 52 rue Francois Miron, tel. 01 48 87 15 40).

Lively **rue de Lappe** is what the Latin Quarter wants to be. This street, just beyond the more stately place de la Bastille, is one of the wildest night spots in Paris. You'll walk past a dizzying array of wacky eateries, bars, and dance halls. Then, sitting there like a van Gogh painting, is the popular, zinc-bar-classic **Bistrot les Sans Culottes**—a time-warp bistro serving traditional French cuisine with a proper respect for fine wine (€20 3-course *menu*, 27 rue de Lappe, tel. 01 48 05 42 92). Stay out past your bedtime. Eat here. Then join the rue de Lappe party.

Le Studio is near the Pompidou Center on a 17th-century courtyard below a dance school. It's best to sit outside, but the salads, €12 *plats du jour*, and Tex-Mex meals are good day or night (daily, 41 rue de Temple, tel. 01 42 74 10 38).

Eating at the east end of the Marais: **Camille,** a traditional corner brasserie, is another neighborhood favorite with great indoor and sidewalk seating. White-aproned waiters serve €9 salads and very French *plats du jour* for €15 to a down-to-earth but sophisticated clientele (daily, 24 rue des Francs Bourgeois at corner of rue Elzévir, tel. 01 42 72 29 50). **Au Petit Fer à Cheval,** named for its horseshoe-shaped bar, is an authentic gem with mirrored walls and tiled floors. The tight, woody interior takes you back to the 1930s—and you'll sit on old wooden Métro seats. The sidewalk tables put you in the front row at the neighborhood's trendy and gay promenade (€10 salads, €15 *plats du jour*, explore the fun chalkboard menu, reasonable wines by the glass, daily until 24:00, 30 rue Vieille du Temple, tel. 01 42 72 47 47).

Cheap eating in the Marais: You'll find several hard-working **Chinese fast food** places along rue St. Antoine, great for a €5 meal or quick late-night snack. **Café de la Poste** is a tight little place serving good €11 *plats du jour* from a small but reliable menu (closed Sun, near place de la Bastille at 13 rue Castex, tel. 01 42 72 95 35). For dirt-cheap French cooking, try €8 *plats du jour* at the charmingly basic **Petite Gavroche** (15 rue Sainte Croix de la Bretonnerie, tel. 01 48 87 74 26). **Au Temps des Cerises,** a *très* local wine bar, is relaxed and amiably run by the incredibly mustachioed Monsieur Vimard. This place is great for a colorful lunch or a very light dinner of cheese or cold meats with good wine (Mon–Fri until 20:00, closed Sat–Sun, at rue du Petit Musc and rue de la Cerisaie).

Picnicking: Picnic at peaceful place des Vosges (closes at dusk) or on the Ile St. Louis quai (see below). Stretch your euros at the basement supermarket of the **Monoprix** department store (near place des Vosges on rue St. Antoine). Two small grocery shops are open until 23:00 on rue St. Antoine (near intersection with rue Castex). For a cheap breakfast, try the tiny *boulangerie/ pâtisserie* where the hotels buy their croissants (coffee machine-€0.70, baby quiche-€1.50, 1 block off place de la Bastille, corner of rue St. Antoine and rue de Lesdiguières).

Nightlife: The best scene is the bars and dance halls of rue de Lappe (beyond place de la Bastille, see above). Trendy cafés and bars also cluster on rue Vielle du Temple, rue des Archives, and rue Ste. Croix de la Bretonnerie (close about 2:00), and are popular with gay men. **Le Vieux Comptoir** is tiny, lively, and just hip enough (off place des Vosges at 8 rue de Biraque). **La Perla** is full of Parisian yuppies in search of the perfect margarita (26 rue François Miron). **The Quiet Man** is a traditional Irish pub with happy hour from 16:00 to 20:00 (5 rue des Haudriettes).

Eating on Ile St. Louis

The Ile St. Louis is a romantic and peaceful place to window-shop for plenty of promising dinner possibilities. Cruise the island's main street for a variety of options, from cozy *crêperies* to Italian (intimate pizzeria and upscale) to typical brasseries (several with fine outdoor seating face the bridge to Ile de la Cité). After dinner, sample Paris' best sorbet. Then stroll across to the Ile de la Cité to see an illuminated Notre-Dame. All listings below line the island's main drag, the rue St. Louis en l'Ile (see map on page 55). Consider skipping dessert to enjoy a stroll licking the best ice cream in Paris.

These two little family-run places serve top-notch traditional French cuisine with white-tablecloth, candlelit elegance in small, 10-table rooms under heavy wooden beams. Their *menus* start with three courses at €26 and offer plenty of classic choices that change with the season for freshness. **Le Tastevin** at #46, run by Madame Puisieux, is a little more intimate (daily, tel. 01 43 54 17 31). **Auberge de la Reine Blanche** is a bit more touristy—but in the best sense—with friendly Françoise and her crew working hard to please in a characteristic little place with dollhouse furniture on the walls and a two-dove welcoming committee at the door (daily, 30 rue St. Louis en l'Ile, tel. 01 46 33 07 87). Reservations are smart for each.

Café Med, closest to Notre-Dame at #77, is best for inexpensive salads, crêpes, and lighter *menus* in a tight but cheery setting (daily, tel. 01 43 29 73 17, charming Eva SE). Very limited wine list.

Two side-by-side places are famous for their rowdy, medieval cellar atmosphere, serving all-you-can-eat buffets with straw baskets of raw veggies (cut whatever you like with your dagger), massive plates of pâté, a meat course, and all the wine you can stomach for €34. The food is just food; burping is encouraged. If you want to eat a lot, drink a lot of wine, and holler at your friends while receiving smart-aleck buccaneer service, these food fests can be fun. **Nos Ancêtres les Gaulois** ("Our Ancestors the Gauls," daily from 19:00, tel. 01 46 33 66 07) has bigger tables and seems made-to-order for local stag parties. If you'd rather be surrounded by drunk tourists than locals, pick **La Taverne du Sergeant Recruteur.** The "Sergeant Recruteur" used to get young Parisians drunk and stuffed here, then sign them into the army (daily from 19:00, #41, tel. 01 43 54 75 42).

Riverside picnic: On sunny lunchtimes and balmy evenings, the quai on the Left Bank side of Ile St. Louis is lined with locals who have more class than money, spreading out tablecloths and even lighting candles for elegant picnics. The grocery store on the main drag at #67 is open daily until midnight if you'd like to join them. Otherwise, it's a great stroll.

Ice cream dessert: Half the people strolling Ile St. Louis are licking an ice cream cone, because this is the home of "*les glaces Berthillon.*" The original Berthillon shop, at 31 rue St. Louis en l'Ile, is marked by the line of salivating customers. It's so popular that the wealthy people who can afford to live on this fancy island complain about the congestion it causes. For a less famous but at least as tasty treat, the homemade Italian gelato a block away at **Amorino Gelati** is giving Berthillon competition (no line, bigger portions, easier to see what you want, and they offer little tastes—Berthillon doesn't need to, 47 rue Saint Louis en l'Ile). Having some of each is a fine option.

Eating in the Contrescarpe Neighborhood

There are a few diamonds for fine dining in this otherwise rough area. Most come here for the lively and cheap eateries that line rues Mouffetard and du Pot-de-Fer. Study the many menus, compare crowds, then dive in and have fun (see map on page 278).

Near the Panthéon, **Les Vignes du Panthéon** is a homey, traditional place with a zinc bar and original flooring. It serves a mostly local clientele and will make you feel you're truly in Paris (allow €23 for à la carte, closed Sat–Sun, 4 rue des Fossés St. Jacques, tel. 01 43 54 80 81). **Le Bistro des Cigales,** between the Panthéon and place de la Contrescarpe, offers an escape to Provence, with deep yellow and blue decor and a purely Proven-çale *menu*, helpful staff, and air-conditioned rooms (€17–22 *menus*, daily, 12 rue Thouin, tel. 01 40 46 03 76). **Gaudeamus,** with a low-profile café on one side and a pleasant bistro on the other, has friendly owners and cheap, €15 *menus* (daily, behind the Pan-théon, 47 rue de la Montagne Ste. Geneviève, tel. 01 40 46 93 40). **L'Ecurie,** almost next door, is for those who prefer ambience and setting over top cuisine, with inexpensive and acceptable meals served on small, wood tables around a zinc bar in an unpreten-tious setting with a few outdoor tables (daily, *menus* from €15, 58 rue de la Montagne Ste. Geneviève, tel. 01 46 33 68 49).

Right on place de la Contrescarpe, sprawling **Café Delmas** is the place to see and be seen with a broad outdoor terrace, tasty salads, and good *plats du jour* from €12 (open daily). **Le Jardin d'Artemis** is one of the better values on rue Mouffetard, at #34 (€15–23 *menus*, closed Tue). **Le Jardin des Pates** is popular with less strict vegetarians, serving pastas and salads at fair prices (daily, near Jardin des Plantes, 4 rue Lacépède, tel. 01 43 31 50 71).

Cafés: The cafés on place de la Contrescarpe are popular until late (see Café Delmas, above). Both indoors and outdoors provide good people-watching. **Café le Mouffetard** is in the thick of the street-market hustle and bustle (at corner of rue Mouffetard and rue de l'Arbalète). The outdoor tables at **Cave de la Bourgogne** are picture-perfect (at the bottom of rue Mouffetard on rue de Bazeilles). At **Café de la Mosque,** you'll feel like you've been beamed to Morocco. In this purely Arab café, order a mint tea, pour in the sugar, and enjoy the authentic interior and peaceful outdoor terrace (behind mosque, 2 rue Daubenton).

Eating on Montmartre

The Montmartre is extremely touristy, with many mindless mobs following guides to cancan shows. But the ambience is undeniable, and an evening up here overlooking Paris is a quintessential experience in the City of Lights.

To avoid the crowds and enjoy a classic neighborhood corner, hike from the Sacré Coeur church away from the tourist zone down the stairs to **L'Eté en Pente Douce** with fine indoor and outdoor seating, €9 *plats du jour* and salads, veggie options, and good wines (23 rue Muller, tel. 01 42 64 02 67). Just off the jam-packed place du Tertre, **Restaurant Chez Plumeau** is a touristy yet cheery, reasonably priced place with great seating on a tiny characteristic square (€18 *menu*, place du Calvaire, tel. 01 46 06 26 29). Along the touristy main drag and just off, several fun piano bars serve reasonable crêpes with great people-watching. More Montmartre eateries are mentioned in the Montmartre Walk chapter.

Eating in Versailles

In the pleasant town center, around place du Marché Notre-Dame, you'll find a variety of reasonable restaurants, cafés, and a few cobbled lanes (market days Sun, Tue, and Fri until 13:00; see map on page 216). The square is a 15-minute walk from the château (veer left when you leave château). From the place du Marché, consider shortcutting to Versailles' gardens by walking 10 minutes west down rue de la Paroisse. The château will be to your left after entering, the main gardens, Trianon palaces, and Hameau straight ahead. The quickest way to the château's front door is along avenue de St. Cloud and rue Colbert.

These places are on or near place du Marché Notre-Dame, and all are good for lunch or dinner. **La Boeuf à la Mode** is a bistro with traditional cuisine right on the square (€23 *menu*, open daily, 4 rue au Pain, tel. 01 39 50 31 99). **Fenêtres sur Cour** is the romantic's choice, where you dine in a glass gazebo surrounded by antique shops, just below the square in the "antique village," on place de la Geôle (closed all day Mon and Tue–Wed eves, tel. 01 39 51 97 77). **A la Côte Bretonne** is the place to go for crêpes in a cozy setting (daily, a few steps off the square on traffic-free rue des Deux Ponts, at #12).

Rue Satory is another pedestrian-friendly street lined with restaurants, on the south side of the château near the Hôtel d'Angleterre (10-min walk, angle right out of the château). **Le Limousin** is a warm, traditional restaurant on the corner nearest the château, with mostly meat dishes (lamb is a specialty, allow €30 with wine, 4 rue de Satory, tel. 01 39 50 21 50).

LES GRANDS CAFÉS DE PARIS
Please see "Café Culture" (above) for tips on Parisian cafés.

History of Cafés in Paris
The first café in the Western world was in Paris—established in 1686 at Le Procope (still a restaurant today, see below). The French had just discovered coffee, and their robust economy was growing a population of pleasure-seekers and thinkers looking for places to be seen, to exchange ideas, and to plot revolutions both political and philosophical. And with the advent of theaters like La Comédie-Française, the necessary artsy, coffee-sipping crowds were birthed. By 1700, more than 300 cafés had opened their doors; at the time of the Revolution (1789), there were over 1,800 cafés in Paris. Revolutionaries from Marat and Napoleon to Dalí enjoyed the spirit of free-thinking that the cafés engendered.

Café society took off in the early 1900s. Life was changing rapidly, with the Industrial Revolution and wars on a global scale. Many retreated to Parisian cafés to try to make sense of the confusion. Vladimir Lenin, Leon Trotsky, Igor Stravinsky, Ernest Hemingway, Scott Fitzgerald, James Joyce, Albert Einstein, Jean-Paul Sartre, Gene Openshaw, and Albert Camus were among the devoted café society. Some virtually lived at their favorite café, where they kept their business calendars, entertained friends, and ate every meal. Parisian apartments were small, walls were thin (still often the case), and heating (particularly during war times) was minimal, making the warmth of cafés all the harder to leave.

There are more than 12,000 cafés in Paris today, though their numbers are shrinking. They're still used for business meetings, encounter sessions, political discussions, and romantic interludes. Most Parisians are loyal to their favorites and know their waiter's children's names. And with the recently approved 35-hour workweek, most will have even more time to linger longer over their *café crème*.

Here's a short list of grand Parisian cafés, worth the detour only if you're not in a hurry and don't mind paying outrageous prices for a shot of espresso. Think of these cafés as museums. Try to understand why they matter just as much today as they did yesterday.

Grand Cafés by Neighborhood

St. Germain
Where the boulevard St. Germain meets rue Bonaparte (Mo: St. Germain-des-Prés), you'll find two famous cafés. **Les Deux Magots** offers great outdoor seating and a warm interior. Once a favorite of Ernest Hemingway (in *The Sun Also Rises*, Jake met

Brett here) and of Jean-Paul Sartre (he and Simone de Beauvoir met here), the café is today filled with international tourists. **Le Café de Flore,** right next door, feels much more local, hip, and literary—wear your black turtleneck. Picasso was a regular while painting *Guernica.* The smoky interior is popular with Europeans.

For great outdoor seating and the same great view for less, skip these places and set up for coffee or a light lunch at **Café Bonaparte** (big salads, from Les Deux Magots 1 block down rue Bonaparte toward river). You're farther from the large boulevards, but still in the thick of this pleasant café-sitting area.

Paris' first and most famous, **Café le Procope** lies an enchanting five-minute stroll away. From Café Bonaparte, walk down the rue de l'Abbaye (consider a 20-step detour to rue de Furstembourg en route), then continue onto rue de Bourbon le Château, veer left on the picturesque rue de Buci (more cafés), and turn right just after crossing rue de l'Ancienne Comédie. Go up the passageway at 59–61 to find Le Procope. This place drew a crowd that reads like a *Who's Who* of French literati, including Voltaire, Rousseau, Balzac, Zola, Robespierre, Victor Hugo, and two Americans, Benjamin Franklin and Thomas Jefferson (beautiful restaurant and café, open Mon–Sat 10:00–24:00, closed Sun, 13 rue de l'Ancienne Comédie, tel. 01 40 46 79 00).

Boulevard du Montparnasse

An eclectic assortment of historic cafés gathers along the busy boulevard du Montparnasse near its intersection with boulevard Raspail (Mo: Vavin). Combine these historic cafés with a visit to the Luxembourg Garden that lie just a few blocks away down rue Vavin (next to Café le Select).

La Coupole, built in the 1920s, was decorated by aspiring artists (Léger, Brancusi, and Chagall, among others) in return for free meals. This cavernous place feels like a classy train station, with grand chandeliers, velvet booths, brass decor, and waiters by the dozen. Today, an unappealing glass building towers above. Bring your friends and make noise. The food is fine, but not the reason you came. In fact, I prefer coffee and drinks rather than dinner here (allow €35 per person with wine, 102 boulevard du Montparnasse, tel. 01 43 26 70 50).

Le Dome is right at the intersection of boulevards Raspail and du Montparnasse and forms a dramatic contrast to the party atmosphere of La Coupole. Smaller, more elegant, and refined in every way, this place makes me want to dress up and look better than I do. Have a drink at the tables just inside, facing the sidewalk. While La Coupole is not known for its cuisine, Le Dome is. Come here for a splurge dinner (figure €40/person with wine, tel. 01 43 35 25 81).

Le Select was popular with the more rebellious types—Leon Trotsky, Jean Cocteau, and Pablo Picasso loved it. It feels more conformist today, with good salads, outdoor seating, and pleasant tables just inside the door (99 boulevard du Montparnasse, across from La Coupole).

Champs-Elysées

Ladurée is the classic 19th-century tea salon/restaurant/*patissier* on Paris' grandest boulevard (a block below avenue George V at #75). Its interior is right out of the 1860s. Wander around . . . you can even peek into the cozy rooms upstairs. A coffee here with a selection of four little macaroons is *très élégant*. The bakery makes traditional macaroons, cute little cakes, and gift-wrapped finger sandwiches.

Le Fouquet's, a block uphill, opened in 1899 as a coachman's bistro. It gained fame as the hangout of France's WWI biplane fighter pilots—those who weren't shot down by Germany's infamous "Red Baron." It also served as James Joyce's dining room. Today, it's pretty stuffy—unless you're a film star. The golden plaques at the entry are from winners of France's film awards (like the Oscars), the Césars. While the intimidating interior is impressive, the outdoor setting is Champs-Elysées great—and you can buy the most expensive shot of espresso I found in Paris (€4.50). Fouquet's was recently saved from foreign purchase and eventual destruction when the government declared it a historic monument (99 avenue des Champs-Elysées, Mo: George V).

Near the Louvre

Within a short walk of the Louvre, you'll find melt-in-your-chair cafés (Mo: Palais Royal/Musée du Louvre). The staunchly Parisian **Café le Nemours,** serving pricey but good light lunches, is tucked into the corner of the Palais-Royal adjacent to the Comédie-Française (leaving the Louvre, cross rue Rivoli and veer left). Brass–and–Art Deco elegant, with outdoor tables under an arcade two minutes from the pyramid, this place makes a great post-Louvre retreat (2 place Colette, tel. 01 42 61 34 14).

On Place de la Concorde

Hôtel Crillon's four-star elegance can be yours for an afternoon. Considered the most exclusive hotel in Paris (and the last of the great hotels to be French-owned), this is the place to experience château life. Wear the best clothes you packed, arrive after 15:00, let the bellhop spin the door, and settle into the royal blue chairs in the *salon du thé* (€9 for a pot of tea or double *café au lait*, €30 for high tea served daily 15:30–19:00 with a live harp serenade). You'll be surrounded by famous people you won't recognize.

At Gare de Lyon

Le Train Bleu is a vast restaurant with a small café-bar area
built right into the train station for the Paris Exhibition of 1900
(which also saw the construction of the pont Alexandre and the
Grand and Petit Palais). It's a simply grand-scale-everything
experience with over-the-top, belle-époque decor that speaks of
another age—when going to dinner was an event, a chance to
see and be seen, and intimate dinning was out. Forty-one massive
paintings of scenes along the old rail lines tempt diners to consider
a short getaway. Reserve ahead for dinner, or drop in for a drink
before your train leaves (*menus* from €40, tel. 01 43 43 09 06,
www.le-train-bleu.com).

PARIS WITH CHILDREN

Paris is surprisingly kid-friendly. After enjoying so many parks, squares, and sights, your children may want to return to Paris before you do. Consider these tips.

Before You Go:
- Get your kids in the spirit (rent or read Madeleine stories, *The Hunchback of Notre-Dame*, or *The Man in the Iron Mask*).
- Hotel selection is critical. Stay in a kid-friendly area near a park. The rue Cler neighborhood is ideal. If you're staying a week or more, rent an apartment (see "For Longer Stays," page 281).
- Bring plenty of kids' books; they're hard to find and expensive in Paris.

In Paris:
- Don't overdo it. Tackle one key sight each day (Louvre, Orsay Museum, Versailles) and mix with a healthy dose of fun activities. The double-decker bus tours (see page 26) are a great way to start your visit.
- Follow this book's crowd-beating tips to a tee. Kids despise long lines more than you do.
- Eat dinner early (19:00–19:30 at restaurants, earlier at cafés). Skip famous places. Try relaxed cafés (or fast-food restaurants) where kids can move around without bothering others. Picnics work well.
- The best, cheapest toy selection is in the large department stores, such as Bon Marché (see Shopping chapter, page 310).
- French marionette shows, called *guignols*, are fun for everyone. They take place in several locations in Paris, mostly in big parks. See *Pariscope* or *L'Officiel des Spectacles* (sold at newsstands), under "Marionettes," for times and places. Even in French, the plots are easy to follow. Arrive 20 minutes early for good seats.

- Involve your children in the trip. Let them help choose daily activities, lead you through the Métro, and so on.
- Some Paris parks host temporary amusement parks. The summer Ferris wheel and rides in the Tuileries are the best— my daughter preferred it to Disneyland Paris (for Disneyland details, see page 255).

TOP TEN KIDS' SPOTS IN PARIS

1. Luxembourg Garden: This is my favorite place to mix
kid business with pleasure. This perfectly Parisian park has it all: an extensive big-toys play area with imaginative slides, swings, and jungle gyms (kids-€3, adults-€2, good for all day, open daily, many parents watch from chairs outside the play area); pedal go-carts; a fun merry-go-round; toy sailboats in the main pond (€3/hr, daily in summer, otherwise Wed and Sat–Sun); and big open areas perfect for kicking a ball. Near the main building is a toddler wading pool and sandpit (free). Adults and kids enjoy the terrific puppet shows (*guignols*) held in the afternoons (Mo: St. Sulpice, Odéon, or Notre-Dame-des-Champs, tel. 01 43 26 46 47).

2. Jardin des Plantes: These pleasant, colorful gardens
are short on grass but have a small zoo, a plant maze, and several kid-friendly natural-science museums (closed Tue). Kids love the dinosaur exhibit at the *Galerie d'Anatomie Comparée et de Paléontologie* (no English explanations, but no real need, kids-€3.10, adults-€5, Wed–Mon 10:00–17:00, closed Tue, includes *Musée de Minéralogie*). The *Grande Galerie de l'Evolution* at the non-river end of the park is a dazzling museum describing the evolution of animals, with huge models and fun exhibits (no English explanations, kids-€5, adults-€6.50, Wed–Mon 10:00–18:00, closed Tue). From the park entrance on place Valhubert, the museums line the left side of the park (Mo: Gare d'Austerlitz or Jussieu).

3. Eiffel Tower, Champ de Mars Park, and
Trocadéro: You can easily fill an entire kid-fun day here.
Come early and ride the elevator up the tower before crowds appear, or ride it above the lights at night (see "Southwest Paris" in Sights chapter, page 33). The Champ de Mars park stretches out from the tower's base, with picnic-perfect benches, big toys, sand pits, and pony rides near the southwestern corner of the park. The center strip of grass is accessible only after the police leave (about dusk), though the corner grass pockets are fine anytime (Mo: Ecole Militaire or bus #69).

All ages enjoy the view from Trocadéro across the river to

the Eiffel Tower, especially after dark (Mo: Trocadéro). In-line skaters and skateboarders make the area below the Trocadéro a teenage scene, particularly during afternoons and evenings. Two kid-friendly museums flank Trocadéro: the Naval Museum *(Musée de la Marine)* and the extensive Museum of Man *(Musée de l'Homme)*. Neither offers much information in English, but both are pretty self-explanatory. An impressive collection of ship models, submarines, torpedoes, and naval you-name-it—including a small boat made for Napoleon—are docked at the Naval Museum (kids-€4, adults-€7, covered by museum pass, Wed–Mon 10:00–17:50, closed Tue, on the left side of the Trocadéro Square with your back to the Eiffel Tower). On the other side of the square, the sprawling Museum of Man is an anthropologist's dream, as cultures from Thailand to Lapland are creatively displayed on several floors with tools, costumes, and musical instruments (under 27-€3, adults-€5, not covered by museum pass, Wed–Mon 9:45–17:15, closed Tue).

4. Notre-Dame, Towers, and Crypt: Paris' famous Gothic cathedral doesn't have to be dry and dull. Replay Quasimodo's stunt and climb the tower. Kids love being on such a lofty perch with a face-to-face look at a gargoyle (go early or face long lines). The crypt on the square in front of Notre-Dame is quick and interesting. Kids can push buttons to highlight remains of Roman Paris and leave with a better understanding of how different civilizations build on top of each other. The small but beautiful park along the river and behind Notre-Dame has sandboxes, picnic benches, and space to run (Mo: Cité). ✪ See Historic Paris Walk, page 47.

5. Seine River Boat Rides: A variety of boats offer one-hour Seine cruises on huge glass-domed boats, with departures until 23:00. Or hop on a Bâtobus, a river bus connecting six stops along the river: Eiffel Tower, Orsay/place de la Concorde, Louvre, Notre-Dame, Hôtel de Ville, and St. Germain-des-Prés. Use the Bâtobus by day, and take a twilight cruise on a Bâteau-Mouche. See "Boat Tours," page 26.

6. Arc de Triomphe and Champs-Elysées: This area is popular with teenagers. Watch the crazy traffic rush around the Arc de Triomphe for endless entertainment, then stroll the Champs-Elysées, with its car dealerships (particularly Renault's concept-car exhibit), Virgin Megastore (music), Disney Store, and the river of humanity that flows along its broad sidewalks. Take your teenager to see a movie on the Champs-Elysées ("*v.o.*" next to the show time means it's shown in the original language). ✪ See Champs-Elysées Walk, page 69.

7. Versailles: This massive complex of palaces, gardens, fountains, and forest can be a good family getaway—if well-planned. Do the gardens first and the interior late, when crowds subside. Rent a bike for the gardens or a rowboat for the canal. The Hameau has barnyard animals nearby. Be careful of weekend crowds when the fountains are flowing. ✪ See Versailles Tour, page 215.

8. Pompidou Center: The Pompidou Center appeals more to teens, with its crazy outdoor entertainers, throngs of young people, happening cafés, and fun fountains next door. Inside, the temporary exhibits on the main floor are visually impressive. The *Star Wars* escalator to the top is fun for all ages, but you need to have a museum pass or a ticket for the modern art museum to escalate (Mo: Rambuteau). ✪ See Pompidou Center Tour, page 148.

9. The Cité des Sciences in the Parc de la Vilette: This is like a city of its own, filled with hands-on science museums (closed Mon). It's well-organized, with something for all ages, and provides some information in English—though it helps to have a good understanding of basic science or French to best decipher the exhibits. Walk up from the Métro Porte de la Vilette into the huge metal building and stop at the information desk to explore your options. Pick up the essential brochure ("The Keys to the Cité") explaining the exhibits, which include separate discovery/play areas for kids ages 3–5 and 5–11, and a Technocité for those ages 12 and up (each €5); the Explora museum (€7.50, helpful English audioguide-€3.80); an aquarium (€5); the Geode (a giant spherical movie screen, €7); and a planetarium (a €2.50 add-on to the Explora museum). All but the Geode are covered by the museum pass and kids under seven enter free. The Explora museum and the Geode are the most popular. Most of these areas have allotted times when you can enter, generally limited to 90 minutes per area (Tue–Sat 10:00–18:00, Sun until 19:00, closed Mon, tel. 01 40 05 12 12).

10. Aquaboulevard: Paris' best pool/water slide/miniature golf complex is easy to reach and a great escape from the museum scene. Indoor/outdoor pools with high-flying slides, waves, geysers, and Jacuzzis draw kids of all ages. It's a pricey but fun opportunity to see soaked Parisians at play. Ride the Métro to the end of line 8, Balard stop, walk two blocks under the elevated freeway, veer left across the traffic circle, and find Aquaboulevard in a complex of theaters and shops (kids under 12-€10/6 hrs, adults-€20/6 hrs, cheaper rates for more than one visit, staff SE, keep a €1 coin for lockers, boys and men need Speedo-style swimsuits—€6 at the Decathlon sporting goods store right there, tel. 01 40 60 10 00).

SHOPPING

Shopping can provide a good break between Paris' heavyweight museums and monuments. And, if approached carefully, shopping can be a culturally enlightening experience. Here you'll find information on shopping for souvenirs, clothing, food, and bargains.

Most travelers are interested in finding a few souvenirs and maybe an article of clothing. Here's a simplified approach that works for most:

1) If you just need souvenirs, find a souvenir shop or consult your neighborhood's supermarket for that Parisian box of tea, jam, or cookies—perfect for tucking into your suitcase at the last minute.

2) For more elaborate purchasing plans, the city's large department stores offer relatively painless one-stop shopping in elegant surroundings.

3) Neighborhood boutiques offer the greatest reward at the highest risk. While clerks and prices can be intimidating, the selection is more original and the experience totally Parisian.

Tips

Before you enter a Parisian store, remember:

- In small stores, always say *"Bonjour, Madame/Mademoiselle/ Monsieur"* when entering and *"Au revoir, Madame/Mademoiselle/ Monsieur"* when leaving.
- The customer is not always right. In fact, figure the clerk is doing you a favor by waiting on you.
- Except in department stores, it's not normal for the customer to handle clothing. Ask first if you can look at an item.
- Forget returns (and don't count on exchanges).
- Saturdays are busiest.
- Observe French shoppers. Then imitate.

Key Phrases

Just looking. - *Je regards.* (pron. zhuh ruh-gar)

How much is it? - *Combien?* (pron. kohm-bee-ehn)

Too big/small/expensive - *Trop grand/petit/cher.*
(pron. troh grahn/puh-tee/sher)

May I try it on? - *Je peut l'essayer?* (pron. zhuh puh
luh-say-yay)

Can I see more? - *Puis-je en voir d'autres?* (pron. pweezh
en vwahr doh-truh)

I'll think about it. - *Je vais y penser.* (pron. zhuh vay
zee pahn-say)

I'd like this. - *Je voudrais ça.* (pron. zhuh voo-dray sah)

On sale - *Soldé* (pron. sold-ay)

Discounted price - *Prix réduit* (pron. pree ray-dwee)

Big discounts - *Prix choc* (pron. pree shock)

Souvenir Shops

Avoid souvenir carts in front of famous monuments. Prices and
selection are better in shops. Look under the arcades of rue de
Rivoli (across from Tuileries Garden), around the Pompidou
Center, on the streets of Montmartre, and in department stores
(see below). The riverfront stalls near Notre-Dame sell a variety
of used books, magazines, and tourist paraphernalia in the most
romantic setting.

Department Stores *(Les Grandes Surfaces)*

Like cafés, department stores were invented here (surprisingly, not
in America). While the stores seem overwhelming at first, they generally work like ours, and those listed here are accustomed to wide-
eyed foreign shoppers and generally have English-speaking staff.
These stores are not only beautiful monuments to a more relaxed,
elegant era, but also a great lesson in how others live. It's fun to see
what's in style, check out Parisians' current taste in furniture, and
compare the selection with Nordstrom's. Parisian department stores
begin with their spectacular perfume sections, almost always at
ground zero and worth a visit to see how much space is devoted to
scented water. Helpful information desks are usually near the perfume section (pick up the handy floor plan in English). Most stores
have a good selection of souvenirs and toys at fair prices, plus reasonable restaurants; some have great view terraces. Stores are generally
open Monday through Saturday from 10:00 to 19:00. Choose from
these four great Parisian department stores:

Galeries Lafayette and Printemps

You'll find both Galeries Lafayette and Printemps (pron. pran-tom) department stores in several Parisian neighborhoods. The most convenient and busiest are side by side behind the old Opéra (Mo: Chaussée d'Antin, Havre-Caumartin, or Opéra). Both stores sprawl over three buildings and consume entire city blocks. The selection is huge. Don't miss the belle-époque dome at Galeries Lafayette or the rooftop view café on the top floor of Printemps. Fashion shows open to the public are held at both stores all year on Tuesdays at 11:00 and from April to October on Fridays at 14:30 (call 01 48 74 02 30 to reserve). Continue your shopping by walking from this area to the place Vendôme (see "Boutiques," below).

Samaritaine

Samaritaine (pron. sah-mah-ree-ten) is Paris' most central department store (on the Seine at Pont Neuf, Mo: Pont Neuf, see Historic Paris Walk, page 47). Old World elegant yet not high-priced, this is a handy place to take care of shopping business and enjoy one of the best views of Paris. Review the history of the store in dioramas at the top of the elevator, then climb to the panorama terrace on the 11th floor (€2).

Bon Marché

Combine this smaller, less touristy, and more manageable department store with a great neighborhood shopping experience. Take the Métro to Sèvres-Babylone and find the Bon Marché behind a small park. Start at the perfume section in the center, then escalate up a few floors for a better perspective. Consider a new couch (furniture on top floor) and review the toy selection in the basement. Graze the gourmet groceries in the store's second building (next door, ideal for food souvenirs like mustards, teas, and chocolates). I buy a small picnic here for the park in front. To find my favorite boutique streets (see "Sèvres-Babylone to St. Sulpice," below), walk through the small park, then walk down rue de Sèvres, passing the grand Hôtel Lutècia on your right.

Boutiques

I enjoy window-shopping on city streets, pausing at cafés, and observing the rhythm of neighborhood life. While the shops are more intimate, sales clerks are more formal—mind your manners. Here are four very different areas to sample:

Sèvres-Babylone to St. Sulpice

This shopping stroll allows you to sample smart, classic clothing boutiques while enjoying one of Paris' prettier neighborhoods.

VAT Refunds

Wrapped into the purchase price of your Parisian souvenirs is a Value Added Tax (VAT) that's generally about 17 percent. If you make a purchase of more than €175 at a store that participates in the VAT refund scheme, you're entitled to get most of that tax back. Personally, I've never felt that VAT refunds are worth the hassle, but if you do, here's the scoop.

If you're lucky, the merchant will subtract the tax when you make your purchase (this is more likely if the store ships the goods to your home). If not, follow these steps:

Get the paperwork. Have the merchant completely fill out the necessary refund document, called a "cheque." You'll have to present your passport at the store.

Have your cheque(s) stamped at the border at your last stop in the European Union (usually the airport) by the customs agent who deals with VAT refunds. It's best to keep your purchases in your carry-on for viewing, but if they're too large or considered too dangerous to carry on, then track down the proper customs agent to inspect them before you check your bag. You're not supposed to use your purchased goods before you leave. If you show up at customs wearing your chic new French outfit, officials might look the other way—or deny you a refund.

To collect your refund, you'll need to return your stamped documents to the retailer or its representative. Many merchants work with a service such as Global Refund or Cashback, which have offices at major airports, ports, or border crossings. These services, which extract a 4 percent fee, can refund your money immediately in your currency of choice or credit your card (within 2 billing cycles). If you have to deal directly with the retailer, mail the store your stamped documents, then wait. It could take months.

This easy, 40-minute saunter starts at the Bon Marché department store (described above) and ends at the church of St. Sulpice. From the Bon Marché store (or Sèvres-Babylone Métro stop), cross boulevard Raspail and start down the rue de Sèvres.

Au Sauvignon Café, on the left at 10 rue de Sèvres, is good for lunch or a drink and is perfectly situated for watching the conveyor belt of shoppers glide by. For dessert, cross over to **La Maison du Chocolat** (19 rue de Sèvres), selling handmade chocolates in exquisitely wrapped boxes.

A few blocks farther down the rue de Sèvres is a half-man, half-horse statue. From here, boutique-lined streets fan out like spokes on a wheel. Rues du Dragon, du Cherche Midi, de Grenelle, and du Vieux Colombier come together here, and each merits a detour if you're a serious shopper. Rue du Cherche Midi offers an ever-changing but always chic selection of shoe, purse, and clothing stores. Many stores on rue du Vieux Colombier offer just one or two items, but in a variety of colors and patterns: Check out **Vilebrequin** if the man or *petit-garçon* in your life needs a swimsuit, or **Hervé Chapelier** or **Longchamps** for a stylish bag in any color. Veer briefly onto rue Bonaparte, and at #57, watch ivory pieces being intricately carved or meticulously restored. Circle back to rue du Vieux Colombier and end your shopping stroll at the church of St. Sulpice (a short hop from the Luxembourg Garden; see page 37).

Place de la Madeleine, Rue Royale, and Place Vendôme

The ritzy streets connecting these high-priced squares are a miracle mile of gourmet food shops, jewelry stores, four-star hotels, perfumeries, and exclusive clothing boutiques. No area better shows the value Parisians place on outrageously priced gourmet products. If done in its entirety (with brief stops to shop), this walk takes about two hours, though it also works well in smaller bites.

Place de la Madeleine: Start at the place de la Madeleine (Mo: Madeleine; see map on page 31) for a gourmet food fantasy. Work your way counterclockwise around the square, starting at the faded pink awnings of **Fauchon's,** behind the basilica. This bastion of over-the-top food products has faded from its glory days and today caters to a largely tourist clientele (mostly Japanese)—though it can still make your mouth water and your pocketbook ache. Four separate shops are necessary to meet demand: a tea room (*salon de thé*), meat (*charcuterie*), pastry (*pâtisserie*), and a grocery (*épicerie*). The *charcuterie* and *pâtisserie* are each worth a quick glance (you'll see better elsewhere), but the *épicerie* is a must. Stroll downstairs to find €7,000 bottles of Cognac (in the small glass case at the rear—who buys this stuff?) and a wall of water demonstrating the French preoccupation with what goes in their mouths (bottled waters come in countless varieties and are evaluated with reverence). Ride the padded pink elevator up to the aromatic tea shop and exotic spice room.

Turn right out of Fauchon's and find **Hediard's** across the square (#21). This older, more appealing, and more accessible gourmet food shop was founded in 1854 and offers elegantly displayed produce and meats, a slick atrium wine shop, and a nifty café above (take the glass elevator up for a coffee or lunch).

You'll find small red containers (good for souvenirs) with flavored mustards, jams, coffee, candies, and tea.

Next to Hediard's at #19 is **La Maison des Truffes,** the house of truffles. Check the window display of black mushrooms that sell for about €180/pound. Inside, you'll find five cozy little tables and every food that can be made with truffles, as well as white truffles from Italy that sell for €2,500/pound. Tempted?

At #17, **Caviar Kaspia,** you can add caviar, eel, and vodka to your truffle collection. The restaurant upstairs serves (at exorbitant prices) what you see downstairs.

Rue Royale: Passing the Baccarat crystal shop on your right, cross the place de la Madeleine and trade gourmet food for material possessions. Pass the three-star restaurant **Lucas Carton** (allow €300 for dinner—per person) and strut down the rue Royale (Royal Street). Don't miss a detour into **Le Village Royale** for a cozy lineup of fine shops and a peaceful café break at **Le Coffee Shop.** Continue down rue Royale to one of *the* premier shopping street intersections in the world (rue Royale and rue St. Honoré). For fine crystal and silver, continue down rue Royale another block, then return to rue St. Honoré to continue the walk.

Rue St Honoré: At the northeast corner of rue St. Honoré and Rue Royale, **Dalloyau Pâtisserie** offers an out-of-this-world pastry break. Since 1802, their goal has been to lure shoppers away from expensive fashions with luscious cakes and pastries (open daily until 21:00). From here, walk east up rue St. Honoré (toward place Vendôme). Classic clothing, shoes, coiffeurs, and a great toy store (**Au Nain Bleu,** #406, 3 floors of top-notch, top-price toys) occupy the windows of this upscale shoppers' row. A left on rue de Castiglione leads into . . .

Place Vendôme: The *très* elegant place Vendôme is home to the Ritz Hôtel on the left (Hemingway liberated the bar in World War II) and upper-crust stores on the right, including jewelry by Van Cleef, clothes by Armani, and watches by Swatch (if you have to ask how much . . .). This square was created by Louis XIV in the 17th century as a setting for a statue of himself. One hundred and fifty years later, Louis was replaced by a statue of Napoleon.

Leave place Vendôme by walking up rue de la Paix—strolling by still more jewelry, high-priced watches, and crystal—and enter place de l'Opéra. Now that you're well-clothed, well-coiffed, and well-jeweled, you're ready to be seen in this most fashionable of belle-époque settings, Le Palais Garnier (see "Northwest Paris" in Sights chapter, page 39). Behind the grand, golden-topped Opéra are the Galeries Lafayette and Printemps department stores (see "Department Stores," above).

Le Marais

For more eclectic, avant-garde stores, peruse the artsy shops between the Pompidou Center and place des Vosges. Stick to the west-to-east axes formed by rue Ste. Croix de la Bretonnerie, rue des Rosiers, rue des Francs Bourgeois, and rue St. Antoine. (These streets are part of the Marais Walk on page 78; see map on page 79.) Rue des Francs Bourgeois bustles with trendy boutiques between place des Vosges and the Carnavalet Museum. On Sunday afternoons, when the rest of Paris naps, this area is jammed with shoppers and café crowds.

Bercy Village

For a contemporary, more casual, and less frenetic shopping experience, and to see Paris' latest urban renewal project, come to Bercy Village (daily 11:00–21:00 year-round). Once a thriving wine warehouse district, it traded barrels for boutiques and has been transformed into an outdoor shopping mall. The linear square, cour St. Emilion (named for one of Bordeaux's wine villages), is lined with cafés and appealing shops. Rail tracks are still embedded in the cobbles, and photos of its original purpose hang under the passages. Club Med greets you with its "*zone de plaisir*" complex of shops and restaurants that positively throb at night (quiz nights, concerts, and "Friday Night Fever" keep a young clientele well-entertained). Don't miss the French National Museum store and the Animalis pet shop.

Sleeping in Bercy Village: Hotel Ibis** is a chain hotel offering very cheap and small but clean, modern, and efficient rooms across from cour St. Emilion (Db-€63, 2 place de l'Europe, tel. 01 49 77 11 97, fax 01 49 77 81 91).

Getting to Bercy Village: Take Paris' newest Métro line (14) to the futuristic station at cour St. Emilion (just 2 stops east sof Gare de Lyon), where signs lead you into the cour St. Emilion shopping area. The well-manicured parc de Bercy, with flowers and ponds, is next to the Métro stop.

Flea Markets

Paris plays host to several sprawling flea markets (*marché aux puces*; pron. mar-shay oh-poos; literally translated, since *puce* is French for flea). These oversized garage sales were started in the Middle Ages, when middle-men would sell old, flea-infested clothes and discarded possessions of the wealthy at bargain prices to eager peasants. Buyers were allowed to rummage through piles of aristocratic garbage.

No event better brings together the melting-pot population of Paris than these almost carnival-like markets. Some find them claustrophobic, crowded, monster versions of those back home, though others find their French diamonds-in-the-rough and return happy. All of Paris' flea markets take place over weekends, and a few are open Mondays (the calmest days). Come early for the best deals and fewest crowds. You can bargain a bit, and you'll generally do better by paying with cash. Note: Wear your moneybelt; pickpockets enjoy these wall-to-wall shopper events.

The **Puces St. Ouen** (pron. poos sahn-wahn) is the biggest and oldest of them all, with more than 2,000 vendors selling everything under the sun, from flamingos to faucets (Sat 9:00–18:30, Sun–Mon 10:00–18:30, closed Tue–Fri, Mo: Porte de Clingancourt). **Puces de Vanves** is comparatively tiny and civilized (Sat–Sun 7:00–13:00, closed Mon-Fri, Mo: Porte de Vanves). The mega-**Puces de Montreuil** is the least organized and most traditional of them all, with chatty sellers and competitive buyers (Sat–Mon 8:00–18:00, closed Tue–Fri, Mo: Porte de Montreuil).

Street Markets

Several traffic-free street markets (like on the rue Cler) overflow with flowers, produce, fish vendors, and butchers, illustrating how most Parisians shopped until the invention of supermarkets and department stores. Browse these markets for picnics, or find a corner café from which to appreciate the scene.

Here is a list of Paris' most appealing street markets (open daily except Sun afternoons and Mon; also closed for lunch 13:00–15:00):

Rue Cler is a refined street market serving an upscale neighborhood near the Eiffel Tower (Mo: Ecole Militaire, for details, see Rue Cler Walk, page 85).

Rue Montorgueil is less touristy but central to many sights, and famous as the last vestige of the once-massive Les Halles market (just north of St. Eustache church, Mo: Etienne Marcel).

Rue Mouffetard is touristy but fun. Combine a visit to this market with the Luxembourg Garden (start at place de la Contrescarpe and work your way down, Mo: Cardinal Lemoine or Censier-Daubenton; for more, see Luxembourg Garden, page 38, and "Contrescarpe Orientation," page 276).

Rue Daguerre, near the Catacombs, is the least touristy of the four (off avenue du Général Leclerc, Mo: Denfert-Rochereau, for Catacombs description, see page 39).

Weekly Markets: Offering cheaper prices and more selection, weekly markets take over selected boulevards and squares throughout Paris (8:00–13:00). Expect a lively combination of flea and street market atmosphere and items.

Marché de la place d'Aligre, a few blocks behind the Opéra

de la Bastille, runs daily and is a more intimate, locally popular open-air market (daily 9:00–12:00, place d'Aligre, Mo:
Ledru-Rollin).

Marché de la Bastille is huge, with a vast selection of products (Thu and Sun, Mo: Bastille); consider combining either of
these two markets with a stroll through the Promenade Plantée
park (see page 44) and the Marais Walk route (see page 78).

Marché Place Monge is comparatively minuscule, specializing in high-quality foods (Wed, Fri, and Sun, near rue Mouffetard,
Mo: Monge).

Marché Boulevard de Grenelle, a few blocks southwest
of the Champ de Mars park and the rue Cler area, is packed with
produce, non-perishable goods, and Parisians in search of a good
value (Wed and Sun, between Dupleix and La Motte Picquet-
Grenelle Métro stops).

Marché Belleville is big and very untouristy (Tue and
Fri, Mo: Belleville).

NIGHTLIFE

Paris is brilliant after dark. Save energy from your day's sightseeing and get out at night. Whether it's a concert at the Sainte-Chapelle, a boat ride on the Seine, an elevator up the Arc de Triomphe, or a late-night café, experience the City of Lights lit. *Pariscope* magazine (€0.50 at any newsstand, in French) offers a complete weekly listing of music, cinema, theater, opera, and other special events—I decipher this useful periodical for you below. The *Paris Voice* newspaper, in English, has a monthly review of Paris entertainment (available at any English-language bookstore, French-American establishments, or the American Church, www.parisvoice.com).

A Tour of *Pariscope*

The weekly *Pariscope* (€0.50) and *L'Officiel des Spectacles* (€0.35) are both cheap and essential if you want to know what's happening. Pick one up at a newsstand and page through it. For a head start, *Pariscope* has a Web site: www.pariscope.fr (in French).

Each begins with culture news. Skip the bulky "Théâtres" and "Dîners/Spectacles" sections and anything listed as "des environs" (outside of Paris). "Musique" or "Concerts Classiques" follow, listing each day's events (program, location, time, and price). Venues with phone numbers and addresses are listed in an "Adresses des Salles de Concerts" sidebar. Touristic venues (such as Sainte-Chapelle and Eglise de la Madeleine) are often featured in display ads. "Opéras, Musique Traditionelle, Ballet/Danse," and "Jazz/Rock" listings follow.

Half of these magazines are devoted to cinema—a Parisian forte. After the "Films Nouveaux" section trumpets new releases, the "Films en Exclusivité" pages list all the films playing in town. While a code marks films as "Historique," "Karate," "Erotisme," and so on, the key mark for tourists is "v.o.," which means *version*

originale (American films have their English soundtracks). Films
are listed alphabetically, with theaters and their *arrondissements* at
the end of each entry. Then films are listed by neighborhood
("Salles Paris") and by genre. First-runs are shown at cinemas on
the Champs-Elysées and on place de l'Odéon; art films and older
films are best found in the Latin Quarter. To find a showing near
your hotel, simply match the *arrondissement*. (But don't hesitate to
hop on the Métro for the film you want.) "Salles Périphérie" are
out in the suburbs.

　　Pariscope has a small English "Time Out" section listing the
week's events. The "Musées" sections ("Monuments," "Jardins,"
"Autres Curiosités," "Promenades," "Activités Sportives," "Pis-
cines") give the latest hours of the sights, gardens, curiosities,
tours, sports, swimming pools, and so on ("tlj" stands for *tous les
jours*—daily). "Clubs de Loisirs" are various athletic and social
clubs. "Pour les Jeunes" is for young people (kids' films, anima-
tions/cartoons, marionettes, circuses, and amusement parks such
as Astérix and Disney). "Conferences" are mostly lectures. For
cancan mischief, look under "Paris la Nuit," "Cabarets," or the
busty "Spectacles Erotiques."

　　Finally, you'll find a TV listing. Paris has four countrywide
stations: TF1, France 2, France 3, and the new Arte station (a
German/French cultural channel). M6 is filled with American
series. Canal Plus (channel 4) is a cable channel that airs an
American news show at 7 in the morning and an American
sports event on Sunday evenings.

Music

Jazz Clubs: With a lively mix of American, French, and international musicians, Paris has been an internationally acclaimed jazz
capital since World War II. You'll pay €6–24 to enter a jazz club
(1 drink may be included; if not, expect to pay €5–9 per drink;
beer is cheapest). See *Pariscope* magazine under "Musique" for
listings, or better, the American Church's *Paris Voice* paper for a
good monthly review, or drop by the clubs to check out their calendars posted on the front door. Music starts after 21:00 in most
clubs. Some offer dinner concerts from about 20:30 on. Here are
several good bets:

　　Caveau de la Huchette, a characteristic old jazz club, fills
an ancient Latin Quarter cellar with live jazz and frenzied dancing
every night (€9 weekday, €12 weekend admission, €5 drinks,
Tue–Sun 21:30–2:30 or later, closed Mon, 5 rue de la Huchette,
Mo: St. Michel, recorded info tel. 01 43 26 65 05).

　　For a hotbed of late-night activity and jazz, go to the two-
block-long rue des Lombards, at boulevard Sebastopol, midway

between the river and the Pompidou Center (Mo: Chatelet). **Au Duc des Lombards,** right at the corner, is one of the most popular and respected jazz clubs in Paris, with concerts generally at 21:00 (42 rue des Lombards, tel. 01 42 33 22 88). **Le Sunside** offers more traditional jazz—Dixieland and big band—and fewer crowds, with concerts generally at 21:00 (60 rue des Lombards, tel. 01 40 26 21 25).

At the more down-to-earth and mellow **Le Cave du Franc Pinot,** you can enjoy a glass of chardonnay at the main-floor wine bar, then drop downstairs for a cool jazz scene (good dinner-and-jazz values as well, located on Ile St. Louis where pont Marie meets the island, 1 quai de Bourbon, Mo: Pont Marie, tel. 01 46 33 60 64).

Classical Concerts: For classical music on any night, consult *Pariscope* magazine; the "Musique" section under "Concerts Classiques" lists concerts (free and fee). Look for posters at the churches. Churches that regularly host concerts (usually March–Nov) include St. Sulpice, St. Germain-des-Prés, Basilique de la Madeleine, St. Eustache, St. Julien-le-Pauvre, and Sainte-Chapelle. It's worth the €15–23 entry for the pleasure of hearing Mozart while surrounded by the stained glass of the tiny Sainte-Chapelle (it's unheated—bring a sweater). Look also for daytime concerts in parks, such as the Luxembourg Garden. Even the Galeries Lafayette department store offers concerts. Many concerts are free *(entrée libre),* such as the Sunday atelier concert sponsored by the American Church (18:00, not every week, Sept–May, 65 quai d'Orsay, Mo: Invalides, RER: Pont de l'Alma, tel. 01 40 62 05 00).

Opera: Paris is home to two well-respected opera venues. The Opéra de la Bastille is the massive modern opera house that dominates place de la Bastille. Come here for state-of-the-art special effects and modern interpretations of classic ballets and operas. In the spirit of this everyman's opera, unsold seats are available at a big discount to seniors and students 15 minutes before the show (Mo: Bastille, tel. 01 43 43 96 96). The Opéra Garnier, Paris' first opera house, hosts opera and ballet performances. Come here for less expensive tickets and grand belle-époque decor (Mo: Opéra, tel. 01 44 73 13 99). For tickets, call 01 44 73 13 00, go to the opera ticket offices (open 11:00–18:00), or best, reserve on the Web at www.opera-de-paris.fr (for both opera houses).

Bus Tours

Paris Illumination Tours, run by Paris Vision, connect all the great illuminated sights of Paris with a 100-minute bus tour in 12 languages. Double-decker buses have huge windows, but customers continuing to the overrated Moulin Rouge get the most desirable front seats.

You'll stampede on with a United Nations of tourists, get an audioguide, and listen to a tape-recorded spiel (interesting but occasionally hard to hear). Uninspired as it is, this provides an entertaining first-night overview of the city at its floodlit and scenic best (bring your city map to stay oriented as you go). Left-side seats are marginally better. Visibility is fine in the rain. You're always on the bus except for one five-minute cigarette break at the Eiffel Tower viewpoint (adults-€23, kids under 11 ride free, departures at 20:30 nightly all year, also at 21:30 April–Oct only, departs from Paris Vision office at 214 rue de Rivoli, across the street from Mo: Tuileries).

The same company will take you on the same route for twice the price by minivan—pick-up is at your hotel, the driver is a qualified guide, and there's a maximum of seven clients (adult-€46, kids ages 4–11-€23).

These trips are sold through your hotel (brochures in lobby) or at Paris Vision (214 rue de Rivoli, tel. for bus and minivans 01 42 60 30 01, fax 01 42 86 95 36, www.parisvision.com).

Seine River Cruises

The Bâteaux-Mouches offers one-hour cruises on huge glass-domed boats with departures along the Seine, including from the Eiffel Tower (every 20–30 min 10:00–22:30; see "Organized Tours of Paris" on page 26).

Night Walks and Scenes

Go for a walk to best appreciate the City of Lights. Break for ice cream, pause at a café, and enjoy the sidewalk entertainers as you join the post-dinner Parisian parade. Consider these walks:

Champs-Elysées and the Arc de Triomphe—✪ See Champs-Elysées Walk, page 69. This is brilliant after dark. Start at the Arc de Triomphe, then stroll down the lively Champs-Elysées. A right turn on avenue George V leads to the Bâteaux-Mouches river cruises. A movie on the Champs-Elysées is a fun experience (weekly listings in *Pariscope* under "Cinema").

Trocadéro and Eiffel Tower—These monuments glimmer at night. Take the Métro to the Trocadéro stop and join the party on place de la Trocadéro for a magnificent view of the glowing Eiffel Tower. It's a festival of gawkers, drummers, street acrobats, and entertainers. Pass the fountains and cross the river to the base of the tower, worth the effort even if you don't go up. See "Eiffel Tower," page 33.

From the Eiffel Tower, you can stroll through the Parc du Champ de Mars past Frisbees, soccer balls, and romantic couples and take the Métro home (Ecole Militaire stop, across avenue de la Motte Piquet from the far southeast corner of the park). Or, to head home sooner, there's a handy RER stop (Champ de Mars–Tour Eiffel) two blocks west (downriver) of the Eiffel Tower.

Ile St. Louis and Notre-Dame—✪ See Historic Paris Walk, page 47. Take this beautiful evening stroll after having dinner on Ile St. Louis (see page 298 of the Eating chapter).

To get to Ile St. Louis, take the Métro (line 7) to the Pont Marie stop, then cross pont Marie to Ile St. Louis. Turn right up rue St. Louis en l'Ile, stopping for dinner—or a Berthillon ice cream at #31. At the end of Ile St. Louis, cross pont St. Louis to Ile de la Cité with a great view of Notre-Dame. Cross to the left bank on quai de l'Archevêché and drop down to the river to the right for the best floodlit views. End your walk on place du Parvis in front of Notre-Dame or continue across the river to the Latin Quarter.

Rue de Lappe—Take a walk on Paris' wild side along the three-block stretch of rue de Lappe, behind the Bastille from boulevard Richard Lenoir to rue de Charonne (Mo: Bastille). Nightclubs, bouncer-staffed bars, and youthful, boy-meets-girl energy power this late-night scene until the wee hours.

TRANSPORTATION
CONNECTIONS

This chapter covers Paris' two airports, six train stations, and main bus station, plus parking tips for drivers.

When leaving Paris, arrive at your departure point early to allow time for waiting in lines (3 hours for an overseas flight, or 1 hour before a flight within Europe, a train trip—including Eurostar—or a bus ride). For the latest information on Paris airports, check www.adp.fr.

CHARLES DE GAULLE AIRPORT

Paris' primary airport has three main terminals: T-1, T-2, and T-9. British Air, SAS, United, US Air, KLM, Northwest, and Lufthansa all normally use T-1. Air France dominates T-2, though you'll also find Delta, Continental, American, and Air Canada. Charter flights leave from T-9. Airlines sometimes switch terminals, so verify your terminal before flying. Terminals are connected every few minutes by a free *navette* (shuttle bus, line #1). The RER (Paris subway) stops near the T-1 and T-2 terminals, and the TGV (stands for *train à grande vitesse;* pron. tay-zhay-vay) station is at T-2. There is no bag storage at the airport.

Those flying to or from the United States will almost certainly use T-1 or T-2. Below is information for each terminal. For flight information, call 01 48 62 22 80.

Terminal 1 (T-1): This round terminal covers 3 floors—arrival (top floor), departure (one floor down) and shops (basement level). The ADP (quasi–tourist office) provides helpful tourist information on the arrival level at gate 36 (look for *Meeting Point* signs). They have museum passes and free maps and hotel information (daily 7:00–22:00). A nearby Relay store sells phone cards. A bank (with lousy rates) is near gate 16. An American Express cash machine and a generic ATM are near gate 32.

Car-rental offices are on the arrival level from gates 10–24; the SNCF (train) office is at gate 22.

Shuttle buses to the RER and to terminal 2 (and the TGV station) leave from outside gate 36—take the elevator down to level (*niveau*) 2, walk outside to find the buses (line #1 serves T-2 including the TGV station, line #2 goes directly to the RER station). The **Air France bus** departs outside gate 34. The **Roissy Bus** leaves outside gate 30 (buy tickets inside at gate 30). **Taxis** wait outside gate 20 and the **Disneyland Express** bus departs from gate 32 (see "Transportation between Charles de Gaulle airport and Paris," below).

Those departing from T-1 will find restaurants, a PTT (post office), a pharmacy, boutiques, and a handy grocery store one floor below the ticketing desks (level 2 on the elevator).

Terminal 2 (T-2): This long, horseshoe-shaped terminal is divided into several sub-terminals (or Halls), each identified by a letter. Halls are connected with each other, the RER, the TGV station, and T-1 every five minutes with free *navettes* (shuttle buses, line #1 runs to T-1). Here is where you should find these key carriers: in Hall A—Air France, Air Canada, and American Airlines; in Hall C—Delta, Continental, and more Air France. The RER and TGV stations are below the Sheraton Hotel (access by *navettes* or on foot). Stops for *navettes*, Air France buses, and Roissy Buses are all well-marked and near each Hall (see "Transportation between Charles de Gaulle airport and Paris," below). ADP information desks are located near gate 5 in each Hall. Car-rental offices, post offices, pharmacies, and ATMs (*point argent*) are also well-marked.

Transportation between Charles de Gaulle airport and Paris: Three efficient public-transportation routes, taxis, and airport shuttle vans link the airport's terminals with central Paris. All are marked with good signs and their stops are centrally located at all terminals. The **RER,** with stops near T-1 and at T-2 (€8), runs every 15 minutes and stops at Gare du Nord, Chatelet, St. Michel, and Luxembourg Garden in central Paris. When coming from Paris to the airport, T-1 is the first RER stop at Charles de Gaulle; T-2 is the second stop.

Roissy Buses run every 15 minutes to Paris' Opéra Garnier (€8, 40 min); the Opéra stop is on rue Scribe at the American Express office). Three **Air France bus** routes serve central Paris about every 15 minutes (Arc de Triomphe and Porte Maillot-€11, 40 min; Montparnasse Tower/train station-€12, 60 min; or the Gare de Lyon station-€12, 40 min).

Taxis with luggage will run €40–55. If taking a cab to the airport, ask your hotel to call for you (the night before if you must leave early) and specify that you want a real taxi (*un taxi normal*) and not a limo-service that costs €20 more.

Airport **shuttles** offer a stress-free trip between either of Paris' airports and downtown, ideal for single travelers or families of four or more (taxis are limited to three). Reserve from home and they'll meet you at the airport (€23 for 1 person, €27 for 2, €41 for 3, €55 for 4, plan on a 30-min wait if you ask them to pick you up at the airport). Choose between **Airport Connection** (tel. 01 44 18 36 02, fax 01 45 55 85 19, www.airport-connection.com) and **Paris Airport Services** (tel. 01 55 98 10 80, fax 01 55 98 10 89, www.parisairportservice.com).

Sleeping at or near Charles de Gaulle Airport: Hôtel Ibis**, outside the RER Roissy Rail station for T-1 (the first RER stop coming from Paris), offers standard and predictable accommodations (Db-€85, CC, near *navette* stop, free shuttle bus to either terminal, tel. 01 49 19 19 19, fax 01 49 19 19 21, e-mail: h1404sb@accor-hotels.com). **Novotel***** is next door and the next step up (Db-€130–145, CC, tel. 01 49 19 27 27, fax 01 49 19 27 99, e-mail: h1014@accor-hotels.com).

To avoid rush-hour traffic, drivers may consider sleeping north of Paris in either **Auvers-sur-Oise** (30 min west of airport, see page 247 in More Day Trips chapter), or in the pleasant medieval town of **Senlis** (15 min north of airport) at **Hostellerie de la Porte Bellon** (Db-€70, CC, in the center at 51 rue Bellon, near rue de la République, tel. 03 44 53 03 05, fax 03 44 53 29 94).

ORLY AIRPORT

This airport feels small. Orly has two terminals: Sud and Ouest. International flights arrive at Sud. After exiting Sud's baggage claim (near gate H), you'll see signs directing you to city transportation, car rental, and so on. Turn left to enter the main terminal area, and you'll find exchange offices with bad rates, an ATM, the ADP (a quasi–tourist office that offers free city maps and basic sightseeing information, open until 23:00), and an SNCF French rail desk (closes at 18:00, sells train tickets and even Eurailpasses, next to the ADP). Downstairs are a sandwich bar, WCs, a bank (same bad rates), a newsstand (buy a phone card), and a post office (great rates for cash or American Express traveler's checks). Car-rental offices are located in the parking lot in front of the terminal. For flight info on any airline serving Orly, call 01 49 75 15 15.

Transportation between Paris and Orly Airport: Several efficient public-transportation routes, taxis, and a couple of airport shuttle services link Orly and central Paris. The gate locations listed below apply to Orly Sud, but the same transportation services are available from both terminals.

Bus services to central Paris: The **Air France bus** (outside gate K) runs to Paris' Invalides Métro stop (€8, 4/hr, 30 min) and is handy for those staying in or near the rue Cler neighborhood (from Invalides bus stop, take the Métro 2 stops to Ecole Militaire to reach recommended hotels, see also under RER access below).

The **Jetbus #285** (outside gate H, €5, 4/hr) is the quickest way to the Paris subway and the best way to the Marais and Contrescarpe neighborhoods (take Jetbus to Villejuif Métro stop, buy a *carnet* of 10 Métro tickets, then take the Métro to the Sully Morland stop for the Marais area, or the Censier-Daubenton or Monge stops for the Contrescarpe area. If going to the airport, make sure your train serves Villejuif, as the route splits at the end of the line). The **Orlybus** (outside gate H, €6, 4/hr) takes you to the Denfert-Rochereau RER-B line and the Métro, offering subway access to central Paris.

These routes provide access to Paris via **RER trains:** an ADP shuttle bus takes you to RER line C, with connections to Austerlitz, St. Michel, Musée d'Orsay, Invalides, and Pont de l'Alma stations (outside gate G, 4/hr, €5.5). The **Orlyval trains** are overpriced (€9) and require a transfer at the Antony stop to reach RER line B (serving Luxembourg, Chatelet, St. Michel, and Gare du Nord stations in central Paris).

Taxis are to the far right as you leave the terminal, at gate M. Allow €26–35 for a taxi into central Paris.

Airport shuttle minivans are ideal for single travelers or families of four or more (see "Charles de Gaulle Airport," above, for the companies to contact; from Orly, figure about €18 for 1 person, €12/person for 2, less for larger groups and kids).

Sleeping near Orly Airport: Hôtel Ibis** is reasonable, basic, and close by (Db-€60, CC, tel. 01 56 70 50 60, fax 01 56 70 50 70, e-mail: h1413@accor-hotels.com). **Hôtel Mercure***** provides more comfort for a price (Db-€120–135, tel. 01 49 75 15 50, fax 01 49 75 15 51, e-mail: h1246@accor-hotels.com). Both have free shuttles to the terminal.

PARIS' TRAIN STATIONS

Paris is Europe's rail hub, with six major train stations, each serving different regions: Gare de l'Est (eastbound trains), Gare du Nord (northern France and Europe), Gare St. Lazare (northwestern France), Gare d'Austerlitz (southwest France and Europe), Gare de Lyon (southeastern France and Italy), and Gare Montparnasse (northwestern France and TGV service to France's southwest). Any train station can give you schedule information, make reservations, and sell tickets for any destination. Buying tickets is handier from an SNCF neighborhood office (e.g., Louvre, Invalides, Orsay, Versailles, airports) or at your neighborhood travel agency—worth the small fee (SNCF signs in their window indicate they sell train tickets). For schedule information, call 08 36 35 35 35 (€0.50/min, English sometimes available).

All six train stations have Métro, bus, and taxi service. All have banks or change offices, ATMs, information desks, telephones, cafés, baggage storage *(consigne automatique)*, newsstands, and clever pickpockets. Each station offers two types of rail service: long distance to other cities, called *Grandes Lignes* (major lines); and suburban service to outlying areas, called *banlieue* or RER. Both *banlieue* and RER trains serve outlying areas and the airports; the only difference is that *banlieue* lines are operated by SNCF (France's train system) and RER lines are operated by RATP (Paris' Métro and bus system). Paris train stations can be intimidating, but if you slow down, take a deep breath, and ask for help, you'll find them manageable and efficient. Bring a pad of paper for clear communication at ticket/info windows. All stations have helpful *accueil* (information) booths; the bigger stations have roving helpers, usually in red vests.

Station Overview

Here's an overview of Paris' major train stations. Métro, RER, buses, and taxis are well-signposted at every station. When arriving by Métro, follow signs for *Grandes Lignes*-SNCF to find the main tracks.

Gare du Nord: This vast station serves cities in northern France and international destinations north of Paris, including Copenhagen, Amsterdam (see "To Brussels and Amsterdam by Thalys Train," below), and the Eurostar to London (see "The Eurostar Train to London," below) as well as two of the day trips described in this book (Auvers-sur-Oise and Chantilly). Arrive early to allow time to navigate this station. From the Métro, follow *Grandes Lignes* signs (main lines) and keep going up until you reach the tracks at street level. *Grandes Lignes* depart from tracks 3–21, suburban *(banlieue)* lines from tracks 30–36, and RER trains depart from tracks 37–44 (tracks 41–44 are 1 floor below). Glass train information booths *(accueil)* are scattered throughout the station and information staff circulate to help (all rail staff are required to speak English). Information booths for the **Thalys** (high-speed trains to Brussels and Amsterdam) are opposite track 8. All non-Eurostar ticket sales are opposite tracks 3–8. Passengers departing on **Eurostar** (London via Chunnel) must buy tickets and check in on the second level, opposite track 6. (Note: Britain's time zone is 1 hour earlier than the Continent's; times listed on Eurostar tickets are local times.) A peaceful café/bar hides on the upper level past the Eurostar ticket windows. Lockers,

Paris' Train Stations

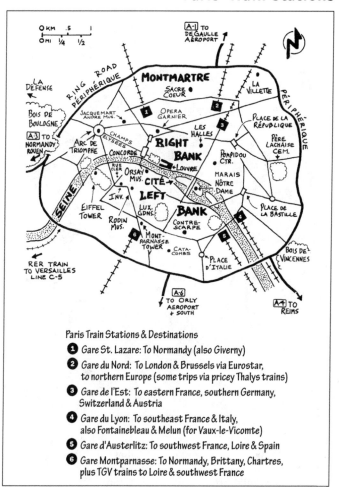

0 KM .5 1
0 MI 1/4 1/2

A-1 TO
DE GAULLE
AÉROPORT

LA
DÉFENSE

RING ROAD
PÉRIPHÉRIQUE

MONTMARTRE

SACRÉ
COEUR

LA
VILLETTE

PÉRIPHÉRIQUE

BOIS DE
BOULOGNE

JACQUEMART
ANDRÉ MUS.

1

OPÉRA
GARNIER

2

PLACE DE LA
RÉPUBLIQUE

A-3 TO
NORMANDY
ROUEN

ARC DE
TRIOMPHE

CHAMPS
ELYSÉES

CONCORDE

LES
HALLES

3

PÈRE
LACHAISE
CEM.

RIGHT
BANK

+ LOUVRE

POMPIDOU
CTR.

RUE
CLER.

ORSAY
MUS.

CITÉ

SEINE

INV.

EIFFEL
TOWER

RODIN
MUS.

LEFT

LUX.
GDNS.

BANK

MARAIS
NÔTRE
DAME

PLACE DE
LA BASTILLE

4

CONTRE-
SCARPE

6

MONT-
PARNASSE
TOWER

CATA-
COMBS

5

PLACE
D'ITALIE

BOIS DE
VINCENNES

RER TRAIN
TO VERSAILLES
LINE C-5

A-6
TO ORLY
AÉROPORT
+ SOUTH

A-4 TO
REIMS

N

Paris Train Stations & Destinations

1 Gare St. Lazare: To Normandy (also Giverny)

2 Gare du Nord: To London & Brussels via Eurostar,
to northern Europe (some trips via pricey Thalys trains)

3 Gare de l'Est: To eastern France, southern Germany,
Switzerland & Austria

4 Gare du Lyon: To southeast France & Italy,
also Fontainebleau & Melun (for Vaux-le-Vicomte)

5 Gare d'Austerlitz: To southwest France, Loire & Spain

6 Gare Montparnasse: To Normandy, Brittany, Chartres,
plus TGV trains to Loire & southwest France

baggage check, taxis, and rental cars are at the far end, opposite
track 3 and down the steps.

Key destinations served by Gare du Nord *Grandes Lignes:*
Brussels (21/day, 1.5 hrs, see "To Brussels and Amsterdam
by Thalys Train," below), **Bruges** (18/day, 2 hrs, change in
Brussels, 1 direct), **Amsterdam** (10/day, 4 hrs; see "To Brussels
and Amsterdam by Thalys Train," below), **Copenhagen** (1/day,
16 hrs, 2 night trains), **Koblenz** (6/day, 5 hrs, change in Köln),

Train Routes

London Eurostar via Chunnel (17/day, 3 hrs, tel. 08 36 35 35 39; see "The Eurostar Train to London," below). By *banlieue*/RER lines: **Chantilly-Gouvieux** (hrly, fewer on weekends, 35 min), **Charles de Gaulle** airport (2/hr, 30 min, runs 5:30–23:00, track 4), Auvers-sur-Oise (2/hr, 1 hr, transfer at Pontoise).

Gare Montparnasse: This big and modern station covers three floors, serves lower Normandy and Brittany, and offers TGV service to the Loire Valley and southwestern France, and suburban service to Chartres. At street level, you'll find a bank, *banlieue* trains (serving Chartres; you can also reach the *banlieue* trains from the second level), and ticket windows in the center, just past the escalators. Lockers *(consigne automatique)* are on the mezzanine level

Key Train Phrases

accueil (pron. ah-koy) = information/assistance
niveau (pron. nee-voh) = level
billets (pron. bee-yay) = tickets
départs (pron. day-par) = departures
arrivées (pron. ah-ree-vay) = arrivals
aller simple (pron. ah-lay sam-pluh) = one-way
aller-retour (pron. ah-lay ruh-toor) = round-trip
voyageurs munis de billets = travelers with tickets
Grandes Lignes (pron. grahnd leen) = major domestic
      and international lines
RER (pron. air-ay-air) = suburban lines
banlieue (pron. bahn-lee-yuh) = suburb
quai (pron. kay) = platform
voie (pron. vwah) = track
retard (pron. ruh-tar) = delay
salle d'attente (pron. sahl dah-tahnt) = waiting room
consigne automatique (pron. kohn-seen oh-to-mah-teek) =
      storage lockers
première classe (pron. pruhm-yair klahs) = first class
deuxième classe (pron. duhz-yehm klahs) = second class

between levels 1 and 2. Most services are provided on the second level, where the *Grandes Lignes* arrive and depart (ticket windows to the far left with your back to glass exterior). *Banlieue* trains depart from tracks 10 through 19. The main rail information office is opposite track 15. Taxis are to the far left as you leave the tracks.

Key destinations served by Gare Montparnasse: Chartres (20/day, 1 hr, *banlieue* lines), **Pontorson-Mont St. Michel** (5/day, 4.5 hrs, via Rennes, then take bus; or take train to Pontorson via Caen, then bus from Pontorson), **Dinan** (7/day, 4 hrs, change in Rennes and Dol), **Bordeaux** (14/day, 3.5 hrs), **Sarlat** (5/day, 6 hrs, change in Bordeaux, Libourne, or Souillac), **Toulouse** (11/day, 5 hrs, most require change, usually in Bordeaux), **Albi** (7/day, 6–7.5 hrs, change in Toulouse, also night train), **Carcassonne** (8/day, 6.5 hrs, most require changes in Toulouse and Bordeaux, direct trains take 10 hrs), **Tours** (14/day, 1 hr).

Gare de Lyon: This huge and bewildering station offers TGV and regular service to southeastern France, Italy, and other international destinations (for more trains to Italy, see "Gare de Bercy," below). Frequent *banlieue* trains serve Melun (near

Vaux-le-Vicomte) and Fontainebleau (some depart from the main *Grandes Lignes* level, more frequent departures are from one level down, follow RER-D signs, and ask at any *accueil* or ticket window where the next departure leaves from).

Grande Ligne trains arrive and depart from one level but are divided into two areas (tracks A-N and 5-23). They are connected by the long platform along tracks A and 5, and by the hallway adjacent to track A and opposite track 9. This hallway has all the services, ticket windows, ticket information, banks, shops, and access to car rental. *Banlieue* ticket windows are just inside the hall adjacent to track A *(billets Ile de France)*. *Grandes Lignes* and *banlieue* lines share the same tracks. A Paris TI (Mon–Sat 8:00–20:00, closed Sun) and a train information office are opposite track L. From the RER or Métro, follow signs for *Grandes Lignes Arrivées* and take the escalator up to reach the platforms. Train information booths *(accueil)* are opposite tracks G and 11. Taxis lines are well-marked in front of the station and one floor below.

Key destinations served by Gare de Lyon: Vaux-le-Vicomte (train to Melun, hrly, 30 min), **Fontainebleau** (nearly hrly, 45 min), **Beaune** (12/day, 2.5 hrs, most require change in Dijon), **Dijon** (15/day, 1.5 hrs), **Chamonix** (9/day, 9 hrs, change in Lyon and St. Gervais, direct night train), **Annecy** (8/day, 4–7 hrs), Lyon (16/day, 2.5 hrs), **Avignon** (9/day in 2.5 hrs, 6/day in 4 hrs with change), **Arles** (14/day, 5 hrs, most with change in Marseille, Avignon, or Nîmes), **Nice** (14/day, 5.5–7 hrs, many with change in Marseille), **Venice** (3/day, 3/night, 11–15 hrs, most require changes), **Rome** (2/day, 5/night, 15–18 hrs, most require changes), **Bern** (9/day, 5–11 hrs, most require changes, night train).

Gare de Bercy: This smaller station handles some rail service to Italy during renovation work at the Gare de Lyon (Mo: Bercy, 1 stop east of Gare de Lyon on line 14).

Gare de l'Est: This single floor station (with underground Métro) serves Eastern France and European points east of Paris. Train information booths are at tracks 1 and 26; ticket windows and the main exit to buses and Paris are opposite track 8; luggage storage is opposite track 12.

Key destinations served by the **Gare de l'Est: Colmar** (12/day, 5.5 hrs, change in Strasbourg, Dijon, or Mulhouse), **Strasbourg** (14/day, 4.5 hrs, many require changes), **Reims** (12/day, 1.5 hrs), **Verdun** (5/day, 3 hrs, change in Metz or Chalon), **Munich** (5/day, 9 hrs, some require changes, night train), **Vienna** (7/day, 13–18 hrs, most require changes, night train), **Zurich** (10/day, 7 hrs, most require changes, night train), **Prague** (2/day, 14 hrs, night train).

Gare St. Lazare: This relatively small station serves Upper Normandy, including Rouen and Giverny. All trains arrive and depart one floor above street level. Follow signs to *Grandes Lignes* from the Métro to reach the tracks. You'll pass a mini-mall. Ticket windows and a Thomas Cook exchange are in the first hall on the second floor. The tracks are through the small hallways (lined with storage lockers). *Grandes Lignes* (main lines) depart from tracks 17–27; *banlieue* (suburban) trains depart from 1–16. The train information office *(accueil)* is opposite track 15; the reservation office is opposite track 16. Baggage consignment and the post office are along track 27, and WCs are opposite track 19. Key destinations served by the **Gare St. Lazare: Giverny** (train to Vernon, 5/day, 45 min; then bus or taxi 10 min to Giverny), **Rouen** (15/day, 75 min), **Honfleur** (6/day, 3 hrs, via Lisieux, then bus), **Bayeux** (9/day, 2.5 hrs, some with change in Caen), **Caen** (12/day, 2 hrs).

Gare d'Austerlitz: This small station provides non-TGV service to the Loire Valley, southwestern France, and Spain. All tracks are at street level. The information booth is opposite track 17, and a Thomas Cook exchange and all ticket sales are in the hall opposite track 10. Baggage consignment and car rental are near Porte 27 (along the side, opposite track 21).

Key destinations served by the **Gare d'Austerlitz: Amboise** (8/day in 2 hrs, 12/day in 1.5 hrs with change in St. Pierre des Corps), **Cahors** (7/day, 5–7 hrs, most with changes), **Barcelona** (1/day, 9 hrs, change in Montpellier, night trains), **Madrid** (2 night trains only, 13–16 hrs), **Lisbon** (1/day, 24 hrs).

Crossing the Channel by Eurostar Train

The fastest and most convenient way to London is by rail. Eurostar is the speedy passenger train that zips you from downtown Paris to London (17/day, 3 hrs) faster and easier than flying. The train goes 190 mph in France but a doddering 80 mph in England. (When the English segment gets up to speed, the journey time will shrink to 2 hours.) The actual tunnel crossing is a 20-minute, black, silent, 100-mile-per-hour nonevent. Your ears won't even pop. Eurostar trains also run to London from Charles de Gaulle Airport (requires change in Lille) and Disneyland Paris (direct).

Channel fares are reasonable but complicated. As with airfares, the most expensive and flexible option is a full-fare ticket with no restrictions on refunds. Cheaper tickets come with more restrictions—and sell out more quickly.

Prices vary depending on when you travel, whether you can live with restrictions, and whether you're eligible for any discounts (youth, seniors, and railpass holders all qualify). The various second-class Leisure Tickets are a good deal, but many require a round-trip purchase. Compare one-way fares with cheap round-trip fares (you can forget to return).

You can check and book fares by phone or online:

U.S.: 800/EUROSTAR, www.raileurope.com (prices listed in dollars).

France: Tel. 08 36 35 35 39, www.voyages-sncf.com (prices listed in euros). In France, you also can buy tickets at any of the train stations, neighborhood SNCF offices, and most travel agencies (expect a booking fee).

Depending on where you book, you'll find different prices and discount deals on similar tickets (see below)—if you order from the United States, check out both. It can be a better deal to buy your ticket from a French company instead of a U.S. company—or vice versa. If you buy from a U.S. company, you'll pay a FedEx charge for ticket delivery in the United States. If you order over the phone or online in Europe, you'll pick up your tickets at the train station— be sure to read the fine print to find out how long you have to pick up the tickets. You can purchase a Eurostar ticket in person at most European train stations, but passholder discounts are only available at Eurostar stations (such as the Gare du Nord, Lille, and Calais in France).

Note that France's time zone is one hour later than Britain's. Times listed on tickets are local times.

Here are typical fares available in 2002. For 2003 fares, check the Eurostar and SNCF phone numbers and Web sites listed above.

Eurostar Full-Fare Tickets

Full-fare tickets are fully refundable even after the departure date. As with plane tickets, you'll pay more to have fewer restrictions. In 2002, one-way Business First *(affaires)* cost €315 in France/ $279 in the United States and included a meal (a dinner departure nets you more grub than breakfast). Full-fare second-class tickets (Standard Flexi or *Seconde Affaires*) cost €255/$199.

Cheaper Tickets

Since full-fare, no-restrictions tickets are so expensive, most travelers sacrifice flexibility for a cheaper ticket with more restrictions. Second class is plenty comfortable, making first class an unnecessary expense for most; prices listed below are for second class unless otherwise noted. Some of these tickets are available only in France, others only in the United States. They are listed roughly from most expensive to cheapest (with more restrictions as you move down the list).

Leisure Flexi *(Loisir Flexi):* €215 round-trip (round-trip purchase required, partially refundable before departure date, not available in U.S.)

U.S. Leisure: $139 one-way (partially refundable before departure date, not available in France)

Leisure *(Loisir):* €145 round-trip (round-trip purchase required, nonrefundable, not available in U.S.)

Leisure 7 *(Loisir 7):* €115 round-trip (round-trip purchase required, nonrefundable, purchase at least 7 days in advance, not available in U.S.)

Leisure 14 *(Loisir 14):* €95/$178 round-trip (round-trip purchase required, nonrefundable, purchase at least 14 days in advance, stay 2 nights or over a Sat, available in U.S. and France)

Weekend Day Return *(Loisir Journée):* €85 for same-day round-trip on a Saturday or Sunday (round-trip purchase required, nonrefundable, not available in U.S.). Note that this round-trip ticket is cheaper than many one-way tickets.

Eurostar Discounts

For Railpass Holders: Discounts are available in the United States or France to travelers holding railpasses that include France or Britain ($75 one-way for second class, $155 one-way for first class).

For Youth and Seniors: Discounts are available in the United States and France for children under 12 (€45/$69 one-way for second class) and youths under 26 (€75/$79 one-way for second class). Only in the United States can seniors over 60 get discounts ($189 one-way for first class).

To Brussels and Amsterdam by Thalys Train

The pricey Thalys train has the monopoly on this route. The cheapest way to connect Paris with Brussels and Amsterdam is by bus (see "Buses," below). Without a railpass, you'll pay about €80–100 second-class for the Paris–Amsterdam train (compared to €35 by Eurolines bus) or about €60–80 second-class for the Paris–Brussels train (compared to €25 by Eurolines bus). Even with a railpass, you need to pay for reservations (€14/second class, €30/first class). Book at least a day ahead as seats are limited. Or hop on the bus, Gus.

BUSES

The main bus station is the Gare Routière du Paris-Gallieni (28 avenue du Général de Gaulle, in suburb of Bagnolet, Mo: Gallieni, tel. 01 49 72 51 51). Buses provide cheaper—if less comfortable and more time-consuming—transportation to major European cities.

Driving in France: Distance and Time

Eurolines' buses depart from here (tel. 08 36 69 52 52, www
.eurolines.com). Eurolines has a couple of neighborhood offices:
in the Latin Quarter (55 rue Saint-Jacques, tel. 01 43 54 11 99)
and in Versailles (4 avenue des Sceaux, tel. 01 39 02 03 73).

PARKING IN PARIS

Street parking is free after 19:00, on weekends, and in August. For a
longer stay, consider parking for less at an airport (about €10/day)
and taking public transport or a taxi into the city. You'll pay more to
park in a downtown lot (€17–25/day) and it's a good idea to reserve
ahead (the lot under Ecole Militaire is good for rue Cler–area hotels,
€17/day, €38/3 days, and €9/day more after that, www.vincipark
.com). Otherwise, ask your hotelier for suggestions.

FRENCH
HISTORY

Celts and Romans (52 B.C.–A.D. 500)

Julius Caesar conquered the Parisii, turning Paris from a tribal fishing village into a European city. The mix of Latin (southern) and Celtic (northern) cultures, with Paris right in the middle, defined the French character.

Paris Sights: Cluny Museum (Roman baths), Louvre (Roman antiquities), and Archaeological Crypt near Notre-Dame.

Dark Ages (500–1000)

Roman Paris fell to German pirates ("Franks" = France) and later to the Vikings ("Norsemen" = Normans). During this turbulent time, Paris was just another island state ("Ile de France") in the midst of many warring kingdoms. The lone bright spot was the reign of Charlemagne (A.D. 768–814), who briefly united the Franks, giving a glimpse of the modern nation-state of France.

Paris Sights: Cluny Museum artifacts and statue of Charlemagne near Notre-Dame.

Border Wars with England (1066–1500)

In 1066, the Norman duke William ("the Conqueror") invaded and conquered England. This united England, Normandy, and much of what is today Western France, sparking centuries of border wars and producing many kings of England who spoke French. In 1328, King Charles IV died without an heir, and the Norman king of England tried to claim the throne of France, leading to more than 100 years of Franco-Anglo battles (called the Hundred Years' War). Rallied by the teenage visionary Joan of Arc in 1429, the French finally united North and South, driving the English across the Channel in 1453. Modern France was born, with Paris as its capital.

Paris Sights: Notre-Dame, Sainte-Chapelle, Cluny Museum tapestries, Carnavalet Museum, and the Sorbonne and the Latin Quarter.

Renaissance and Religious Wars (1500s)

A strong centralized France emerged, with French kings setting Europe's standard. François I made Paris a cultural capital, inviting Leonardo and *Mona Lisa* to visit. Catholics and Protestants fought openly, and 2,000 Parisians were slaughtered in the St. Bartholomew's Day Massacre in 1572. The Wars of Religion subsided for a while when the first Bourbon king, Henri IV, took the throne in 1589, after converting to Catholicism (he signed the Edict of Nantes in 1598, instituting freedom of worship).

Paris Sights: Louvre (palace and Renaissance art), pont Neuf, place des Vosges, and Fontainebleau.

Louis XIV, the Absolute Monarch (1600s)

Louis XIV centralized the power, neutered the nobility, revoked the Edict of Nantes, and moved the capital to Versailles, which also became the center of European culture. France's wealth sparked "enlightened" ideas that became the seeds of democracy.

Paris Sights: Versailles, Vaux-le-Vicomte, Les Invalides, paintings by Poussin and Lorraine.

Decadence and Revolution (1700s)

This was the age of Louis XV, Louis XVI, Marie-Antoinette, Voltaire, Rousseau, Robespierre, and Napoleon. A financial crunch from wars and royal excess drove the French people to revolt. On July 14, 1789, they stormed the Bastille. A couple years later, the First French Republic arrested and then beheaded the king and queen. Thousands lost their heads—guillotined if suspected of hindering progress. A charismatic commoner rose amid the chaos, promising stability—Napoleon Bonaparte.

Paris Sights: Versailles, place de la Concorde, place de la Bastille, Conciergerie, and paintings by Watteau, Boucher, Fragonard, and David.

Elected Emperors and Constitutional Kings (1800s)

Napoleon conquered Europe, crowned himself emperor, invaded Russia, was defeated on the battlefields of Waterloo, and ended up exiled to an island in the South Pacific. The monarchy was restored, but rulers toed the democratic line—or were deposed in the popular uprisings of 1830 and 1848. The latter resulted in the Second French Republic, whose first president was Napoleon's nephew. He rewrote the constitution with himself as Emperor Napoleon III, and presided over a wealthy, middle-class nation with a colonial empire in slow decline. Although he trod carefully, the disastrous Franco-Prussian War in 1870 ended his reign, leading to the Third Republic. France's political clout was fading, even as Paris remained the world's cultural center during the belle époque, or beautiful age.

Paris Sights: Arc de Triomphe, Haussman's wide boulevards, Eiffel Tower, Les Invalides and Napoleon's Tomb, pont Alexandre, Grand and Petit Palais, Montmartre, Opéra Garnier, paintings by Ingres and Delacroix at the Louvre, and Impressionist and Post-Impressionist paintings (Manet, Monet, Renoir, Degas, Toulouse-Lautrec, Cézanne, and so on) at the Orsay, Marmottan, and Orangerie (scheduled to reopen in 2004).

War and Depression (1900–1950)

France began the turn of the century as top dog, but the two World Wars with Germany (and the earlier Franco-Prussian War) wasted the country. France lost millions of men in World War I, sank into a depression, and was easily overrun by Hitler in World War II. Paris, now dirt cheap, attracted foreign writers and artists.

This was the age of Picasso, Ravel, Debussy, Satie, Stravinsky, Nijinsky, Hemingway, Fitzgerald, Stein, Pound, Sartre, Edith Piaf, and Maurice Chevalier.

Paris Sights: Picasso Museum, Deportation Memorial, Pompidou Center (contains art from this period).

Postwar France (1950–Present)

After the war, France reestablished a democracy with the Fourth Republic. But France's colonial empire dissolved after bitter wars in Algeria and Vietnam, which helped mire an already unsteady government. Wartime hero Charles de Gaulle was brought back to help in 1958, and he rewrote the constitution, beginning the Fifth (and current) Republic. Immigrants from former colonies flooded Paris. The turbulent '60s, progressive '70s, socialist-turned-conservative '80s, and the middle-of-the-road '90s bring us to the *début de siècle*, or the beginning of the century.

Paris Sights: Montparnasse Tower, La Défense, Louvre's pyramid, and Pompidou Center (modern art).

Contemporary Politics in France

The key political issues in France today are high unemployment (about 9 percent), a steadily increasing percentage of ethnic minorities, and the need to compete in a global marketplace. The challenge is to address these issues while maintaining the social benefits the French expect from their government. As a result, national policies seem to conflict with each other (e.g., France supports the lean economic policies of the European Union, but recently reduced the French workweek to 35 hours).

The unification of Europe has been powered by France and Germany. The 15-member European Union, well on its way to becoming a "United States of Europe," is dissolving borders and freeing up trade. Most EU members share one currency—the euro.

French national politics are fascinating. While only two parties dominate American politics, France has five major parties. From left to right, these include the reformed Communists (PCF—Parti Communiste Française), the moderate Socialists (PS—Parti Socialiste), the aristocratically conservative UDF (Union pour la Démocratie Française), the center-right RPR (Rassemblement pour la République), and the racist and isolationist Front National. In general, the UDF and RPR split the conservative middle ground and the Socialists dominate the liberal middle ground. But in France, unlike in the United States, informal coalitions are generally necessary for any party to "rule."

At the fringes, you'll read about the Front National party, led by Jean-Marie Le Pen. Le Pen's "France for the French" platform calls for the expulsion of ethnic minorities and broader police powers. Although the Front National has a staunch voter base of about 12 percent, the recent rise in unemployment and globalization worries have increased its following somewhat. In the 2002 presidential primary, 16 candidates (a new record) vied for office, and Le Pen's loyal following put him in second place—ahead of the Socialist party candidate Lionel Jospin (who had been prime minister), but behind conservative incumbent Jacques Chirac (a former mayor of Paris). While Chirac won the regular election easily, Le Pen has been able to nudge the political agenda to the right. On the far left, the reformed Communists, still recovering from the fall of the Soviet Union, have had to work more flexibly with the less radical Socialists and the environmental (Green) parties, who see their fortunes rise when the economy is strong and fall when it's weak.

While the French president is elected by popular vote every seven years, he is more of a figurehead than his American counterpart. The more powerful prime minister is elected by the parliament (Assemblée Nationale) and confirmed by the new president. With five major parties, a single majority is rare—it takes a coalition to elect a prime minister. Currently, the right is working together better than the left, as President Jacques Chirac and Prime Minister Jean-Pierre Raffarin are both conservatives.

APPENDIX

Let's Talk Telephones

Here are general instructions for making phone calls. (For information specific to France, see page 10). International access codes and country codes are listed below.

Making Calls within a European Country: About half of all European countries use area codes (like we do); the other half uses a direct-dial system without area codes.

To make calls within a country that uses a direct-dial system (France, Belgium, Czech Republic, Denmark, Italy, Portugal, Norway, Spain, and Switzerland), you dial the same number whether you're calling across the country or across the street.

In countries that use area codes (such as Austria, Britain, Finland, Germany, Ireland, Netherlands, and Sweden), you dial the local number when calling within a city, and you add the area code if calling long-distance within the country.

Making International Calls: You always start with the international access code (011 if you're calling from America or Canada, or 00 from virtually anywhere in Europe), then dial the country code of the country you're calling (see chart below).

What you dial next depends on the phone system of the country you're calling. If the country uses area codes, drop the initial 0 of the area code, then dial the rest of the number.

Countries that use direct-dial systems (no area codes) vary in how they're accessed internationally by phone. For instance, if you're making an international call to the Czech Republic, Denmark, Italy, Norway, Portugal, or Spain, simply dial the international access code, country code, and phone number. But if you're calling France, Belgium, or Switzerland, drop the initial 0 of the phone number.

European Calling Chart

Just smile and dial, using this key:
AC = Area Code, LN = Local Number.

European Country	Calling long distance within...	Calling from the U.S.A./ Canada to...	Calling from another European country to...
Austria	AC (Area Code) + LN (Local Number)	011 + 43 + AC (without the initial zero) + LN	00 + 43 + AC (without the initial zero) + LN
Belgium	LN	011 + 32 + LN (without initial zero)	00 + 32 + LN (without initial zero)
Britain	AC + LN	011 + 44 + AC (without initial zero) + LN	00 + 44 + AC . (without initial zero) + LN
Czech Republic	LN	011 + 420 + LN	00 + 420 + LN
Denmark	LN	011 + 45 + LN	00 + 45 + LN
Estonia	LN	011 + 372 + LN	00 + 372 + LN
Finland	AC + LN	011 + 358 + AC (without initial zero) + LN	00 + 358 + AC (without initial zero) + LN
France	LN	011 + 33 + LN (without initial zero)	00 + 33 + LN (without initial zero)
Germany	AC + LN	011 + 49 + AC (without initial zero) + LN	00 + 49 + AC (without initial zero) + LN
Gibraltar	LN	011 + 350 + LN	00 + 350 + LN From Spain: 9567 + LN
Greece	LN	011 + 30 + LN	00 + 30 + LN

European Country	Calling long distance within...	Calling from the U.S.A./ Canada to...	Calling from another European country to...
Ireland	AC + LN	011 + 353 + AC (without initial zero) + LN	00 + 353 + AC (without initial zero) + LN
Italy	LN	011 + 39 + LN	00 + 39 + LN
Morocco	LN	011 + 212 + LN (without initial zero)	00 + 212 + LN (without initial zero)
Nether- lands	AC + LN	011 + 31 + AC (without initial zero) + LN	00 + 31 + AC (without initial zero) + LN
Norway	LN	011 + 47 + LN	00 + 47 + LN
Portugal	LN	011 + 351 + LN	00 + 351 + LN
Spain	LN	011 + 34 + LN	00 + 34 + LN
Sweden	AC + LN	011 + 46 + AC (without initial zero) + LN	00 + 46 + AC (without initial zero) + LN
Switzer- land	LN	011 + 41 + LN (without initial zero)	00 + 41 + LN (without initial zero)
Turkey	AC (if no initial zero is included, add one) + LN	011 + 90 + AC (without initial zero) + LN	00 + 90 + AC (without initial zero) + LN

- The instructions above apply whether you're calling a fixed phone or cell phone.
- The international access codes (the first numbers you dial when making an international call) are 011 if you're calling from the U.S.A./Canada, or 00 if you're calling from virtually anywhere in Europe. Finland and Lithuania are the only exceptions. If calling from either of these countries, replace the 00 with 990 in Finland and 810 in Lithuania.
- To call the U.S.A. or Canada from Europe, dial 00 (unless you're calling from Finland or Lithuania), then 1 (the country code for the U.S.A. and Canada), then the area code and number. In short, 00 + 1 + AC + LN = Hi, Mom!

International Access Codes

When dialing direct, first dial the international access code. For the United States and Canada, it's 011. Virtually all European countries use 00 as their international access code; the only exceptions are Finland (990) and Lithuania (810).

Country Codes

After you've dialed the international access code, then dial the code of the country you're calling.

Austria—43	Greece—30
Belgium—32	Ireland—353
Britain—44	Italy—39
Canada—1	Morocco—212
Czech Repub.—420	Netherlands—31
Denmark—45	Norway—47
Estonia—372	Portugal—351
Finland—358	Spain—34
France—33	Sweden—46
Germany—49	Switzerland—41
Gibraltar—350	United States—1

Handy Phone Numbers

Directory Assistance for Paris and France (some English spoken): 12

Collect Calls to the U.S.: tel. 00 00 11

Lost Property (Bureau des Objets Trouvés, at the police station): Open Tue and Thu 8:30–20:00, 36 rue des Morillons, Mo: Convention, tel. 01 55 76 20 20

American Church: Open daily 9:00–22:00, 65 quai d'Orsay, tel. 01 40 62 05 00

Office of American Services (lost passports, etc): See "U.S. Consulate," below

Sunday Banks: 115 and 154 avenue des Champs-Elysées

Emergency/Medical Needs

Police: 17

Emergency medical assistance: 15

American Hospital: 63 boulevard Victor Hugo, in Neuilly suburb, Mo: Porte Maillot, then bus #82, tel. 01 46 41 25 25

English-speaking pharmacy: tel. 01 45 62 02 41 (Pharmacie les Champs, 24 hrs, 84 avenue des Champs-Elysées, Mo: Georges V)

Chiropractic Centers: tel. 01 43 54 26 25 or 01 43 87 81 62

SOS Doctors: tel. 01 47 07 77 77 or 01 48 28 40 04

SOS Help (English-speaking hotline): Open daily 15:00–23:00, tel. 01 47 23 80 80

Rape Crisis Hotline: 24-hr tel. 08 00 05 95 95
Ambulance: tel. 01 45 67 50 50

Consulates/Embassies
U.S. Consulate: Open Mon–Fri 9:00–12:30 & 13:00–15:00, 2 rue
St. Florentin, Mo. Concorde, tel. 01 43 12 22 22
U.S. Embassy: 2 avenue Gabriel (to the left as you face Hôtel
Crillon), Mo: Concorde, tel. 01 43 12 22 22
Canadian Consulate and Embassy: 35 avenue Montaigne, Mo:
Franklin-Roosevelt, tel. 01 44 43 29 00

Tourist and Transportation Information
Paris Tourist Information: tel. 08 92 68 31 12
   (recorded info with long menu)
Ile de France Tourist Information (Paris area, for example,
   Fontainebleau, Vaux-le-Vicomte, Chantilly): tel. 01 42 60 28 62
Train (SNCF) Information: tel. 08 36 35 35 35
   (some English usually spoken)
Bus and Métro (RATP) Information: tel. 08 36 68 77 14
   (French only)

Travel Companies
American Express: 11 rue Scribe, Mo: Opéra, tel. 01 47 77 77 07

Cheap Flights
Access Voyages: 6 rue Pierre Lescot, Mo: Chatelet,
   tel. 01 44 76 84 50
Any Way: 46 rue des Lombards, Mo: Chatelet or Hôtel de
   Ville, tel. 01 40 28 00 74
Cash & Go: 34 avenue des Champs-Elysées, Mo: Franklin D.
   Roosevelt, tel. 01 53 93 63 63
USIT Voyages: 12 rue Vivienne, Mo: Bourse, tel. 01 42 44 14 00
Booking service (for hotels, restaurants and other tourist activi-
   ties): 1212 avenue des Champs-Elysées, tel. 01 43 59 12 12

Lost or Stolen Credit Cards
Visa: tel. 08 00 90 11 79
MasterCard: tel. 08 00 90 13 87
American Express: tel. 01 47 77 72 00
Diner's Club: call U.S. collect 00-1-702-797-5532

Airports
Charles de Gaulle: general info tel. 01 48 62 22 80, lost
   luggage tel. 01 48 62 10 46
Orly: tel. 01 49 75 15 15

Airlines
Aer Lingus: tel. 01 55 38 38 55
Air Canada: tel. 08 25 88 08 81
Air France: tel. 08 20 82 08 20
Alitalia: tel. 08 02 31 53 15
American Airlines: tel. 08 10 87 28 72
British Airways: tel. 08 25 82 54 00
BMI British Midlands: tel. 01 41 91 87 04
Continental: tel. 01 42 99 09 09
Delta: tel. 08 00 35 40 80
Iberia: tel. 08 02 07 50 75
Icelandair: tel. 01 44 51 60 51
KLM: tel. 08 10 55 65 56
Lufthansa: tel. 08 20 02 00 30
Northwest: tel. 08 10 55 65 56
Olympic: tel. 01 44 94 58 58
Portugal Airlines: 08 03 08 38 18
SAS: tel. 08 10 25 25 25
Swiss: tel. 08 20 04 05 06
United: tel. 08 10 72 72 72
US Airways: tel. 08 10 63 22 22

Classes

French Language Classes
- American University of Paris (tel. 01 40 62 07 20,
  fax 01 47 05 34 32, www.aup.edu)
- France Ecole Langue (tel. 01 45 00 40 15, fax 01 45 00
  53 41, www.france-langue.fr)

Cooking Schools
These have demonstration courses:
- Le Cordon Bleu (tel. 01 53 68 22 50,
  fax 01 48 56 03 96)
- Ritz Escoffier Ecole de Gastronomie Française
  (tel. 01 43 16 30 50)

Paris' Climate
First line, average daily low; second line, average daily high; third
line, days of no rain.

J	F	M	A	M	J	J	A	S	O	N	D
34°	34°	39°	43°	49°	55°	58°	58°	53°	46°	40°	36°
43°	45°	54°	60°	68°	73°	76°	75°	70°	60°	50°	44°
14	14	19	17	19	18	19	18	17	18	15	15

2003

JANUARY
S	M	T	W	T	F	S
			1	2	3	4
5	6	7	8	9	10	11
12	13	14	15	16	17	18
19	20	21	22	23	24	25
26	27	28	29	30	31	

FEBRUARY
S	M	T	W	T	F	S
						1
2	3	4	5	6	7	8
9	10	11	12	13	14	15
16	17	18	19	20	21	22
23	24	25	26	27	28	

MARCH
S	M	T	W	T	F	S
						1
2	3	4	5	6	7	8
9	10	11	12	13	14	15
16	17	18	19	20	21	22
23/30	24/31	25	26	27	28	29

APRIL
S	M	T	W	T	F	S
		1	2	3	4	5
6	7	8	9	10	11	12
13	14	15	16	17	18	19
20	21	22	23	24	25	26
27	28	29	30			

MAY
S	M	T	W	T	F	S
				1	2	3
4	5	6	7	8	9	10
11	12	13	14	15	16	17
18	19	20	21	22	23	24
25	26	27	28	29	30	31

JUNE
S	M	T	W	T	F	S
1	2	3	4	5	6	7
8	9	10	11	12	13	14
15	16	17	18	19	20	21
22	23	24	25	26	27	28
29	30					

JULY
S	M	T	W	T	F	S
		1	2	3	4	5
6	7	8	9	10	11	12
13	14	15	16	17	18	19
20	21	22	23	24	25	26
27	28	29	30	31		

AUGUST
S	M	T	W	T	F	S
					1	2
3	4	5	6	7	8	9
10	11	12	13	14	15	16
17	18	19	20	21	22	23
24/31	25	26	27	28	29	30

SEPTEMBER
S	M	T	W	T	F	S
	1	2	3	4	5	6
7	8	9	10	11	12	13
14	15	16	17	18	19	20
21	22	23	24	25	26	27
28	29	30				

OCTOBER
S	M	T	W	T	F	S
			1	2	3	4
5	6	7	8	9	10	11
12	13	14	15	16	17	18
19	20	21	22	23	24	25
26	27	28	29	30	31	

NOVEMBER
S	M	T	W	T	F	S
						1
2	3	4	5	6	7	8
9	10	11	12	13	14	15
16	17	18	19	20	21	22
23/30	24	25	26	27	28	29

DECEMBER
S	M	T	W	T	F	S
	1	2	3	4	5	6
7	8	9	10	11	12	13
14	15	16	17	18	19	20
21	22	23	24	25	26	27
28	29	30	31			

Numbers and Stumblers

- Europeans write a few of their numbers differently than we do. 1 = *1* , 4 = *4* , 7 = *7* . Learn the difference or miss your train.
- In Europe, dates appear as day/month/year, so Christmas is 25/12/03.
- Commas are decimal points and decimals commas. A dollar and a half is 1,50, and there are 5.280 feet in a mile.
- When pointing, use your whole hand, palm down.
- When counting with fingers, start with your thumb. If you hold up your first finger to request one item, you'll probably get two.
- What Americans call the second floor of a building is the first floor in Europe.
- Europeans keep the left "lane" open for passing on escalators and moving sidewalks. Keep to the right.

Metric Conversion (approximate)

1 inch = 25 millimeters
1 foot = 0.3 meter
1 yard = 0.9 meter
1 mile = 1.6 kilometers
1 centimeter = 0.4 inch
1 meter = 39.4 inches
1 kilometer = .62 mile

32 degrees F = 0 degrees C
82 degrees F = about 28 degrees C
1 ounce = 28 grams
1 kilogram = 2.2 pounds
1 quart = 0.95 liter
1 square yard = 0.8 square meter
1 acre = 0.4 hectare

French Pronunciation Guide for Paris

Arc de Triomphe ark duh tree-oh<u>nf</u>
arrondissement ah-roh<u>n</u>-dees-moh<u>n</u>
Art Nouveau art noo-voh
Auvers-sur-Oise oh-vehr-sur-wahz

Bâteaux Mouches bah-toh moosh
Bon Marché boh<u>n</u> mar-chay
boulangerie boo-lah<u>n</u>-zheh-ree

Carnavalet kar-nah-val-eh
Champ de Mars shah<u>n</u> duh mar
Champs-Elysées shah<u>n</u>-zay-lee-zay
Chantilly shah<u>n</u>-tee-yee
charcuterie shar-koo-tuh-ree
Chartres shar-truh
château(x) shah-toh
Cité see-tay
Cité des Sciences see-tay day see-ah<u>n</u>s
Conciergerie kon-see-ehr-zhuh-ree
Contrescarpe koh<u>n</u>-truh-scarp

droguerie droh-guh-ree

Ecole Militaire eh-kohl mee-lee-tehr
Egouts ay-goo

Fauchon's foh-shoh<u>n</u>
Fontainbleau foh<u>n</u>-tehn-bloh
fromagerie froh-mah-zhuh-ree

Galeries Lafayette gah-luh-ree lah-fay-yet
gare gar
Gare d'Austerlitz gar doh-ster-leets
Gare de l'Est gar duh less
Gare de Lyon gar duh lee-oh<u>n</u>
Gare du Nord gar dew nor
Gare St. Lazare gar sah<u>n</u> lah-zar
Garnier gar-nee-ay
Giverny zhee-vehr-nee
Grand Palais grah<u>n</u> pah-lay
Grande Arche de la Défense grah<u>n</u>d arsh duh lah day-fah<u>n</u>s

histoire ees-twar
Hôtel d'Aignan oh-tehl day-nyah<u>n</u>
Hôtel de Sully oh-tehl deh soo-lee
Hôtel Salé oh-tehl sah-lay

Ile de la Cité eel duh lah see-tay
Ile St. Louis eel sah<u>n</u> loo-ee

Jacquemart-André zhahk-mar-ah<u>n</u>-dray
jardin zhar-da<u>n</u>
Jardin des Plantes zhar-da<u>n</u> day plah<u>n</u>t
Jeu de Paume juh duh pohm

La Madeleine lah mah-duh-lehn
La Marseillaise lah mar-seh-yehz
Le Hameau luh ah-moh
Les Halles lay ahl
Les Invalides lay-za<u>n</u>-vah-leed
Loire lwar
L'Orangerie loh-rah<u>n</u>-zhuh-ree
Louvre loov-ruh

Marais mah-ray
Marché aux puces mar-chay oh poos
Marmottan mar-moh-tah<u>n</u>
Métro may-troh
Monge moh<u>n</u>zh
Montmartre moh<u>n</u>-mart
Montparnasse moh<u>n</u>-par-nas
Moulin Rouge moo-la<u>n</u> roozh
musée mew-zay
Musée de l'Armée mew-zay duh lar-may
Musée d'Orsay mew-zay dor-say

Nôtre-Dame noh-truh-dahm

orangerie oh-rah<u>n</u>-zhuh-ree
Orsay or-say

palais pah-lay
Palais de Justice pah-lay duh zhew-stees
Palais Garnier pah-lay gar-nee-ay
Palais Royal pah-lay roh-yahl
Parc de la Vilette park duh la vee-leht
Parc Monceau park moh<u>n</u>-soh
Père Lachaise pehr lah-shehz
Petit Palais puh-tee pah-lay
Pigalle pee-gahl
place plahs
Place Dauphine plahs doh-feen
Place de la Bastille plahs duh lah bah-steel
Place de la Concorde plahs duh lah koh<u>n</u>-kord
Place de la République plahs duh lah ray-poo-bleek
Place des Vosges plahs day vohzh
Place du Tertre plahs dew tehr-truh
Place St. André des Arts plahs sah<u>n</u> tah<u>n</u>-dray day zart
Place Vendôme plahs vah<u>n</u>-dohm
Pompidou poh<u>n</u>-pee-doo
pont poh<u>n</u>
pont Alexandre poh<u>n</u> ah-leks-ah<u>n</u>-druh
pont Neuf poh<u>n</u> nuhf
Promenade Plantée proh-moh<u>n</u>-ahd plah<u>n</u>-tay

quai kay

Rive Droite reeve dwaht
Rive Gauche reeve gohsh
Rodin roh-da<u>n</u>
rue rew
Rue Cler rew klehr
Rue Daguerre rew dah-gehr
Rue des Rosiers rew day
    roz-ee-ay
Rue Montorgueil rew moh<u>n</u>-tor-goy
Rue Mouffetard rew moof-tar
Rue de Rivoli rew duh ree-voh-lee

Sacré-Couer sah-kray-koor
Sainte-Chapelle sah<u>nt</u>-shah-pehl
Samaritaine sah-mah-ree-tehn
Seine sehn

Sèvres-Babylone seh-vruh-bah-
    bee-lohn
Sorbonne sor-buhn
St. Germain-des-Prés sah<u>n</u> zhehr-ma<u>n</u>-
    day-pray
St. Julien-le-Pauvre sah<u>n</u> zhew-lee-
    ahn-luh-poh-vruh
St. Séverin sah<u>n</u> say-vuh-ra<u>n</u>
St. Sulpice sah<u>n</u> sool-pees

Tour Eiffel toor ee-fehl
Trianon tree-ah<u>n</u>-oh<u>n</u>
Trocadéro troh-kah-day-roh
Tuileries twee-lah-ree

Vaux-le-Vicomte voh-luh-vee-koh<u>nt</u>
Venus de Milo vuh-new duh mee-loh
Versailles vehr-sigh

Basic French Survival Phrases

English	French	Phonetics
Good day.	Bonjour.	bohn-zhoor
Mrs. / Mr.	Madame / Monsieur	mah-dahm / muhs-yur
Do you speak English?	Parlez-vous anglais?	par-lay-voo ahn-glay
Yes. / No.	Oui. / Non.	wee / nohn
I understand.	Je comprends.	zhuh kohn-prahn
I don't understand.	Je ne comprends pas.	zhuh nun kohn-prahn pah
Please.	S'il vous plaît.	see voo play
Thank you.	Merci.	mehr-see
I'm sorry.	Désolé.	day-zoh-lay
Excuse me.	Pardon.	par-dohn
(No) problem.	(Pas de) problème.	(pah duh) proh-blehm
It's good.	C'est bon.	say bohn
Goodbye.	Au revoir.	oh vwahr
one / two	un / deux	uhn / duh
three / four	trois / quatre	twah / kah-truh
five / six	cinq / six	sank / sees
seven / eight	sept / huit	seht / weet
nine / ten	neuf / dix	nuhf / dees
How much is it?	Combien?	kohn-bee-an
Write it?	Ecrivez?	ay-kree-vay
Is it free?	C'est gratuit?	say grah-twee
Included?	Inclus?	an-klew
Where can I buy / find...?	Où puis-je acheter / trouver...?	oo pwee-zhuh ah-shuh-tay / troo-vay
I'd like / We'd like...	Je voudrais / Nous voudrions...	zhuh voo-dray / noo voo-dree-ohn
...a room.	...une chambre.	ewn shahn-bruh
...the bill.	...l'addition.	lah-dee-see-ohn
...a ticket to ___.	...un billet pour ___.	uhn bee-yay poor
Is it possible?	C'est possible?	say poh-see-bluh
Where is...?	Où est...?	oo ay
...the train station	...la gare	lah gar
...the bus station	...la gare routière	lah gar root-yehr
...tourist information	...l'office du tourisme	loh-fees dew too-reez-muh
Where are the toilets?	Où sont les toilettes?	oo sohn lay twah-leht
men	hommes	ohm
women	dames	dahm
left / right	à gauche / à droite	ah gohsh / ah dwaht
straight	tout droit	too dwah
When does this open / close?	Ça ouvre / ferme à quelle heure?	sah oo-vruh / fehrm ah kehl ur
At what time?	À quelle heure?	ah kehl ur
Just a moment.	Un moment.	uhn moh-mahn
now / soon / later	maintenant / bientôt / plus tard	man-tuh-nahn / bee-an-toh / plew tar
today / tomorrow	aujourd'hui / demain	oh-zhoor-dwee / duh-man

When using the phonetics, try to nasalize the n sound.

For more user-friendly French phrases, check out *Rick Steves' French Phrase Book and Dictionary* or *Rick Steves' French, Italian & German Phrase Book and Dictionary.*

Road Scholar Feedback for PARIS 2003

We're all in the same travelers' school of hard knocks. Your feedback helps us improve this guidebook for future travelers. Please fill this out (or use the online version at www.ricksteves.com/feedback), attach more info or any tips/favorite discoveries if you like, and send it to us. As thanks for your help, we'll send you our quarterly travel newsletter free for one year. Thanks! Rick

Of the recommended accommodations/restaurants used, which was:

Best _____

     Why? _____

Worst _____

     Why? _____

Of the sights/experiences/destinations recommended by this book, which was:

Most overrated _____

     Why? _____

Most underrated _____

     Why? _____

Best ways to improve this book:

_____

_____

I'd like a free newsletter subscription:

_____ Yes   _____ No   _____ Already on list

_____
Name

_____
Address

_____
City, State, Zip

_____
E-mail Address

Please send to: ETBD, Box 2009, Edmonds, WA 98020

Faxing Your Hotel Reservation

Use this handy form for your fax, or find it online at
www.ricksteves.com/reservation. Photocopy and fax away.

One-Page Fax

To: _____ @ _____
              hotel   *fax*

From: _____ @ _____
              name   *fax*

Today's date: ____ / ____ / ____
                day   *month*   *year*

Dear Hotel _____,

Please make this reservation for me:

Name: _____

Total # of people: _____   # of rooms: _____   # of nights: _____

Arriving: ____ / ____ / ____ My time of arrival (24-hr clock): _____
          day *month* *year*   (I will telephone if I will be late)

Departing: ____ / ____ / ____
            day *month* *year*

Room(s): Single___ Double___ Twin___ Triple___ Quad___

With: Toilet___ Shower___ Bath___ Sink only___

Special needs: View___ Quiet___ Cheapest___ Ground Floor___

Credit card: Visa___ MasterCard___ American Express___

Card #: _____

Expiration date:_____

Name on card: _____

You may charge me for the first night as a deposit. Please fax, e-mail, or
mail me confirmation of my reservation, along with the type of room
reserved, the price, and whether the price includes breakfast. Please also
inform me of your cancellation policy. Thank you.

_____
Signature

_____
Name

_____
Address

_____
City   *State*   *Zip Code*   *Country*

_____
E-mail Address

INDEX

FREE-SPIRITED TOURS FROM
Rick Steves

Great Guides

Big Buses

Small Groups

No Grumps

Best of Europe ■ Village Europe ■ Eastern Europe ■ Turkey ■ Italy ■ Village Italy ■ Britain
Spain/Portugal ■ Ireland ■ Heart of France ■ South of France ■ Village France ■ Scandinavia
Germany/Austria/Switzerland ■ London ■ Paris ■ Rome ■ Venice ■ Florence ■ Prague

Looking for a one, two, or three-week tour that's run in the Rick Steves style? Check out Rick Steves' educational, experiential tours of Europe.

Rick's tours include much more in the "sticker price" than mainstream tours. Here's what you'll get with a Europe or regional Rick Steves tour ...

- **Group size:** Your tour group will be no larger than 26.

- **Guides:** You'll have two guides traveling and dining with you on your fully guided Rick Steves tour.

- **Bus:** You'll travel in a full-size bus, with plenty of empty seats for you to spread out and read, snooze, enjoy the passing scenery, get away from your spouse, or whatever.

- **Sightseeing:** Your tour price includes all group sightseeing. There are no hidden extra charges.

- **Hotels:** You'll stay in Rick's favorite small, characteristic, locally-run hotels in the center of each city, within walking distance of the sights you came to see.

- **Price and insurance:** Your tour price is guaranteed for 2003. Single travelers do not pay an extra supplement (we have them room with other singles). ETBD includes prorated tour cancellation/ interruption protection coverage at no extra cost.

- **Tips and kickbacks:** All guide and driver tips are included in your tour price. Because your driver and guides are paid salaries by ETBD, they can focus on giving you the best European travel experience possible.

Interested? Call (425) 771-8303 or visit www.ricksteves.com for a free copy of Rick Steves' 2003 Tours booklet!

Rick Steves' Europe Through the Back Door
130 Fourth Avenue North, PO Box 2009, Edmonds, WA 98020 USA
Phone: (425) 771-8303 ■ Fax: (425) 771-0833 ■ www.ricksteves.com

Trafalger man
Night out.
Metro to museums
Cuban cigars

Free, fresh travel tips, all year long.

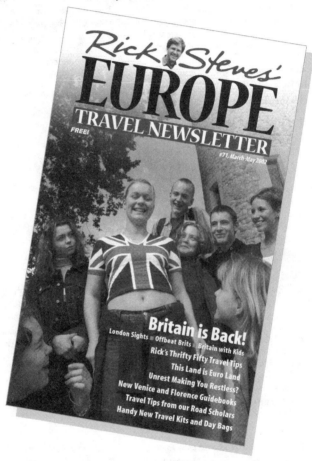

Visit **www.ricksteves.com**
to get Rick's free
64-page newsletter... and more!